The Supreme Court
and Partisan Realignment

TRANSFORMING AMERICAN POLITICS
Lawrence C. Dodd, Series Editor

Dramatic changes in political institutions and behavior over the past two decades have underscored the dynamic nature of American politics, confronting political scientists with a new and pressing intellectual agenda. The pioneering work of early postwar scholars, while laying a firm empirical foundation for contemporary scholarship, failed to consider how American politics might change or to recognize the forces that would make fundamental change inevitable. In reassessing the static interpretations fostered by these classic studies, political scientists are now examining the underlying dynamics that generate transformational change.

Transforming American Politics will bring together texts and monographs that address four closely related aspects of change. A first concern is documenting and explaining recent changes in American politics—in institutions, processes, behavior, and policymaking. A second is reinterpreting classic studies and theories to provide a more accurate perspective on postwar politics. The series will look at historical change to identify recurring patterns of political transformation within and across the distinctive eras of American politics. Last and perhaps most importantly, the series will present new theories and interpretations that explain the dynamic processes at work and thus clarify the direction of contemporary politics. All of the books will focus on the central theme of transformation—transformation in both the conduct of American politics and in the way we study and understand its many aspects.

TITLES IN THIS SERIES

The Supreme Court and Partisan Realignment

A MACRO- AND MICROLEVEL PERSPECTIVE

John B. Gates

Westview Press

BOULDER • SAN FRANCISCO • OXFORD

Transforming American Politics

Copyright © 1992 by Westview Press, Inc.

Published in 1992 in the United States of America by Westview Press, Inc., 5500 Central Avenue, Boulder, Colorado 80301-2847, and in the United Kingdom by Westview Press, 36 Lonsdale Road, Summertown, Oxford OX2 7EW

Library of Congress Cataloging-in-Publication Data
Gates, John Boatner.
  The Supreme Court and partisan realignment : a macro- and microlevel perspective / John B. Gates.
    p.   cm.—(Transforming American politics series)
  Includes bibliographical references and index.
  ISBN 0-8133-0919-0
  1. United States. Supreme Court—History.   2. Judicial review—United States—History.   3. Political questions and judicial power—United States—History.   4. United States—Politics and government.
I. Title.   II. Series
KF8742.G285   1992
347.73′26—dc20
[347.30735]   91-21592
                                                                               CIP

Printed and bound in the United States of America

(∞) The paper used in this publication meets the requirements of the American National Standard for Permanence of Paper for Printed Library Materials Z39.48-1984.

10   9   8   7   6   5   4   3   2   1

To Melissa

Contents

Tables and Figures

Figures

Preface and Acknowledgments

The general public rarely encounters the jargon of political science. In most cases, this is just as well. Partisan realignment is an exception. Over the past decade, realignment has become a topic for commentary and debate in the national media. Did the elections of Ronald Reagan in 1980 and 1984 as well as that of George Bush in 1988 signal a new Republican majority that had become more conservative and dominant in national policymaking? Was the Republican party destined to control the national government in the coming decades as the Democratic party had after the election of Franklin Roosevelt in 1932? Political analysts of all stripes gave their opinions on the possibility of partisan realignment in the 1980s.

The emergence of partisan realignment in common lexicon is unusual but quite understandable. Realignment of the American party system is an intriguing and provocative idea for several reasons. Realignment of the American party system has long-term consequences for the major parties' electoral support and the general shape or direction of national policy. Also, partisan realignments point to periodic connections between vote choice and public policy that are consistent with visions of democratic governance. Perhaps the most important reason the term *partisan realignment* is shared by scholars, analysts, and pundits alike is that it provides a panoramic view of American political history and political change.

Recent journalistic debate over realignment as an *event* can be exciting, hostile, and sometimes misguided. One columnist points to change in the electorate's partisan identification and announces that realignment is not proved; another offers a different piece of evidence and hails the arrival of a new majority party. The reason for such continuing debate is simple; political scientists and historians are still developing a complete explanation or theory of the complex *process* of realignment. Even today, the academic community disagrees on the question of whether realignment occurred in the 1980s.

Outside of the current events of the past decade, however, political scientists know a great deal about the dynamics of realignment from 1800 to the mid-1960s, including electoral changes and, to a lesser extent, the dynamics of realignment and congressional policymaking. Conversely, very little is known regarding the dynamics of judicial policymaking in times of realignment. This book is an attempt to fill some of the void by examining realignment and policymaking by the U.S. Supreme Court.

The relationship between the decisionmaking of the U.S. Supreme Court and realigning presidential elections has not gone unnoticed. Some argue that the Supreme Court may serve two different, but not necessarily mutually exclusive, roles. First, Supreme Court decisions can contribute to the volatile issue agenda *before* realigning elections. Second, the Court may come into conflict with the popularly elected branches *following* realigning elections because a new majority party controls the elected branches but the Court's membership changes slowly. Hence, some argue that the Supreme Court stands as a barrier to, or a protector against, majoritarian reform. An examination of these two roles provides the unifying threads in the analysis.

The validity of these two propositions across four different party eras is tested primarily by examining the 743 cases in which federal statutes, state statutes, and state constitutional provisions were declared unconstitutional between 1837 and 1964. Admittedly, this approach does not include every aspect of Supreme Court policymaking. Nevertheless, in combination with historical and interpretative analysis, examination of these dramatic and important cases improves our understanding of the connections between Supreme Court policymaking and the process of realignment. Quantitative analysis of the issues in these cases, the timing of the decisions, and the voting of justices yields new information on the Supreme Court and partisan realignment. The results provide a basis for understanding the Supreme Court and partisan realignment and also provide insights for the development of a theory of Supreme Court policymaking and realignment.

I am grateful to a number of institutions, colleagues, and friends. The National Science Foundation provided essential financial assistance for the content analysis of judicial opinions (NSF SES-8318155). It is doubtful that this research would have come to fruition without this support. In addition, the Graduate School and Law School of the University of Maryland and the Office of Research at the University of New Orleans also contributed financial support. The University of California, Davis, gave me an intellectually rich environment for the revision and rewriting of the manuscript. The efforts of Randy Siverson, Larry Berman, and Phil Dubois are especially appreciated. Finally, funding from the Committee on Research of the Davis Division of the Academic Senate of the University of California is gratefully acknowledged.

Portions of this manuscript have been previously published. I appreciate the permission to reprint select parts of these publications. Duke University Press granted permission for reprinting some of the material in "The American Supreme Court and Electoral Realignment: A Critical Review" and "Supreme Court Voting and Realigning Issues," originally published in *Social Science History.* Some of the material in "Partisan Realignment, Unconstitutional State Policies, and the U.S. Supreme Court, 1837–1964" first appeared in the *American Journal of Political Science* and is used with the permission of the University of Texas Press.

I wish to thank several graduate assistants for their assistance: Roy Dawes; Marti Klemm; Dennis Krystek (University of New Orleans); David Houser and Charles Dannehl (University of California, Davis). They were extremely helpful at various stages. Most important, however, were two new law school graduates who assisted in the content analysis: John Andre and Gregory Kallen. Linda Potoski of the Department of Political Science, University of California, Davis, typed the final manuscript with good humor, efficiency, and accuracy.

Individuals at Westview were also instrumental. Jennifer Knerr and Diana Luykx skillfully managed the project through the review and production stages. Diane Hess provided very valuable insights as copy editor.

I appreciate the comments, criticisms, and encouragement of many colleagues and friends. Foremost are Richard Claude, Wayne McIntosh, and Eric Uslaner of the University of Maryland. Also, David Adamany (president, Wayne State University) first aroused my interest in the subject. I hope the mention of the following people will adequately convey my appreciation for their assistance, advice, and comments on various parts of this research: Charles Barrilleaux (Florida State University); Larry Baum (Ohio State University); Gregory Caldeira (Ohio State University); Jeffrey Cohen (University of Illinois); M. Margaret Conway (University of Florida); Benjamin Ginsberg (Cornell University); William Flanigan (University of Minnesota); Charles Hadley (University of New Orleans); Stephen Halpern (SUNY at Buffalo); Stuart Hill (University of California, Davis); Garry Jennings (St. Mary's College); Charles Johnson (Texas A&M University); William Lasser (Clemson University); Earlean McCarrick (University of Maryland); Stuart Nagel (University of Illinois); David Neubauer (University of New Orleans); Steve Shull (University of New Orleans); Larry Wade (University of California, Davis); and John Wildgen (University of New Orleans).

My personal debts are extremely large. My parents continue to be a source of encouragement and support. Melissa Lavigne Gates and our son Eric gave constant support and counsel in their unique ways. Only Melissa knows the depth and importance of her contribution.

John B. Gates

The American Supreme Court, Partisan Realignment, and the Invalidation of State and Federal Policies

The ultimate function of the Supreme Court is nothing less than the arbitration between fundamental and ever-present rival forces or trends in our organized society.

—Robert H. Jackson
The Struggle for Judicial Supremacy

[Realignments] arise from emergent tensions in society which, not adequately controlled by the organization or outputs of party politics as usual, escalate to a flash point; they are issue-oriented phenomena, centrally associated with these tensions and more or less leading to resolution adjustments; they result in significant transformation in the general shape of policy; and they have relatively profound after effects on the roles played by institutional elites.

—Walter Dean Burnham
Critical Elections and the Mainsprings of American Politics

New political issues arise every day, such as comparable worth, a balanced budget, or the homeless. The public's attention is often short-lived. Some issues, however, do not grow, decay, and die. Certain types of political issues polarize the public and the leaders of the major parties for decades. If the response of party leaders is to take polar positions, these issues may realign the party system and shift electoral support as well as institutional control to one of the major parties. These changes have long-term consequences for national policymaking.

Realigning issues are uncommon in American political history. There have been only a few instances when such issues consumed public and elite attention and a transformation of the American party system ensued. The most recent full-scale realignment was the New Deal. The issue of the depression and government management of the economy polarized the party system and the general public. The election of Franklin Roosevelt marked the beginning of an extended period of Democratic rule at the national level and a redirection of policymaking toward a mixed system of welfare-capitalism.

We know a great deal about changes in the electorate and congressional policymaking surrounding partisan realignment. Much less is known, however, regarding judicial policymaking. This book examines Supreme Court policymaking and partisan realignment and addresses several questions. What has been the role of the Supreme Court in partisan realignment in the past two centuries? Does Supreme Court policymaking reflect the volatile issues that polarize the political parties and precipitate a critical presidential election? Does Supreme Court policymaking stand as a barrier to realignment of the party system following these major elections and the installation of a new majority party in Congress and the presidency? Historical and interpretative analyses are in disagreement on these questions.

The relationship between the decisionmaking of the U.S. Supreme Court and partisan realignment has generated considerable debate (e.g., Nagel, 1965; Adamany, 1973; 1980; Funston, 1975; Beck, 1976; Canon and Ulmer, 1976; Handberg and Hill, 1980; Caldeira and McCrone, 1982). Scholars ascribe two roles to the Supreme Court during partisan realignment. First, traditional historical and doctrinal analyses suggest that Supreme Court decisionmaking contributes to the volatile issue agenda before realignment (Adamany, 1980; Lasser, 1983). Second, there is some evidence of policy conflict between the Supreme Court and the party that gains control of the popularly elected branches because a new majority party controls the latter but the Court's membership changes slowly (Adamany, 1973; 1980). Hence, the Supreme Court stands as a barrier to, or a protector against, majoritarian reform.

This study tests the validity of these two roles and several other questions regarding Supreme Court policymaking in periods of realignment. Specifically, Supreme Court policymaking is gauged primarily through an analysis of the 743 cases in which federal and state policies were declared unconstitutional between 1837 and 1964. Each case is classified into various issue categories including those critical or highly salient to realignment of the party system. The number and pattern of salient cases provides an important, if not essential, view of Supreme Court policymaking. Moreover, analysis of the voting of the justices yields considerable insight into the internal dynamics of the Supreme Court and partisan realignment. The rate of division among the justices in deciding cases involving the critical issues of a realignment period and the degree to which the justices' partisan affiliations structure their response to these volatile questions are important for understanding Supreme Court behavior in times of major crisis. In sum, this study constitutes a macro- and microlevel analysis of the relationship between Supreme Court policymaking and partisan realignment.

REALIGNMENT AND AMERICAN POLITICS

The study of realignment in American politics has its roots in the analysis of electoral behavior. In the mid-1950s, V.O. Key (1955) focused attention on presidential elections that coincide with a long-term redistribution of partisan support and begin distinctive periods in American political history. Political historians identify five fairly precise party systems in American history. They coincide with the rise and fall of majority parties: the Federalist-Jeffersonian (1789–1828); the Jacksonian (1828–1860); the First Republican (1860–1896); the Second Republican (1896–1932); and the New Deal party era (1932–1968).

A critical presidential election is one in which "the depth and intensity of electoral involvement are high, in which more or less profound readjustments occur in the relation of power within the community, and in which new and durable electoral groupings are formed" (Key, 1955: 4). The forces behind such changes may be long-term issues and tensions in society or they can arise from a sudden crisis or dramatic event (Key, 1959).[1] A critical election occurs when there is a durable and significant redistribution of party support within reasonably defined time limits (McMichael and Trilling, 1980: 23).

Sundquist (1973) examines the stimulus to rapid change in the political agenda and the dynamics of polarization, critical elections, and realignment. According to Sundquist, the central dynamics of critical elections and partisan realignments reside in the rise of new and volatile political issues and in the response of party leaders. These new political issues do not raise partisan passions over the long-term policy differences between the major parties. Instead, these issues cut across existing lines of ideological cleavage in the parties. New regional, class, or ideological cleavages in each party are created by issues such as governmental action with respect to slavery in the 1850s, the inequality of wealth and the money supply in the 1880s and 1890s, regulation of the economy and economic interests in the 1930s, as well as racial equality, rising crime, school prayer, and matters of life-style in the 1960s (Sundquist, 1973: 276–278).

These dynamics are fundamental to realignment. A graphic presentation of these changes illustrates the point. Note in Figure 1.1A that the candidates differ substantially on sectional issues. The degree to which these positions capture electoral support is shown by the active axis of conflict. The position of this axis within the universe of voters shows that the Republican candidate has majority status. Most important, note that the position of the candidates on the economic dimension is identical. This is precisely the positioning of most Republican and Democratic candidates following the Civil War realignment of the 1860s.

As the economic issues of the 1880s and 1890s polarized the parties, however, the lines of cleavage between and within the parties changed, as did the position of presidential candidates. This is illustrated in Figure 1.1B. The dimension of conflict changes with crosscutting issues. The line dividing the parties' coalitions changes and the active axis shifts. This produces new coalitions for both candidates. Hence, critical issues disrupt traditional partisan loyalties.

Crosscutting issues may eventually consume political debate and polarize the parties and the electorate. When party leaders take distinctive and polar

FIGURE 1.1

The Impact of Crosscutting Issues on the
Dimensions of Partisan Conflict

1A.

ACTIVE
AXIS

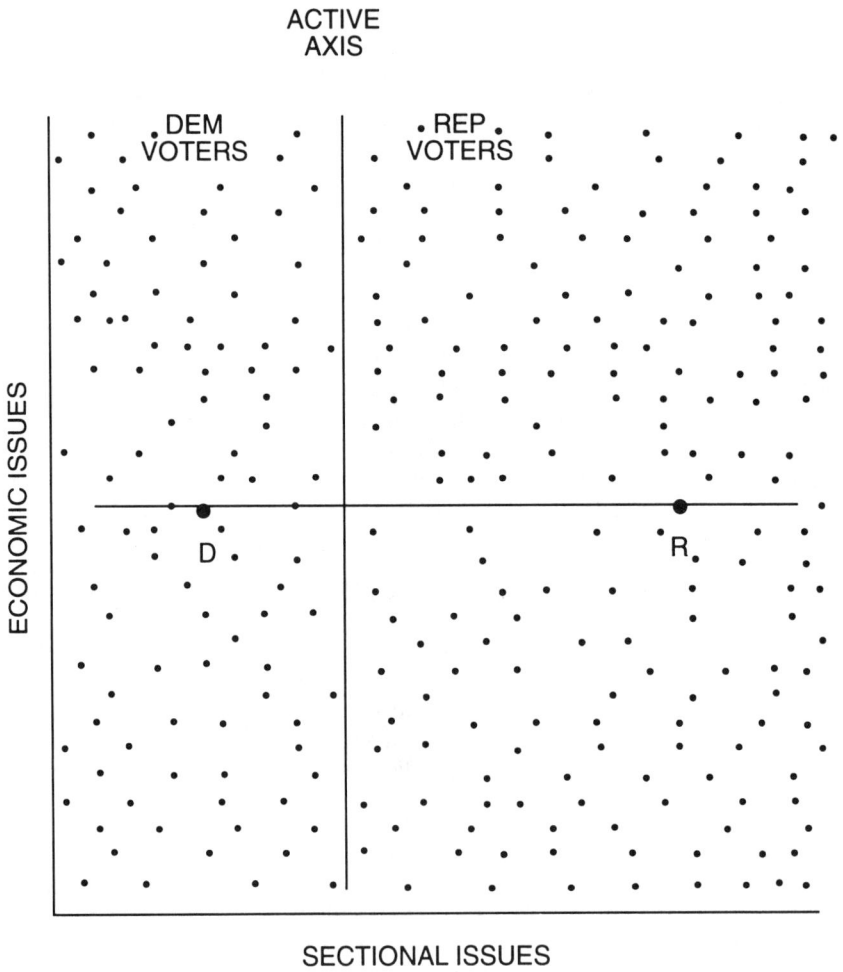

SECTIONAL ISSUES

FIGURE 1.1 (Continued)

1B.

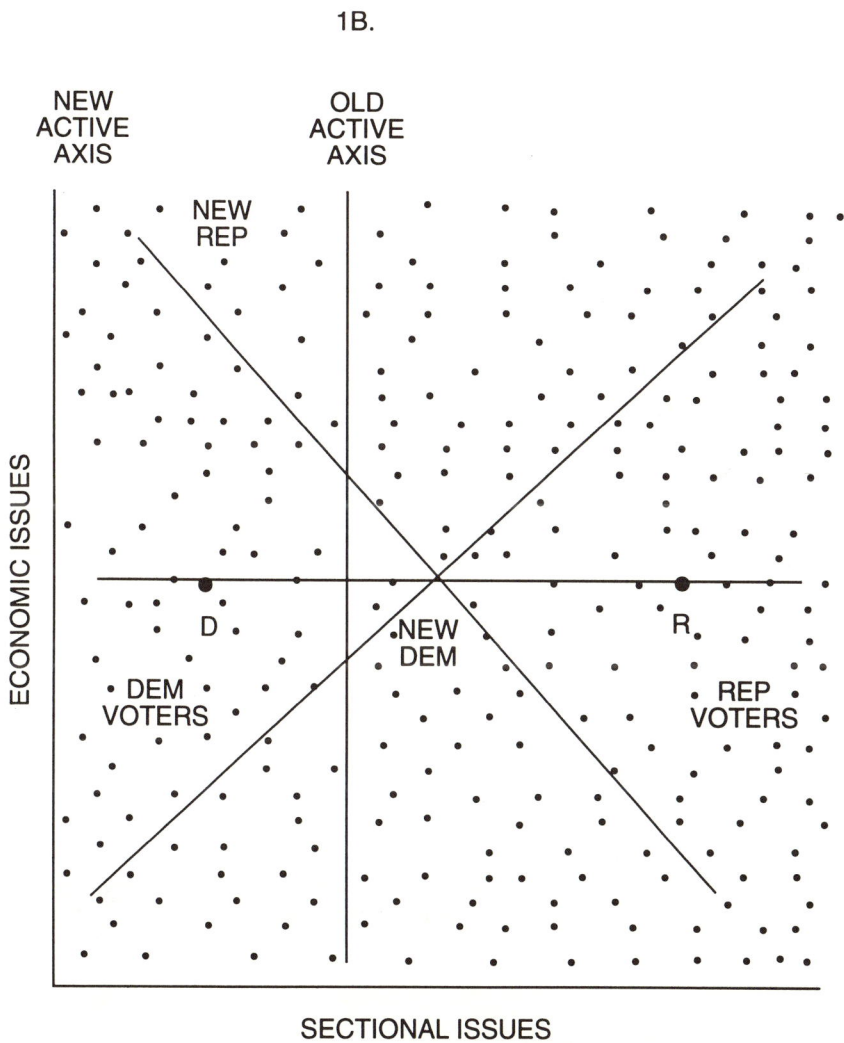

Source: Compiled by author.

positions, political rhetoric over the issue or cluster of issues takes on a passionate and moralistic quality. The polarization continues, and how party leaders respond determines the course of realignment. Polarization will continue only if the nature of the issue allows groups to take truly polar positions. Some new and volatile issues, of course, do not produce party polarization because the very nature of the issue prohibits truly polar positions such as anticommunism in the cold war era. Although many members of Congress and groups found it easy to take positions in favor of stopping the "march of communism," few could be found on the other side urging the country to join in step. Critical issues must, by their nature, allow for polar positions within the general classical liberal tradition (Hartz, 1955).

Leadership is especially important to the dynamics of polarization in the party system. For example, President Grover Cleveland's refusal to compromise on the monetary question in the 1890s increased polarization and contributed to the capture of his party by the Silver Democrats and the Populists in 1896. Initially, party leaders will often seek to avoid or straddle new and divisive issues (Sundquist 1973: 283–284). Unlike President Cleveland, party leaders usually respond by taking moderate stands and silencing issues through compromise. Demands for government action and changes in policy meet with concern among established party leaders in both major parties, and this may continue for years. Third parties often develop that are unsatisfied with the continuing moderate or centrist course of the major parties (Sundquist, 1973: 289–290). The demands for reform persist until crisis occurs. "A realignment crisis is precipitated when the moderate centrists lose control of one or both of the major parties—that is, of party policy and nominations—to one or the other of the polar forces" (Sundquist, 1973: 290).

Critical presidential elections are the result of the polarization process when the parties take distinct, passionate stands on the volatile issues of the day and the voters make a reasonably clear choice between the parties. The result is a major redistribution of electoral support and change in the long-term control of the national government. Following the critical election, the victorious party attempts to resolve concern over the issue and polarization gradually subsides as the parties seek conciliation. Although stable and nonpolarized politics eventually returns, the electoral base of the parties has changed and one party dominates national politics for an extended period of time. This portrayal of political change is important. It demonstrates the centrality of certain political issues to the dynamics of critical elections and realignment.

AN OVERVIEW OF CRITICAL ISSUES IN
FOUR PERIODS OF PARTISAN REALIGNMENT

This study examines partisan realignment in four party eras marked by the critical elections of 1860, 1896, 1932 and 1936, and 1960 and 1964.

The four periods of realignment between the 1830s and 1960s illustrate the disruptive nature of crosscutting political issues and the importance of party leadership. The second party system in the Civil War era was composed of Whigs and Democrats. It was torn apart as national attention focused on the critical issue of slavery, or more precisely, the expansion of slavery into the territories (Sundquist, 1973: 39–244). Initially, each party sought silence or compromise on the critical issue to maintain party unity. As the question of slavery grew in importance and the major parties did not respond, third parties formed, such as the Liberty party, the Barnburners in New York, and the Free-Soil party. Throughout the 1850s, the Whigs and the Democrats did not accommodate the abolitionist movement. This led to a restructuring of the Democratic party and to the demise of the Whigs. In 1856, the new Republican party formed through a coalition of northern leaders from both parties, most especially the Whigs.[2] The party's antislavery stance and strong expansionist position on economic policy produced major victories throughout the northern region. By 1860, Republican governors were elected in every northern state and Republicans won both the presidency and Congress.

With the onset of war, the slavery issue became intertwined with the issue of secession. Policymaking during Reconstruction strengthened the geographical cleavage between the parties as the Republicans lost support in the border states. The parties divided over what Sundquist (1973: 91–92) labels the "slavery–secession–war–reconstruction–Negro rights" cluster of issues.

This cluster of issues gradually faded with the end of Reconstruction. By 1878, both parties shared similar views on the role of blacks in American life and the importance of industrialization. In the years following Reconstruction, however, new forces challenged the First Republican party system. By the 1880s and 1890s, the political agenda was marked by agrarian issues centering on government control of economic interests. Farmers periodically entered the political arena with great distrust in the financiers and entrepreneurs who controlled grain elevators, railroads, and the money essential for purchasing farm supplies and equipment. With neither party offering support for these concerns, the agrarian revolt produced a variety of groups including the Granger movement and the Populist party. This period saw substantial differences between the parties on the gold-silver question, the control of businesses, the protective tariff, and expansionism.

The conflict between the two major parties on one side and numerous minor parties on the other reflects the crosscutting nature of critical issues. The First Republican party system of the Civil War era was organized on the issue of slavery and produced a clear line of geographic division between the parties. The demands of the farmer, however, represented primarily a class struggle dividing both parties and blurring geographic lines of partisan support. While the "bloody shirt" of the Civil War was continuously waved by the strong eastern wing of the Republican party, farmers in the Republican Midwest came to share many of the concerns of Democratic farmers in the

Southwest. The new economic issues cut across the strong sectional lines created by slavery and the Civil War (see Figure 1.1).

Similar to the Whigs and the Democrats of the 1850s, the Republicans and Democrats of the Civil War era sought to placate the agrarian demands by evasive positions. Throughout the 1870s and 1880s, the two parties were challenged by minor parties. The Panic of 1893 further polarized the party system as each party ousted the leaders of its minority factions. The Democrats adopted the principles of the Populist party and the Republicans took opposing positions. The election of President William McKinley in 1896 signals a shift in support for the Republican party as urban and blue-collar voters in the East and Midwest cast their ballots for the Republican party (Ladd, 1972: 109–177). Unlike the critical election of 1860 in which a new third party rose to the status of majority party, the critical election of 1896 strengthened a declining majority party. Following the election, Republican majorities enacted such measures as the gold standard and protective tariffs.

In the Progressive era of 1900 to 1920, the Republican party protected its majority party status despite attacks by Populists, urban political reform movements, and groups demanding legislation aimed at perceived social problems. The party could not, however, withstand the sudden and dramatic impact of the Great Depression. The Republican policy of limited economic intervention during the farm depression of the 1920s was consistent with the party's post-Reconstruction stance that government should not interfere with the business of industry. This position brought no relief from the economic trauma. As the election of 1932 approached, the Democratic party did not endorse radical departures from the Republican approach. As Sundquist (1973: 196) notes, "The key variable in the 1930s was not leadership but the overwhelming intrinsic power of the Great Depression as a realigning issue." Substantial shifts in Democratic support by urban, working-class, and ethnic voters in 1932 gave Roosevelt the victory and the Democratic party hope for majority status.

New Deal programs such as the Agriculture Adjustment Act, the National Recovery Act, and the Works Progress Administration were fairly pragmatic attempts to deal with severe economic problems (Hofstadter, 1948: 315–352). Nevertheless, the Democratic party presented itself as the guardian of the managerial state, and Roosevelt's victory in 1936 demonstrated a solidification of the changes in party support seen in the 1932 election. The differences between the Democratic and Republican parties in the New Deal era centered on the aggregation of wealth and government management of the economy (Ginsberg, 1976; Brady and Stewart, 1982). The New Deal realignment highlights a critical facet of the partisan realignment process; successful action by the government is necessary to "complete" or solidify the electoral changes. As Clubb, Flanigan, and Zingale (1980: 39) note, "Policy action by the government that can be perceived as a meaningful and effective response to societal problems is a further and necessary component of the realignment."

The last critical election period covered in this study are the periods before the elections of 1960 and 1964. These periods witnessed new crosscutting issues including race and the vague "social issue" (Pomper, 1975). In the 1950s, the new issues included civil rights, law and order, and perceived social permissiveness, or traditional versus countercultural values. Controversy over these issues intensified in the early 1960s. Eventually these issues polarized the major parties in the 1960 and 1964 elections. The victory of the Democratic party was accomplished by gains among both northern and southern blacks as well as northern middle-class whites. Unlike the previous eras of partisan realignment, the critical elections of 1960 and 1964 did not produce full-scale partisan realignment in which long-term control of the national government passed to a new or strengthened majority party. Instead, these elections signaled a major dealignment from the major parties including significant shifts in the Democratic party's support among certain groups and regions (e.g., Campbell, 1977).

Critical elections and partisan realignments are clearly significant changes in the electoral universe. But such electoral change is only part of partisan realignment. Usually, major and enduring shifts in partisan support entail significant changes in public policy (Ginsberg, 1972; 1976; Burnham, 1965; 1970; Beck, 1979; Brady, 1978; 1985; Brady and Stewart, 1982; 1984; Sinclair, 1982). Analysis of party platforms, federal statutes, and congressional behavior shows vividly how partisan realignments bring changes in the parties, the congressional party system, and policy outputs.[3] Brady and Stewart (1982: 81), for example, examine congressional realignment in the 1890s and the 1930s and find that both periods witness a decline in two major barriers to party government: party-constituency cross-pressures and the committee system. "Critical elections change the constituency bases of the congressional parties along a continuum which reflects the changes that are occurring in the 'party in the electorate,' thereby helping to diminish party-constituency cross-pressures. Such elections also effectively rearrange the committees of the House so that the party leadership is able to perform its function of organizing coherent majorities for legislative programs." Brady and Stewart stress the large personnel turnover as a major factor in the altered style of congressional policymaking.[4] These changes in congressional policymaking produce major policy changes focusing on the issues that provoked partisan realignment. Studies of political party platforms and federal statutes provide additional evidence in support of the theory of realignment. Examining the positions of the major parties as stated in the party platforms shows that the ideological difference between the parties is greatest in the years before and after critical elections (Ginsberg, 1972). Further, an analysis of federal statutes testifies to the policymaking ability of Congress on the realignment question (Ginsberg, 1976).[5]

These studies support Burnham's portrayal of realignments. He writes (1970: 10): "Realignments arise from emergent tensions in society which, not adequately controlled by the organization or outputs of party politics as usual, escalate to a flash point; they are issue-oriented phenomena, centrally associated with these tensions and more or less leading to resolution adjustments; they result in significant transformations in the general shape of policy; and they have relatively profound after effects on the roles played by institutional elites." He argues further that realignments are the primary means of tension management in the American political system. Societal conflicts grow more and more intense as highly diffuse governmental institutions and coalitional political parties are unable to respond effectively to the consequences of natural and rapid change in the social and economic spheres of national life. Underlying critical issues is rapid socioeconomic change. Figure 1.2 graphically summarizes the dynamics of partisan realignment.

Realignments are not simply instruments of tension management but are a "constituent act" (Burnham, 1970: 10). As an indicator of popular sovereignty, the theory of realignment provides clear linkages between mass behavioral change and public policy. These periodic events allow voters to set "the outer boundaries of policy in general, though not necessarily of policies in detail" (Burnham, 1970: 10). Traditional democratic theory views democratic governance as a continuous process whereby voters constantly inform the policymaking process and through elections hold officials accountable. The theory of realignment offers a different conception of democratic governance. Citizen control of public policy is not constant but periodic, and "it is the fact that control *can* occur that makes a system democratic" (Trilling and Campbell, 1980: 3). And as E.E. Schattschneider (1975: 136) writes, "The power of the people is not made less by the fact that it cannot be used for trivial matters. The whole world can be run on the basis of a remarkably small number of decisions. The power of the people in a democracy depends on the *importance* of the decisions made by the electorate, not the *number* of decisions they make."

THE SUPREME COURT AND PARTISAN REALIGNMENT

The Political View of Judicial Policymaking

What role does the U.S. Supreme Court play in critical elections, partisan realignment, and changes in national policy? The traditional idea of the judicial function is that it is essentially nonpolitical. Judges merely apply the existing law to the facts of a case in a neutral and objective fashion. According to this view, judges are simply legal technicians. Unlike the legislative and executive branches, the judiciary does not possess the responsibility for determining the ideological direction of policy. In resolving legal disputes, the Supreme Court decides on the basis of clear rules and principles established by prior cases, or stare decisis.

This portrayal of the judicial function, however, is rejected by social scientists. As early as the 1930s, legal realists such as Karl Llewellyn (1962) and Thurman Arnold (1935) analyzed the discretionary element in judicial decisions.[6] They argued that precedents do not necessarily constrain judges because legal principles are often contradictory, vague, or completely absent. The realists observed that when precedents are available as a guide to

FIGURE 1.2

The Dynamics of Partisan Realignment

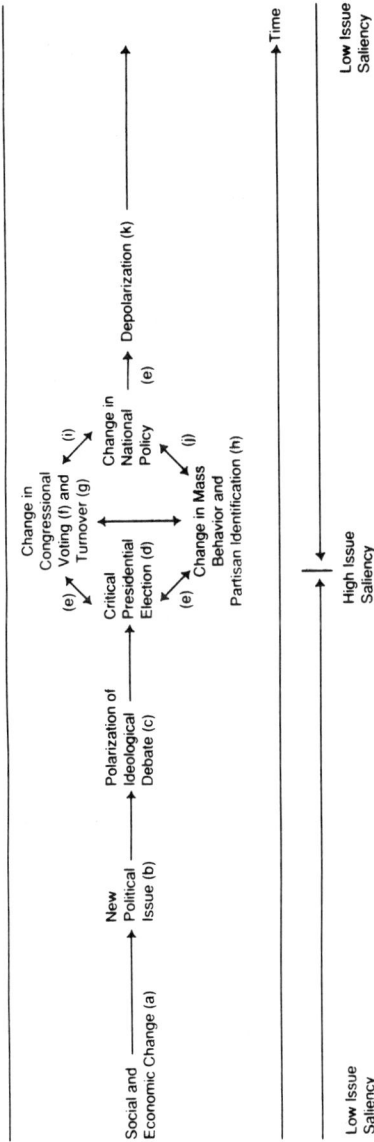

Social and Economic Change (a) → New Political Issue (b) → Polarization of Ideological Debate (c) → Critical Presidential Election (d) → Change in Mass Behavior and Partisan Identification (h)

(e) → Change in Congressional Voting (f) and Turnover (g)

(e) → Change in National Policy

(i) → Depolarization (k)

Time

Low Issue Saliency — High Issue Saliency — Low Issue Saliency

(a) E.g. Burnham (1970).
(b) E.g. Sundquist (1973); Schattschneider (1975).
(c) E.g. Ginsberg (1972); Carmines and Stimson (1986).
(d) E.g. Pomper (1975); McMichael and Trilling (1980).
(e) E.g. McDonald and Rabinowitz (1987).
(f) E.g. Sinclair (1982); Clubb, Flanigan, and Zingale (1990)
(g) E.g. Brady (1978).
(h) E.g. Campbell (1977); (1980); Anderson (1979); Erikson and Tedin (1981).
(i) E.g. Brady and Stewart (1982); Sinclair (1982); Ginsberg (1976).
(j) E.g. Clubb, Flanigan, and Zingale (1990)
(k) E.g. Ginsberg (1972); Brady (1985); Ladd (1972).

Source: Compiled by the author from sources listed in notes.

resolving a legal dispute, judges can often distinguish or overrule precedents. Implicit in this view is the assumption that the attitudes and values of individual judges affect their perception of valid claims. Judicial behavioralists began in the 1950s to explore these attitudinal factors in judicial decision-making and gave empirical support to many of the realists' claims (e.g., Rohde and Spaeth, 1976; Spaeth, 1976; Gibson, 1983; Howard, 1981). As one student of judicial decisionmaking writes, the political view of the Supreme Court does not deny that there is "a kind of *stare decisis* underlying the Supreme Court's decision but that it is based on *personal* rather than institutional precedents" (Schubert, 1974: 20).

In the modern view of the judicial process there is also a recognition that courts make policy simply as a matter of function. Judicial decisions will aid certain values and societal interests over others. This does not deny that judicial policymaking is different in some ways from legislative or executive policymaking. Seldom do partisan rivalries surface in judicial opinions. Moreover, cases often involve minor disputes in which the legal principle is clear and judges make only slight modifications (Dubois, 1980: 21). Nevertheless, discretion is often available to judges, and at the level of Supreme Court adjudication, few cases are unimportant.

Supreme Court Policymaking and Partisan Realignment

Given this political view, there are several reasons for arguing a connection between Supreme Court policymaking and partisan realignment. Although justices of the U.S. Supreme Court are not elected, the appointment process provides clear linkages between the justices, the appointing president, and political parties. Supreme Court justices are recruited for their ideological congruence with the appointing president (Scigliano, 1971). Over 90 percent of all justices nominated share the political party affiliation of the appointing president (Scigliano, 1971).[7] Moreover, it appears that the vast majority of justices live up to the president's partisan expectations on those political issues important to the president (Rohde and Spaeth, 1976; Tate, 1981; Gates and Cohen, 1988; 1989). In controversial nominations to the Court, Senate votes on confirmation will proceed in an ideological fashion (Sulfridge, 1980; Songer, 1978/1979). In sum, there are very good reasons to argue that Supreme Court policymaking is connected in some way to major political transformations such as partisan realignment.[8]

The precise role of the U.S. Supreme Court in each period of realignment is a topic worthy of analysis. Extant research focuses on two probable roles the Court may serve during realignment and critical elections. It is necessary to examine these various roles and how an in-depth analysis of judicial review of state and federal policies and interpretative evidence will provide empirical grounding for an understanding of the Supreme Court and re-alignment. At both the institutional and individual levels, there is much to be learned from studying the Court during times of critical change. The major theories are important for understanding the dynamics of partisan realignment, the range of Supreme Court policymaking, and the persistent question of the congruence of judicial review with democratic principles.[9]

THE LEGITIMATION THESIS

One of the more pervasive roles ascribed to the Supreme Court is that it serves to legitimate the policies of the popularly elected branches. Dahl (1957) advanced this position explicitly some thirty years ago and Black (1960) shortly thereafter. According to this view, the Court's primary role is to affirm the policies of the popularly elected branches. Because of public reverence for the Constitution and the myth of the justices as a "mouthpiece of a self-interpreting, self-enforcing law," these affirmations give constitutional approval to congressional and executive policies (Corwin, 1936: 1080). By upholding the actions of the popularly elected branches, the Court confers a special symbolic legitimacy to those actions and aids in creating consensus on public policies. The symbolic quality of Supreme Court adjudication enhances majority rule.

Dahl analyzes all cases in which the Supreme Court declared congressional policies unconstitutional. He finds that the Court struck down national legislation in conflict with the Bill of Rights in only ten of forty cases. Consequently, Dahl rejects the popular notion that the Court serves to protect minorities. He shows that nearly half of the overturned congressional policies were held unconstitutional within four years of their enactment. Virtually all of the "important" policies were shortly reversed by either congressional action or constitutional amendments or by subsequent decisions of the Court. Dahl attributes this to the president's ability to appoint new justices to the Court, a power exercised an average of once every twenty-two months. As he notes (1957: 294), "The Supreme Court is inevitably a part of the dominant national alliance."

For students of Supreme Court policymaking and realignment, the most important conclusion is that "policy views dominant on the Court are never for long out of line with the policy views dominant among the law making majorities of the U.S." (Dahl, 1957: 285). Instead of serving as a protector of minority interests, the Court serves to enhance majoritarian democracy by conferring the approval of the much-revered Constitution on the policies of the other branches.[10]

The legitimation thesis has many problems. First, as a logical matter it is not clear that it is necessary for the Supreme Court, an unelected body, to approve policies enacted by electorally accountable institutions (Adamany, 1973: 792). Since Chief Justice Marshall's declaration of the Supreme Court's authority to void congressional action in *Marbury v. Madison* (1803), there has been a continuous debate on the democratic character of Court policymaking. Some argue that the Court is removed from traditional democratic processes because the justices are not subject to removal by the electorate and because various political controls are ineffective, such as congressional control of the size and jurisdiction of federal courts (Berger, 1977). To these critics, Dahl's analysis suggests that such concerns are unwarranted because the forces of majority rule prevail. The Court can strike down congressional actions, but these few cases are quickly reversed. The problem with this "quick overturn" defense is that it does not demonstrate the necessity of judicial review in a democracy (McCleskey, 1966). If Court policymaking, and judicial review specifically, have not served to thwart majority will, are such activities necessary at all?

A second problem with the legitimation thesis is that it is extremely doubtful that Supreme Court decisionmaking can confer a special legitimacy on congressional and executive policies. Studies of public opinion cast doubt on the Court's ability to legitimate policy. Although legitimacy is an elusive concept, Murphy and Tannenhaus (1968: 357–359) identify three conditions for judicial legitimization: (1) the Court must be visible to the public; (2) the public must recognize that it is proper for the Court to interpret and apply constitutional principles; and (3) the Court must be viewed as both competent and objective. Public opinion surveys find that the vast majority of the public are unaware of the Court's activities and its constitutional role of interpreting and applying the Constitution (Dolbeare and Hammond, 1968; Kessel, 1966; Murphy, Tannenhaus, and Kastner, 1973). Moreover, the public's awareness of Supreme Court decisions is greater when the decisions involve striking down legislative policy rather than when decisions affirm such policies (Murphy, Tannenhaus, and Kastner, 1973). Surveys conducted in the 1960s show that many of the most visible Court actions entailed invalidations of policies dealing with civil rights, school prayer, and the rights of criminal defendants. A panel study shows that these issues remain visible to the public for some time (Murphy and Tannenhaus, 1981).

An important question beyond the Supreme Court's visibility is whether the public views these policies favorably or unfavorably and the factors that account for such reactions. The evidence to date does not support Dahl's assertion of a legitimacy-conferring capacity. Respondents to surveys in the 1960s and 1970s gave consistently more unfavorable than favorable evaluations of Supreme Court decisions (Murphy and Tannenhaus, 1981). In visible policy areas, the percentage of panel respondents giving unfavorable ratings rose from 1966 to 1975.[11] Although there is a growing body of evidence showing that Supreme Court decisions are often consistent with public opinion since 1935 (Barnum, 1985: 656–659; Marshall, 1989: 88–90), the public is often closely divided on highly salient or visible issues such as desegregation or abortion. Moreover, although there is a very small body of research showing that the Supreme Court can shift aggregate distributions of public opinion (Franklin and Kosaki: 1989), there are several studies showing that Supreme Court decisions do not move opponents to support the Court's policy position (Murphy and Tannenhaus, 1968: 359; Adamany, 1973: 804; Marshall, 1989: 131–166; Baas and Thomas, 1984: 335). A legitimacy-conferring power is simply doubtful given contemporary survey research.

Casper (1976) also criticizes the legitimation thesis but on different grounds. He argues that Dahl underestimates the Court's policymaking authority by relying solely on the Court's invalidations of federal policies. According to Casper, the Court plays an important role in national policymaking when it invalidates state laws or engages in statutory interpretation. He argues that state policy invalidations are not simply "narrow, local or regional issues" (1976: 61). Often, the overturn of state policies raises major national issues. One could cite many examples. Policies ranging from the regulation of business to civil rights and liberties illustrate the importance of these issues for national politics. Most recently, the Supreme Court decisions striking down state policies involving school desegregation, school prayer, and abortion have been at the center of partisan debate. It is impossible to consider the policy questions at stake in state policy invalidation as matters of only local interest. Finally, the national character of many invalidations is reinforced because these decisions often invalidate similar policies in other states.[12]

Given recent evidence, it seems unlikely that the Supreme Court's primary role is to legitimate national policy across one or numerous party eras. The legitimation thesis constitutes only one of three possible roles for the Supreme Court in national policymaking and partisan realignment. In the following sections we turn to the two remaining roles ascribed to the Court. First, some argue that the Court will stand in conflict with the policies of a new party majority installed in a critical election. Second, Supreme Court policymaking may contribute to the issue agenda that precipitates realignment. This study addresses both of these roles, relying on interpretative and quantitative evidence.

POLICY CONFLICT FOLLOWING CRITICAL ELECTIONS: THE "DELEGITIMIZING" ROLE

Some assert that the Supreme Court will find itself in conflict with Congress following a critical election (e.g., Funston, 1975). The role of the Court may be to impede the policymaking of new majorities ushered into power in one or more critical elections. The logic of this "delegitimizing," or policy conflict, role is straightforward. During the long stable period when one party dominates national politics, this party controls most appointments to the Supreme Court. A critical election, however, rapidly brings a new lawmaking majority to Congress. In contrast, the Supreme Court remains as custodian of the old regime's ideology. Hence, policy conflict is most likely following a critical election and until the victorious party replaces a majority of the justices. Richard Funston has termed this period as the "lag" period, when the Court is ideologically behind majoritarian forces.

Historical and quantitative analyses have sought to measure the level of conflict between the Supreme Court and the new majority party. Adamany (1973) shows that the new party confronts a Supreme Court staffed by a majority of justices appointed by the vanquished party in every partisan realignment except that of the 1890s. Moreover, historical evidence of interbranch relations and constitutional doctrine suggests that there was some level of conflict between the Court and the new regime in the realignments of 1800, 1828, 1860, and 1932. According to Adamany, the highest level of conflict was during the rise of the Jeffersonian and New Deal coalitions. During the early 1800s, partisan rivalries surfaced on issues of judicial structure and Supreme Court policy. The passage of the Circuit Court Act of 1801, its repeal, the impeachment of Justice Samuel Chase, and various anti-Republican decisions such as *Marbury v. Madison* (1803) are examples of partisan struggles involving the judiciary.

The more famous clash between the Court and the popularly elected branches occurred during the 1930s. The Democratic party faced a conservative Supreme Court willing to invalidate numerous federal statutes aimed at resolving the economic crisis. The Court struck down legislation such as the National Recovery Act and the Agricultural Adjustment Act only to face Roosevelt's famous attempt to increase the size of the nine-member Court.

Conflict was also seen in the critical elections of 1828 and 1860. The strong nationalist stance of the Marshall Court was at odds with the Jacksonian desire for greater state authority. Although there were many Supreme Court decisions and circuit court decisions in the 1860s that either avoided or affirmed Republican policies, there was intense conflict on certain issues such as military occupation of the South; see, for example, *Ex parte Merryman* (1861), *Ex parte Milligan* (1866), and *Ex parte Yerger* (1869). Congress retaliated by enacting measures that reduced the size of the Court and narrowed its jurisdiction.

Adamany (1980: 246–247) argues that these temporary periods of conflict are important for understanding the dynamics of realignment. First, the old Court appointed by the previous majority party presents the new regime with a barrier to major policymaking. The most ideological entity of the new regime, usually the presidential wing of the majority party, attempts to reverse or curb the Court. These attacks are unlikely to be successful, however, because the Court is viewed as the legitimate institution for constitutional interpretation, and members of Congress frown on an assault on constitutional structure. The forces of reform dissipate as the assault on the Court divides the new regime and weakens the image of the presidential wing of the party, and perhaps of the president as well.[13]

The question of interbranch conflict during critical election periods has also been subject to quantitative analysis in an effort to provide more precise assessments of this delegitimizing role. Funston (1975) examines the number of invalidations of federal statutes in the four-year period before a critical election and the number of invalidations after the election until the new coalition appoints a majority of new justices. During these "lag" periods of realignment, he finds that the level of conflict was especially high before a critical election. By averaging invalidations in all of these periods, he found that the level of conflict was much greater than suggested by Dahl, especially for recently enacted federal laws. Funston argues that the role of the Supreme Court during realignment is to delegitimate the policies of the new regime.[14]

Studies of the Supreme Court based on the delegitimation, or conflict, thesis are incomplete. For example, only one study examines the cases in which state policies are declared unconstitutional (Caldeira and McCrone, 1982). Ignoring state policy invalidation raises problems for assessing ideological conflict during realignment. State legislatures were the primary forums for most legislation until the early part of the twentieth century, especially with respect to economic matters. Also, state legislation enacted by partisan majorities frequently related to national political issues, and the Court's invalidation of such measures often alarmed national party leaders. For example, the contemporary national concern with abortion primarily involves state legislation regulating the availability of abortion services. The concern of national leaders with Supreme Court overturn of state policies is understandable because these decisions often implicitly invalidate similar policies throughout the nation. Finally, the cases invalidating state policies expand the range of evidence for assessing Supreme Court policymaking in periods surrounding critical elections. Between 1937 and 1964, 73 federal statutes were struck down compared to 640 state policies.

The invalidation of state policies has not gone unnoticed by scholars concerned with the relationship between Supreme Court policymaking and partisan realignment. Caldeira and McCrone (1982) examine the pattern of invalidations for both federal and state statutes between 1800 and 1973. Although the analysis is sophisticated, it illustrates a major problem in conceptualizing and measuring Supreme Court policymaking in times of partisan realignment. Caldeira and McCrone find that the number of federal and state laws invalidated appear in an episodic and nonsystematic fashion before the Civil War. There is, however, significant and gradual growth in the number of cases over time. Some cycles are noted in both state and federal cases. Periods that saw a large number of federal laws invalidated are the late 1860s, 1881 to 1909, 1919 to the late 1930s, and during the 1960s. Although the analysis does not demonstrate a statistically significant relationship between the cycles of federal and state invalidation cases, there are periods when the Court invalidated a large number of both federal and state laws. These periods are the late 1860s, the 1870s, the mid–1920s, and the late 1950s and 1960s. Caldeira and McCrone argue that the relationship between critical elections and judicial invalidations of federal and state laws is far from straightforward.

As in previous studies, this conclusion rests on a misspecified indicator of conflict between the Court and popular majorities in times of realignment. Historical analyses are sensitive to the important issues dominant on the parties' agendas and to the relationship of these issues to certain Supreme Court decisions. Unfortunately, those who seek precise estimates have paid little attention to the policy issues raised by Supreme Court decisions. As Burnham (1970: 10) reminds us, partisan realignments "are issue oriented phenomena." Ignoring the issues raised by a particular case is problematic for assessing either the impact of the Supreme Court on the realignment process or the consequences of realignment for Supreme Court policymaking.

For instance, an inspection of Table 1.1 reveals the considerable problems of inference one encounters when the issues surrounding a case are ignored. The number of federal and state policies reported during the periods of "lag" between the time the new party takes control of the popularly elected branches and the time a majority of new justices are appointed by this party are only suggestive. The number of state laws invalidated rose from seven in the period 1850–1859 to twenty-three in the period 1860–1869. This increase is not significant for the Civil War realignment unless the legal and political issues raised in these cases reflect the issues at the core of partisan conflict. Some Supreme Court decisions may not be important for the ongoing partisan debate in the party system. Although the number of invalidations increases after 1860, these decisions could involve policies regulating the conditions of real estate transfer for private homeowners or other policies that are of little concern to party leaders or the partisan struggle. This point is equally applicable in more recent years. Decisions regarding affirmative action and abortion provoke partisan comment today, but many Supreme Court decisions go unnoticed except by the legal community.

Macrolevel relationships are important, and uncovering relationships between Court decisions and systemic change is theoretically intriguing. Relying exclusively on aggregate macrolevel data, however, does not uncover the internal dynamics of the Court in critical election periods. Studies of congressional voting continue to show that party-line voting increases in critical election periods in the salient or realigning issue areas (Brady, 1985; Brady and Stewart, 1982; Sinclair, 1982). In contrast, studies of the Supreme Court and partisan realignment do not examine individual or microlevel data that could illuminate macrolevel relationships or the lack of such relationships (Gibson, 1983).[15] Although judicial voting is perhaps more complex than congressional voting,[16] the response of individual justices to the crosscutting issues of realignment may provide important clues to the role of the Supreme Court during major change in the party system. For example, those who ascribe the delegitimizer role to the Supreme Court assume that the political party affiliation of the old regime in the Court will be solid and cohesive and, consequently, in conflict with the new regime. This study examines the justices' voting for all cases of judicial review related to the critical issues across four periods of realignment.

Those who ascribe a second role to the Supreme Court do recognize that only certain types of policies or decisions are relevant to partisan realignment. Inherent in the delegitimizer role is a focus on policy conflict between the Court and the new majority party *following* a critical election. Some have argued that Supreme Court decisions may help to shape partisan debate *before* critical elections. Because in each role the Court deals with different phases of partisan realignment, the roles are not necessarily contradictory. The important point is that in each role the justices focus on only specific types of decisions or issues. This is consistent with the issue dynamics of partisan realignment and the issue-focused approach of congres-

TABLE 1.1

Summary of Supreme Court Invalidations of Federal and State Policies,
Realignment Periods, Lag Periods, and High Frequency Court-Curbing Periods

	Number of Unconstitutional Federal Policies	Number of Unconstitutional State Policies	Periods of Electoral Realignment	Periods of Lags	High Frequency Court-Curbing Periods (No. of bills)
1790-1799	0	0			
1800-1809	1	1			1802-1804 (2)
1810-1819	0	7			
1820-1829	0	8	1821-1828	1829-	1823-1831 (12)
1830-1839	0	3		-1836	
1840-1849	0	9			
1850-1859	1	7	1853-		1858-1869 (22)
1860-1869	4	23	1860	1861-1865	
1870-1879	8	37			
1880-1889	4	45	1889-		
1890-1899	5	36	1896		1893-1897 (9)
1900-1919	5	118			
1920-1929	15	140	1929-		1922-1924 (11)
1930-1939	13	91	1936	1933-	1935-1937 (37)
1940-1949	2	58		1940	
1950-1959	4	69			1955-1959 (53)
1960-1969	18	140			
1970-1979	16	177			
Total	150	1007			

Sources: Library of Congress (1978); Beck (1976: 1215 - 1218); Nagel (1969).

sional realignment. In all of the subsequent analyses, the instances of judicial review are categorized as either salient to the partisan struggle or nonsalient. This is a crucial distinction in assessing the relationships between the Supreme Court and partisan realignment. Appendix B includes a discussion of the content analytic methods that identify the salient cases of judicial review.

POLICYMAKING BEFORE CRITICAL ELECTIONS: THE AGENDA-SETTING ROLE

Most research centers on policy conflict between the Supreme Court and the popularly elected branches following a critical election. The period before a critical election is, however, very important. As crosscutting issues polarize the parties, the behavior of the party leaders will determine the intensity, duration, and timing of the realignment. In this regard, Adamany (1980) and Lasser (1983) offer different analyses of the Court's probable role before critical elections.

Adamany (1980) observes that there are a number of reasons to expect that the Supreme Court will be part of the majority party leadership before critical elections. Near the end of a party system, the Supreme Court will be composed of justices appointed primarily by the dominant alliance because the majority party had many opportunities to appoint justices. Further, Adamany argues that as the party polarizes and the coalition becomes unstable, the Court is likely to join the presidential wing of the party because of the appointment process. This alliance is also strengthened by the fact that both branches engage in enforcing, executing, and applying the law (Scigliano, 1971).[17] Therefore, during times of instability in the parties, the Court has an unusual opportunity to shape the majority party's position on the realigning issues. This is consistent with Dahl's (1957: 294) observation over twenty-five years ago: "There are times when the coalition is unstable with respect to certain key policies; at very great risk to its legitimacy powers, the Court can intervene in such cases and may succeed in establishing policy."

Adamany's analysis of the historical record portrays a Court making highly salient and volatile decisions in the years before the critical elections of 1828, 1860, 1932, 1960–64. In two presidential critical election periods, 1896 and 1960–1964, Adamany finds that the Court played a "significant role" in setting the majority party's position, which was vindicated at the ballot box. The critical election of 1896, for example, strengthened the financial and industrial interests in the Northeast and Midwest as well as the dominance of the Republican party. From the 1870s, the Court handed down cases that gave protection to industrial interests through its interpretation of the commerce and contract clauses. These major policies of the Second Republican party system continued until their repudiation in the New Deal realignment of the 1930s.

Lasser (1983) also argues that Supreme Court policymaking before critical elections is important for the process of party polarization and realignment.

His analysis of cases involving slavery and the invalidation of federal laws shows the Court played an important role in the realigning eras of the 1860s, 1890s, and the 1930s. He finds that in each era the Court made one or more "important and controversial decisions on constitutional issues that provoked realignment" (1983: 26–32). These include the 1857 decision in *Scott v. Sanford* (1857), the income tax case of *Pollock v. Farmer's Loan and Trust Co.* (1895), and the New Deal cases in the 1930s.[18] These decisions accelerated polarization in the party system.

A focus on a select number of major cases in times of critical elections is important. Nevertheless, these cases are only a very small portion of the Court's policymaking. Before even tentative acceptance of a theory of the Supreme Court and critical elections is possible, a systematic and more complete examination of the Court's policymaking is necessary. As Casper (1976) notes, the Court makes important policies through statutory interpretation and the invalidation of state laws. In these cases, the Court may incrementally build to a dramatic case such as *Dred Scott*. Further, although many cases may be deemed historically "minor" or "unimportant," a systematic examination of all cases could reveal incremental policy changes that have an important thrust. A systematic examination of Supreme Court cases involving statutory interpretation is beyond the scope of this study, although interpretative analysis of such cases is examined. The various roles ascribed to the Supreme Court during partisan realignment are examined primarily through a systematic analysis of the 743 cases in which federal or state policies were struck down as unconstitutional. The following section sets forth the propositions found in extant research and how our inferences regarding the Court and realignment may be enhanced through a systematic analysis of judicial review.

POLICYMAKING DURING PERIODS OF PARTISAN CHANGE

Previous studies of Supreme Court policymaking during realigning eras ignore the different types of issues raised by Supreme Court decisions. The lack of firm empirical support for a delegitimating role may stem from an inattention to the issue-oriented dynamics of realignment. However, historical analyses are sensitive to the diversity and complexity of legal institutions and their environment. More precise analysis must address in a conceptually meaningful way the interesting and theoretically rich hypotheses that emerge from these historical studies. Moreover, individual-level analyses are absent from extant studies, despite the admitted power of this approach and its use in the study of congressional realignment.

The following chapters focus on different realigning eras and the propositions arising from the two primary roles ascribed to the Court in periods of critical elections and partisan realignment. The first role centers on Supreme Court policymaking in the years before a critical election. As noted, Supreme Court policymaking may contribute to the majority party's stance regarding the critical issues (Adamany, 1980). Using Sundquist's (1973) description of the issue dynamics of critical elections, Adamany (1980) argues that the Court is part of the majority party leadership as it confronts new and crosscutting issues. This role leads to a number of propositions concerning the invalidation of state and federal policies. First, it is expected that many of the state and federal policies struck down by the Court relate directly to the critical issue or cluster of policy questions provoking critical elections.

Expectation 1: In the years surrounding party polarization and realignment, the critical issues will be found in the cases of state and federal policy invalidation.

This study also examines the partisan composition of the state governments enacting policies subsequently struck down by the Court. As noted, the study of the Supreme Court focuses primarily on the relationship between the Court and national majorities and/or a concern with the overturning of federal policies. State legislatures were the source of most legislation in the nineteenth century, and in many cases, the only source of government policy in volatile areas. Further, it has been shown in various studies that the partisan changes at the state level often preceded changes at the national level (Burnham, 1970; Kleppner, et al., 1979; Sundquist, 1973). As the critical issues and polar groups coalesce around the issues, state governments and state elections often witness realignment before critical national elections. Populists and farmers in the 1880s and 1890s as well as abolitionist groups from the 1830s to the 1860s initially demanded policy change from state governments rather than from the national government.

Expectation 2: The salient state policies declared unconstitutional in each period arise from states whose partisan or ideological character is different than the partisan majority on the Supreme Court.

A final concern at the aggregate or macrolevel will be directed at the Funston (1975) hypothesis: The Court will be more prone to strike down legislation in the period after a critical election. This study builds upon this notion of policy conflict following a critical election but differs in two ways. First, only the cases pertaining to the era's critical issues are treated as evidence of conflict because the invalidation of nonsalient policies receives little partisan attention. Only the salient cases represent policy conflict precipitated by realignment. For example, in terms of the number of cases, the Court did strike down a significant number of federal policies following the critical election of 1932. Included in the raw number of cases, however, is the invalidation of a temporary reduction in the retirement pay of federal judges, which is not important to the critical question of the 1932–1936 elections—the question of government management of the economy and economic interests.

A second difference in addressing the policy conflict between the Court and a new majority party is that this study examines conflict based on state policy invalidation. As noted, state governments were often the source of important legislation, and the Court may strike at the ideology of the new majority party as it finds expression at the state level.

Expectation 3: The number of salient state and federal policies will increase significantly following a critical election and continue until a majority of the justices are replaced.

To evaluate the previous expectations, one focuses on decision outcomes or cases over time. This type of aggregate analysis is powerful. Nevertheless, it is also necessary to explore the individual-level relationships that may account for the aggregate-level findings. Moreover, the portrayal of electoral realignment and change in congressional policymaking raises a number of questions regarding Supreme Court behavior at the individual level. First, to what extent does the Supreme Court divide over the crosscutting political questions as the party system polarizes? More specifically, it is expected that the level of nonunanimous cases will be higher in the salient cases, which deal with the basic realigning political questions, rather than in the nonsalient or more routine cases. There are several theoretical reasons for this expectation.

The theory of electoral realignment focuses on the saliency and level of political conflict over new and unforeseen political questions. These realigning political questions are very volatile, and political rhetoric becomes tenacious. Given the voluminous research on the importance of political attitudes in judicial decisionmaking, it is reasonable to expect that the justices will also divide on the new and difficult political questions similar to members of Congress and other party leaders (e.g., Gibson, 1983; Spaeth, 1976).

In addition, dissent is more likely in salient cases because of the underlying dynamics of realignment. Burnham argues that the American party system cannot cope with rapid and major change in the social and economic spheres of national life because of a desire to maintain party coalitions (1970: 10). During these systemic changes, the Supreme Court confronts not only more difficult and novel political questions but it also entertains more difficult questions of law. There is evidence that more difficult legal questions produce higher levels of conflict or dissent in appellate courts (e.g., Songer, 1986: 121–123).

The control of economic interests is a major crosscutting issue in the realignment of the 1890s. The Supreme Court faced novel legal questions including the development of certain financial instruments, the constitutional status of certain economic arrangements, and the development of government mechanisms for economic regulation (Keller, 1977; Warren, 1932; Twiss, 1942; Westin, 1953). The new issues present dramatic political questions and also raise troubling legal questions for the Supreme Court in the 1890s. This is not a minor tension in judicial policymaking or in jurisprudence generally. A fundamental and troubling question in the philosophy of law is the proper judicial response to maintaining legal stability in the midst of social change (e.g., Unger, 1976; Cardozo, 1921).

Finally, the justices will be highly divided in deciding realigning issues because these issues represent changing social values. The legal activity of certain political groups (e.g., McIntosh, 1985, O'Connor, 1980) and the rise of third parties (e.g., Rosenstone, Behr, and Lazarus, 1984) are symbolic of fundamental value change. The abolitionist movement before 1860 and the formation of the Farmers' Grange in the 1880s and 1890s are instructive (see also, Twiss, 1942; Warren, 1932; Dolan, 1964; Barker, 1967). Hence, there are several reasons for arguing that the Court will be similar to Congress in its level of polarization and internal division. Another expectation is that Supreme Court policymaking at the individual level will reflect increased divisiveness.

Expectation 4: The Supreme Court will decide salient cases or realigning cases nonunanimously more often than other invalidation cases and more often than all cases decided with opinion.

Research on congressional realignment and the scant evidence on the Court and realignment points to a second question at the micro-, or individual, level. Although the justices may divide more often in deciding realigning or salient cases, it is imperative to examine whether each justice's partisan affiliation structures his or her individual vote in these cases. This is important for two reasons. First, there is a large body of evidence on party voting in Congress and realigning issues. A comparison with Supreme Court voting aids in cross-institutional comparison and theoretical development. Second, the extent to which the justices' partisan affiliations structure their responses to these volatile political questions provides useful information on the microlevel behavior of the Court and the macrolevel linkages suggested by others (Gibson, 1983; 1986: 154–156). Previous studies make important assumptions regarding individual-level behavior, but there has been no precise testing of such assumptions.

The role of the justices' partisan affiliations in judicial decisionmaking has been a subject of much study (e.g., Goldman, 1975; Tate, 1981). Few would argue that a justice's partisan affiliation is the only aspect of judicial voting. Judicial decisionmaking is complex and multifaceted. Research continues to show the importance of nonpartisan elements such as role orientations, legal cues, and legal facts (cf. Baum, 1988; Gibson, 1978; Goldman, 1975; Goldman and Lamb, 1986; Howard, 1981; Segal, 1984, 1986; Tate, 1981). Nevertheless, the theory of realignment brings the role of the justices' partisan affiliations to the forefront of concern. Previous studies of the Court and realignment assume that the justices' partisan affiliations play a major role in deciding realigning questions.

For example, Dahl's (1957) classic work on the Supreme Court argued that the key to understanding Court policymaking historically is the recruitment of justices during long, stable phases of the party system. During such periods, the Court is composed of justices generally appointed by the majority party and the Court is a supportive ally (Dahl, 1957).

Dahl's emphasis on the role of partisan appointment and judicial behavior is also stressed by the other two major studies of the Court and realignment. Both Adamany (1973) and Funston (1975) emphasize the role of a justice's partisan affiliation before a critical election. They argue that the Court will be composed primarily of justices recruited by the "old regime," and hence, the justices share the perspective of the party that is often vanquished by a critical election. When a new majority party is installed in the popularly elected branches, there will be conflict over the critical issues between the Court and the new majority party. This notion of conflict assumes that *before* a critical election, the party of the justices is important in deciding critical issues. There is some quantitative evidence drawn from one period of realignment supporting this perspective.

Schmidhauser (1961) examines twenty-nine nonunanimous decisions handed down between 1837 and 1860. The cases are regionally divisive and relate to the sectional tensions of the pre–Civil War realignment. He finds that the partisan affiliations of the justices were quite important in understanding their voting in these cases. For example, on these regionally divisive issues, both southern and northern Democrats were the strongest supporters of the proslavery position. This buttresses the importance of a justice's partisan affiliation, just as partisan affiliation is stressed in the more extensive literature on congressional voting.

Expectation 5: In cases related to the realigning issues before critical elections, the justices' partisan affiliations will be a significant and powerful predictor of their votes in cases raising the salient, or realigning, political questions.

In the following chapters I examine Supreme Court policymaking in four eras of realignment. In each chapter the various levels of analyses necessary to address and answer the questions outlined above are presented. Appendix B is a discussion of the data sources and methodological concerns. In Chapters 2, 3, 4, and 5 are examinations of realigning eras marked by critical elections. Chapter 6 is a summary and evaluation of the findings of the previous chapters and an assessment of the implications for understanding Supreme Court policymaking and partisan realignment.

NOTES

1. To these insights, Campbell (1966) adds a crucial element to critical election theory. He asserted that the new agenda of realigning periods was sufficiently intense to change the partisan orientation of the electorate in the elections of 1860 and 1932 as well as to increase substantially support for the Republican party in 1896. This provides an important link between critical elections and changes in the party system.

This dramatic "conversion" of the electorate has been questioned by Kristi Anderson (1979) and others. This alternative position focuses on the gradual "mobilization" of inactive or ineligible citizens. These alternatives may actually reflect the different dynamics involved in critical elections and realignments. That is, the cleavages that occur in secular realignments appear consistent with the less dramatic mobilization thesis; the sharp cleavages in critical realignments appear consistent with the conversion thesis. Of course, Anderson's work attempts to demonstrate how mobilization was crucial to the critical realignment of the 1930s. For evidence to the contrary, see Erikson and Tedin (1981).

2. There is some evidence that economic rather than moral interests played a role in this shift by party leaders. Some argue that the northern Whigs represented the liberal capitalist wing of the party and saw their own financial interests involved in the party struggle. This is part of a revisionist view of the Civil War that ranks slavery as a secondary political issue to the economic clash of the agrarian South and the industrial North (Binkley, 1958). Nevertheless, the preponderance of evidence and historians conclude that the question of slavery was more important than the economic issues involved in the sectional controversy (e.g., Ladd, 1972).

3. The policy outputs normally associated with partisan realignment are not a characteristic of the period of electoral realignment in the 1960s; instead, these critical elections mark a long-term dealignment of the party system when partisan loyalties are disrupted but not reoriented to a new or existing majority party. Although this period witnessed many of the factors associated with partisan realignment including major turnover in Congress and a short period of policymaking activity relating to the critical issues, some have argued that the early 1960s can only be considered a period of electoral realignment. Long-term control of the government did not occur and policymaking relating to critical issues faded. As Clubb, Flanigan, and Zingale (1980) argue, partisan realignment occurs when critical elections are followed by sustained policy action. Due to the Democratic coalition in Congress and perhaps to the diffuseness of the "social issue," the 1960–1964 period can only be thought of as a period of electoral realignment rather than as a period containing all aspects of partisan realignment seen in the 1860s, 1890s, and 1930s (Brady and Stewart, 1982).

4. Sinclair (1982) argues that such a turnover is not a prerequisite to change in the congressional agenda. Significant change occurs because of highly salient issues that force a behavioral change in incumbent members; however, this highly charged atmosphere also results in significant personnel turnover.

5. Some periods of realignment demonstrate different intensity. Ginsberg (1976) examined all federal statutes enacted between 1789 and 1959 and concluded that clusters of policy change occurred during the traditional realigning eras of 1800, 1828, 1860, 1896, and 1932. But there were differences in the degree of partisanship in each realignment. In his content analysis of party platforms, Ginsberg (1972) finds that the difference between the two parties' positions on the salient issues was greatest in the Civil War realignment and much less during the New Deal realignment. In a similar vein, Brady and Stewart (1982) show that the partisan affiliation of members of Congress structured voting more in the Civil War and the 1890s realignments than in the New Deal realignment.

6. The legal realist movement, however, did not always present consistent positions. Moreover, there are major limits to legal realism as an alternative jurisprudence. See especially Tushnet (1980b).

7. This figure includes all nominations up to the appointment of Chief Justice William Rehnquist in 1986.

8. There are a number of factors regarding Supreme Court procedure that point to a more limited role during periods of partisan realignment. In contrast to Congress, the Court does not have absolute control over its agenda because it must wait for litigation to move through the appellate process. The Supreme Court's agenda may be changed because of changes in the Court's jurisdiction, personnel, doctrines, or

changes in the structure of the federal court system. Legal and doctrinal developments also contribute to agenda change. The Civil War amendments, for example, undoubtedly provided an expanded basis for litigation. Moreover, the decisions of the Supreme Court may affect the types of cases heard. The Court's interpretations of jurisdictional statutes and its doctrines regarding justiciability such as standing, ripeness, and "political questions" affect not only the types of cases heard but also the mobilization of interests provoking litigation. As Casper and Posner (1974, 1976) argue, these doctrines and the announcement of new legal rights provide important clues to potential litigants.

The structure of the judicial system is yet another factor that affects the flow of cases to the Supreme Court. One of the major structural changes in the federal judicial system was the Circuit Court of Appeals Act of 1891, which created the intermediate appellate courts. Frankfurter and Landis (1928) argue that this policy led to a reduction in the number of "trivial" cases brought before the Court.

The main point regarding these agenda-building factors is that partisan realignment is only one type of environmental factor related to the types of issues heard by the Supreme Court.

9. The Court could be judged harshly from a majoritarian perspective if it attempted to veto or delay the policies of the new majority party at a time of heightened partisanship and issue intensity (see especially Adamany, 1973: 844–845).

10. Dahl does not suggest that there is never conflict between the Court and the popularly elected branches. Without supporting data, he deduces that the periods of conflict occur when the old "alliance" is declining and a new one is rising. Dahl asserts that when the alliance to which the Court belongs is unstable, the Court can establish important policy. Nonetheless, his analysis of constitutional reversal in cases overturning federal laws suggests that the majoritarian forces will ultimately prevail.

11. These evaluations are ideological. Those who identify themselves as political liberals are more prone to favor the decisions of the Warren Court on issues such as school desegregation than respondents who identify themselves as political conservatives. These findings are perhaps the most damaging for Dahl's theory (Adamany, 1973: 818–820). If the Court cannot serve through its perceived guardianship of the Constitution to reconcile those who disagree with a particular decision—probably the most critical facet of legitimacy—then the notion of the Court as a legitimator stands on frail and unstable grounds. Limiting analysis to those who are "activists," "politically aware," or "elites" does not change the unproven case for the legitimacy-conferring capacity of the Court (Adamany, 1977). Even the politically active possess limited knowledge of the Supreme Court; attention focuses on invalidations rather than affirmations; and positive reactions covary with ideological agreement with the particular judicial policy. Using the criteria noted previously, Murphy and Tannenhaus (1968: 378) find that the Court confers legitimacy on national policy for only 12.8 percent of the respondents. It is difficult to specify the necessary level of support before inferring a legitimacy-conferring function to the Court. Nevertheless, it is reasonable to assume that at least a majority of the public should satisfy the criteria, because legitimacy is based on consensus. In sum, survey evidence does not support the legitimacy-conferring function of the Court.

12. Casper also criticizes Dahl's portrayal of the policymaking process as a zero-sum game in which there are clear winners and losers. For instance, the reversal of the Court's invalidations does not mean that the judicial action has had no effect on policymaking. The original judicial policy may mobilize interests that could affect the shape of future struggles. In addition, Dahl ignores the unsuccessful efforts to

curb or reverse judicial policy. The role of the Supreme Court, according to Casper, is greater than suggested by Dahl's analysis because of the evidence neglected in his measure of Supreme Court policymaking and the subtle play of influence in the policymaking process.

13. Adamany notes (1980: 246–247): "Burnham may be correct to characterize realignments as 'constituent acts' which temporarily concentrate sufficient political power to force rapid change in governmental policies that brings them into line with the unfettered and rapid developments that have already occurred in the nation's social and economic sectors. But this political development always remains incomplete, because the concentration of political power is broken on the issue of judicial review. And, by the time that issue is resolved, not by permanent revisions in judicial power but rather by eventual presidential appointment of a majority of justices from the new coalition, the forces of reform in the nation and the government have spent themselves."

14. Unfortunately, Funston's analysis is problematic. The "realigning" or "lag" period includes the period of electoral realignment before a critical election. This is inappropriate for measuring conflict because control of the popularly elected branches has not passed to the new majority party. The appropriate time frame for examining conflict must begin with the installation of the new party into the popularly elected branches (Beck, 1976). Further, it is inappropriate to average all of the invalidations over each realigning period (Canon and Ulmer, 1976). By separating the different realignment periods and the respective number of invalidations, they prove that only during the New Deal period was there a statistically significant increase in the number of overturned federal policies. The other quantitative studies are equally inconclusive.

Nagel (1969), for example, attempts to gauge the level of conflict by the incidence of bills introduced to curb or reverse the Supreme Court and the number of such measures reported from congressional committees from 1789 to 1959. His division of high and low periods of Court-curbing do not correspond perfectly to traditional critical election periods, when one would expect high levels of conflict. Nevertheless, at least three of the high Court-curbing periods overlap with these periods: 1823–1831, 1858–1869, and 1935–1937.

Another study builds on Nagel's work, but the findings are also inconclusive. Handberg and Hill (1980) examine the periods of Court-curbing and all cases in which the federal government participated as a principal litigant from 1801–1957. The cases accepting the federal government's position were identified. Over this 1801–1957 period, the Supreme Court upheld the government's position in 62 percent of the cases. More important, the Court is less likely to decide in favor of the federal government during periods of high Court-curbing. The low level of support is also evident in the years before the high Court-curbing period. Handberg and Hill (1980) argue that this earlier period of low support for the government's position leads to a congressional attempt to curb the Court.

15. Schmidhauser (1961) provides the only quantitative study. He examines Supreme Court voting between 1837 and 1860. Hence, the study examines only one part of one realignment. Further, a reanalysis of his data in Chapter 2 shows his conclusions may be unwarranted.

16. Outside of the justices' partisan affiliations, many factors impinge on judicial voting. Role orientations, for example, are the values constituting a judge's orientation to the role of judging and the validity of legally relevant and irrelevant facts (Gibson, 1978: 917; Howard, 1981). The basic question is whether nonlegal factors should be considered in deciding a particular dispute. Judges with "broad" role orientations will consider nonlegal factors; judges with "narrow" orientations will try to rely solely on precedent and the relevant legal facts.

17. Recent work explores the formal links provided by the U.S. solicitor general's office and the federal government's success rate as a litigant or through participation by amicus curiae briefs (Puro, 1981; O'Connor, 1981; Segal, 1986).

18. E.g., *Schechter Poultry Corp. v. United States*, 295 U.S. 495 (1935); *Panama Refining Co. v. Ryan*, 293 U.S. 388 (1935).

2

The Civil War Realignment, 1837–1878

It matters not what way the Supreme Court may hereafter decide as to the abstract question whether slavery may or may not go into a Territory under the Constitution, the people have the lawful means to introduce it or exclude it as they please, for the reason that slavery cannot exist a day or an hour anywhere, unless it is supported by local police regulations.

—Stephen Douglas
Lincoln-Douglas Debates

So what had appeared initially as a relatively simple single issue now became a cluster of related issues—slavery-secession-war—and once the shooting began the combined issue had far more polarizing power than the original issue alone had had. After the war, a new set of issues arose, and the cluster became slavery-secession–war–reconstruction–Negro rights.

—James L. Sundquist
Dynamics of the Party System

Partisan realignment in the 1850s and 1860s was the culmination of long-term sectional tensions between the North and the South. The critical issues of slavery, the Civil War, and later, Reconstruction tore apart the Jacksonian party system and led to the establishment of Republican dominance in national policymaking. The critical election of 1860 marks the beginning of what is often referred to as the First Republican party system.

The study of the Supreme Court and critical elections has focused on two possible roles. First, some have asserted that the Court will make judicial policy that contributes to the majority party's stance on the crosscutting issues before critical elections (Adamany, 1980: 249–251; Lasser, 1983: 33–113). The case of *Dred Scott* clearly supports the idea that the Court, as a member of the majority coalition, can participate in shaping the crosscutting issues on which critical elections and realignment depend. In *Scott v. Sanford* (1857), the Court declared the Missouri Compromise unconstitutional and limited federal power over the institution of slavery. The decision was handed down by a Supreme Court dominated by Democratic justices and was a controversial proslavery statement (Warren, 1932: 303–319; Hyman and Wiecek, 1982; Curry, 1969). The decision forbidding congressional control of slavery in the territories was consistent with President James Buchanan's position on the control of slavery, a position that led to the defeat of the Democratic party in three short years.

Those who ascribe a second policy role to the Supreme Court in periods of critical elections and partisan realignment focus on the period after the critical election. In the years following a critical election, a new majority party is brought to power in the popularly elected branches. Some analysts argue that there will be policy conflict between the Court and the new majority party (Nagel, 1965; Funston, 1975; Adamany, 1973; 1980). Because the membership of the Court changes slowly, the new majority party faces a Supreme Court staffed primarily of justices appointed by the vanquished majority party. The "old regime" posture of the Court is in potential conflict with the new and energetic majority party. There is certainly some evidence of conflict after 1860, such as *Hepburn v. Griswold* (1870). In *Hepburn*, the Supreme Court invalidated one aspect of a Republican Reconstruction act dealing with the important postwar issue of legal tender.

The number and pattern of cases striking down state and federal policies related to the critical issues after a critical election affords a more precise test of these roles. This approach differs from but builds upon previous research on the Supreme Court and partisan realignment in numerous ways. First, previous studies include examinations of only the cases involving the invalidation of federal statutes for assessing policy conflict between the Supreme Court and the new majority party. This study is an examination not only of the cases of federal policy invalidation but also of the more numerous instances in which state statutes are invalidated. State statutes are included because they raise controversial national issues and because policymaking at the national level was limited in scope in the nineteenth century (Ladd, 1972: 86–93, 73). State legislatures were the centers of the bulk of legislation, especially that aimed at economic regulation (Beth, 1971: 29–31). Thus, a more accurate analysis is provided by focusing on state policy invalidation rather than exclusively on federal invalidations.

This study also builds upon prior work by focusing on the types of issues raised in the policies struck down by the Court. To determine the relationship between the invalidation of state and federal policies and realignment, it is necessary to examine whether the policies struck down raise the crosscutting issues. The dynamics of realignment are closely connected with certain critical political issues that divide the party system along new ideological lines (Burnham, 1970: 10; Sundquist, 1973: 11–38). As Sundquist (1973: 31–32) has shown, the responses of party leaders to these crosscutting issues are crucial for understanding the timing and magnitude of party polarization and critical elections. As a member of the majority party coalition during the long stable phase of the Jacksonian party system, the Court could participate in shaping these issues before and after the critical election of 1860.

In addition, analysis of justices' voting provides important individual-level information that may help explain the pattern of decisionmaking. First, will the justices divide more often in the cases in which the Court strikes down a policy raising the central issues of the realignment than in nonsalient cases? Critical issues serve to fundamentally transform the political party system, and it seems reasonable to expect that these issues will also divide the justices to a greater extent than cases raising other types of policy questions. Therefore, the percentage of nonunanimous cases will be compared in the salient cases of invalidation, the nonsalient cases of invalidation, and in all cases handed down by the Court.

A second question is, To what extent do the justices' partisan affiliations structure their voting in salient cases? The partisan affiliations of judges and justices is a subject of much study outside of a concern with partisan realignment (Goldman, 1975; Tate, 1981). Although there are many factors related to judicial voting (e.g., Gibson, 1977; 1978; Howard, 1981; Rohde and Spaeth, 1976), there are reasons to expect that partisan voting will be evident in deciding to strike down salient policies as the party system polarizes. First, party-line voting in Congress has been shown in the analysis of votes on bills raising the salient issues (Brady and Stewart, 1982; Sinclair, 1982). Second, partisan voting appears probable because of the intensity of the critical issues polarizing the party system and the changing social values attendant to realignment. These changes bring novel political and legal issues, as discussed in Chapter 1 (Adamany, 1973; Schmidhauser, 1961).[1]

The eighty-seven cases of judicial nullification decided between 1837 and 1878 are the primary, but not exclusive, focus of this chapter. The number of cases in each is graphically displayed in Figure 2.1. In 1837, there was a new majority of Democratic justices when President Andrew Jackson added two additional justices including Chief Justice Roger B. Taney. Hence, 1837 marks the beginning of a Court whose members were recruited by the Democratic party. By 1878, the critical issues of the 1860 realignment were fading in importance as the Republican party retreated from its attempt to remake southern society through Reconstruction. Both parties also came to advocate similar positions on many general economic issues (Sundquist, 1973: 94, 101–113). This chapter is divided into two parts reflecting the period before the critical election of 1860 and the period immediately after the election until 1878. Before the cases of invalidation in the prewar era are examined, the changes in the Jacksonian parties that realigned the party system in the Civil War era are discussed.

THE CROSSCUTTING ISSUES AND THE ESTABLISHMENT OF REPUBLICAN DOMINANCE IN 1860

From the election of President Jackson in 1828 to the late 1840s, the second party system was competitive in the electoral arena. The Democratic party majority and the Whigs competed over several issues including the protective tariff, the expansion of the national economy, and the role of the

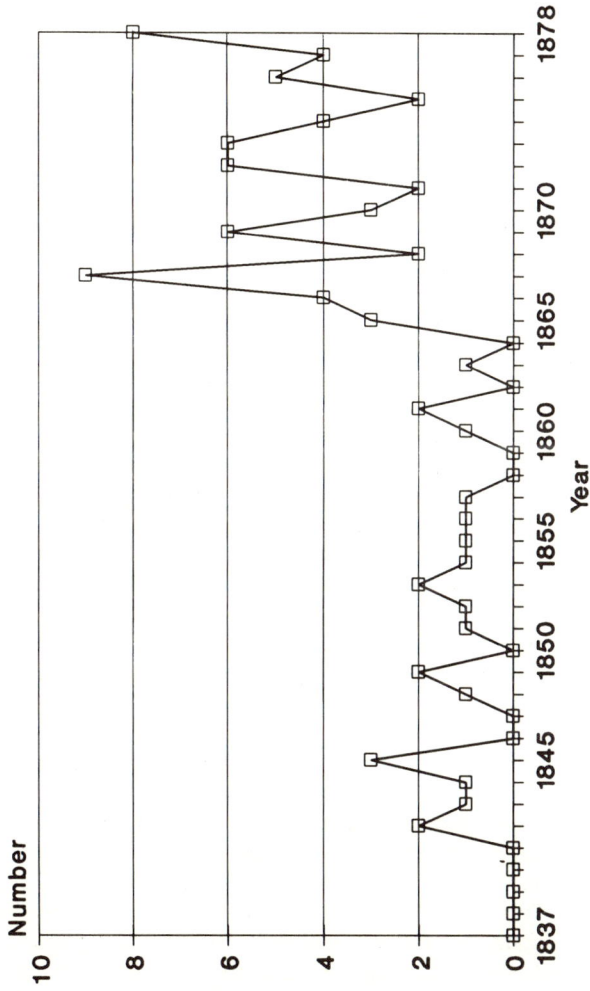

Figure 2.1
Number of Federal and State Policies
Declared Unconstitutional, 1837–1878

Source: Library of Congress (1978).

federal government in various types of internal improvements such as railroad construction and the improvement of canals and harbors (Sundquist, 1973: 39–91). The Democratic party in the "Age of Jackson" is associated with a disdain for monopoly and special privilege.Further, the party was committed in varying degrees to state autonomy, economic individualism, and the extension of democratic principles.[2] The central issues expressed in party platforms during the era include the long-standing question of the tariff as well as the role of the national government in the economy and general internal improvements (Johnson and Porter, 1970).

The differences between the Democrats and Whigs are seen in party platforms and select national policies such as President Jackson's veto of the rechartering of the National Bank and vetoes of high protective tariffs by Democratic presidents from the 1840s through the 1850s.[3] Although there were discernible differences between the Whigs and the Democrats before the 1850s, the parties were often pragmatic in their policy positions and cannot be considered programmatic. Moreover, the coalitions within each party represented a wide-ranging set of interests. For example, the Whig party has generally been portrayed as a party of eastern, commercial, industrial, and financial interests. Yet, the party also found support among western farmers and large-scale planters in the South.

As the Democrats and Whigs competed in national elections from 1837 to 1860, the Supreme Court was led by President Jackson's former attorney general, Chief Justice Roger B. Taney.[4] The Court was staffed from 1837 to 1860 with twelve Democrats and four Whig justices (Schmidhauser, 1961: 621). As in the popularly elected branches over this period, the Democrats were a stable majority on the court.[5] Some note a distinctive shift in Court policymaking under Taney away from the nationalism of the Marshall Court (Warren, 1932). Other analysts have emphasized the lines of continuity in Court policy in such areas as litigation under the contract clause (Newmyer, 1968; McCloskey, 1960: 81–100; Hyman and Wiecek, 1982: 55–85; Schmidhauser, 1961: 617–620). Although the debate over specific policy areas will continue, there does appear to be a general correspondence between the constitutional policy of the Taney Court and the general principles of the Jacksonian party system. For example, the Supreme Court treated corporate enterprise with greater suspicion consistent with President Jackson's retreat from the neomercantilist system (Swisher, 1954: 186–229; Funston, 1975: 801–802). Further, there is scattered evidence of a general unwillingness to invalidate state legislation consistent with the Democratic party's concern with states' rights.[6] For most of the pre–Civil War era, the Supreme Court and the popularly elected branches reflected the values of Jacksonian democracy.

The Jacksonian party system could not, however, contain the sectional issue of slavery. Questions regarding slavery and the slave trade rose at the constitutional convention and again during the events surrounding the Compromise of 1820. In both instances, the party leaders dealt with the issue through compromise. In each case, the compromise was temporary.

Throughout the 1830s to the early 1850s, the Democrats and Whigs sought to compromise the slavery issue, an issue promising to divide the coalitions of each major party. This evasive strategy is seen, for example, in the 1836 "gag" rule in the House of Representatives requiring the tabling of abolitionist petitions. In addition, President Jackson's order prohibiting abolitionist publications from being carried by U.S. mail illustrates the attempts by party leaders to silence the growing antislavery forces.

In the 1850s, the continued efforts of abolitionists and various legislative measures intensified sectional rivalries. The acquisition of new territory continued to raise the question of free versus slave territories throughout the period. The events precipitating civil war and realignment in the party system are well known. The defeated Wilmot Proviso of 1848 was an early sign of crisis, as it sought to make Mexican territory free of slavery. Shortly, issues involving the annexation of Texas, the admission of California, and the slave trade in the District of Columbia resulted in Henry Clay's patchwork of proslavery and antislavery provisions known as the Compromise of 1850. Although the leaders of both parties placed hope in this measure, the passage of the Kansas-Nebraska Act in 1854 further polarized the party system. Endorsing Stephen Douglas's much studied theory of popular sovereignty, the Kansas-Nebraska Act led to the establishment of rival governments and bloodshed in the Kansas territory.

The events of the decade prior to the Civil War divided each political party as the slavery issue cut across existing lines of partisan and ideological cleavage. As early as 1848, New York Democrats divided into two groups, the antislavery Barnburners and the moderate Hunkers. The volatile Kansas-Nebraska Act also strengthened growing sectional lines among Democrats as western Democrats moved to a Whig position. The impact of crosscutting issues was even greater on the loose coalition of groups in the Whig party. By the election of 1856, southerners deserted the party and northern Whigs split into two rival groups, the Nationals and the Conscience Whigs. The Conscience Whigs were the core of the new Republican party born in 1854, and the party made impressive electoral gains in the congressional elections of 1854 and 1856. By the presidential election of 1856, the Republican party was able to bring many diverse groups into the party and demonstrated considerable electoral strength.

Lincoln's victory in 1860 was the result, in part, of the splintering of Democrats in the four years before the election. Polarization within the Democratic party was spurred by "bleeding Kansas," where the issue of state control of slavery had precipitated domestic warfare. When the Democrats met in Charleston in 1860, the northern Democrats headed by Stephen Douglas split from the southern element, which favored President Buchanan's endorsement of the proslavery constitution in Kansas. Some argue that this split was inevitable because of the Supreme Court's decision in *Scott v. Sanford* (1857) (Hyman and Wiecek, 1982: 190–192); Lasser, 1983: 33–46). Speaking through Chief Justice Taney, the Court ruled that blacks could not be citizens and therefore did not have standing in federal court. Most important, Taney ruled, by way of dicta, that Congress did not have the power to exclude slavery from the territories and hence the Missouri Compromise of 1820 was unconstitutional. The Missouri Compromise of 1820 was not a minor law. The admission of Missouri as a slave state and Maine as a free state provided a sectional balance of free and slave states.

Dred Scott dealt a severe blow to the position of moderate Democrats who sought compromise on the slavery issue, hoping to maintain its multi-regional coalition (Hyman and Wiecek, 1982: 86–114). This sectional split within the Democratic party certainly increased Republican electoral hopes. Indeed, the Supreme Court historian, Charles Warren, has gone so far as to conclude that *Dred Scott* was crucial to Lincoln's victory in 1860 (1932: 357): "It may fairly be said that Chief Justice Taney elected Abraham Lincoln to the Presidency."

Scott v. Sanford (1857) is one of the most studied and debated cases in the history of the Court. It is not crucial to resolve the question of the intent of Chief Justice Taney or the six justices who wrote separate concurrences (Adamany, 1980: 250). In declaring the Missouri Compromise of 1820 unconstitutional, *Dred Scott* undoubtedly strengthened the constitutional position of the proslavery wing of the Democratic party and appears as a rallying point for the antislavery forces in Congress (Warren, 1932: 324).[7] The fact that the Court was composed of eight Democrats and one Whig only reinforced the partisan debate over the decision. Even before *Dred Scott*, the proslavery reputation of the Court was illustrated by Senator John P. Hale's (Rep.-Maine) characterization of the Court as a "citadel of slavery" (Warren, 1932: 268). *Dred Scott* can be seen as an exemplary case of Supreme Court policymaking related to realigning issues. It is also very supportive of the thesis that Supreme Court policymaking contributes to the realignment process *before* a critical election. Further support for this position may be found in analyzing all cases in which state and federal policies are declared unconstitutional.

The Critical Issues and the Invalidation of State and Federal Policies, 1837–1860

The exercise of judicial review over both state and federal legislation during the prewar period occurred episodically and nonsystematically (Caldeira and McCrone, 1982: 111–120). The Civil War marked a significant and fundamental change in the level of invalidations (Caldeira and McCrone, 1982). This change is graphically illustrated in Figure 2.1. The graph displays yearly data on the total number of cases striking down state or federal policies from 1837 to 1878. The cases of state and federal policy invalidation in the years preceding 1860 were not only small in quantity but haphazard in occurrence. The pre–Civil War era was before the "institutionalization" of judicial review (Polsby, 1968; Caldeira and McCrone, 1982; Gates, 1987). As such, the pre–Civil War era was a transitional period. In the prewar era the Supreme Court struck down eighteen state statutes and only one federal law, the important Missouri Compromise invalidated in *Dred Scott*.

The State and Federal Cases, 1837–1860. Are the statutes invalidated in the pre–Civil War period directly related to the issues involved in the Civil War realignment? Examining these cases leads one to announce the old Scottish verdict "not proved." Of the eighteen cases, only two related to the volatile issue of slavery: *Prigg v. Pennsylvania* (1842) and *Scott v. Sanford* (1857). In *Prigg*, the Supreme Court invalidated a Pennsylvania personal liberty law that placed procedural barriers for the recapture of fugitive slaves. The Court ruled that the policy was in conflict with the federal Fugitive Slave Law of 1793 and the slave owner's right to recapture fugitive slaves. Along with the Court's decision in *Dred Scott, Prigg* is consistent with the proslavery position commonly associated with the Taney Court (Warren, 1932: 212).[8] The Court did not invalidate a large number of federal or state laws directly related to the critical issues in the prewar era.

The small number of salient cases in the prewar period could be attributed to a number of factors. First, the power of the Supreme Court to invalidate state and federal policies was wielded too irregularly in this period to be useful for assessing Court policymaking. Second, the jurisdiction of the Court was more limited in the 1840s and 1850s than in the postwar period (Frankfurter and Landis, 1928: 4–55; Wiecek, 1969: 333–334). For instance, the Supreme Court lacked the power to remove state cases for trial in federal courts. Before 1867, federal habeas corpus power did not extend to judicial proceedings. Also, despite abolitionist efforts in state courts, few slavery cases reached the Supreme Court because these state cases often involved conflicts over the laws of the same state as opposed to a conflict over the laws of different states. Hence, the parties to the litigation lacked standing in federal courts (Hyman and Wiecek, 1982: 98–101).[9]

Although only two cases dealt directly with slavery, there is ample historical evidence demonstrating that cases involving other types of policies were indirectly related to the slavery issue. A study by Schmidhauser (1961) suggests that many cases, though not directly involving slavery policies, were regionally divisive and indirectly related to slavery. These cases dealt with the commerce clause as a limit on the states' police power and with the contract clause as a limit on the states' authority to control corporations. Cases relating to the general field of commerce and the legal status of corporations have been mentioned by various analysts in connection with the long-standing tensions between the North and South (Warren, 1932: 168–174; Swisher, 1954: 230).[10]

There are compelling reasons for deeming the invalidation of state policies related to commerce and corporations as salient or related to the critical issue of slavery. First, as a regional issue, slavery became intertwined with long-standing regional tensions. These tensions originated in the different economic bases of the regions. Indeed, these economic differences were so strong that some historians have concluded that the Civil War resulted primarily from the clash of southern agricultural interests with northern industrial and corporate interests (Binkley, 1958: 187; Sundquist, 1973: 75–78). The power of the state government to control corporations did reflect regional tensions connected with the control of slavery. For example, Justice John Campbell, a strong southern Democrat, noted in dissenting from a procorporation decision in 1853 (*Marshall v. Baltimore and Ohio Railroad Co.*, 1853: 353):

> It may be safely assumed that no offering could be made to the wealthy, powerful, and ambitious corporations of the populous and commercial states of the Union so valuable and none which would so serve to enlarge the influence of those states as the adoption, to its full import, of the conclusion, that to all intents and purposes, for the objects of their incorporation, these artificial persons are capable of being treated as a citizen as much as a natural person.

Although statutes attempting to regulate corporate business are not directly related to the critical issue of slavery in the prewar period, it is clear that the regional tension surrounding slavery also included economic issues (Hyman and Wiecek, 1982: 24–30). Constitutionally, these regional tensions were not confined to cases raising questions with a slavery statute.[11]

In addition, statutes related to state power over commerce became intertwined with the regional antagonisms surrounding slavery. Cases relating to the state government's control over commerce were important to southern slave interests because many state laws regulating and maintaining slavery could be jeopardized. If the Supreme Court held to a broad federal power over commerce, then that power could possibly lead to limits on the states' control of slaves, free blacks, as well as the interstate movement by blacks. As Warren (1932: 168) notes in regard to the hostile reaction of southerners to a particular commerce decision: "Once more it was clearly shown that the opposition of Southern statesmen to the expansion of power of Congress over commerce was based but slightly on abstract political doctrines relative to strict or broad constructions of the Constitution, and very greatly on the concrete fear as to its effect on the power of Southern States over slavery."

In general, Schmidhauser's (1961) point is important for discussing the relevance of commerce and corporation cases to the sectional tensions of the 1850s. Nevertheless, a focus on important constitutional issues is not without problems for the analysis of the Court's invalidation of state laws in this period. For example, cases involving commerce and corporation issues are only indirectly related to the policy issues of the critical election of 1860. The statutes involved in these cases seldom relate to critical sectional issues in terms of their overt policy goals. For example, three of the fifteen state laws invalidated by the Court from 1836 to 1860 were struck down on commerce-clause grounds. In the *Passenger Cases* (1849), the Supreme Court invalidated New York and Massachusetts per capita taxes on alien and domestic passengers arriving in their ports. Warren (1932: 178) argues that these northern immigration policies also raised the general question of the power of the southern states to control the travel of free blacks. The connection between these immigration statutes and the sectional issue of slavery is indirect.

Unlike for subsequent periods of partisan realignment, the historical evidence is voluminous in support of Schmidhauser's approach, which identifies commerce and corporation cases as indirectly related to critical issues. As such, these cases can be considered critical to the issue of slavery. Between 1842 and 1860, the Supreme Court invalidated four state statutes on commerce grounds[12] and six state statutes involving the status of corporations.[13] When the two slavery cases are also included with the commerce and corporation cases, twelve of the eighteen (66.7%) invalidations in this period related directly or indirectly to the sectional tensions in the realignment of the 1860s. The remaining cases dealt with such policies as a state tax on a federal officer,[14] mortgage moratoriums,[15] and state tolls on the Cumberland road.[16] The explicit goals of these policies did not relate directly to slavery nor is there historical evidence that could support an indirect relationship with the critical issues. Therefore, these cases are deemed nonsalient to the central issues in the 1860 election.

The Voting of Justices, 1837–1860. Clearly, the small number of invalidation cases decided before 1860 obviates precise statistical estimates of the justices' voting. It is possible, however, to analyze the voting of the justices. Such microlevel analysis provides insight into the dynamics of the Supreme Court and realignment. The highly volatile nature of these critical issues can be reflected in the divisiveness of the justices. Given research on congressional policymaking and realignment, one expects that the justices will dissent in these salient cases of invalidation more frequently than in nonsalient invalidation cases or in all cases decided by the Court.

The volatility of realigning issues is vivid when the salient cases are compared with the nonsalient cases. The level of dissent in slavery, commerce, and corporation cases is much higher than the level of dissent in all cases decided by the Court.[17] Table 2.1 displays the results. Nine of the eleven cases decided between 1840 and 1860 were nonunanimous. Only 50 percent of the nonsalient cases of invalidation and only 16 percent of all cases were decided nonunanimously. In sum, the justices were more prone to divide in invalidation cases raising salient issues than in other types of cases handed down in this period. Further, the high level of dissent is not due to the presence of a lone dissenter. Although Justice Peter Daniel has long been known for his solo dissents on the Taney Court (Frank, 1964), the dissenting behavior in these salient invalidation cases rests on two, and more often, three justices. The high level of dissent and the presence of joint dissents are consistent with Dolan's (1964) study of dissent during the Taney Court period. Dolan (1964: 284) notes: "After 1850 the pattern of dissent changed from sporadic, isolated instances of individual judges entering minority opinions . . . to one in which three or four judges took strong issue with the political assumptions of the majority."[18]

The divisiveness of realigning political questions is intriguing, but it is crucial to examine the degree to which partisan affiliation structures each justice's response to these issues.[19] Schmidhauser (1961) addresses the question of partisan unity in the Court in his study of the twenty-nine

TABLE 2.1

Percentage of Nonunanimous Cases in Regionally Divisive
Invalidation Cases Compared with All Cases Decided with Opinion,
1840-1860

Period	Cases Deemed Regionally Divisive		All Cases Decided [a]	
	Percent	Number	Percent	Number
1840-1845	00.0	1	17.2	232
1846-1850	100.0	3	17.4	317
1851-1855	100.0	4	20.6	373
1856-1860	66.7	3	11.9	369
Overall	66.7 (mean)	11	16.8 (mean)	1291

[a]These percentages were compiled from data in Dolan (1964: 286).

Source: Compiled by the author from *United States Reports.*

nonunanimous cases raising issues of slavery, commerce, and the status of corporations between 1837 and 1860. The cases were cited by one or more political historians and considered regionally divisive. The cases include the invalidation cases discussed and cases involving statutory construction.

The results of Schmidhauser's scaling analysis are displayed in Table 2.2. The table also categorizes the justices into groups ranging from strong pronorthern justices to strong prosouthern justices based on the scale score, or ranking, of pronorthern votes. The weakest supporters of the northern position in these cases included only northern and southern Democratic justices. These justices are classified as moderate or strong prosouthern. This may not be surprising, because appointments to the Court in this period are described as nominating "northern men of southern principles" (Adamany, 1980: 250). Although both southern and northern Democrats can be found in the neutral category, there are none who were pronorthern, with the exception of Justice Baldwin. Justice Henry Baldwin, however, has been characterized as a "maverick" and to some extent eccentric in his judicial career (Schmidhauser, 1961: 627). Also, the voting of all the Whigs serving on the Court is either moderately or strongly in support of the northern position.

The fact that both northern and southern Democratic justices were the strongest supporters of the prosouthern position in cases of slavery, commerce, and corporations supports the view that the justices are likely to divide along partisan lines. This is certainly true of the voting of justices in *Dred Scott,* when both northern and southern Democratic justices joined in striking down the Missouri Compromise. Adamany, for example, argues (1980: 248):

If one views the presidential wing of the dominant party as having a stable base of support within the party and the electorate during the long eras

TABLE 2.2

Schmidhauser's Categorization of the Voting of the Justices
in Slavery, Commerce, and Corporation Cases,
1837-1860

Category	Scale Score	Justice	Section and Party
Strong Pronorthern Score	29	Story	Northern Whig
	28	McLean	Northern Whig
Moderate Pronorthern Score	22	Curtis	Northern Whig
	22	Baldwin	Northern Democrat
	20	Wayne	Southern Whig
Neutral Score	16	McKinley	Southern Democrat
	14	Clifford	Northern Democrat
	14	Woodbury	Northern Democrat
	14	Taney	Southern Democrat
Moderate Prosouthern Score	12	Grier	Northern Democrat
	10	Nelson	Northern Democrat
	10	Thompson	Northern Democrat
Strong Prosouthern Score	4	Catron	Southern Democrat
	1	Campbell	Southern Democrat
	0	Daniel	Southern Democrat
	0	Barbour	Southern Democrat
			n=29

Source: Adapted from Schmidhauser (1961: 624).

between critical elections, then one expects also that the justices named by succeeding presidents of the same party will usually share a coherent executive perspective on crucial national issues. Hence, as new issues create the potential for a critical election, the Supreme Court will ordinarily side with the presidential wing of the party in shaping a strategy for dealing with those issues.

It is unclear, however, whether Schmidhauser's (1961) results yield firm support for this argument. The scale scores cover an extended period of time, and these scores do not consider partisan voting in cases decided by the same group of justices; that is, the scale scores for southern and northern Democratic justices do not depict the actual voting alignment of the justices when these justices sat together in deciding the cases.

It was possible to reanalyze Schmidhauser's data through the use of bloc analysis for six cases involving commerce and corporation issues decided between 1853 and 1856 (Bolner, Feldman, and Gates, 1982). In three of these cases, the Court invalidated state laws, and in the other three instances, the Court upheld state laws. During this period, the membership of the Court did not change. The remaining natural court periods contained too few cases for analysis. In these select but regionally divisive cases, there were two solid blocs of justices.[20] The partisan composition of these blocs does not support Adamany's (1980: 248) argument. The blocs demonstrate an almost perfect division between northern and southern Democratic justices. From 1853 to 1856, the Court was composed of three Whigs, two northern Democrats, and four southern Democrats. The first bloc identified is composed of all but one of the southern Democrats and includes Justices John Catron, John Campbell, and Peter Daniel. The other bloc consists of all of the remaining justices including the Whig justices, John McLean, Benjamin Curtis, and James Wayne;[21] the northern Democratic justices, Robert Grier and Samuel Nelson; and the one southern, or border-state, Democrat, Chief Justice Taney.

Although the small number of cases over natural court periods prohibits extending bloc analysis for a larger proportion of Schmidhauser's cases, these results cast some doubt on the probability that the justices of the long dominant majority party will join together in resolving all cases that raise the central issues of the critical election of 1860. The bloc analysis suggests that the issues of state power cut across the Democrats on the Court, with the exception of Chief Justice Taney, in the same regional fashion as occurred within the party system. Further, the proportion of prosouthern votes of these justices is similar to their voting in all twenty-nine cases considered by Schmidhauser.[22] The results of the bloc analysis are more consistent with Lasser's (1983) analysis of all slavery cases; only in the case of *Dred Scott* do northern and southern Democratic justices join together in support of the presidential wing of the party on the critical issue of slavery. The results show that the salient cases raise issues that cut across party lines in the same crosscutting fashion as seen in congressional voting and in the changing electoral coalitions of the parties.

It should be emphasized, however, that these cases are an extremely small number of the regionally divisive cases. In addition, the voting of the justices in all cases decided by the Court is not examined, which makes it impossible to note whether similar alignments occur in all types of nonunanimous cases. Most important, the confidence in the bloc analysis results is weakened because fifteen of the thirty-six pairwise agreement scores for the justices cannot be considered different from what one would obtain by chance agreement assuming random voting (Willetts, 1972).[23] The examination of the justices' voting should be viewed as tentative. Nevertheless, the disagreements between northern and southern Democratic justices appear much more complex than depicted by Schmidhauser's (1961) analysis.

Conclusion: The Pre-1860 Period

In closing the examination of judicial review in the prewar era, a number of summary points are in order. First, analysis of the eighteen cases does support the hypothesis that the Court did invalidate state statutes related to the central issues prior to the critical election of 1860. The invalidation agenda is marked by a large number of cases that directly or indirectly raised the issue of slavery or slavery interests. Also, one cannot ignore the importance of *Dred Scott* for the growing sectional crisis. When the commerce and corporation cases are included with the slavery cases, the percentage of regionally divisive cases is 66.7 percent, or twelve of the eighteen cases.

The absence of a large number of salient cases is because judicial review had yet to become "institutionalized" as a regular component of Supreme Court policymaking. Indeed, *Dred Scott* represents the first case invalidating a federal law since the establishment of judicial review in *Marbury v. Madison* (1803). Whatever the reason, the fact remains that few cases of invalidation occurred in the prewar era, but these often related to the central issue that resulted in the realignment of the Jacksonian party system.

The justices' voting patterns in the invalidation cases and Schmidhauser's class of more numerous regionally divisive cases produces only limited support for the proposition that the justices will divide along party lines on realigning questions. It is clear that the justices were more prone to divide in such cases than in other types of cases. Schmidhauser's (1961) analysis of support scores for all justices over the entire period shows ideological congruence between both northern and southern Democratic justices. But the results of the bloc analysis for the cases decided by the same group of justices between 1853 and 1856 casts some doubt on the degree of congruence among Democratic justices. The bloc analysis suggests strongly that the divisive issues divided the Democratic justices along regional lines similar to the division of the political party system.

We can see at the individual level that the realigning issues are divisive. The level of dissent in regionally divisive cases is quite high compared to other types of cases. Given the previous emphasis on the Supreme Court as part of the majority party, it is quite surprising that the justices do not appear to divide along partisan lines. The latter point is especially important when we turn to Supreme Court policymaking and judicial review following a critical election.

NEW INDICATORS OF CONFLICT BETWEEN THE COURT AND A NEW MAJORITY PARTY

The critical election of 1860 ushered in not only a Republican president but a new Republican Congress. The Republican party maintained control of the popularly elected branches throughout the Civil War period and throughout most of Reconstruction. Indeed, the Republican party controlled both chambers of Congress and the presidency from 1860 to 1874, when the Republicans lost their majority in the House. Moreover, the partisan control of state governments reflected a greater sectional alignment; the Republicans controlled most state governments in the North and the Democrats controlled most state governments in the South (Clubb, Flanigan, and Zingale, 1980: 189–215).

Following President Lincoln's election, partisan rivalries persisted over war-related matters such as Lincoln's suspension of habeas corpus, the establishment of martial law, the emancipation of blacks, the income tax, and conscription. By the war's end, the sectional division between the political parties was strengthened by the divisive issues of loyalty oaths, civil rights, and the course of Reconstruction (Sundquist, 1973: 85–86; Hyman and Wiecek, 1982: 232–294). The platforms of the parties from 1864 to 1876 also reflect differences over the flow of immigrants and public land grants to corporations (Johnson and Porter, 1970). These issues remained on the agenda of both parties until the Compromise of 1877. The Republican agreement to stop military occupation of the South signaled the decline of the critical issues of slavery, secession, war, and Negro rights, which had fundamentally realigned the American party system.

Students of the Supreme Court and critical elections focus considerable attention on the probability of policy conflict between the Supreme Court and the new majority party. The rationale for this policy conflict rests on various premises. First, the justices on the Court at the time a new majority rises to power were appointed by presidents of the old majority party and remain a solid and cohesive bloc of the "old regime" (Adamany, 1973: 823–825). Second, the justices of the old regime continue to serve after the critical election and until the victorious party is able to appoint a new majority.[24] These conditions are clearly met in the period immediately following the election of 1860; the Supreme Court was staffed by eight Democrats and one Whig. Also the appointment of new justices by Lincoln was not immediate. A majority of Republican-appointed justices was not achieved until 1864.[25]

Judicial politics during the Civil War and Reconstruction is a subject of much debate among political historians. Many stress the policy conflicts between the Supreme Court and the new majority party (Warren, 1932; McCloskey, 1960; Swisher, 1954). The Republican Congress, for example, changed the jurisdiction of the Court in order to prevent a decision testing the constitutionality of the Republican Habeas Corpus Act. Although the Court upheld congressional power to change its jurisdiction in *Ex parte McCardle* (1869), the episode is symbolic of the clash of partisan perspectives. The Republican Congress also increased the size of the Court to ten justices in March of 1863.[26] This change increased Lincoln's appointment opportunities, which were already numerous due to the deaths of Justices Daniel and McLean as well as to Justice Campbell's vacancy. There is also evidence that President Lincoln attempted to prevent certain war-related issues from arising on the judicial agenda. At the same time, Chief Justice Taney was writing opinions in *anticipation* of certain controversial issues such as arbitrary arrests, conscription, and emancipation (Hyman and Wiecek, 1982: 250).

During the 1860s, Congress sought to curb judicial power. One measure was an 1868 proposal requiring a two-thirds majority on the Supreme Court when invalidating a congressional statute. This reflects a concern among Republicans, a concern fueled by some notable Supreme Court decisions. In a circuit court decision, for example, Chief Justice Taney issued a writ ordering the release of a civilian arrested by the military. *Ex parte Merryman* (1861) was subsequently ignored and repudiated by Lincoln as he asserted executive emergency powers. In 1866, the Republican plans to use military forces in reconstructing the South were dealt a "staggering blow" in *Ex parte Milligan* (1866) (Warren, 1932: 423). The Court voided the use of military trials when civilian trial courts were operating. The use of state and federal loyalty oaths were also struck down as a precondition for professional practice.[27]

Republican legal tender policies also met with judicial hostility. Although the Court denied jurisdiction to an earlier challenge to the Legal Tender Acts in 1863[28] and skirted the issue in 1869,[29] it provoked partisan passions in *Hepburn v. Griswold* (1870). Chief Justice Samuel Chase, Justice Stephen Field, and the two remaining Democratic justices held that paper money could not be used for payment of debts contracted prior to the passage of the Legal Tender Acts. The criticism that was leveled against the Court focused not only on the dissents of the three Republican justices but also on the very broad language of the majority opinion. The opinion questioned the constitutionality of all aspects of the Legal Tender Acts (Adamany, 1973: 835; Warren, 1932: 466–67). The decision was overruled sixteen months later as a vacancy and the creation of a new seat provided President Ulysses Grant the opportunity to appoint two justices (Ratner, 1935). In *Knox v. Lee* (1871), the constitutionality of the Legal Tender Acts was upheld and the four-man majority in *Hepburn* composed of Chief Justice Chase and the Democratic justices became the dissenters.

The conflict between the Supreme Court and the new majority party from the 1860s to 1870–71 can be seen in these selected cases and congressional actions. Yet, the historical record is not overwhelming in support of a policy conflict. The Court was not continually at odds with the Republican party. Indeed, the Republican Congress appeared to have faith in the judiciary, as it gave extensive authority to the federal courts over the new loyalty oath program. The jurisdiction of federal courts and the Supreme Court was also greatly extended through a series of acts from 1863 to 1875 (Wiecek, 1969).

Further, the Court's major decisions do not reflect a consistent stand against Republican policies. The Supreme Court refused to rule or denied jurisdiction in cases involving the constitutionality of certain reconstruction policies.[30] Despite Taney's circuit court opinion in *Ex parte Merryman* (1861), the entire Court refused to hear the question of military trials in 1864.[31] The Court also upheld Republican policies dealing with the Civil War and Reconstruction. For example, the Court upheld President Lincoln's exercise of executive authority in the blockade of the South in *Prize Cases* (1862) (Warren, 1932: 416–417). In sum, the historical record does not demonstrate a consistent period of conflict following the critical election of 1860. An analysis of the Supreme Court's invalidation of state and federal statutes, however, may yield further evidence of policy conflict.

The State and Federal Cases, 1861–1878. Between 1860 and 1878, the Supreme Court struck down fifty-eight state policies and ten federal statutes. Compared to the sporadic and nonsystematic character of judicial review

TABLE 2.3

Policy Issues in the Supreme Court's
Invalidation of State and Federal Policies,
1861-1878

Policy Area	Number of Policies	Percent of Total Cases	Percent Nonunanimous
Civil War & Reconstruction	11	16.4	90.9
Business Taxation & Regulation	27	40.3	33.3
General Market Relations	9	13.4	11.1
Public Land Disputes	3	4.5	00.0
Immigration	4	5.8	00.0
Federalism	9	13.4	22.2
Miscellaneous	5	7.5	20.0
Total	68	100.0	25.3 (Mean)

Sources: Compiled by the author from *United States Reports.*

in the prewar era, this level of invalidations is extremely high. The number of invalidations of both state and federal statutes grew systematically and gradually following the Civil War (Caldeira and McCrone, 1982). This rather abrupt change in the level of state law invalidations was not due to the addition of new states (Caldeira and McCrone, 1982: 116).

Although this significant increase is suggestive of potential conflict between the Court and the new majority party, an examination of the issues raised in the cases and their relation to the critical election is necessary. Table 2.3 presents the distribution of the cases by various policy areas. Of the sixty-eight cases of invalidation, eleven cases involved statutes raising either slavery, Reconstruction, or war-related issues. There are seven state policies and four federal statutes included.[32] Therefore, although invalidations of state and federal policies increased in the post-1860 period, only 16.2 percent of the cases raised critical issues related to realignment.

The largest class of cases related to the regulation or taxation of businesses. Of the sixty-eight cases, twenty-seven or 39.7 percent, involved statutes that taxed or regulated businesses. Included in this category are state statutes such as a Louisiana statute imposing a tax on ships entering its ports;[33] a Maryland statute levying a higher trading license fee for nonresidents than for residents of the state;[34] and a Missouri statute imposing a tax on a railroad before a grant of exemption had expired.[35] The only federal statute involved in this area was an 1867 statute regulating the sale of flammable lamp oil, which the Court struck down as a police regulation reserved to the states.[36]

The remaining cases raised a variety of issues including banking, general contracts and debts, public land disputes, immigration, as well as federalism or conflicts between state and national government units. The cases relating to federalism included six state statutes imposing taxes on U.S. notes, securities, or national bank stock.[37] Also, three of the federalism cases overturned statutes that had vested in rem jurisdiction in admiralty disputes to their respective state court systems. The Court invalidated the statutes on the basis of the Judiciary Act of 1789, which conferred exclusive admiralty jurisdiction on the federal courts.[38]

The Court also invalidated seven state and two federal statutes involving issues of general market relations such as debt collection and contractual relations.[39] Three cases involved the invalidation of state laws that were found to interfere with congressional control over public lands or state taxes on land reserved by treaty to certain Indian tribes.[40] Also, state statutes establishing immigration policy through shipping regulations were struck down by the Court.[41]

In short, there were a variety of issues in the sixty-eight cases of state and federal laws decided between 1860 and 1878. The increase in the level of invalidations is simply not attributable to a Democratic court striking out at policies of a new majority party as that party's policies find expression at the national or state level. Nonetheless, it is necessary to turn to the eleven cases that raised Reconstruction issues in order to determine whether these invalidations are suggestive of policy conflict with the Republican party during the lag period from 1860 to 1870–71. The yearly pattern of these cases may support Funston's (1975) hypothesis of conflict during the policy "lag" period.

There is some evidence of policy conflict during this period as measured by the salient state and federal policies invalidated. In 1867, for example, the Supreme Court struck down a federal loyalty oath directed at attorneys seeking to practice before federal courts in *Ex parte Garland* (1867). At the same time, the Court struck down constitutional provisions imposing similar oaths on clergymen in the state in *Cummings v. Missouri* (1867). In 1870, the infamous case of *Hepburn v. Griswold* (1870) was decided and produced bitter criticism in the partisan press. The Court struck down the application of the Legal Tender Acts as applied to the payment of debts contracted prior to the passage of the acts. The majority opinion by Chief Justice Chase appeared to call into question the constitutionality of all aspects of the acts. Partisan concerns raised in *Hepburn* were put to rest in the following year, however, as Grant appointed two new justices and the Court overruled *Hepburn* in *Knox v. Lee* (1871).

In the two loyalty oath cases of 1867, the four justices appointed prior to Lincoln were joined by Justice Field in striking down these Reconstruction measures. In the legal tender case of *Hepburn*, both Chief Justice Chase and Field joined the two remaining Democratic justices. These three cases, however, are the only salient federal and state invalidations during the lag period, when the highest level of policy conflict might be expected. The remaining eight cases that raised Reconstruction issues were decided between 1872 and 1878. By 1872, Republican presidents and Republican senates had selected eight new justices, and only Justice Nathan Clifford remained from the prewar Court. The large proportion of invalidations during this period illustrates that there is little relationship between the number of federal and state invalidations dealing with Reconstruction policies and the policy lag period. Moreover, the eight cases decided between 1872 and 1878 reflect an affirmation of federal jurisdiction over the Reconstruction program as well as a gradual withdrawal from radical Reconstruction policies.

In *U.S. v. Klein* (1872), the Court struck down an 1870 congressional act that made presidential pardons inadmissible in the court of claims and required the dismissal of appeals from the Supreme Court if the litigant had not shown loyalty to the Union. The Court also invalidated three state Reconstruction policies in 1872. Each case arose from the Deep South and involved Reconstruction policies aimed at contractual relations. In *Delmas v. Insurance Company* (1872), a Louisiana constitutional provision prevented the enforcement of a contract by the state courts when a consideration in the contract was confederate money. The Court found this provision to be in conflict with the contract clause. In *White v. Hart* (1872) and *Osborne v. Nicholson* (1872), the Court also found violations of the contract clause in constitutional provisions from Georgia and Arkansas that prohibited state courts from enforcing any contract involving a slave.

White v. Hart (1872) represents judicial nullification of a state Reconstruction policy but also an affirmation of federal control over the Reconstruction program. One of the primary concerns of Republicans with regard to the Supreme Court was whether the Court would strike down the general power of Congress over the entire Reconstruction program, not simply whether the Court would strike down specific types of policies such as the use of military commissions at question in *Ex parte Milligan* (1866). The legal status of states during the period of secession was the crucial constitutional issue for Reconstruction. The specifics of the debate do not need elaboration, but it was precisely this important question that the Court addressed in *White v. Hart* (1872). As it struck down a state-level Reconstruction measure, the Court dismissed the question of the status of the states during the war as a political question to be determined by Congress. Therefore, the decision tacitly endorsed the Republican theory of secession, which was used to justify congressional power over Reconstruction. The outcome of *White v. Hart* (1872) is complicated because the Court struck down a state-level reconstruction measure at the same time it gave its approval to congressional power over Reconstruction.[42]

The remaining three cases of invalidation of state and federal laws relating to Reconstruction were decided following the appointment of Justice Joseph Bradley and Chief Justice Morrison Waite from 1876 to 1878. The decisions were handed down three to five years after the retirement of Chase and the overturn of the first legal tender case. During this period, the Republican party was moving away from close adherence with the doctrines of the radical Republicans. As Carl Brent Swisher (1954: 344) has noted, "At a time the federal government was growing weary of the task of policing the South and when the ineffectiveness of its efforts was becoming clear to the

TABLE 2.4

Distribution of Salient[a] and Nonsalient State Cases by Partisan
Control of State Government at Time of Policy Enactment,
1861-1878

Partisan Status by Region	Number of Salient	Percent	Number of Nonsalient	Percent
Democratic-East[b]	0	00.0	1	3.6
Democratic-West[c] & South[d]	1	14.3	4	14.3
Mixed[e]-East	0	00.0	7	25.0
Mixed[e]-West & South	1	14.3	2	7.1
Republican-East	0	00.0	4	14.3
Republican-West & South	5	71.4	10	35.7
Total	7	100.0	28	100.0
Missing data	0		33	

[a]Includes cases dealing with Reconstruction and Civil War-related policies.
[b]Includes the northeastern and middle Atlantic regions.
[c]Includes the northeast central and northwest central regions.
[d]Includes the solid South and border states.
[e]States governments classifies as mixed in terms of partisan control had different parties in each chamber of the legislature or the legislature was controlled by one party and the governorship by another party. Control is signified by either a solid majority or a simple plurality.

Source: Clubb, Flanigan, and Zingale (1990); *United States Reports.*

country, it [the invalidation of Reconstruction laws] undoubtedly had the effect of discouraging the remaining sponsors of Radical Reconstruction."

In *U.S. v. Reese* (1876), the Supreme Court invalidated two sections of the Enforcement Act of 1870 and narrowly construed the meaning of the Fifteenth Amendment. The Enforcement Act provided for the punishment of local election officials if the officials refused to permit qualified voters to vote or hindered individuals seeking to qualify. The Court ruled that these provisions were not within the scope of congressional power derived from the Fifteenth Amendment. Two years later, in *Hall v. DeCuir* (1878), the Court struck down a Louisiana Reconstruction act prohibiting interstate common carriers from discriminating on the basis of race. And in the same term, the Court ruled a Tennessee constitutional provision unconstitutional in *Keith v. Clark* (1878). This Reconstruction policy voided the bills of the state bank for the payment of taxes and declared all bills issued during the Civil War to be void.

An examination of the partisan control of the state governments enacting these salient policies demonstrates that these statutes or constitutional provisions were enacted primarily by Republican governments in the solid South and border states. As Table 2.4 illustrates, five of the seven state policies originated in the new Republican governments established in the South. All of the seven policies were enacted within three years after the Civil War.

It is evident that these cases represent complex outcomes. It is fair to characterize the cases as reflecting a dual concern: namely, the affirmation of congressional control over Reconstruction policy as demonstrated in the cases of state invalidation and a gradual withdrawal from the national Reconstruction program. Nonetheless, the major point is that the examination of the sixty-eight cases of federal and state law invalidation yields only minimal support for the delegitimizer, or policy conflict, role so often ascribed to the Court in times of realignment. There is no evidence of concerted and sustained conflict between the Court and the new majority party in popularly elected branches. Although slightly over 16 percent of the cases raised the critical issues of realignment, the extent of conflict is questionable as indicated by the raw number of federal and state invalidations and their timing. Eight of the eleven Reconstruction cases handed down between 1860 and 1878 were decided after the new majority party had made numerous appointments. The delegitimizing role is simply not shown in the invalidation of state and federal policies either in terms of the number of cases or the issues presented.[43] The reasons Supreme Court policymaking does not always stand as a barrier to a new majority party are undoubtedly complex. Part of the answer may well be found by examining the justices' voting in the cases raising crosscutting issues. The delegitimizer-role theory assumes a fairly solid group of justices who stand firmly as a barrier to the new majority party. The following section examines Supreme Court voting following the crtical election of 1860.

The Voting of the Justices, 1861–1878. As in the pre-1860 period, cases raising realigning issues provoked high levels of dissent on the Supreme Court. The Court decided nine of the eleven salient cases (90.9%) unanimously. The second-highest level of dissent in any class of cases was 33.3 percent in the twenty-seven cases dealing with business taxation and regulation policies. The overall level of dissent in the Reconstruction cases was higher than the Court's average rate of division for selected years during the period. Yearly data on all cases decided with opinion are not available for the 1860 to 1878 period. The dissent rate, however, was 10.1 percent in 1870 and 11 percent in the 1872–73 term (Halpern and Vines, 1977; Goldman, 1982: 108). This supports the conclusion that the level of dissent in cases dealing with reconstruction policies was much greater than in the average case in this period.[44]

The crosscutting, realigning questions provoked much greater internal division on the Court than nonsalient cases of invalidation or all cases decided with opinion. This is further testament to the intensity of these issues. But does this increase in internal division reflect partisan division among the justices? Certainly those who argue that the Court will stand as the "old regime" emphasize partisan division. In the pre–1860 period, we saw how solid partisan blocs may not characterize Supreme Court voting on realigning issues. In the post–1860 period, the small number of decisions prevents a precise statistical assessment. A simple inspection of the voting alignments in the salient cases is not supportive of partisan voting. Only in the loyalty oath cases and in the case dealing with legal tender does one find a visible division between Democrats and Republicans. In these three cases handed down during the policy lag period, we find that only the voting of Chief Justice Chase and Justice Field obscures a perfect party-line division among the justices. The partisan voting of the justices is not shown, however, in the eight remaining cases. In sum, there are no apparent partisan patterns in the voting of the justices in cases relating to Reconstruction measures. The cases provoked a high level of dissent, but simple inspection of the alignments does not show consistent partisan voting.

These results are not encouraging for those who posit a solid "old regime" position to the Supreme Court. The evidence from the post–Civil War period points to a highly divided Court, certainly a testament to the nature of realigning issues. It does not, however, appear to be a Court dividing along party lines. The evidence paints a contrary portrait. The Supreme Court divided in new ways as the new crosscutting issues blurred partisan lines on the Court and in the larger party system.

CONCLUSION: THE CIVIL WAR REALIGNMENT

The Supreme Court's nullification of federal and state policies from 1837 to 1878 provides mixed results for the roles ascribed to the Court during the Civil War realignment. First, the critical issues of slavery, the Civil War, and Reconstruction represent a small proportion of the sixty-seven cases. At least for the period surrounding the Civil War realignment, there is not a strong relationship between the highly salient issues precipitating the critical election of 1860 and the Supreme Court's invalidation of state and federal policies.

Second, identifying the salient cases and the patterns before and after the 1860 election produces only marginal support for the two primary roles attributed to the Court in periods of partisan realignment. The number and timing of salient cases do not support the view that the Supreme Court helped shape the policy stance of the majority party. Instead, only a select number of cases related directly to slavery interests or policies.

These results, however, cannot be viewed in isolation from the very important *Dred Scott* case. The Court handed down perhaps the most controversial decision in its history, a decision related to the critical issue and, arguably, to the onslaught of the Civil War. Nonetheless, expanding the range of cases to include all cases in which state policies were struck down does not give additional support to the view that the Court's invalidation agenda was marked by a large number of salient cases. These results for the pre–1860 period may be a function of the limited class of cases examined. The cases of judicial nullification occurred in a nonsystematic fashion before the Civil War, which perhaps limits the usefulness of these cases for even a partial assessment of Supreme Court policymaking.

The aggregate analysis also has implications for the second role attributed to the Court. Following the 1860 election, the Supreme Court invalidated three volatile Reconstruction measures at the state and national level. This supports the view that following a critical election there will be policy conflict between the Court, dominated by justices of the old regime, and the new majority party. Perhaps as important is the fact that the eight remaining salient cases were handed down after the lag period when the Court was composed primarily of Republican justices appointed after the rise of Lincoln. Earlier studies of the raw number of invalidations have shown little relationship between the invalidation of state and federal policies and periods of critical elections and partisan realignment (Caldeira and McCrone, 1982). Separating salient cases from nonsalient invalidation cases also shows little relationship between the Court's invalidation of state and federal policies and partisan realignment.

Analysis of the justices' voting also yields mixed results. In the pre–Civil War period, the voting of the justices in the salient cases was extremely divisive compared to either the nonsalient invalidation cases or to all cases handed down by the Taney Court. It is not clear, however, that the justices' voting represents party-line voting as commonly assumed. Reanalysis of a subset of Schmidhauser's (1961) regionally divisive cases demonstrates that southern and northern Democratic justices appear to divide along regional as opposed to party lines. These results suggest that only in *Dred Scott* did the justices join with the presidential wing of the party as suggested by Adamany (1980). Instead, the justices appear to divide in this limited class of cases along new lines of division similar to those resulting from the impact of crosscutting issues in the larger party system. Although the justices continued to divide among themselves in deciding cases raising Civil War and Reconstruction issues, their voting does not appear partisan based, albeit the small number of cases prevents rigorous analysis.

The historical evidence and the analysis of judicial review of state and federal policies is an admittedly incomplete portrayal of Supreme Court policymaking. Even considering the mixed results, the evidence points to the highly divisive nature of realigning questions in the ultimate judicial forum. For the 1837–1878 period, no significant patterns appear in Supreme Court decisions and the occurrence of partisan realignment. This changes dramatically, however, as judicial review becomes a common practice. The following chapters present such evidence, which allows for a more precise analysis of the roles ascribed to the Supreme Court during realignment in the party system.

NOTES

1. There will be no attempt to resolve long-standing debates on the historical status of the Supreme Court and its relation to the other branches of the government. Further, determining the precise impact of these decisions on the *process* of realignment is beyond the scope of this study. The possible impact of these decisions on the various coalitions and party leaders within the parties, however, will be discussed. In addition, it is probable that some of the cases related to the critical issues are more important to realignment than others.

2. Historians have justly debated the importance and impact of these ideas. There is consensus that these ideas were prevalent at one time or another among individuals considering themselves Democrats prior to 1860.

3. Further, the temper of the party was reflected in state constitutional changes such as the elimination of property qualifications for voting as well as the direct election of state judges (Beth, 1971: 83).

4. The policymaking and doctrinal developments of the Taney Court continue to generate intense debate regarding its relations with the other branches and the significant developments in the early body of constitutional law.

5. Of course students of the Court continue to disagree over the extent to which the Court under Taney reflected the values of Jacksonian democracy.

6. This general congruence stands at the center of Dahl's (1957) classic study of the role of the Supreme Court in national policymaking. Dahl (1957: 294) concluded that "the main task of the Court is to confer legitimacy on the fundamental policies of the successful coalition." Dahl (1957: 294) also noted that "there are times when the coalition is unstable with respect to certain key policies; at a very great risk to its legitimacy powers, the Court can intervene in such cases and may even succeed in establishing policy."

The period prior to a critical election is clearly a period of instability in the party system because a critical issue or cluster of issues divide the parties into contending blocs of leaders (Sundquist, 1973). Dahl's (1957) observation that the Court assumes a leadership role in policymaking during times of instability is especially meaningful for discussing Supreme Court policymaking on the eve of realignment. As Adamany (1980: 248) notes, "The Supreme Court, as a center of power within the dominant coalition, has an uncharacteristic leadership opportunity of power within the dominant coalition."

7. Two years later in the *Booth Cases*, 21 How. 506 (1859), the Court continued this proslavery stance. The cases originated in Wisconsin, where the state judiciary issued a writ of habeas corpus allowing for the discharge of a fugitive slave from federal jurisdiction on the grounds that the federal Fugitive Slave Law was unconstitutional. The Supreme Court overruled the Wisconsin Supreme Court and upheld the constitutionality of the federal law. On the doctrinal contrast between the *Booth Cases* (1859) and *Dred Scott* (1857), see Hyman and Wiecek, 1982: 198–202.

8. This of course does not mean that the Supreme Court was uninvolved in slavery issues in other cases decided before the Civil War. One of the first slave cases to come before the Court was *Groves v. Slaughter* (1841). *Groves* represented the first and only slave-trade case. In a decidedly proslavery decision, the Supreme Court upheld the state's power over international trade. Abolitionist interests were also disappointed by a decision in 1851 noting that sojourner slaves' rights were to be determined ultimately by the laws of their respective states. Therefore, federal courts lacked jurisdiction in matters relating to a sojourner's rights. Although the decisions of the slavery cases before 1857 favored proslavery states and provoked some partisan outcry, many argue that the decisions were moderate because the Court did not address the legal status of slaves and their possible rights. Further, the Court did not hold that slaves were articles of commerce, a holding that could have raised difficult constitutional issues because state laws regulating slaves could possibly have been challenged on the grounds of interfering with congressional control over interstate commerce. However, this "moderate" course was altered in 1857 with the decision in *Dred Scott*.

9. Finally, abolitionists and other societal interests may have been unwilling to litigate in the federal courts because of various factors such as the simple additional cost (Casper and Posner, 1976).

10. As Schmidhauser (1961: 619) argues: "Commerce clause interpretations upholding the internal police power of the states were related in Southern thinking, to the Southern desire to regulate the ingress and egress of Negroes, whether slave or free, in order to safeguard the social structure of the region. Furthermore, since virtually the only public regulation of business during this period was by the governments of the states, advocacy of exclusive federal control of interstate commerce, became associated, in the Southern plantation aristocracy, with the goals of an antagonistic Northern capitalism. . . . [Also,] judicial interpretations of the status of corporations, whether in contract clause or diversity of citizenship cases, reflected regional economic and cultural antagonisms."

11. This is also supported by historical accounts, which have demonstrated that the partisan press of the period often addressed commerce or corporation cases as a part of the general question of state power. For example, the prosouthern press was hostile to the Supreme Court's decision in a case dealing with the legal status of corporations. In *Dodge v. Woolsey* (1856), the Court nullified an Ohio bank tax levied on a corporation at a higher rate than specified in the original charter (Warren, 1932: 254).

12. *Passenger Cases*, 7 How. 283 (1849) *Hays v. The Pacific Mail Steamship Co.*, 17 How. 596 (1855). *Sinnot v. Davenport*, 22 How. 227 (1860).

13. E.g., *Dodge v. Woolsey*, 18 How. 331 (1856); *State Bank of Ohio v. Knoop*, 16 How. 369 (1854); *Planters Bank v. Sharp*, 6 How. 301 (1848), *Woodruff v. Trapnall*, 10 How. 190 (1851).

14. *Dobbins v. The Commissioners of Erie County*, 16 Pet. 435 (1842).

15. *Bronson v. Kinzie*, 1 How. 311 (1843); *McCracken v. Hayward*, 2 How. 608 (1844).

16. *Searight v. Stokes*, 3 How. 151 (1845); *Neil, Moore & Co. v. Ohio*, 3 How. 720 (1845); *Achison v. Huddleson*, 12 How. 293 (1852).

17. Tests of statistical significance are omitted. These tests would not be meaningful because the population, rather than a sample, is used. Tests of statistical significance are certainly appropriate for random samples. Significance tests are also necessary when the population is drawn from a universe that is normally distributed. The caseload of the Supreme Court (the universe) cannot, under even the most lenient of standards, be considered a normal distribution (see McLauchlan, 1984; Frankfurther and Landis, 1928).

18. Dolan's (1964: 294) conclusion is not given overwhelming support by his data; the percentage of all nonunanimous cases decided with opinion in which two or more justices joined in dissent rose from 38.3 percent in the 1837–1849 period to 50.0 percent in the 1850–1864 period.

19. Bloc analysis requires that membership on the Court remains stable because it is based on the proportion of agreement between pairs of justices. Unfortunately, the number of salient invalidation cases is so small that analysis is impossible either by year or over "natural" court periods when the membership of the Court is unchanged (Bolner, Feldman, and Gates, 1982; Handberg, 1976).

20. The mean of all pairs of agreement in each bloc was more than ten percentage points above the criterion for considering a group of justices to constitute a bloc.

21. On the classification of Justice Wayne as a Whig as opposed to a Democrat, see Schmidhauser (1961: 624).

22. When all twenty-nine cases presented by Schmidhauser (1961) are considered, the proportion of prosouthern votes for southern Democrat justices is Daniel, 95.7 percent; Campbell, 80.0 percent; Catron, 76.9 percent; and Taney, 51.7 percent. For northern Democrats the figures are Grier, 47.8 percent and Nelson, 39.1 percent.

The proportion of prosouthern votes is lowest for the Whigs serving on the Court during the 1835-1856 period: Wayne, 20.7 percent; Curtis, 7.7 percent; and McLean, 3.5 percent.

23. The low number of cases means that significant levels of agreement between any two justices must be extremely high, such as perfect agreement or agreement in five of the six cases. Alternatively, very low levels of agreement are significant only when two justices do not agree in all cases or agree in only one of the six. Using these criteria, there is evidence of discord between northern and southern justices, with the exception of Chief Justice Taney. Southern Democrats Daniel and Catron agreed with northern Democrats Grier and Nelson in either no cases or only one. Southern Democrat Campbell agreed only once with Nelson and in two of the six cases with Grier.

24. A simple majority of newly appointed justices may not, however, signal a Court reflecting the values of the new majority party, because some of the newly appointed justices may fail to meet the expectations of the appointing president. These presidential "misses" could further extend the period of policy conflict with the new majority party (Adamany, 1973: 824, 833).

25. Of course, the "lag" period between the critical election and a Court ideologically supportive of the new majority party may be longer. This certainly appears to be the case in the period following 1864, when Justice Field as well as Chief Justice Chase continually disappointed Lincoln's hopes for a favorable Court (Warren, 1932: 197). Adamany (1973: 833) suggests a lag period from 1860 to the appointments in 1870-71.

26. The size of the Supreme Court was changed in 1863, 1866, and 1869. In 1863, the size increased from nine to ten justices, allowing Lincoln an additional appointment to the Court. In 1866, Congress reduced the number of justices to eight with a Union Democratic president. Finally, under President Grant and following the first legal tender decision by the Court, Congress added an additional justice. The partisan character of these changes has been greatly debated. Some argue that nonpartisan concerns such as concern for tie votes on the Court dominated in 1869 and were also present in 1863 and 1866 (e.g., Ratner, 1935).

27. *Cummings v. Missouri*, 4 Wall. 277 (1867); *Ex parte Garland*, 4 Wall. 333 (1867).

28. *Roosevelt v. Meyer*, 1 Wall. 512 (1863).

29. *Lane County v. Oregon*, 7 Wall. 71 (1869).

30. See, *Georgia v. Stanton*, 6 Wall. 50 (1867); *Mississippi v. Johnson*, 4 Wall. 475 (1867).

31. *Ex parte Vallandigham*, 1 Wall. 243 (1864).

32. It should be noted that four of the seven state cases actually involved constitutional provisions rather than legislative statutes. These provisions in southern states were included as part of the Reconstruction program. The four different provisions were part of the new state constitutions following the Civil War. See *Cummings v. Missouri*, 4 Wall. 277 (1867); *White v. Hart*, 13 Wall. 646 (1872); *Osborne v. Nicholson*, 13 Wall. 654 (1872); *Delmas v. Insurance Company*, 14 Wall. 661 (1872).

33. *Steamship Company v. Portwardens*, 6 Wall 31 (1867).

34. *Ward v. Maryland*, 12 Wall. 418 (1871).

35. *Pacific Railroad Company v. Maguire*, 20 Wall 36 (1874).

36. *U.S. v. Dewitt*, 9 Wall. 41 (1870).

37. E.g., *Bank of Commerce v. New York City*, 2 Bl. 620 (1863); *Van Allen v.The Assessors*, 3 Wall. 573 (1866); *Bank v. Supervisors*, 7 Wall 26 (1868).

38. *The Moses Taylor*, 4 Wall. 411 (1867); *The Hine v. Trevor*, 4 Wall. 555 (1867); *The Belfast*, 7 Wall. 624 (1869).

39. *E.g., Christmas v. Russell,* 5 Wall. 290 (1867); *Edwards v. Kearzy,* 96 U.S. 595 (1878); *Howard v. Bugbee,* 24 How. 461 (1861); *McGee v. Mathis,* 4 Wall. 143 (1867).

40. *The Kansas Indians,* 5 Wall. 737 (1867); *The New York Indians,* 5 Wall. 761 (1867); *Gibson v. Chouteau,* 13 Wall. 92 (1872).

41. *E.g., Inman Steamship Co. v. Tinker,* 94 U.S. 238 (1877); *Foster v. Masters of New Orleans,* 94 U.S. 246 (1877).

42. See also, *Texas v. White,* 7 Wall. 700 (1869).

43. The reader will be spared the avalanche of numbers that give an estimate of no increase in the number of salient policies handed down in the lag period.

44. There are also higher rates of dissent in certain nonsalient categories than in the average level of dissent in all cases decided with opinion. This higher rate of dissent may illustrate the concern of certain justices in deciding to displace legislative choice. Many studies have shown that judges' role orientations interact with their political attitudes and values. Justices may dissent more frequently in the overturn of policies not related to the critical issues because such a decision involves an unusual exercise of judicial authority; that is, the Court overturns the policy choice of a majority legislature that is electorally accountable.

3

Partisan Realignment
in the 1890s

If there is any problem yet unsettled, it is whether the bench is able to bear the great burden of supporting under all circumstances, the fundamental law against popular or supposed popular, demands for enactments in conflict with it. It is the loftiest function and the most sacred duty of the judiciary. . . . This is the only breakwater against the haste and the passions of the people—against the tumultuous ocean of democracy. It must, at all costs, be maintained.

—Judge Dillon
"Address of the President"
American Bar Association, 1892

Corruption dominates the ballot box, the legislatures, the Congress, and touches even the ermine of the bench.

—People's Party
St. Louis Platform, 1892

By the late 1870s, the issues of slavery, secession, and Reconstruction were no longer relevant to the policy stances of the two major political parties. Political turmoil in the western states, however, raised new issues—issues that would polarize and realign the party system in two decades. The new and crosscutting issues of corporate power and industrialization became central to partisan debate because of populism in the West and the Southwest and the labor movement in the urban centers of the Northeast. The critical election of 1896 was the culmination of populism as Republican William McKinley defeated the Democrat-Populist William Jennings Bryan. McKinley's victory strengthened his weakening majority party. The realigning election of 1896 also signaled a long-term national commitment to laissez-faire.

The study of the Supreme Court and the critical election of 1896 focuses, in part, on the period before the critical election of 1896. Some analysts argue that the Supreme Court contributed to the developing crisis and party polarization (Westin, 1953; Adamany, 1980: 247–249; 253–254; Lasser, 1983: 114–117). One observer notes (Adamany, 1980: 256–257): "The Court's conservatism on economic issues after 1876 contributed to shaping a party stance that, in 1896 consolidated a new Republican majority in the nation."

Supreme Court policymaking following the realigning election is also likely to be conservative. From the Civil War to the 1940s, the Court was staffed by a fairly solid Republican majority. It remains to be seen precisely whether judicial review was connected with the partisan realignment of the 1890s. Before examining these connections, it is fruitful to examine the dynamics of partisan change in the late nineteenth century and the general character of Supreme Court policymaking.

THE RISE OF POPULISM AND THE AGENDA OF THE CRITICAL ELECTION OF 1896

By the end of Reconstruction in the late 1870s, the forces of industrialization and corporate capitalism brought rapid social and economic change to the country. Many factors contributed to unheralded economic development from the 1870s to the turn of the century including the combination of emerging technology, new financial instruments for investment, and cultural values consistent with free enterprise (Keller, 1977: 162–196; 371–408). These developments produced remarkable wealth for a few, a marginal change in the standing of living for some, and severe economic dislocations for many in the agricultural and industrial labor sectors of the economy. Generally the Republican and Democratic parties shared a basic consensus on furthering these developments until the polarization of the parties in the late 1880s and early 1890s (Sundquist, 1973: 92, 105–106).

New political forces rose in response to these economic changes. Farmers in the western and southwestern states organized and protested the perceived abuses of corporate capitalism. Labor movements in the East also entered the political arena, but somewhat hesitantly. Farmers periodically sought policy change beginning in the 1870s as business cycles lowered agricultural prices and aggravated other long-term financial problems. Groups such as the Grange, the Farmers' Alliance, the Greenback party, and later, the People's, or Populist, party were diverse attempts to cope with the various economic evils. Farmers blamed their economic problems on vague eastern money power. As Sundquist (1973: 93) notes: "In the newer states of the West, in particular, tens of thousands of farmers were developing an intense class consciousness and an acute hostility toward the powerful class of financiers and entrepreneurs that appeared to control not only the economy but the polity as well." Specifically, the agrarian protest movements were concerned with the business practices of railroads and large corporations and the farmers' persistent debts.

For example, one of the major concerns for farmers was the rates charged by railroad companies for hauling agricultural goods. The railroads commonly charged higher rates to farmers by basing their rate schedule on shipping points. These discriminatory rates were sometimes attacked in midwestern states by establishing rate-setting commissions. The farmers also confronted railroads unwilling to lease rights-of-way in property to build grain elevators (Westin, 1953). Without these independent elevators, the farmers faced high monopoly prices for grading and storing grain.

The farming interests in the West and Southwest grew increasingly bitter over another issue that was linked to the diffuse evil of corporate power: the public debt. The tremendous railroad expansion of the nineteenth century was financed in part through municipal bonds. The promoters of railroad and roadbuilding would obtain municipal bonds for construction in exchange for shares in the companies. Often, fraudulent companies did not provide the additional road or rail-line and left municipalities with large bond debts. Some states sought to repudiate these bonds by forbidding municipalities to levy taxes and by prohibiting the issuance of new bonds. The farmer continued to bear the burden of these debts through a land-based system of taxation. The farmers' private debts also fueled the concern with corporate power. Money lenders charged interest rates as high as 20 percent for supplies to farmers (Sundquist, 1973: 93). Again, the villains became the large, eastern financiers.

The protest movement in the 1880s and 1890s also raised issues of equitable taxation and the free coinage of silver. By the formation of the Populist party and its famous St. Louis platform in 1892, the movement against corporate capitalism included many crosscutting issues: government ownership of the means of transportation and communication; free coinage of silver; taxation based on the ability to pay; and a "subtreasury" plan for the conversion of agricultural products into legal tender.

The formation of the Knights of Labor in 1881 also represented a negative response to the rapid industrialization and economic growth following the Civil War. Eastern laborers sought changes dealing with wages and general working conditions. The labor movement and the Populists, however, had difficulty uniting their forces.[1] The lack of a strong union between these two groups is due in part to the cultural differences between eastern laborers and midwestern farmers. Also, the labor movement was inexperienced politically compared with the agrarian alliances. This limited labor's organizational strength. Instead, the farmers' protest movement built coalitions among various ethnocultural groups such as poor whites and blacks in the South and individuals termed "evangelical moralists" in states such as Nebraska (Keller, 1977: 573).

The demands of populism were class oriented. As such, these issues cut across the sectional party system of the Civil War. The North and South continued to vote "as they fought"; the Populist movement came to include farmers in Minnesota, Illinois, Missouri, and Texas.[2] As the Democratic and Republican parties evaded these demands in the 1880s, distinctive western wings developed within each party (Sundquist, 1973: 109–113). Populists were able to work with both parties in selected states, for example, they made alliances with Democrats in Texas and with Republicans in Illinois, Minnesota, and many western states of the Midwest (Goodwyn, 1976: 331–333; Sundquist, 1973: 113–118).

At the national level, the two major parties responded very slowly to the crosscutting issues. Instead, the leaders of both parties sought to silence these issues and emphasized the importance of the long-standing tariff question. The parties could not ignore, however, the strong showing of the Populist party in 1892; the party won a plurality of votes in Colorado, Idaho, Kansas, Nevada, and North Dakota. In addition, the Populist party won three governorships, three Senate seats, and eleven House seats.

The strong electoral showing of the Populist party only set the stage for polarization of the parties in the 1890s. Following the severe economic crisis of 1893, the two major parties became increasingly divided over the silver question. Populists and western Democrats urged the free coinage of silver; Republicans and conservative Democrats held to a firm reliance on the gold standard. Democrats favored the free coinage of silver as a means of expanding the money supply. Following the panic of 1893, the money-supply issue intensified. Attempted compromise was evident in the demand for bimetallism by Democratic members of Congress. This proposal, however, met with little enthusiasm from President Cleveland and the eastern wing of the party. The Silver Democrats were able to capture the party in 1895, and the party's platform and William Jennings Bryan's campaign reflected most, if not all, of the Populist proposals. In turn, the Republican party derisively and emphatically rejected these demands. The polar policy alternatives confronted the electorate in 1896.

William McKinley's election was due in part to Bryan's lack of support among eastern labor and to superior Republican strategy and funding. Whatever the central elements in McKinley's victory, the 1896 election established long-term Republican dominance in national policymaking. Republicans maintained control of the presidency and both chambers of Congress until 1910. The party could expect consistent electoral support from both the Northeast and West. Eastern laborers gave their support to the Republican tariff; favorable economic conditions brought many western farmers back to the more moderate Republican ranks (Sundquist, 1973: 146–153). The intensity of the realignment is also seen by the major shifts that occurred in the control of state governments (Clubb, Flanigan, and Zingale, 1980: 195). The percentage of nonsouthern states with one-party control of the legislature and governorship increased from 27 percent in the 1892–1893 period to over 65 percent in the 1894–1897 period (Clubb, Flanigan, and Zingale, 1980: 200).

A Republican Supreme Court and Corporate Capitalism

In the period before the critical election of 1896, the Supreme Court played a major role in developing and strengthening the Republican commitment to laissez-faire capitalism (McCloskey, 1951; Miller, 1968; Westin, 1953). Although some fine historical accounts ignore the Supreme Court (Goodwyn, 1976), there is ample evidence that the Court established policy related to the critical issues. The judicial response to the farmers' protest was initially favorable before the end of Reconstruction. For example, the

Court upheld some of the early Grange laws in *Munn v. Illinois* (1877). The Court held that state regulation was legitimate when the regulated business was one "affected with the public interest." This profarmer position was gradually changed as Republican presidents appointed new Supreme Court justices in the late 1870s and early 1880s. As Swindler (1969: 31) observes:

> In an age like the twenty-five years concluding the nineteenth century, members of the Supreme Court, who presumably pronounced the law of the Constitution, inevitably bore the imprint of . . . various forces: they were nominated by Presidents who, uniformly from Grant through McKinley, were the choice of party organizations firmly in control of conservative industrial interests of the Northeast and the most industrialized portions of the Midwest. By 1890, seven of the justices in *Munn* had left the Court. The new justices included five Republicans and two Democrats.

The rejection of the *Munn* position by the Court under both Chief Justices Morrison Waite and Melville Fuller has led most analysts to classify the Court as conservative and probusiness (Kelly, Harbinson, and Belz, 1983; McCloskey, 1960; Swindler, 1969; Paul, 1969; Twiss, 1942). The conservativism of the Court is also reflected in the major doctrinal developments in the period, especially the rise of substantive due process under the Fourteenth Amendment (Gunther, 1980: 503–569). The Fourteenth Amendment was originally directed at protecting the civil and political rights of blacks freed by the Civil War. In a series of decisions after Reconstruction,[3] the Court limited the central thrust of the Fourteenth Amendment. Instead, the due process clause of the Fourteenth Amendment became a powerful tool for scrutinizing state policies directed at economic interests. Conservative interests applauded the rise of "substantive due process" under Chief Justices Melville Fuller and Edward White. Specifically, substantive due process allows the Court to rule on the substantive goals of a policy by evaluating the underlying reason for government action; procedural due process focuses primarily on how government may exercise authority over individuals.

The judicial response to the Populist movement was also linked in part to the increased professionalization and activity of the legal profession. The conservative and probusiness American Bar Association called for heightened scrutiny of policies detrimental to the growth of corporate capitalism (Twiss, 1942; Paul, 1969). There were also changes in legal philosophy that gave added impetus to legal conservatism on economic issues (Twiss, 1942). The willingness of business to seek legal counsel and protection in the federal courts is perhaps reflected in the increase in the number of constitutional challenges to state and national legislation. The total number of challenges to state and national statutes increased from 31 over the 1850–1860 period to 192 over the 1880–1890 period (Moore, 1913: 141).

The recruitment of new justices following Reconstruction and the close connection between the business and legal community led Justice Samuel Miller to conclude: "It is vain to contend with judges who have been, at the bar, the advocates of railroad companies and all forms of associated capital, when they are called upon to decide cases in which such interests are in context" (Rodell, 1955: 146). Of the twenty-one justices serving on the Court from 1879 to 1896, fourteen were Republican justices appointed by Republican presidents. There were seven Democratic justices on the Court in the period, and Democratic presidents appointed six of the seven. Throughout this period, the Republican justices remained a stable majority on the Court.

Three dramatic cases handed down by the Supreme Court in 1895 vividly illustrate the Supreme Court's commitment to entrepreneurial liberty, or laissez-faire. Moreover, these cases illustrate the Court's response to the critical issues of partisan realignment. In *United States v. E.C. Knight Co.* (1895), the Court confronted the first constitutional test of the Sherman Antitrust Act. The case originated in the purchase of four sugar companies by the American Sugar Refining Company. This purchase brought the company's share of the American market to 98 percent. The case was rushed to the Supreme Court by Attorney General Richard Olney, a former corporate lawyer. The Supreme Court, ruling in favor of the sugar trust, narrowly construed Congress's power over goods in "commerce" compared with goods in "manufacturing." Although the Court did not invalidate the Sherman Act, corporate interests applauded the decision (Swindler, 1969: 34–36).

The second major case decided in 1895 was *In re Debs* (1895). The case also raised constitutional questions with the Sherman Act, not with respect to manufacturing trusts but with labor unions. Eugene V. Debs was convicted under the Sherman Act for obstructing railroad business during the famous Pullman strike. The Supreme Court upheld the conviction. The decision met with strong Populist protest. Five Populist governors issued an official message declaring that "the federal courts have flagrantly usurped jurisdiction, first to protect corporations and perpetuate their many abuses, and second to oppress and destroy the powers of organized labor" (Westin, 1953: 29).

Finally, the Supreme Court struck down a federal income tax of 1894 enacted by a congressional coalition of Democrats and Populists. The major point is that these three cases reflect a conservative Court striking out at policies supported by Populist and Democrat reformers. As Westin (1953: 40) argues:

> In 1895, the most respectable agency of American government, an agency beyond the reach of ordinary political processes, was dedicated to private property, "due process" of law, and Herbert Spencer's *Social Statics*. In this position as Seneschal of the Status Quo, the Supreme Court strengthened the radical character of the People's Party, weakened the influence of its moderate leadership, and aided immeasurably in capturing the Democratic party.

An analysis of the Supreme Court's invalidation of state and federal legislation from 1879 to 1896 provides additional evidence that the Court stands as a member of the majority coalition in shaping the majority party's position on the crosscutting issues precipitating the critical election of 1896.

The Invalidation of Federal and State Statutes and the Critical Election of 1896

The Supreme Court struck down over sixty state and selected federal policies before the critical election of 1896. Unlike the pre–Civil War period, the instances of judicial nullification of state policies became a regular aspect of Supreme Court policymaking. Specifically, the Court held sixty-two state and eight federal statutes unconstitutional in this period (see Figure 3.1). The invalidated statutes raise a number of political issues including alcohol control, immigration, and general contract and debt policies.

As Table 3.1 reveals, however, most cases related directly to many of the central questions on the critical election agenda. The largest class of cases voided legislative attempts to regulate or tax businesses. The Court struck down thirty-seven state and two federal statutes relating to the general field of business regulation and taxation. In addition, ten of the state cases were statutes dealing with municipal bonds. Only four of these statutes involved state attempts to repudiate municipal bond obligations. As noted earlier, western farmers sought the repudiation of such obligations. Finally, the invalidation of the federal income tax in 1895 is important or salient to the critical election. Therefore, forty-four of the seventy cases, or 62.9 percent of the state and federal statutes struck down, are salient to the issues dividing the political party system.

A closer examination of the cases shows that the Supreme Court attempted to preserve entrepreneurial liberty consistent with the probusiness reputation of the Republican party in the late nineteenth century. Second, an examination of the partisan control of the state governments that enacted salient policies and the regional distribution of these states demonstrates that a vast majority of these salient policies arose either in western and southern Democratic states or midwestern Republican states. This also supports the theory of ideological conflict in the salient invalidation cases, because the conservative Supreme Court struck down policies supported by Populists and Democratic reformers.

The State Cases, 1879–1896. The vast majority of the invalidations from 1879 to 1896 involved state statutes, as seen in Table 3.1, which presents the number and percentage of cases by policy area. The Supreme Court's hostility toward state regulation and taxation of businesses is evident in two widely cited cases. By *Wabash, St. Louis and Pacific Railway Company v. Illinois* (1886), the Supreme Court had moved far from its position in *Munn v. Illinois* (1877). The Court declared a Populist-backed Illinois statute unconstitutional. The statute prohibited railroads from charging lower rates for hauling goods over longer distances, a practice that hurt smaller farmers who were often competitive only in a small geographical area and thus subject to higher rates. The Court reasoned that the state lacked the power to establish rates for railroads engaged in interstate commerce.[4]

The response of Populists to the *Wabash* decision was predictably unfavorable. The Populist presidential candidate in 1892, James B. Weaver, wrote in response to the decision, "A State—three millions of people (sic),

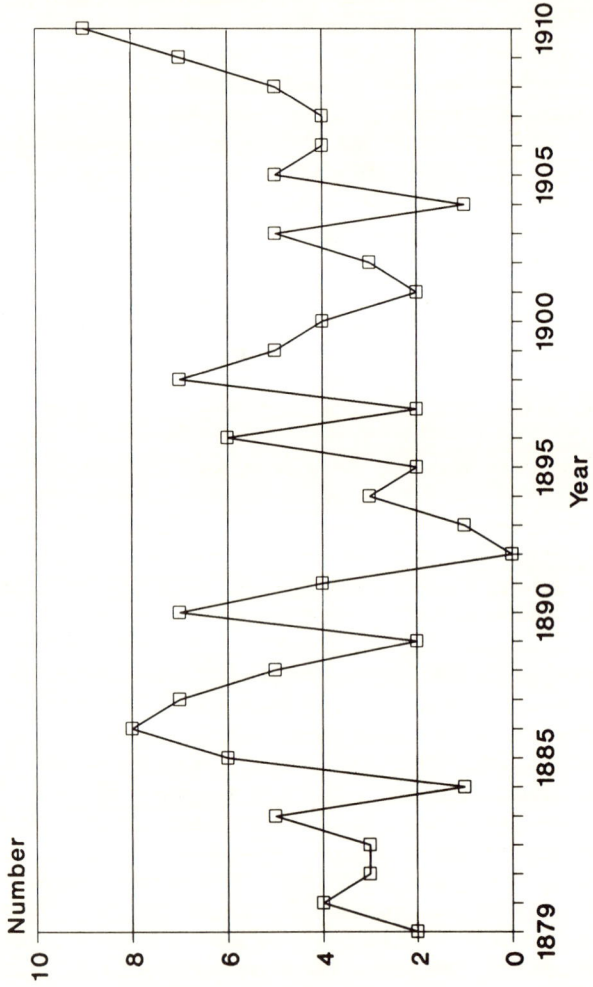

Figure 3.1
Number of Federal and State Policies
Declared Unconstitutional, 1879–1910

Source: Library of Congress (1978).

TABLE 3.1

Number and Percentage of State and Federal Cases
by Policy Area,
1879-1896

Policy Area	Number of State Cases	Number of Federal Cases	Total Number of Cases	Percentage of Total Cases
Business Regulation & Taxation	37	2	39	55.7
Municipal Bonds	10	0	10	14.3
Labor	0	0	0	00.0
General Contracts-Debts	5	0	5	7.1
Reconstruction	2	2	4	5.7
Criminal Justice/ Civil Liberties	2	2	4	5.7
Alcohol Control	3	0	3	4.3
Personal General Taxation	0	1	1	1.4
Miscellaneous[a]	3	1	4	5.7
Total	62	8	70	100.0

[a]Policy areas and the number of cases are public lands, 1; immigration, 1; federalism, 1; and the rights of aliens, 1.

Source: Compiled by author from *United States Reports.*

their Legislature and courts—stood at the bar, summoned hither at the beck of a corporation which this same state had created, but which now denied the authority of its creator to circumscribe it, conduct or set limits to its actions" (Westin, 1953: 16).

In four years, the Supreme Court announced another dramatic railroad decision that provided momentum to the development of substantive due process as a doctrinal tool for limiting state control of business. In *Chicago, Milwaukee, and St. Paul Railway Co. v. Minnesota* (1890), the Court invalidated a Minnesota statute that had vested a state commission with rate-setting authority and limited the right of railroads to seek judicial review of the commission's rates. The Court argued that the "reasonableness" of railroad rates was ultimately a judicial determination. Again the Populist forces objected to judicial policy. The newspapers of the Farmers' Alliance labeled the decision "the second Dred Scott decision" (Paul, 1969: 222).

Wabash and the Minnesota Rate Case are the most cited and discussed cases of railroad regulation and related constitutional doctrines in the pre–1896 period. The Court, however, struck down an additional ten state statutes regulating or taxing railroads. The Court voided attempts by Tennessee and Pennsylvania to impose taxes for the privilege of doing business within the state.[5] In addition, the Court invalidated statutes that imposed taxes on railroads at a higher rate than originally specified in the railroads' charters.[6] The remaining cases involving railroad regulation or taxation include an Illinois law regulating the routes of passenger lines;[7] a Texas statute requiring all railroads to pay the court costs and attorney fees of litigants who were successful in a claim against the railroad;[8] and a Nebraska law compelling a railroad to allow a third party to build a grain elevator on its chartered land.[9]

The cases of business regulation and taxation that did not involve railroads included more general forms of business regulation. The Supreme Court invalidated these statutes by limiting state power over interstate commerce. The Court struck down policies designed to tax either out-of-state merchants[10] or the gross receipts of businesses.[11] The Court also invalidated state laws establishing regulations for the handling and sale of certain goods.[12] These cases of business regulation and taxation show that the Court used its power to invalidate state laws consistent with the Republican position of preserving entrepreneurial liberty.

The salient state cases also include four statutes that involved state attempts to repudiate municipal bond indebtedness. As Westin (1953: 3) has shown, state attempts to avoid paying bond debts incurred in support of internal improvements were attempts to relieve farmers of a heavy local tax burden. Through its interpretation of the contracts clause, the Supreme Court struck down statutes from Missouri, Louisiana, and Alabama that withdrew county and city taxing power for raising revenue to meet bond interest payments.[13] Also, a Missouri statute placing procedural barriers on the amortization of bond issues was struck down.[14] The six remaining cases were not salient to the critical issues of the 1896 election involving the regulation of business power and the farmers' demands for reform. Four of these cases centered on the use of bond coupons for the payment of individual taxes[15] and requirements for localities to issue bonds in the aid of manufacturing.[16] In the four cases involving the repudiation of municipal bonds, however, the Supreme Court fueled partisan clashes over the extent and desirability of state control over business (Westin, 1953: 4–9). In response to these and other bond cases, the Governor of Missouri urged the state legislature to "assert the outraged dignity of the State against usurpation of power by the Federal judiciary" (Westin, 1953: 8).

The hostility generated by these judicial decisions is clear. In *Barron v. Burnside* (1887), for example, the Supreme Court struck down an 1886 Iowa law that conditioned the entry of foreign corporations on an agreement not to invoke diversity of citizenship jurisdiction for hearings in federal courts. Many saw the decision as antagonistic to the interests of the western states.[17] Although this case is not widely cited in comparison with *Wabash*, it shows that judicial invalidation of state attempts to control business led to state legislative attacks on federal judicial power.[18] The Iowa statute was similar to the various congressional proposals to limit the Court's jurisdiction and constituted a state attempt to "curb," or restrict, the Court's power.

Barron is also important because it illustrates the hostility of some states to judicial control over a broad class of legislation aimed at business regulation. This gives added support to the importance of the cases striking down general regulatory and taxation legislation. The continued hostility of certain

TABLE 3.2

Distribution of Salient[a] and Nonsalient State Cases
by Partisan Control of State Governments at the
Time of Policy Enactment,
1879-1896

	Number of Salient	Percent	Number of Nonsalient	Percent [b]
Democratic--East[c]	0	00.0	0	00.0
Democratic--West[d] & South[e]	17	51.5	5	27.8
Mixed[f]--East	1	3.0	1	5.6
Mixed[f]--West & South	3	9.1	4	22.2
Republican--East	3	9.1	0	00.0
Republican--West & South	9	27.3	8	44.4
Total	33	100.0	18	100.0
Missing Data	8		3	

[a]Includes cases of business regulation and taxation and the repudiation of municipal bond obligations.
[b]The percentages are based on a small number of cases.
[c]Includes the northeastern and middle Atlantic regions.
[d]Includes the northeast central and northwest central regions.
[e]Includes the solid South and border states.
[f]State governments classified as mixed in terms of partisan control had different parties in each chamber of the legislature or the legislature was controlled by one party and the governorship by another party. Control is signified by either a solid majority or a simple plurality.

Source: Clubb, Flanigan, and Zingale (1990); *United States Reports.*

state governments to a broad class of business regulation suggests that these expressions of judicial hostility did not go unnoticed by state party leaders.

The thirty-seven state cases of business regulation and taxation and the four bond cases show a relationship with the central issues leading to realignment in the party system. Examining the regional distribution of the state statutes also reveals that a majority of these statutes arose from regions where populism had made strong inroads (Goodwyn, 1976: 25–50, 87–108; Sundquist, 1973: 94–109, 113–118). Of the forty-one salient state cases involving business regulation and taxation and municipal bond obligations, legislatures in the solid South or the West and northeast regions enacted twenty-nine, or 87.9 percent, of these salient policies. Analysis of the partisan status of the state governments that enacted these policies gives additional support to the thesis that these invalidations were based on ideological differences. Table 3.2 presents the distribution of salient and nonsalient state cases by eastern and noneastern regions and by the partisan status of the state government. It was not possible to obtain the date of enactment for eight of the forty-one salient statutes. Of the remaining thirty-three statutes, 51.5 percent arose from Democratic state governments in the West and solid South.[19] Moreover, the Republican states in the West were the source of an additional nine, or 27.3 percent, of the important statutes. The states in this region—Indiana, Illinois, Minnesota, Michigan, and Nebraska—had moderate to strong Populist movements. Historical evidence has also shown that the Illinois statute involved in the Minnesota Rate Case and the two Minnesota statutes were strongly supported by Populist forces in these states (Swindler, 1969: 61–68).

The distribution of eighteen nonsalient cases displayed in Table 3.2 shows that most of these statutes were also enacted by noneastern states. Republican states and southern states enacted the largest number of statutes (nine) compared with five in Democratic and four in mixed state governments. A large majority (78.8%) of the important or salient cases arose from either Democratic state governments or midwestern Republican states with moderate to strong Populist elements. In addition, the distribution of the notable cases may suggest the mobilization of interests into judicial forums at the state level; that is, the political "losers" at the state level may move their conflicts into the state and federal court systems after losing in the state legislative and judicial arena.

In sum, the analysis of the state law invalidations shows that the Court struck down policies directly dealing with the critical political questions that realigned the party system. These statutes were enacted primarily by Democratic or midwestern Republican states. Although the data do not allow for uncovering the precise impact of these cases on the process of realignment, it is reasonable to conclude that the Court continued to frustrate Populist demands from 1879 to 1896 and contributed to the increasingly radical character of the Populist party in the 1890s. Also, the Court's policy stance in these cases strengthened the constitutional position of the most conservative wing of the Republican party, the same wing in firm control of the party in 1896.

The Federal Cases, 1879–1896. The cases overturning federal statutes between 1879 and 1896 are few. There are only eight cases, and more important, only three of these cases pertain to the realigning questions of 1896. The larger number of salient state statutes reflects how state legislatures were the primary forums for economic legislation throughout most of the nineteenth century. The forces of reform in the 1880s and 1890s initially turned to the state governments rather than to the federal government. As Beth (1971: 30) has noted: "While the farmer's troubles produced political revolts such as the Granger movement and later the Populist party, for the most part (at least until the nineties) the demands were aimed primarily at the state governments, some of which tried in various ways to respond. The farmers turned to federal action only after it was clear that these states would not, or could not, provide relief." Although invalidations were few in number, the invalidations of two federal statutes in 1879 and 1893 reflected judicial hostility toward business regulation, and in 1895, the Court struck directly at the forces of reform by voiding the Democratic-Populist income tax.

In the *Trade Mark Cases* (1879), the Court voided a congressional act aimed at the registration of trademarks. In *Monongahela Navigation Co. v. United States* (1893), a congressional provision for the compensation of companies whose locks and dams were either purchased or condemned was struck down because the scheme of compensation omitted the estimates of the tolls collected by the company. Both of these cases were of only limited importance to the growing forces of reform. The final federal statute invalidated before 1896, however, was of major importance to the partisan struggle.

In *Pollock v. Farmer's Loan and Trust Co.* (1895), the Supreme Court addressed the important question of money and the federal deficit, a question the Democratic platform of 1896 described as "paramount to all others at this time" (Johnson and Porter, 1970: 97). The income tax was part of the Democratic tariff reduction program. The bill compensated for lost tariff revenue and sought to reduce the growing federal deficit through the levy of a 2 percent tax on all incomes above $4,000. Many supporters in Congress saw this as desirable for the tariff and because the tax recognized the growing gap between the rich and the poor. Before 1894, federal taxes were regressive in nature and eventually led to the Populist demands for a graduated income tax.

The congressional debates on the income tax were intense, and division over the question appears class based. Western and southern Democrats and Populists argued that the tax was overdue and necessary to address the concentration of wealth in the upperclass. Eastern Democrats and Republicans branded the measure "socialistic," "class legislation," and "in the spirit of communism" (Paul, 1969: 185–220). Even before its passage, opponents to the tax provision were looking forward to a hearing before the Supreme Court. A New York senator remarked in debate on the bill in 1894 "that with the Supreme Court as now constituted this income tax will be declared unconstitutional" (Swisher, 1954: 444). These conservative opponents had little support for such a constitutional judgment given one hundred years of Supreme Court precedent. The Court had previously upheld a variety of taxes, including an income tax in 1881.[20]

Nonetheless, the Court swept away these precedents and ruled the income tax unconstitutional. Overruling its previous interpretations regarding direct and indirect taxes, the Court held 5–4 that the tax was a direct tax, and thus, it was necessary to apportion the tax on the basis of population as explicitly required by the Constitution. The language in many of the opinions bears testament to the volatility of the income tax question. Justice Field's separate concurrence, for example, describes the tax as an "assault upon capital" (1895: 607). The reaction was equally strong from those sympathetic to the income tax: ". . . the triumph of selfishness over patriotism. It is another victory of greed over need"; "it calls upon the fair-minded of the Country precisely as did the Dred Scott decision forty years ago" (Swindler, 1969: 3). Legal journals such as the *American Law Review* also responded bitterly to the decision: "*Pollock* has not strengthened the confidence of the American people in their Federal Court of last resort . . . the decision is in favor of the rich and the talk is freely bandied about that the Court is and always has been a rich man's court and a corporation court" (Swindler, 1969: 4).

That salient state policies were struck down reinforces the conservative reputation of the Supreme Court from the late 1870s to 1896. The dramatic quality of *Pollock*, however, heightened concern over judicial policy, and the Supreme Court became a campaign issue in 1896 (Westin, 1953: 22–37). Because of the efforts of Populists such as William Jennings Bryan, the Democratic platform had anti-Court planks expressing disagreement with the Court's policies on the income tax and labor rights (Johnson and Porter, 1970). The planks noted implicitly that these policies could change with a Democratic victory and later appointments. The conservative press and Republican politicians, however, attacked the platform as an assault on constitutional structure.[21]

The invalidation of the income tax and the two previously discussed cases of federal law invalidation show policies bearing directly upon the central issues of government control of business interests and populism. In sum, forty-four of the seventy cases of judicial review, or 62.9 percent, were important to the central issues surrounding the critical election of 1896. Figure 3.2 displays the yearly number of important cases dealing with business regulation-taxation, the repudiation of municipal bonds, and the federal personal income tax. The Supreme Court invalidated an increasingly larger number of salient or important statutes as the critical election of 1896 approached. The increase however, is not a simple linear one.[22] The number and proportion of salient invalidation cases support the view that the Supreme Court helps to shape the majority party's stance on the critical realigning issues consistent with its agenda-setting role (e.g., Adamany, 1980). The Supreme Court participated in forming the majority party's response to crosscutting issues through the exercise of judicial review. Yet, there is little known about the individual behavior of the justices in times of realignment. The following section examines one aspect of the internal dynamics of the Court during critical election periods, the voting of the justices.

The Voting of the Justices, 1879–1896. The issues polarizing the political party system and precipitating critical elections are unique in their intensity. Political rhetoric over these issues becomes passionate (Sundquist, 1973: 278–281). These crosscutting and volatile issues and the responses of party leaders constitute the driving forces behind major transformations in the political party system. It would be surprising if the justices on the Supreme Court did not divide more often in cases overturning state and federal policies that raise these realigning questions than in other types of cases. The level of formal dissent in the salient cases should therefore be higher than in other types of cases handed down by the Supreme Court. These data illuminate the impact of the volatile issues on the justices as these issues divide the electorate and the party system.

A second concern centers on the extent to which the justices' partisan affiliations structure their responses to the basic question of business power and its control by government. Studies of congressional voting on salient bills have shown consistently that party-line voting increases along these

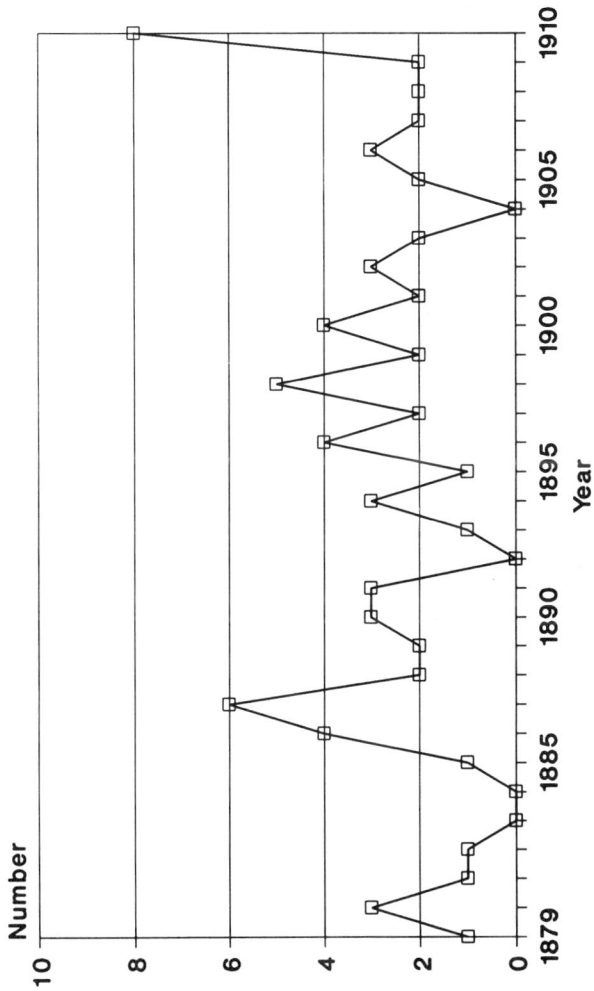

Figure 3.2
Number of Salient Policies
Declared Unconstitutional, 1879–1910

Source: Compiled by the author.

dimensions (Brady and Stewart, 1982; Sinclair, 1982). In response to the crosscutting issues, some have suggested that the justices will align with the presidential wing of the majority party in cases raising critical issues (Adamany, 1980: 248). Similar to members of Congress, justices may divide along partisan lines when deciding salient cases, as do party leaders and the party system generally. However, one can argue that the crosscutting nature of critical issues disrupts the expression of traditional partisan ideologies as the justices confront new, crosscutting issues (see also, Lasser, 1983; Gates, 1989). The justices' voting provides not simply additional descriptive information on the period before 1896 but information that aids in generalizing about Supreme Court policymaking and partisan realignment.

The analysis of the justices' voting in the seventy state and federal cases handed down between 1879 and 1896 yields mixed support for these propositions. The justices divided in twenty-two, or 33.4 percent, of all invalidation cases. This level of division as measured by the proportion of solo or joint dissents is higher than the 10 percent estimated rate of division for all cases decided by the Waite Court (1874–1888) and an estimated 20 percent for all cases decided by the Fuller Court (1888–1910).[23] The nonunanimous invalidations are examined by these chief justice periods. Of all cases handed down under Chief Justice Waite (1874–1888), 32.3 percent were nonunanimous. Under Chief Justice Fuller (1888–1910), the level of nonunanimous cases was 53.9 percent. The justices divided more often in striking down state and federal legislation than in the average case decided in the late nineteenth century. This higher level of dissent in all of the cases of judicial review reflects, perhaps, disagreement regarding the overturn of legislative choice as the justices divided over the proper judicial role.

The rate of dissent in the forty-four cases salient to the 1896 realignment, however, is higher than the rate of dissent in all cases of invalidation. Of the salient cases, 53.4 percent had at least one registered dissent. This is slightly higher than the dissent rate for all cases of judicial review and much higher than the level of division in all cases decided with opinion.

The level of nonunanimous cases is suggestive of the conflict generated by realigning political questions. To what extent, however, do the justices vote along partisan lines? Table 3.3 presents the dissent rates for all justices serving in the period for both the salient cases and all cases of judicial review. The table portrays the rank of each justice from those with the highest dissent rate to the lowest in the salient and nonsalient cases of judicial review. Because all the salient cases represent the voiding of policies inconsistent with Republican policy, a high dissent rate suggests little disagreement with the overturn of policies relating to business regulation-taxation, the repudiation of municipal bonds, and the Democratic income tax. Surprisingly, the rankings of the justices show Democratic justices dissenting at both high and low levels. Two Democrats, White and Fuller, were the strongest supporters of these policies, judged by their high rates of dissent. These justices disagreed more often than the remaining Democratic justices in overturning business regulation and taxation policies and state

TABLE 3.3

Dissent Rates of the Justices in Salient Invalidation
Cases Compared to All Cases of Invalidation,
1879-1896

Justice (Party)	Dissent Rate in Salient Cases		Dissent Rate in All Cases	
	Percent	Number	Percent	Number
White, J. (D)	22.2[a]	9	18.2[a]	11
Fuller, C.J. (D)	21.1[a]	19	15.4	26
Gray, J. (R)	16.7	36	15.7	66
Brewer, J. (R)	12.5[a]	16	21.7	23
Waite, C.J. (R)	10.0	20	12.2	41
Shiras, J. (R)	10.0[a]	10	8.3[a]	12
Lamar, J. (D)	8.3[a]	12	5.3[a]	19
Bradley, J. (R)	6.5	31	8.6	57
Miller, J. (R)	3.6	28	7.4	54
Harlan, J. (R)	2.4	41	8.6	70
Field, J. (D)	00.0	41	4.3	70
Blatchford, J. (R)	00.0	27	00.0	50
Brown, J. (R)	00.0[a]	13	00.0[a]	16
Matthews, J. (R)	00.0[a]	17	00.0	35
Jackson, J. (D)	00.0[a]	6	00.0[a]	6
Peckham, J. (D)	00.0[a]	4	00.0[a]	6
Strong, J. (R)	00.0[a]	3	00.0[a]	6
Clifford, J. (D)	00.0[a]	5	11.1[a]	9
Hunt, J. (R)	00.0[a]	5	00.0[a]	9
Swayne, J. (R)	00.0[a]	3	00.0[a]	7
Woods, J. (R)	00.0[a]	14	00.0	31

[a]Percentages computed with less than 20 cases.

Source: Compiled by author from *United States Reports.*

attempts to repudiate municipal bond obligations. The remaining Democratic justices were moderate to weak in support of the policies, as their low level of dissent illustrates. The level of association between the dissent rates in the salient cases and the partisan affiliation of the justices is also low. Analysis of the correlation between the justices' dissent rates and their partisan affiliations yields an eta of 0.194. Party affiliation is generally not found to be a determining factor.

Note as well that three of the five Democratic justices appointed after 1885 regularly dissented in the salient cases. In addition, there was little relationship between the justices' region of origin and their dissent rates. Republican justices from the midwest were both strong and weak supporters of the salient policies, such as Justice Waite (Ohio) and Justice Stanley Matthews (Ohio).

The ranking of the justices is generally consistent with the ideological descriptions of the various justices. Table 3.3 shows that the strongest supporters of these policies were Justices Edward White, Horace Gray, Stephen Field, Wheeler Peckham, and Chief Justice Melville Fuller.[24] In a study of all nonunanimous cases decided by the Fuller Court, Leavitt (1974) found similar rankings, and Justice John Harlan was considered the least conservative justice in a more general class of economic cases.

In sum, the voting of the justices does support the hypothesis that the justices will divide more often in cases raising issues related to the crosscutting questions on the critical election agenda. The justices do not, however, appear to divide in a partisan fashion as measured through their dissent rates. The voting of the justices gives support to the argument that the justices will divide in new ways as the critical issues cut across the existing ideological and partisan cleavages on the Court. This interpretation is consistent with the dynamics of crosscutting, realigning issues and the slow turnover on the Court. Supreme Court justices appointed before the rise of populism or during the moderate response by both parties were unlikely to be appointed because of their views on these issues.

Conclusion: The Pre-1896 Period

The voiding of state and federal statutes by the Supreme Court supports Adamany's (1980: 247–249) speculations regarding the role of the Court on the eve of realignment. As a member of the majority coalition, the Court struck down state and federal laws contributing to the Republican party's position on the critical or realigning issues. Most state policies sought regulation or taxation of businesses or the repudiation of municipal bonds. The partisan and regional distribution of the cases shows that the Court voided policies enacted by either Democratic or midwestern Republican state governments.

Federal statutes struck down by the Supreme Court from 1879 to 1896 did not, for the most part, concern the critical issues. This may reflect the Republican dominance in national policymaking in the years following 1896. It also reflects the strategy of reform movements to seek change initially through state politics. When the Democrats and Populists in Congress passed a personal income tax in 1894, the Supreme Court overrode long-standing precedent and declared it unconstitutional.

In short, analysis of the state and federal statutes struck down shows the Court's contribution to the laissez-faire stance of the Republican party, to the growing radicalization of the protest movements in the midwestern states, and perhaps to the capture of the Democratic party by the Silver Democrats (Westin, 1953: 39–41; but see Lasser, 1983: 170–173). These results give added support to the most recent role ascribed to the Supreme Court in critical election periods. As a member of the majority coalition, the Court contributes to the policy stance of the majority party as party leaders stake out positions before a critical election (Adamany, 1980). Although specifying the precise impact of these decisions on the process of critical elections and realignment awaits historical and interpretive analysis, the results show a relationship between Court policymaking and the salient issues precipitating realignment in the party system. By invalidating these salient policies, the Court ruled Progressive policies unconstitutional and perhaps contributed to the conservative extremists in the intraparty battles at the state and national level. The Court declared Progressive approaches to the basic question unconstitutional and enhanced the constitutional position of the most conservative wing of the party committed to maintaining the status quo.

The analysis of the justices' voting in the salient cases does not yield support for an increase in party-line voting near the critical period of partisan realignment. Although congressional voting studies have shown such increased partisan voting (Sinclair, 1982; Brady and Stewart, 1982; 1984), the evidence presented here does not show a similar pattern in these Supreme Court decisions. The dissent rates of the individual justices in the salient cases show little relationship between party voting and dissents in voiding salient state and federal policies. These results give support to the speculation that the justices will divide in new ways as these intense issues create new and fluid coalitions on the Court.

Although the Supreme Court handed down many cases of judicial review that helped to posture the Republican party before 1896, this conservatism appears not to have been rooted in Republican appointments in the preceding years. The voting records point to a much more complex relationship. The Supreme Court's support for economic conservatism between 1879 and 1896 was buttressed by both Democratic and Republican justices who confronted changing issues and a changing partisan agenda with the onslaught of partisan realignment.

The critical election of 1896 signaled the establishment of an extremely stable party system. The importance of the election is seen in the changing patterns of voting in the electorate, the solid control of the national government by the Republicans until 1910, and the changes in the partisan control of state governments (Burnham, 1970; 1981; Clubb, Flanigan, and Zingale, 1980: 208–212). The Republican commitment to laissez-faire continued with some alterations in the Progressive era until the New Deal. An analysis of the stability of this system and various propositions regarding the Supreme Court after 1896 follows.

THE AFTERMATH OF 1896 AND
THE RISE OF PROGRESSIVISM

Students of the Supreme Court and critical elections have offered different, if not contradictory, roles for the Court in the period following the critical election of 1896. Funston (1975) considers part of the post–1896 era as a period of policy conflict or "lag" between the Court and the popularly elected branches similar to the post–1860 period. Adamany (1980) notes, however, that the realignment of 1896 is fundamentally different from either the 1870s or the 1930s. It is different because the election was a "converting" critical election (Pomper, 1975). A converting election is one that strengthens a declining majority party rather than one that replaces a majority party with a new party. Unlike the period after the 1860 election when the new Republican majority confronted a Supreme Court composed primarily of Democratic or "old regime" justices, in the post-1896 period the Republican party faced a Court composed primarily of Republican justices appointed by Republican presidents in the years surrounding the election of 1896.[25]

From 1886 to 1896, presidents appointed sixteen justices to the Supreme Court. Of these, ten were Republican justices appointed by Republican presidents. The remaining six justices were Democrats, appointed by Democratic presidents except in one instance. A Republican Court thus confronted a Republican president and Congress in the post-1897 period; the justices were probably appointed for their views on the critical issues that realigned the party system in 1896.

For these reasons, Adamany (1980: 227–230) argues that the impact of the Court's policymaking on the majority party's stance on critical issues will be greater following the 1896 election than in periods when a new party replaces a long dominant party. "In a realignment election, existing policy is rejected and the out party wins a mandate to make policy. In converting elections, however, the preexisting majority party remains in power and its policy, while provoking shifts in voter allegiance, endures." Moreover, although the Court may help shape policies before all types of critical elections, "its impact on national policy is usually greater and more enduring in converting elections." This enduring policy impact is present because of the lack of conflict between the Court and the popularly elected branches after critical elections replacing an old majority party.

Therefore, the cases could show a continuation of Supreme Court policymaking dealing with the salient or critical issues. The same approach and measures developed in the first part of this chapter are used to examine the Supreme Court's invalidation of salient state and federal policies. In addition, the extent of division on the Court in resolving these cases is analyzed.

The consistency of these cases and the cases decided before the election is the primary focus. Partisan politics following 1896 are, however, not as straightforward as those following the Civil War. In the post–Civil War era, the parties divided over the cluster of slavery–Civil War–Reconstruction issues. In contrast, shortly after the 1896 election, both parties responded, at least in part, to new reform issues presented by various Progressive movements. By the time the Progressive Theodore Roosevelt became president, both parties were clearly developing Progressive wings.

Progressivism and the Supreme Court

Progressive movements at the turn of the century were similar to the Populist movements of the 1890s because the Progressives focused on the abuses or excesses of corporate capitalism. Both movements shared a concern for workers' rights and labor interests. Also, progressivism involved a diverse set of proposed reforms and appealed to a variety of societal interests across different regions. The proposed reforms dealt with political processes, education, and business monopolies. The movements centered at various times from the Spanish American War to World War I on issues of social justice including protection of women and worker safety in industry, care of the aged and destitute, control of workers' wages and hours, reform of policies relating to child labor, and establishment of workmen's compensation. The various movements also demanded new political reforms such as the direct primary, initiatives, recalls, referenda, and the direct election of senators.

Unlike the crosscutting issues of populism, the issues of the Progressive movement did not result in a critical election. This is because both parties responded to the demands for reform. Both the Republican Theodore Roosevelt and the Democrat Woodrow Wilson were often sympathetic to the Progressive forces. As Sundquist (1973: 159) notes concerning the early years of protest after 1896, "In no state did groups striving for reform . . . find it necessary to go outside of the two-party structure." In Congress, Democrats from urban centers and western Republicans joined forces to enact Progressive legislation from 1900 to 1910. Spurred by Roosevelt's "Square Deal," Congress enacted legislation such as the Employer Liability Act of 1906, which established employer liability for injured workers, the Pure Food and Drug Act of 1906, which established public health regulations for food and drugs, and in the same year it strengthened the Interstate Commerce Commission (ICC) in the Hepburn Act.

The Supreme Court in this period is often characterized as continuing its commitment to laissez-faire principles. Between 1896 and 1910, some major decisions protected business from regulation and worsened the legal position of labor. For example, from 1897 to 1905 the Court decided fifteen cases involving the regulatory authority of the ICC, and in each case the ICC lost (Goldman, 1982: 165). The Court also invalidated New York's maximum hours of labor law in the famous case *Lochner v. New York* (1905). The decision aroused controversy among reformers in the state and in Congress (Warren, 1913; Jackson, 1941: 53–55). As McCloskey (1960: 154) has observed, "The *Lochner* decision represents one of those moments in the Court's twentieth-century history when the judges temporarily embraced the illusion that the regulatory movement could be halted, rather than merely delayed, by judicial pronouncement."

The Court also modified, however, some of its more conservative decisions of the early 1890s. The Court upheld prosecutions of meat trusts in *Swift v. United States* (1905) and approved the Hepburn Act, which strengthened the ICC by giving the commission extensive jurisdiction and control over railroad rates and regulation. In *McCray v. United States* (1904), the Court also expanded taxing power of Congress to include regulatory taxation.

The more moderate course of the Court can be best understood in terms of membership changes. The appointment of justices from 1896 to 1910 is revealing. Although the Court was composed of eight Republicans and five Democrats, three of the Republican justices, Oliver Holmes, William Day, and William Moody, were appointed by Progressive Theodore Roosevelt.

TABLE 3.4

Number and Percentage of State and Federal Cases
by Policy Area,
1897-1910

Policy Area	Number of State Cases	Number of Federal Cases	Total Number of Cases	Percentage of Total Cases
Business Regulation and Taxation	39	1	40	64.5
Labor Rights	1	2	3	4.8
Municipal Bonds	0	0	0	00.0
General Contracts-Debts	3	0	3	4.8
General Taxation	2	0	2	3.2
Reconstruction	0	2	2	3.2
Criminal Justice/ Civil Liberties	2	3	5	8.1
Alcohol Control	2	1	3	4.8
Miscellaneous*	2	2	4	6.5
Total	51	11	62	100.0

*Policy areas include public lands, state banking, public morals, and state protectionism of business.

Source: Compiled by author from *United States Reports.*

Analysis of Supreme Court policymaking following this particular critical election follows an analysis of the cases of state and federal policy invalidation. This entails an examination of the issues involved, the pattern of the salient cases, and the voting of the justices.

The Invalidation of State and Federal Policies
Following the Critical Election of 1896

In the period stretching from McKinley's election in 1896 to the death of Chief Justice Fuller in 1910, the Supreme Court struck down a total of fifty-one state and eleven federal policies.[26] Of the policies invalidated in this class of cases, a large number involved the regulation or taxation of businesses. Table 3.4 displays the distribution of the state and federal cases by various policy areas. Business regulation and taxation policies constituted thirty-nine of the fifty-one state cases. The remaining state and federal cases dealt with policies ranging from general contractual and debt relationships to nonbusiness or general taxation and alcohol control or regulation.[27] The business regulation and taxation cases constituted 62.9 percent of all state and federal cases. It is important to note that the eleven federal cases did not dominate a particular policy area. Only three cases raised issues of importance to the critical issues of the 1890s: business regulation and taxation, the farmers' plight, and labor rights. The issues raised in these cases do not support Funston's (1975) hypothesis of policy conflict following 1896. Instead, the distribution of state and federal cases supports the notion that Supreme Court policymaking was consistent with the national lawmaking majority. Moreover, a closer examination of these cases supports the view that following a converting election, the Supreme Court will continue to make policy surrounding the critical, realigning issues.

The State Cases, 1897–1910. In the period 1892–1910, most of the state statutes struck down by the Supreme Court dealt with business regulation and taxation. As a proportion of all state cases, the cases of business regulation and taxation constituted a larger proportion in the 1897–1910 period (74.5%) than in the 1879–1896 period (56.5%). These data reinforce that the Supreme Court continued its commitment to the principles of laissez-faire.

For example, the Court struck down a Louisiana statute of 1897 that penalized insurance solicitation by out-of-state companies in *Allgeyer v. Louisiana* (1897). The case is widely cited by political historians because the Court announced a new doctrinal tool for the protection of business (Swindler, 1969: 36; Twiss, 1942: 132–133; Kelly, Harbinson, and Belz, 1983: 414). Implicitly adopting the position that corporations were persons for purposes of the due process and equal protection clauses of the Fourteenth Amendment, the Court announced that the Louisiana law violated due process because it interfered with the newly developed "liberty of contract." Decided in the year of McKinley's inauguration, *Allgeyer* is symbolic of a Court willing to expand constitutional rights for the protection of corporate capitalism.

As in the pre-1896 period, the Court struck down state policies relating to claims against foreign corporations[28] and various tax assessment procedures for businesses.[29] The Court invalidated state statutes regulating the business practices of out-of-state corporations based on the contract and commerce clauses and the due process and equal protection clauses of the Fourteenth Amendment.[30] State attempts to regulate the sale and condition of certain products such as oleomargarine were also struck down.[31] Finally, the Supreme Court invalidated an 1893 Illinois statute that regulated monopolies but exempted certain agricultural products in *Connolly v. Union Sewer Pipe Co.* (1902).

A large number of the cases of business regulation and taxation, however, centered on policies directed at railroads. Of the thirty-nine cases, seventeen concerned state policies relating to railroad rates and the general administration of companies. For example, in *Smyth v. Ames* (1898) the Court continued to serve as a judicial guardian of railroad rates. A Nebraska statute enacted in 1893 established rates for the hauling of freight. The Court held that the statutory rates were so low that they constituted deprivation of property forbidden under due process. The Court also struck down the 1894 rate-setting provisions of the Kentucky constitution in *Louisville and Nashville Railway Co. v. Eubank* (1902). Minnesota's long-standing attempts to regulate railroads met a similar fate in *Ex parte Young* (1908). The statute imposed penalties for violating the rate structure and established barriers to testing the validity of the statute in courts. The Court found the statute to constitute a denial of the equal protection of the law guaranteed by the Fourteenth Amendment.

The Supreme Court also invalidated various statutes aimed at general railroad regulation and taxation including the recovery of lands by the State of Texas that were initially chartered to a railroad company,[32] the establishment of passenger rates and railroad routes in Michigan and Illinois,[33] the repeal of tax exemptions to railroads in Minnesota,[34] and various tax policies and general regulations such as requiring railroads to deliver freight cars upon demand.[35]

The final issue of saliency to the progressive movement was labor rights. There was only one state case in the 1897–1910 period raising this general issue. It was not a minor case. In *Lochner v. New York* (1905), the Supreme Court struck down a New York law establishing a ten-hour day in all bakeries located in the state. The state argued that the statute was a reasonable exercise of the state's police power to provide for the health and safety of workers. Although the Court upheld a Utah statute regulating the hours of labor in the mining industry in 1898,[36] the Court's conservative majority voided the New York law arguing that the exercise of state power was not "fair," "reasonable," or "appropriate." The Court concluded that the statute was an interference with the liberty of contract or with the personal liberty of individuals to contract their labor (1905: 45, 52).[37]

The critical issues of the 1890s continued to dominate the class of state law invalidation cases. These cases also illustrate policymaking consistent with the policy stance of the Republican party, which defeated the Populist Bryan in 1896. Some of the statutes reflected Progressive policies such as legislation regulating the hours of labor. The conservativism of the Court is also seen in the cases overturning state policies regulating business.

One could argue that the state cases represented judicial affirmations of national power in these particular policy areas. By 1900, the national government had become involved in some forms of economic regulation. There are reasons, however, that reinforce the view that these were anti-regulatory cases rather than simply pronational power statements. First, the Court struck down these policies on the basis of constitutional limits to state power as interpreted from various constitutional provisions rather than on the basis of conflicts with federal statutes. In only two business regulation cases dealing with state regulation of the shipment of oleomargarine did the Court base its decision in part on a federal statute.

Some analysts of the Court's major decisions have shown that the Court was also hostile to federal efforts from the 1890s to the New Deal. It is instructive to quote at length the doctrinal assessment of the exercise of judicial review by Robert Harris (1948: 1–2). He writes:

> With the impact of industrialization upon government and the attendant clash of state regulatory activity and vested rights, judicial review flourished under a hot-house growth into a full blown instrumentality of laissez faire and the new corporate collectivism. It was employed for the most part by a recourse to the due process clause of the Fourteenth Amendment to strike down state legislation dealing with price-fixing, wage regulation, taxation, and regulatory action generally. At the national level the Tenth Amendment operated as a

serviceable vehicle for laissez faire in the invalidation of child labor legislation, agricultural adjustment, the regulation of industry generally and so on. With reference to such matters as legislation for the District of Columbia and regulatory action by federal administrative agencies the due process clause of the Fifth Amendment could be put into action, but such instances were never too numerous with the consequence that the due process clause of the Fifth Amendment did not always mean the same thing as the due process clause of the Fourteenth, a result which not only rejected the Euclidean proposition that things which are equal to the same thing are equal to each other but also stood for the proposition that a thing is unequal to itself. The conversion of the same thing into different things while retaining each was not the only solecism produced by judicial review. For example, Congress could not regulate minimum wages generally, for that would impair the reserved rights of the states, but the states could not regulate them for that would deprive persons of liberty without due process of law. Putting these two proposals together we arrive at the result that Congress could not exercise certain powers because to do so would be to approach upon the reserved rights of the states under the Tenth Amendment which the states did not really possess under the due process clause of the Fourteenth Amendment. In other words whereas nothing from one would equal one in simple arithmetic, nothing from something would leave nothing in constitutional law.

The number of salient state cases and the timing from 1879 to 1896 is most consistent with Adamany's (1980) speculations: Supreme Court policymaking following a converting election will continue to reflect the new majority party's stance. The Supreme Court's invalidation of state laws strengthened its commitment to laissez-faire, a commitment that at times brought the Court in conflict with Democrats and Progressives in the states.

An examination of the regional distribution of the salient statutes and the partisan control of the state when the statute was enacted reveals results similar to those of the pre-1896 period. Table 3.5 illustrates the distribution of the salient statutes both by the partisan control of the state government and by region. Democratic state governments in the West and South were responsible for fifteen, or 48.4 percent, of the salient cases. Republican state governments in the West and South enacted nine, or 29.0 percent, of the salient statutes. Only one of the nine Republican statutes in the West and South was enacted before 1896 when there was strong Populist activity in the western wing of the Republican party.

As in the pre-1896 period, a large majority (77.4%) of the salient cases arose from either Democratic state governments or midwestern Republican states with moderate to strong Populist movements. The distribution of the small number of nonsalient cases is rather even across the noneastern states. In sum, the analysis of the cases of state policy invalidation shows the Court continuing to strike down state policies concerning the critical issues of the 1890s, and these policies were usually passed by legislatures under partisan control different from the partisan majority on the Supreme Court.

The Federal Cases, 1897–1910. If Funston (1975) is correct, the number of important federal laws raising critical issues should increase significantly

TABLE 3.5

Distribution of Salient[a] and Nonsalient State Cases
by Partisan Control of State Governments at the
Time of Policy Enactment,
1897-1910

	Number of Salient	Percent	Number of Nonsalient	Percent [b]
Democratic--East[c]	0	00.0	0	00.0
Democratic--West[d] & South[e]	15	48.4	3	30.0
Mixed[f]--East	1	3.2	1	10.0
Mixed[f]--West & South	3	9.7	2	20.0
Republican--East	3	9.7	1	10.0
Republican--West & South	9	29.0	3	30.0
Total	31	100.0	10	100.0
Missing Data	9		0	

[a]Includes cases of business regulation and taxation and the repudiation of municipal bond obligations.
[b]The percentages are based on a small number of cases.
[c]Includes the northeastern and middle Atlantic regions.
[d]Includes the northeast central and northwest central regions.
[e]Includes the solid South and border states.
[f]State governments classified as mixed in terms of partisan control had different parties in each chamber of the legislature or the legislature was controlled by one party and the governorship by another party. Control is signified by either a solid majority or a simple plurality.

Source: Clubb, Flanigan, and Zingale (1990); *United States Reports.*

following the election; he argues that this period is a period of policy lag between the Court and the popularly elected branches. Again, the analysis of the issues presented in the cases does not support the delegitimizing role. The distribution of state and federal cases across various policy areas is displayed in Table 3.4. The eleven federal statutes struck down from 1896 to 1910 raised a variety of political issues including criminal justice, the regulation of alcohol, reconstruction, general taxation, and public land disputes. The Court invalidated three federal statutes dealing with criminal justice including an 1875 statute that shifted the presumption of guilt for individuals who received stolen property,[38] a 1900 section of the Alaska territorial code requiring jury trials for misdemeanors,[39] and a 1901 section of the District of Columbia Code relating to the right of appeal.[40] Equally unimportant, or nonsalient, from a critical election perspective are statutes relating to the harboring of alien prostitutes,[41] the approval provision for a second lease on Indian lands,[42] the sale of alcohol to Indians,[43] the Reconstruction Enforcement Acts of 1870,[44] and the enforcement of contracts.[45] In sum, eight of the eleven federal statutes did not concern the realigning issues. Only three statutes were salient to either the partisan issues of populism or progressivism. In *Fairbank v. United States* (1901), the Supreme Court struck down an 1898 stamp tax on foreign bills of lading. The Court held that the tax was an export tax forbidden by Article I. Although these were not as important in a qualitative sense to the personal income tax voided in *Pollock v. Farmers' Loan and Trust Co.* (1895), *Fairbank* reflected the Court's continuing concern with taxation and its general character. The conservative Justice Brewer (1901: 312) wrote, "It is only of late years, when the burdens of taxation are increasing by reason of the great expenses of government that the objects and modes of taxation have become a matter of special scrutiny."

The two remaining federal cases dealt with labor rights. Both illustrate a negative attitude toward prolabor statutes. In 1908, the Court struck down the Employer Liability Act of 1906.[46] The Employer Liability statute, establishing employer liability for certain cases of injured workers, was struck down because the Court found that Congress's authority over interstate commerce did not include intrastate commerce. When Congress amended the legislation, the Court unanimously upheld it in the *Second Employers' Liability Case* (1912). The final federal case was also related to labor interests. In 1908, the Court invalidated a congressional attempt to prohibit employers from using "yellow-dog" contracts. These contracts required workers not to join a union or to engage in strikes or boycotts of the employer's business.[47]

At first glance, these antilabor decisions may appear consistent with the thesis of policy conflict following critical elections advanced by Funston (1975)[48] and Nagel (1969). Policy conflict may be likely because the Court is staffed with justices appointed by the old lawmaking majority. These labor statutes, however, were not consistent with the laissez-faire principles of McKinley republicanism. Instead, they were the product of the Progressive wings of both parties. The accident of Roosevelt's ascendancy to the presidency in 1901 brought with it a new strength and vigor to Progressive forces in the Republican party. Therefore, one cannot consider these cases as evidence of conflict with the new lawmaking majority because the policy stance of the party had changed by the time the Court struck down these laws in 1908. The small number of federal invalidations from 1896 to 1910 and the absence of salient partisan issues may reflect a degree of congruence between the Court and the popularly elected branches. The Court's decisions in two cases of labor rights blunted Progressive forces and kept them aware of the Court's nay-saying power in the area of taxation. At best, one can conclude that the two cases invalidating Progressive labor legislation were statements of judicial policy favoring the conservative wing of the Republican party.

The cases voiding federal statutes do not support the notion of inevitable policy conflict between the Court and Congress following a critical election. The eleven cases suggest instead a congruence between the Court and Congress regarding the critical issues. Eight of the eleven statutes dealt with policy areas of little consequence to the issues of business regulation and the development of corporate capitalism. Of the three cases relating to the issues of 1896, two were primarily a response to the new Progressive movements and labor rights.

A few points are necessary concerning the number of salient issues found in both the state and federal cases. Business regulation and taxation cases continued to dominate in cases of state policy nullification. As Figure 3.2 portrays, the Supreme Court continued to strike down state statutes involving these issues following 1896. The graph illustrates a substantial decrease in the number of invalidations.

The 1890s witnessed the highest level of salient invalidations. This is strikingly consistent with the analysis of polarization in party platforms (Ginsberg, 1972). A more precise test or accounting of whether the salient state cases increased significantly in line with party polarization follows. Regression estimates of a formal equation are the primary tool. The proposition that the 1890s witnessed a significant increase in the salient cases can be formally stated as

$$I_t = a + b_1 \text{ Time1}_t + b_2 \text{ Time2}_t + b_3 R_t + e_t,$$

where I_t is the simple number of cases invalidating state statutes dealing with the critical issues from 1878 to 1910; a is a constant term; Time1_t is the time trend before 1890 and Time2_t is the time trend from 1891 to 1910; R_t is a dummy variable that takes the value of 1 from 1890 to 1900 and 0 in other years because of the critical years of party polarization (Ginsberg, 1972); and e_t is an error term. The coefficients to be estimated are b_1, b_2, and b_3. As discussed in Appendix B, the value of the coefficient for the dummy variable (b_3), representing the period of impact on the series, is the primary focus. If b_3 is greater than 0, then the realignment period of polarization does have the posited effect on the series.

Least-squares regression provides the estimates for the impact of the realignment period except in the presence of serial correlation, or autocorrelation.[49] In such an instance, the estimates of the coefficients were adjusted according to the Cochrane-Orcutt method.[50] This method can provide efficient estimates in the presence of autocorrelation.[51] Table 3.6 displays the estimates for the interrupted time series of salient policies between 1878 and 1910; the t statistics are in the parentheses below the relevant estimates of the coefficients; R^2 is the coefficient of multiple determination (adjusted); D.W. is the Durbin-Watson statistic; p is the value of rho when generalized least squares was necessary; and N is the number of cases.

Note that Table 3.6 displays estimates for both the total number of salient policies and an estimated rate of invalidation. The yearly number of policies is important but it does not take into account the Court's workload in a given year, the number of policies challenged as unconstitutional and upheld, or the number of policies challenged within a given issue area. Ideally, a rate of invalidation would be computed based on the number of challenges to policies relating to the realigning political question. Unfortunately, these data are unavailable. Nevertheless, an estimated rate of invalidation is used based on a measure of the changing workload of the Supreme Court, the log of the number of written opinions handed down by the Court (Blaustein and Mersky, 1978:137).

The results indicate that there was a statistically significant increase in the number of critical cases from 1890 to 1900 because b_3 is greater than

TABLE 3.6

Interrupted Time-Series Estimates for the Total Number
of Salient Policies and an Estimated Rate of Invalidation,
1879-1910

Variable		Total Number of Salient Policies	Estimated Rate of Invalidation
Constant	b	-0.086	-0.210
	SE	0.913	0.163
	t	-0.095	-0.128
Time 1	b	0.271[b]	0.495[b]
	SE	0.127	0.228
	t	2.133	2.170
Time 2	b	0.167[a]	0.032[a]
	SE	0.060	0.017
	t	2.791	3.011
R_t	b	1.625[c]	0.297[c]
	SE	0.805	0.143
	t	2.018	2.076
R^2 =		0.221	0.252
Adj. R^2		0.140	0.175
D.W. =		1.820	1.750
rho =		———	-0.064
n = 33			

[a]$p > t = 0.01$
[b]$p > t = 0.05$
[c]$p > t = 0.10$

Source: Compiled by author.

0. This is true for both the number of policies and the estimated rate of invalidation.[52] These results do not hold for the total number of nonsalient cases that raised other types of issues.[53] The apparent increase in Figure 3.2 is given precise support. A sudden and abrupt increase is also supported by the insignificant results obtained when the dummy value continues to take the value of 1 from 1890 to 1910 instead of 1890 to 1900. Generalized least-squares estimates were insignificant at the .10 level, which suggests that the "impact" of the critical election period cannot be extended from 1890 to 1910.

The significant results for Time 2 also show a modest long-term impact on the series of salient invalidations. Following polarization, the Supreme Court struck down 0.167 more cases each year, which is hardly staggering. Overall, the results show a sudden surge in the invalidation surrounding polarization but only a mild increase in the subsequent decade (1901–1910).

This is not to suggest that partisan realignment somehow "caused" an increase in the number of invalidations dealing with the critical issues. The increase is because of several complex developments such as industrialization, capitalism, and changing attitudes regarding law and the legal profession. These findings do show, however, that the Court invalidated a significantly larger number of statutes related to the types of issues that realigned the party system between 1890 and 1900. In addition, these cases are consistent with the conservative position of the Republican party, vindicated in the 1896 presidential election. In sum, the analysis is quite supportive of the proposition that the Supreme Court is an active participant on the realigning questions and is involved in setting the realignment agenda.

The Voting of the Justices, 1897–1910. The volatile nature of critical issues may divide the justices to a greater extent than nonsalient types of issues and party-line voting in the salient cases. As party leaders stake out polar positions on these issues, the Supreme Court divides as well. The percentage of nonunanimous cases in cases invalidating federal and state laws was higher than in all of the cases handed down by the Court. Of the sixty-two cases, 58.1 percent registered dissent by one or more justices. The level of dissent on the Fuller court was generally higher than the level of dissent on the Waite Court. The percentage of nonunanimous cases rose from 8.9 in the 1890 term to 23.5 percent in the 1900 term, 23.5 in the 1905 term, and 13.0 percent in the 1910 term (Halpern and Vines, 1977). The dissent rate from 1888 to 1910 has been estimated at roughly 43 percent (Goldman, 1982: 175).

Therefore, the class of cases declaring unconstitutionality provoked more dissent than the average case handed down by the Court. Moreover, the cases of invalidation are included in the Court's overall level of dissent and may inflate these figures. As in the 1879–1896 period, the overturn of all types of state and federal policies provoked greater dissent than the average case handed down with opinion. It appears that the justices were more divided in displacing legislative choices. The overturn of legislative choices raises sensitive issues of the Court's proper role vis-à-vis institutions subject to periodic elections.

The justices were often divided in cases of judicial review. Yet, the salient cases of business regulation and taxation and labor rights show an even higher rate of division. Of the forty-two salient cases, nonunanimous cases constituted 59.5 percent. The Court divided more often over these types of issues than it did in either the nonsalient cases of invalidation or all cases decided by the Fuller Court (1888–1910). The volatility of critical issues continued to divide the justices after the resounding choice made in the election of 1896.

The dissent rates of the individual justices serving on the Court is not suggestive of strong partisan voting. Table 3.7 displays the rate of dissent for each justice in all of the cases of judicial nullification and the salient cases. The level of dissent provides a crude indicator of the justices' support or nonsupport for the statutes relating to business regulation-taxation or labor. A lower level of dissent is a more conservative position because less disagreement signifies general approval of the overturn of these Progressive policies.

TABLE 3.7

Dissent Rates of the Justices in Salient Invalidation
Cases and All Invalidation Cases,
1897-1910

Justice (Party)	Dissent Rate in Salient Cases		Dissent Rate in All Cases	
	Percent	*Number*	*Percent*	*Number*
McKenna, J. (R)	32.5	40	25.0	60
Gray, J. (R)	29.4ª	17	27.3	22
Harlan, J. (R)	28.6	42	30.6	62
Holmes, J. (R)	28.0	25	22.5	40
Fuller, C.J. (D)	23.8	42	21.0	62
Moody, J. (R)	18.8ª	16	16.7	24
White, J. (D)	9.5	42	6.5	62
Brewer, J. (R)	5.6	36	8.9	56
Shiras, J. (R)	5.3ª	19	8.3	24
Day, J. (R)	4.3	23	5.4	37
Brown, J. (D)	3.8	26	7.9	38
Peckham, J. (D)	00.0	34	5.8	52
Lurton, J. (D)	00.0ª	8	00.0ª	9
Hughes, J. (R)	00.0ª	2	00.0ª	2
Field, J. (D)	00.0ª	2	00.0ª	2

ªPercentages computed with less than 20 cases.

Source: Compiled by author from *United States Reports.*

The dissent rates show that Republican and Democratic justices can be found as both weak or strong supporters of these policies. Democrats Wheeler Peckham and Horace Lurton, for example, show a very low level of dissent in the salient cases. The correlation between the justices' dissent rates and their partisan affiliations is moderate (0.346, eta), but it is higher than the correlation in the 1879–1896 period.

The results are, however, generally consistent with ideological characterizations of some of the justices. Justices Peckham, Brown, and Day are shown as staunch defenders of laissez-faire. Justices Oliver Holmes, John Harlan, and Joseph McKenna were the least conservative on the Fuller Court (Fairman, 1966: 387; King, 1967).

CONCLUSION:
THE REALIGNMENT OF THE 1890s

Following the Civil War, the Supreme Court began to systematically invalidate federal and state policies. The critical issues of concern to the Populist forces were evident in most of the state policies struck down by the Court before the critical election of 1896. Primarily, the Supreme Court struck down a large number of policies aimed at the regulation and taxation of business and state attempts to repudiate municipal bond obligations.

Although the number of federal policies voided were few, the Court also declared a federal income tax unconstitutional—a policy supported by Populists and Democrats.

The issues of realignment were present on the Court's agenda, and through its power of judicial review the Court contributed to the partisan struggle. The data do not permit specification of the exact causal nature of this relationship, but the analysis does yield support for the propositions advanced regarding the role of the Court in the period before a critical election.

These findings reinforce the proposition that the Supreme Court participates in shaping the majority party's response to the crosscutting issues precipitating critical elections and partisan realignment (Adamany, 1980). The salient cases represent judicial policy statements consistent with the conservative extremist wing of the Republican party vindicated by McKinley's election in 1896. The many state cases also led to greater hostility among Populists and reformers toward the judiciary and the Republican party. The legislative successes of Populists and reformers in the South and West faced a hostile Republican Court. From Minnesota to Kansas to Texas, attempts to control railroads and business generally were struck down. Attempts to relieve farmers of their tax debt by repudiating municipal bond debts met a similar fate before the Court. These cases undoubtedly frustrated reformers and possibly contributed to their growing radicalization and greater concern for reform policies at the national level.[54]

The analysis of the cases decided between 1879 and 1896 also shows important differences between the Supreme Court's treatment of state and federal policies. The number of statutes voided is much lower for federal statutes. This is due, in part, to the concentration of economic legislation at the state level during most of the period. In addition, this suggests some policy congruence between the Court and the national lawmaking majority. The few federal laws struck down is consistent with Robert Dahl's (1957) analysis. As part of the rather stable Republican alliance from 1860 to 1890, the Supreme Court invalidated few federal statutes. Dahl argues, however, that the Supreme Court may take a lead in developing important policy when the alliance or coalition becomes unstable at the national level. This is a fair description of the dramatic income tax decision in *Pollock v. Farmers' Loan and Trust Co.* (1895) in which the Court struck down the recently enacted federal tax supported by Populists, Democrats, and midwestern Republicans. Moreover, the small number of federal statutes bearing upon the central issues reflects how the reformers initially sought policy change from state governments.

Analysis of the 1897–1910 cases supports Adamany's (1980) speculations that the period following a converting election will not show increasing policy conflict. The post-1896 period witnessed the Court's continuing commitment to laissez-faire with some minor changes in the level of activism. Most of the invalidations were of state laws that related to the regulation and taxation of business, especially railroad regulation. Three federal statutes were struck down in this period. The Court held to the principles of business freedom even against the rising tide of progressivism in the early 1900s.

The macro-, or aggregate, results are supportive of the agenda-setting role ascribed to the Supreme Court by Adamany (1980). This agenda-setting role is premised in part on the idea that the Court will reflect the views of the dominant party before the critical election because of several presidential appointments in the preceding years or decades. Although the Supreme Court's decisions are consistent with this view, the individual-level data provide little evidence that the Court's conservatism in the cases of judicial review was supported by a solid group of Republican justices before 1896. The salient cases of judicial review were supported by both Democrats and Republicans who confronted new and crosscutting issues. This strongly suggests that the basis for a linkage to the dominant party before critical elections is extremely complex and the decisions of the Supreme Court on the realigning political questions may not always reflect the ideological views of the dominant party.

Moreover, although strong partisan voting on the critical issues was not found either before or after the critical election of 1896, there is some evidence that there was greater partisan voting in the period following the critical election. Although the evidence is far from conclusive and awaits further confirmation, the results suggest that the linkage between the Supreme Court and the majority party provided by presidential appointment is stronger following a critical election than in the period before a critical election. After 1986, the parties had polarized and staked out definitive and quite different policy positions on the realigning questions. The justices appointed under these conditions would most likely reflect these ideological changes. In contrast, party leaders before 1896 had often avoided, straddled, or compromised on the crosscutting issues in hopes of maintaining their electoral coalitions. Under these conditions, the linkage between the Court and the president's party becomes much more tenuous.

In sum, the analysis of the Supreme Court's invalidation of state and federal policies gives support to the propositions of Adamany (1980) and to Lasser's (1983) analysis of the income tax case. For both, the Supreme Court helped to shape the majority party's position on the critical issues before the election of 1896. Second, the continued efforts of the Court to strike down policies dealing with labor rights and the regulation and taxation of businesses suggest a long-term impact on national policy as the majority party continued in firm control of the Court. Unlike in the periods following the realignment of the 1860s or the 1930s (Adamany, 1980), the impact of the Court may be greater as it continues to make policy surrounding the critical issues. Burnham (1981: 174), for example, attributes to the stability of the Second Republican party system begun in 1896 "the ascendancy of the Supreme Court over legislation affecting corporate capitalism." As he notes, the Republican party system endured until the New Deal because "stable control of key parts of the political system—the presidency and above all the Supreme Court—was sufficient for . . . insulating dominant interests from pressure" (1981: 181).

This conservative stance is vividly seen in the exercise of judicial review before realignment of the party system in the 1930s and most especially in the response to Progressive forces between 1911 and 1920. The Supreme Court's invalidations in this period and the New Deal period are the subject of the following chapter.

NOTES

1. The Greenback party made a deliberate effort to join labor and agrarian interests. Nevertheless, the movement was short-lived. See Goodwyn (1976: 16–17, 21–24).

2. The sectional tensions of the Civil War undoubtedly hindered the spread of populism and diluted its multisectional strength (Keller, 1977: 576-578).

3. E.g., *The Civil Rights Cases*, 109 U.S. 3 (1883); *Plessy v. Ferguson*, 163 U.S. 537 (1896).

4. Implicit in the Court's decision was the proposition that Congress could establish such rates given its power over interstate commerce. Yet, when Congress enacted the Interstate Commerce Act in the following year, the power of the commission was curtailed in subsequent cases. The Court decided fifteen cases involving the ICC between 1897 and 1905 and in each case the ICC lost (Goldman, 1982: 165).

5. *Pickard v. Pullman Southern Car Co.*, 117 U.S. 34 (1886); *Norfolk and Western Railway Co. v. Pennsylvania*, 136 U.S. 114 (1890).

6. *Mobile and Ohio Railroad v. Tennessee*, 153 U.S. 486 (1894); *New York, L.E. and W. Railroad Co. v. Pennsylvania*, 153 U.S. 628 (1894).

7. *Illinois Central Railway v. Illinois*, 163 U.S. 142 (1896).

8. *Gulf, C. and S.F. Railway Co. v. Ellis*, 165 U.S. 150 (1897).

9. *Missouri Pacific Railway v. Nebraska*, 164 U.S. 403 (1896).

10. E.g., *Robbins v. Shelby Taxing District*, 120 U.S. 489 (1887); *Asher v. Texas*, 128 U.S. 129 (1888).

11. *Western Union Telegraph Co. v. Pendelton*, 122 U.S. 347 (1887); *Ratterman v. Western Union Telegraph Co.*, 127 U.S. 4111 (1888); *Western Union Telegraph Co. v. Alabama*, 132 U.S. 472 (1889).

12. *Minnesota v. Barber*, 136 U.S. 313 (1890); *Brimmer v. Rebman*, 138 U.S. 78 (1891); *Scott v. Donald* 165 U.S. 58 (1897).

13. *United States ex. rel. Wolff v. New Orleans*, 103 U.S. 358 (1881); *Ralls County Court v. United States*, 105 U.S. 733 (1881); *Mobile v. Watson*, 116 U.S. 289 (1886).

14. *Seibert v. Lewis*, 122 U.S. 284 (1887).

15. *Hartman v. Greenhow*, 102 U.S. 672 (1880); *Virginia Coupon Cases*, 114 U.S. 269 (1885); *Royall v. Virginia*, 116 U.S. 572 (1886); *McGahey v. Virginia*, 135 U.S. 662 (1890).

16. *Parkersburg v. Brown*, 106 U.S. 487 (1882); *Cole v. LaGrange*, 113 U.S. 1 (1885).

17. The Supreme Court also decided cases involving the creation of "receiverships," which protected corporations from state court systems. See Westin (1953: 17–19).

18. There were two other similar statutes decided outside of the 1879–1896 time frame.

19. For the policies in which the date of enactment was available, two of the thirty-nine statutes were enacted prior to the end of Civil War. This fact, however, may not be an indication that these policies were unimportant to partisan forces. Indeed, in his critique of Dahl's famous study of the cases of federal law nullification, Casper (1976: 55–56) makes this point well. Dahl attempted to assess whether the invalidations of federal law constituted policymaking in the interests of some "minority." He examined the Court's invalidation of only recently enacted federal statutes or those enacted within four years of their invalidation, assuming a lawmaking

majority was a surrogate for majority preferences. This was done to guarantee that the Court was striking down the policy preferences of a "live" majority.

Casper notes that this focus on recently enacted statutes limits analysis of important older statutes that are important to current or live majorities. Also, Casper (1976: 56) notes: "Without its intervention, the original older policy would presumably have been continued." Indeed, Dahl's coding scheme would omit the Missouri Compromise of 1820 struck down in *Dred Scott v. Sanford*, 19 How. 393 (1857). Applying this scheme to the state cases has a similar effect. The salient railroad cases discussed further on often involved policies older than four years.

20. The central question for the Supreme Court is determining whether a tax is a direct tax and subject to being apportioned by population. From *Hylton v. United States*, 3 Dal. 171 (1796) to *Springer v. United States*, 8 Wall 533 (1881), the Court held that only land and poll taxes were direct taxes. Indeed, an income tax was upheld four years prior to *Pollock* in *Springer v. United States*, 8 Wall 533 (1881).

21. Former president Benjamin Harrison noted in a campaign address in 1896: "I cannot exaggerate the gravity and the importance and the danger of this assault upon our constitutional form of government; upon the high minded, independent judiciary that will hold to the line on questions between wealth and labor, between the rich and poor" (Westin, 1953: 34). Of course, there is disagreement on the importance of the Court issue in the campaign. Compare Westin (1953: 22–39) and Lasser (1983: 164–168).

22. Least-squares regression analysis of all important state and federal cases proves the lack of linearity in this pattern. The R^2 of 0.018 shows that roughly 11 percent of the variation in the number of cases can be "accounted" for by time alone. This lack of a simple linear increase during this period is also found for the nonsalient cases.

The proportion of all cases of invalidation involving business regulation and taxation, however, shows an almost steady increase following the Civil War to the 1890s. The percentage of these important questions increased from 33.3 percent in the 1886–1870 period to 80.0 percent in the 1891–1895 period. These questions gradually dominated the Court's invalidation agenda. Generalized least-squares regression analysis of the percentage of total state cases relating to the important issues on time shows that the salient cases increased over the period ($R^2 = 0.614$) as a proportion of all state cases. The small number of cases in some periods may, however, inflate the percentage changes.

23. Halpern and Vines (1977) report that dissent in 1890 was slightly under 10 percent (8.9%). The dissent rate in 1880 was identical (8.9%). In 1900, the dissent rate increased to 23.5 percent.

24. For example, see McCloskey (1960). Chief Justice Fuller, however, has often been considered a generally conservative justice. This may be due to Chief Justice Fuller's opinions in both *United States v. E.C. Knight Co.*, 156 U.S. 1 (1895) and *Pollock v. Farmers' Loan and Trust Co.*, 158 U.S. 601 (1895).

25. One could argue that policy conflict over the critical issues may arise because turnover in Congress has brought into office the most ideological individuals, who confront a more moderate Supreme Court. The Supreme Court's decisions prior to 1896 do not suggest a moderate course in respect to the critical issues. It is useful to remember the decision of *Pollock* in 1895.

26. Three of the state policies were constitutional provisions rather than legislative statutes. These cases are included in the standard source: the list of cases published by the Library of Congress in 1978. As noted earlier, the simple yearly frequency of cases is not based on the dates in the citations of this source. In the citations

found in the Library of Congress list of cases, there is no consistent use of either the Court term year or the calender year in which the decision was handed down.

27. It is perhaps necessary to restate that the cases of general contracts and debts related to nonbusiness interests in the litigation. For example, in *Northwestern University v. Illinois ex rel. Miller*, 99 U.S. 309 (1879), the Court struck down an Illinois statute that changed the charter provisions of Northwestern University. The Court held that the statute violated the contract clause. The Court also struck down state statutes relating to obtaining judgments against governments by individuals (e.g., *Nelson v. St. Martin's Parish*, 111 U.S. 716 [1884]) and real estate transfers (e.g., *Barnitz v. Beverly*, 163 U.S. 118 [1896]).

Although general contractual issues could be viewed as indirectly relating to business interests by strengthening the market and its infrastructure, the interests involved in the litigation and the specific target of the statutes were not business related. My approach or classification scheme is more conservative. The focus is on the explicit goals of the statutes and the interests involved in litigation at the trial and appellate court levels. For an elaboration, see Appendix B.

One could conceivably argue that in addition to the class of general contract and debts, the cases of alcohol control were indirectly related to some forms of business control. In examining the policy goals of these statutes, however, there is evidence that the statutes were designed to restrict or regulate the sale of alcohol. These statutes were struck down on commerce-clause grounds as well as on the basis of federal statutes (e.g., *Leisy v. Hardin*, 135 U.S. 100 [1890]). These restrictions appear on their face to be directed at public morals, and this is supported by historical evidence relating to alcohol and Prohibition movements such as the Anti-Saloon League. Although the issue of alcohol control was a pressing issue in many areas and undoubtedly raised partisan passions, the issue was not crucial to the demands of populism and the monetary question, which served to realign the party system.

28. E.g., *Blake v. McClung*, 172 U.S. 239 (1898).

29. E.g., *Union Transit Co. v. Kentucky*, 199 U.S. 194 (1905).

30. E.g., *Stockard v. Morgan*, 185 U.S. 27 (1902); *American Smelting Co. v. Colorado*, 204 U.S. 103 (1907); *Western Union Telegraph Co. v. Kansas*, 216 U.S. 1 (1910); *International Textbook Co. v. Pigg*, 217 U.S. 91 (1910).

31. E.g., *Schollenberger v. Pennsylvania*, 171 U.S. (1898); *Collins v. New Hampshire*, 171 U.S. 30 (1898); *Ohio v. Thomas*, 173 U.S. 276 (1899).

32. *Houston and Texas Central Railway v. Texas*, 170 U.S. 243 (1898).

33. *Lakeshore and Michigan Southern Railway Co. v. Smith*, 173 U.S. 684 (1899); *Cleveland C.C. & St. Louis Railway Co. v. Illinois*, 177 U.S. 514 (1900).

34. *Stearns v. Minnesota*, 179 U.S. 223 (1900).

35. E.g., *Union Transit Co. v. Kentucky*, 199 U.S. 194 (1905); *Houston & Texas Central Railroad v. Mayes*, 201 U.S. 321 (1906); *Galveston, Houston & San Antonio Railway Co. v. Texas*, 210 U.S. 217 (1908); *St. Louis S.W. Railway v. Arkansas*, 217 U.S. 136 (1910).

36. *Holden v. Hardy*, 169 U.S. 366 (1898).

37. These cases, salient in terms of the 1890s realignment, cannot be viewed in isolation from the Court's other types of decisions if the goal is to assess Supreme Court policymaking in the early years of progressivism (Semonche, 1978; Warren, 1913).

38. *Kirby v. United States*, 174 U.S. 47 (1899).

39. *Rassmussen v. United States*, 197 U.S. 516 (1905).

40. *United States v. Evans*, 213 U.S. 297 (1909).

41. *Keller v. United States,* 213 U.S. 138 (1909).

42. *Jones v. Meehan,* 175 U.S. 1 (1899).

43. *Matter of Heff,* 197 U.S. 488 (1905).

44. *James v. Bowman,* 190 U.S. 127 (1903).

45. *Hodges v. United States,* 203 U.S. 1 (1906).

46. *The Employers' Liability Cases,* 207 U.S. 463 (1908).

47. *Adair v. United States,* 208 U.S. 161 (1908).

48. To be perfectly fair to Funston, it should be noted that at one point he writes (1975: 802): "The result of the realignment of 1888–1896 was to elevate McKinley to a position of preeminence in the political system and the Court began a campaign completely in consonance with the values represented by the dominant party." But the post-1896 period is included in the analysis as a period of policy conflict, or "lag" (1975: 806).

49. If we use a significance level of 0.05, the Durbin-Watson statistic for the ordinary least-squares regression is 1.701. The statistic ranges in value from 0.0 to 4.0. The upper and lower critical values of the statistic can be found in most econometric texts; see Rao and Miller (1971); Pindyck and Rubinfeld (1981). Values of the statistic below the critical values indicate positive autocorrelation; values above the highest critical value indicate negative autocorrelation.

50. The Cochrane-Orcutt method of adjusting the estimated coefficients involves a two-state iteration. First, an estimate of rho is obtained through least-squares regression. Second, the value of rho is used to transform the variables in the equation to obtain uncorrelated residuals for the equation, and a new least-squares analysis is performed.

51. This is true, of course, when there are theoretical reasons for positing a first-order autocorrelation process (e.g., the observation in year 1 is a good indicator of observation in year 2 but not necessarily in year 3). It is also appropriate over a short time series when "trend" and "drift" in the series are minimal. The latter is true in this analysis, and some would argue the former is true as well of the Supreme Court's attention to issues.

52. As noted in Appendix B, the number of salient policies overturned by the Supreme Court is an event count. The most precise estimation strategy is Poisson regression (King, 1989). Poisson estimates of the equation for the total number of salient policies are very similar to those provided by least squares regression: constant $(b = -0.490; S.E. = 0.466)$; Time 1 $(b = 0.147; S.E. = 0.055)$; Time 2 $(b = 0.096; S.E. = 0.030)$; and R_t $(b = 0.800; S.E. = 0.340)$. Although the value of the coefficient for R_t is slightly lower, the statistical significance is higher.

Some could argue on theoretical grounds that the underlying statistical Poisson distribution is inappropriate when applied to the estimated rate of invalidation (e.g., the presence of negative values for the rate). Poisson regression may nonetheless be appropriate in this research because only the number of salient policies is examined.

Poisson estimates of the equation for the estimated rate of invalidation also are very similar to the least-squares estimates: constant $(b = -2.65; S.E. = 1.197)$; Time 1 $(b = 0.185; S.E. = 0.137)$; Time 2 $(b = 0.120; S.E. = 0.0776)$; and R_t $(b = 1.1470; S.E. = 0.835)$.

53. Estimating the equation for the number of nonsalient cases (N-S) yields results that demonstrate a rather abrupt *decrease* in the nonsalient cases. Specifically, the results are

$$N\text{-}S = 2.019 + .0137 \text{ Time1}_t + -.0092 \text{ Time2} + -1.123 \text{ R}_t$$

(2.234)*	(.0981)	(−.1533)	(−1.439)**

$$R^2 = .145 \qquad\qquad D.W. = 2.015$$
$$rho = -.125 \qquad\qquad N = 31$$

*significant at the .025 level
**significant at the .10 level

54. Some caution is in order. First, the cases of judicial nullification represent a very small part of the Court's formal policymaking. A focus on these cases could result in overrepresenting or underrepresenting various types of issues on the Supreme Court's agenda because these cases are extreme expressions of judicial authority. Second, only selected types of critical issues were raised in the policies declared unconstitutional by the Court. The volatile silver question was not tested in an explicit form, albeit the Court addressed the money supply question in voiding the federal income tax of 1894. Labor issues were also completely absent in the cases of invalidation handed down before 1896.

4

The New Deal Realignment, 1911–1945

This vote was determined by the capacity for economic analysis and the views of public policy of five individuals. It is their preference which has rendered minimum-wage legislation invalid. It is not wholly true that the elucidation of the question of its validity cannot be aided by counting heads. Only because in the final vote some heads rather than others are the ones to be counted is minimum-wage legislation invalid.

—Thomas Reed Powell
"The Judiciality of Minimum Wage Legislation"
Harvard Law Review, 1924

Our difficulty with the Court today rises not from the Court as an institution but from human beings within it . . . we cannot yield our constitutional destiny to the personal judgment of a few men who, fearful of the future, would deny us the necessary means of dealing with the present.

—Franklin D. Roosevelt
"Fireside Chat"
March 9, 1937

Major developments occurred in the American party system between 1911 and 1945. First, between 1910 and 1920, the Progressive movement had a significant impact on national policymaking. By the 1920s, however, it had run its course as the country returned to "normalcy" and the Republican party resumed its support for a limited role for government in economic regulation (Swindler, 1969: 222–283). The second major development in this thirty-five year period was the New Deal realignment of the 1930s. The Democratic party under Franklin Roosevelt replaced the Republican party as the nation's majority party. The critical elections of 1932 and 1936 ushered in a period of Democratic dominance in national policymaking.[1] The Great Depression marked an abrupt phase in the partisan realignment of the 1930s.

The study of the Supreme Court and critical elections has focused considerable attention on the New Deal realignment. This is because of the well-known clash between the Democratic party and the Republican majority on the Supreme Court. No other period of realignment demonstrates such overwhelming support for the proposition that the Supreme Court will void a large number of federal statutes following the replacement of a majority party in a critical election. Between 1934 and 1937, the Supreme Court struck down various provisions of New Deal statutes enacted by a Democratic Congress. Further, various congressional attacks on the Court as well as President Roosevelt's pressure to enlarge the size of the Court illustrate the intensity of policy conflict. These attacks upon the Court in response to its anti–New Deal rulings were not ultimately carried out because Justice Owen Roberts departed from his earlier decisions in 1937 and joined the four liberal justices in upholding New Deal policies.

In the second part of this chapter I explore further this period of policy conflict after the critical election of 1932 by examining not only the cases invalidating federal policies but also the cases nullifying state policies. The expectation is that the invalidation of state policies will reflect judicial animosity toward the ideology of the Democratic party as it found expression at the state level. The cases related to the salient or realigning questions during this period of policy conflict or "policy lag" are identified in order to address these questions. In addition, there is an examination of whether the salient cases originated in states ideologically opposed to the Supreme Court. The voting of the justices is also examined as a test of the intensity of the realigning issues. Finally, bloc analysis affords insight into the possible partisan basis of the justices' responses to the salient cases.

The first part of the chapter is an examination of the relationship between the invalidation of state and federal policies and the Court's policy stance before the critical election of 1932. The Court may play some role in periods before critical elections in helping to shape or posture the majority party's stance on the critical issues of realignment. As Adamany (1980: 215) notes, "The Supreme Court's role in shaping the posture of a national coalition was most evident in the decades preceding the realignment of 1932. . . . And it was in that posture that the GOP, despite a vigorous progressive wing, faced a changing electorate and the debacle of the Depression." This proposition will be examined by relying upon the number of salient cases and the justices' voting. A systematic analysis of all federal and state policies declared unconstitutional by the Court between 1911 and 1932 may provide additional evidence of this agenda-setting role. We will examine this evidence after the following section, which provides a brief overview of partisan politics before 1932 and characterizations of Supreme Court policymaking.

THE CROSSCUTTING NATURE OF PROGRESSIVISM
AND THE PERIOD OF "NORMALCY"

The Progressive reformers of the early twentieth century raised a variety of political issues. Composed of interests ranging from urban middle-class reformers to industrial laborers as well as midwestern agrarian interests, the Progressive movement sought numerous reforms in political processes, workmen's compensation, child labor laws, and the control of wages, prices, and hours of labor. As Sundquist (1973: 156–162) notes, these economic and social-justice issues cut across the existing lines of division in the party system inaugurated by the victory of McKinley republicanism in 1896. Progressivism provided the basis for the strongest third-party movement in the entire century; this is certainly testament to the strength of the movement. The presence of crosscutting issues and the rise of third parties are two important factors associated with partisan realignment in the party system (Sundquist, 1973; Clubb, Flanigan, and Zingale, 1980; Trilling and Campbell, 1980).

By the time of America's involvement in World War I, however, the leaders of the movement had become an ineffective minority in both parties. According to Sundquist (1973: 158–162), realignment was "averted" from the early 1900s to 1920 because of the response of leaders in both of the major parties. In other periods before partisan realignment, party leaders took evasive strategies hoping to silence the crosscutting issues completely or to calm reformers through compromise. Polarization occurred because of a combination of events that led party leaders to take decisive and opposing positions on the crosscutting issues. In the Progressive era Democrats and Republicans responded by making some concessions to the reformers. Leadership was important to the course of Progressive issues because of the accidental ascendancy of Theodore Roosevelt to the presidency. Roosevelt brought legitimacy and vigor to the growing Progressive wing in the Republican party. The Democratic party also had a moderately Progressive president in Woodrow Wilson (Sundquist, 1973: 162–164). In short, extreme polarization and realignment did not occur in the Progressive era because each party contained strong Progressive wings before 1920.

Supreme Court policymaking during the Progressive era has been the subject of extended discussions and debates (Warren, 1913; Swindler, 1969; Kelly, Harbinson, and Belz, 1983; Semonche, 1978). On the one hand, a conservative posture for the Supreme Court is clear in various decisions between 1911 and 1920. In 1918, the Court nullified the federal Child Labor Act of 1916 in *Hammer v. Dagenhart* (1918). The Court found that Congress had exceeded its authority under the commerce clause in prohibiting the passage of goods in interstate commerce if the products were made by child labor. In the field of labor rights, the Court handed down conservative decisions such as *Coppage v. Kansas* (1915). In *Coppage*, the Court voided a state law prohibiting the use of antiunion, or "yellow-dog," contracts by employers. These contracts allowed employers to obtain written agreements that laborers would not join unions or engage in strikes or boycotts against the employer.

However, many analysts have noted that the Supreme Court supported or affirmed several Progressive policies (Semonche, 1978). The Court upheld maximum-hours legislation at the state level.[2] Federal regulatory statutes were also sustained, such as the Food and Drug Act of 1906,[3] the Meat

Inspection Acts of 1906 and 1907,[4] and the important Hepburn Act of 1906, which strengthened the Interstate Commerce Commission (ICC) by expanding its jurisdiction and rate-setting authority.[5] As noted, by 1920 the Progressive movement had largely waned. From the election of President Warren Harding until the Great Depression, national politics lacked an effective Progressive element, and Republican dominance in national policymaking resembled the republicanism of McKinley rather than that of Teddy Roosevelt. President Harding's pledge to "return to normalcy" reflected a desire for less government activity, especially that aimed at regulation of economic interests and the economy. By most accounts, the Supreme Court reflected these developments (Swindler, 1969: 222–283; McCloskey, 1960: 121–135; Semonche, 1978: 201–238).

From 1920 to 1932, the Supreme Court voided or restricted the application of Progressive policies and became increasingly opposed to Progressive efforts. This conservative stance is due in part to President Harding's appointments to the Court. He appointed four conservative justices: Chief Justice William Howard Taft as well as Associate Justices George Sutherland, Pierce Butler, and Edward Sanford. Goldman's (1982: 242) characterization of Supreme Court policymaking between 1911 and 1932 is particularly apt:

> The Supreme Court during the progressive period before the war and the reactionary period afterwards generally staked out positions to the right of the mainstream of politics. When national politics moved to the left, the Court was more liberal than before but less liberal than the majority consensus within the other branches of government. When national politics moved to the right, the Court moved even further to the right.

This stance is important for understanding the possible role of the Supreme Court in the period before the New Deal realignment. The Court's decisions relating to labor as well as business regulation and taxation were consistent with the conservative Republican position that confronted the Democratic party in the critical elections of 1932 and 1936. The cases of state and federal policy invalidation show a Court firmly controlled by conservative justices. In cases relating to the salient issues of government regulation of the economy and economic interests in general, the Court helped to shape the Republican party's posture on the basic question of government management of the economy in the midst of depression and critical elections. Indeed, the Supreme Court's invalidation of salient policies represented a position consistent with the conservative wing of the majority party in control of the party in the 1932 and 1936 critical elections. As a member of the majority coalition, the Court demonstrated an unwillingness to depart from the Republican party's traditional laissez-faire position.

The Invalidation of State and Federal Policies
Before the New Deal Realignment

The Supreme Court continued to strike down many more state policies compared to the number of federal policies from 1911 to 1932. There were

248 state invalidation cases compared to 22 federal invalidation cases. In addition, the yearly number of state invalidations was much greater over this twenty-one-year period. Indeed, the Court struck down an average of 11.8 state policies each year compared to an average of 4.2 policies per year between 1890 and 1910. Figure 4.1 presents the total number of state and federal invalidation cases from 1911 to 1945.

As Table 4.1 illustrates, a majority of these cases involved either labor-related issues or the regulation and taxation of businesses. The Supreme Court struck down 147 state and 4 federal policies related to business regulation and taxation. In addition, 20 state and 5 federal policies dealt with labor and labor unions. As noted below, all of these cases cannot be deemed consistent with the conservative reputation of the Court regarding economic- and business-related regulations and therefore salient judicial policy for the period before the New Deal realignment. A closer examination of these cases illustrates that most state policies declared unconstitutional by the Court were salient or related to the issues of government management of the economy and economic interests.

The State Cases, 1911–1932. The unconstitutional state policies ranged from public and Indian land policies to labor rights as well as business regulation and taxation. Similar to the invalidations of state laws in the nineteenth century, the state invalidations in this era were dominated by issues of business regulation and taxation. Of the 249 state policies invalidated by the Court, 149, or 59.8 percent, dealt with the regulation or taxation of business. Policies related to labor also grew as a proportion of all cases— twenty, or 8.0 percent, related to policies directed at labor concerns and involved labor interests in the litigation. In the 1897–1910 period, only 4.8 percent of cases decided dealt with labor issues. Although unrelated to either the issues of progressivism or the role of government in the economy, statutes requiring racial discrimination in transportation[6] and voting were struck down.[7] Also, the Court voided various state policies that discriminated against alien residents.[8] Further, the Court invalidated statutes relating to the publishing rights of newspapers[9] and the display of red flags in the post–World War I era.[10] The Court also nullified fourteen state policies dealing with general nonbusiness contracts and debts such as the attachment of liens on real estate in bankruptcy proceedings.[11] The Court struck down a large number of policies dealing with inheritance taxes[12] and other general nonbusiness policies.[13]

Before examining the state cases in greater detail and identifying salient cases, it is necessary to address the question of state versus federal jurisdiction. Throughout the nineteenth century, the Supreme Court struck down policies primarily on constitutional rather than statutory grounds. When the Court invalidates a state policy because of a similar but conflicting federal law, it becomes difficult to categorize the ideological stance of the case as judicial hostility to the goals of the state policy. State policies struck down on federal statutory grounds may not signal judicial antipathy for a particular state policy but often represent an affirmation of national or federal authority in

Figure 4.1
Number of Federal and State Policies
Declared Unconstitutional, 1911–1945

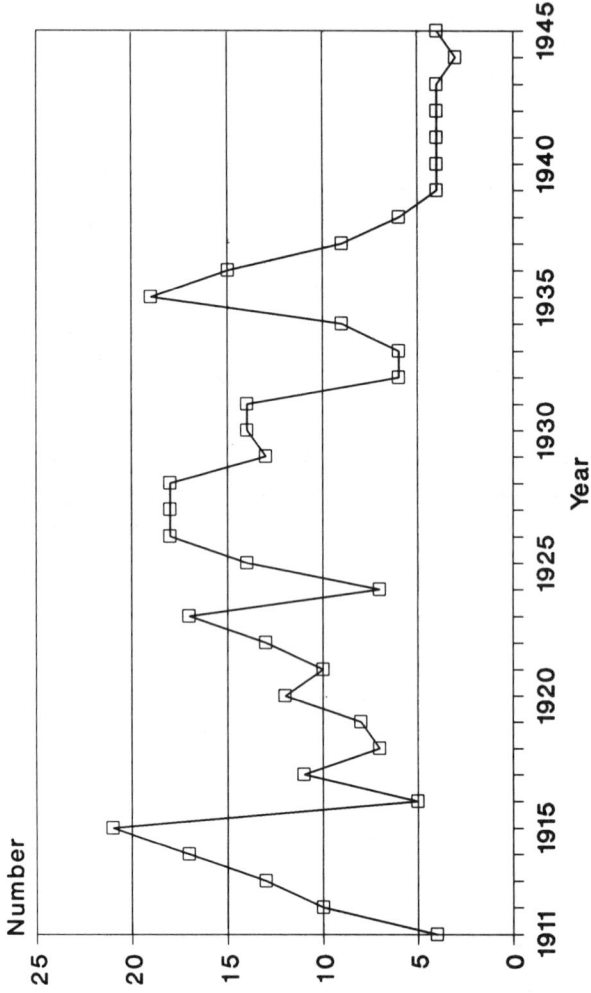

Source: Library of Congress (1978).

TABLE 4.1

Number and Percentages of State and Federal Cases
by Policy Area,
1911-1932

	Total Number of State Policies	Total Number of Federal Policies	Total Number of State & Federal Policies	Percent of Total
Business Regulation & Taxation	147	4	151	55.9
Labor	20	5	25	9.3
General Contracts & Debts	13	1	14	5.2
General Nonbusiness Taxation	20	5	25	9.3
Civil Rights & Liberties	19	1	20	7.4
Banking	11	0	11	4.1
Alcohol Control	5	0	5	1.8
Political Process Reforms	0	1	1	0.4
Miscellaneous[a]	14	4	18	6.7
Total	249	21	270	100.0

[a]Includes the following types of policies: municipal bonds; public land disputes; state protection of in-state businesses; federalism; regulation of game.

Source: Compiled by author from *United States Reports.*

the area. For example, the Court struck down a Minnesota regulation of railroads establishing an obligation to deliver railroad cars.[14] The basis of the Court's decision was the Hepburn Act of 1906, which strengthened and expanded the jurisdiction of the ICC. As such, it is difficult to characterize this case outcome as judicial hostility to railroad regulation.

By the 1920s, there were a growing number of federal statutes related to economic matters and businesses. The Court based its decision to overturn state policies on assorted federal statutes in 57, or 22.9 percent, of the 249 cases handed down between 1911 and 1932. In identifying the salient state cases and their policy outcome, this analysis omits the invalidations based on federal statutes; these cases are considered to raise primarily federalism issues. Federalism issues are included within the miscellaneous category in Table 4.1. The voting of the justices is also supportive of this approach to the federalism issue. In the thirty-two invalidation cases of labor and business regulation and taxation based on federal statute, the Court decided over 71 percent without a single dissent. In cases without a federal statutory basis to the nullification, the Court decided slightly over 58 percent unanimously.

Of special significance for the policy stance of the Republican party before 1932 are the cases classified either as labor-related or as business regulation and taxation. The policies involved in these areas raise the general question of economic regulation or the proper level of government management of the economy and economic interests. Judicial policymaking in these cases is important for discussing the Court's probable role in fostering the position of the Republican party in the prerealignment period. The cases illustrate a continuing conservative posture consistent with the laissez-faire reputation of the Court. The data do not allow for specifying the exact impact of these cases on the process of polarization in the midst of economic crisis. These cases, however, provide general support for the view that the Court, as a member of the majority coalition, contributes to the policy position of the majority party (Adamany, 1980: 251). The Court's conservative position in these salient cases was representative of the Republican position repudiated by the electorate in 1932 and 1936.

Excluding the state labor and business regulation and taxation policies struck down on the basis of a federal statute, there are 135 salient cases.[15] These cases comprise 54.2 percent of all cases invalidating state policies between 1911 and 1932. As in the period before the critical election of 1896, the Court continued to strike down many economic and regulatory statutes. Yet, the yearly number of salient cases was much greater than in the 1890s. The average number of salient cases handed down in this period was 6.4, compared to 3.4 in the 1890–1900 period.

The most notable state cases that reflected the continuing conservatism of the Court involved state policies dealing with labor, price and rate controls, and more general forms of business regulation. In striking down these policies, the Court used a variety of doctrinal tools. In 1915, the Court struck down a Kansas statute prohibiting employers from using antiunion, or "yellow-dog," contracts in *Coppage v. Kansas* (1915). A majority of the Court held that the policy interfered with the contractual rights of the employers by limiting their freedom to establish the conditions of employment. The majority ruled that the policy violated the liberty of contract protected under the due process clause of the Fourteenth Amendment.

The Court also struck down prolabor policies by further restricting the class of businesses that were affected with a "public interest" and subject to regulation. In *Munn v. Illinois* (1877), the Court had ruled that state regulation extended only to businesses "affected with a public interest." In *Wolff Packing Co. v. Industrial Court* (1923), a majority of the Court narrowed the scope of the doctrine and found that a compulsory arbitration statute was unconstitutional because it applied to businesses not affected with a public interest. Therefore, the statute interfered with the property rights of businesses.

Two years before *Wolff*, the Court had struck down an Arizona antiinjunction statute on the basis of the due process and equal protection clauses. The statute prohibited employers from obtaining state court injunctions in order to halt labor picketing and boycotting. In *Truax v. Corrigan* (1921), Chief Justice Taft (1921: 332) argued that due process of law guarantees "equality of law in the sense that it makes a required minimum of protections for everyone's right of life, liberty, and property, which the Congress or the legislature may not withhold." Further, the statute violated the guarantee of the equal protection of the law because it granted an immunity to one class as opposed to another (1921: 333).

In contrast to Taft's conservative interpretation of the due process and equal protection clauses were the interpretations of the Progressive Justices Oliver Holmes, John Clark, and Louis Brandeis as well as Justice Mahlon Pitney who dissented in *Truax*. Brandeis (1921: 355, 357) noted: "Nearly all legislation involves a weighing of public needs as against private desires; and likewise a weighing of relative social values. . . . What, at any particular time, is the paramount public need, is necessarily, largely a matter of judgment." The difference in "judgment" found in the labor cases continued in many other labor and business regulation and taxation cases between 1911 and 1932.

For example, the Court voided state regulations designed to control prices, such as a New York statute dealing with the resale price of theater tickets. In *Tyson Brothers v. Bantom* (1927), the Court ruled 5–4 that the theater business involved was not one affected with a public interest and thus not subject to state regulation. The following year a similar price control on employment agencies was invalidated in *Ribnick v. McBride* (1928). The majority and dissenting opinions in *Tyson* and *Ribnick* reflect very different conceptions of the relationship between government, business, and economic matters.

The conservative Justice Sutherland wrote the opinion of the Court in *Tyson* and further restricted the public-interest doctrine as a doctrinal tool for justifying state economic regulation. He noted in voiding this price control (1927: 430): "A business is not affected with a public interest merely because it is large or the public are warranted in having a feeling of concern with respect to its maintenance, . . ." Further, he argued that only businesses "devoted to public use" and "granted by the public" could be subject to regulation (1927: 350). Commenting on the theater business involved in *Tyson*, Sutherland (1927: 441–442) observed: "It may be true, as asserted, that, among the Greeks, amusement and instruction of the people through drama was one of the duties of the government. But certainly no such duty devolves upon any American government." In dissent in *Ribnick*, Justice Harlan Stone (1928: 359) argued: "Price regulation is within the state's police power whenever any combination of circumstances seriously curtails the regulative force of competition so that buyers and sellers are placed at such a disadvantage in the bargaining struggle that a legislature might reasonably anticipate serious consequences to the community as a whole."

The major point is that these cases of business regulation and taxation raise issues of importance to the Republican policy stance in the New Deal realignment period. In addition to these cases, the Court struck down a variety of regulatory and taxation policies ranging from the regulation of utility rates to the control of bedding materials for safety purposes as well as the regulation of hours and wages. Specifically, the Court voided policies establishing state taxes or regulations on out-of-state corporations.[16] Also, the Court used the commerce clause, the contracts clause, and the due process clause of the Fourteenth Amendment to nullify state regulations and taxes directed at such businesses as insurance, oil, gas, as well as telegraph and telephone companies.[17] The Court also invalidated state policies restricting state court remedies for businesses.[18] These state policies ranged from statutes revoking the license of foreign corporations when the business invoked diversity of citizenship jurisdiction for suits in federal courts[19] to statutes establishing conditions for entry into the state court system for enforcing contracts[20] as well as for reviewing state-established rates.[21] In addition, the Court voided state attempts to control the practice and fees of employment agencies,[22] to regulate certain products and goods,[23] and to tax and regulate in-state businesses.[24] As noted, the Court also struck down attempts to control or set prices.[25]

Excluding the forty-five cases dealing with railroad regulation, the court struck down ten of the state cases relating to business regulation and taxation on the basis of a federal statute.[26] A Wisconsin food labeling law conflicted with the Federal Pure Food and Drug Act.[27] An Oklahoma oil-lease policy interfered with federal statutes relating to Indian lands,[28] and Washington and Maryland statutes regulating motor carriers were struck down on the basis of the Federal Highway Act.[29] The remaining state policies clashed with federal policies dealing with the Interstate Commerce Commission (ICC).[30]

In the banking field, one state policy is considered salient to the critical issues. In *Manley v. Georgia* (1929), a state law making all bank failures fraudulent was declared unconstitutional as violative of due process. The remaining banking statutes involved state taxes on national bank shares. In each case, federal statutes governing the level and procedures for taxation served as the legal source for invalidation.[31]

Included in the class of business regulation and taxation cases are forty-five state policies aimed at railroads. Of these, the Court voided fifteen, or 33.3 percent, on the basis of the legislation relating to the ICC including the Hepburn Act of 1906,[32] the Carmack Amendment,[33] and other ICC rules and regulations.[34] Also nullified were three state policies relating to railroad regulation that were found in conflict with the Federal Safety Appliance Act.[35]

When federal statutes could not be applied as a limit to state policymaking, however, the Court struck down regulatory legislation aimed at the regulation of rates charged by railroads. Here, as in the 1890s, the due process clause of the Fourteenth Amendment served as an instrument for voiding state regulations.[36] The Court struck down state policies aimed at the liability of railroads and procedures for damage suits by citizens and shippers.[37] In addition, the cases included policies relating to railroad taxes, license fees,[38] and general railroad practices.[39]

In the field of labor, the Supreme Court voided state policies relating to minimum wage,[40] workmen's compensation,[41] and labor practices that were found to constitute a form of peonage.[42] The Court declared only one antilabor state policy unconstitutional. In *Fiske v. Kansas* (1927), the Court nullified a Kansas criminal syndicalism statute as it was applied to labor organizations.

The cases identified as salient do not simply raise highly controversial questions of public policy. These cases involve clear conflict with state policies that attempt to control the economy or business interests (Brady and Stewart, 1982: 355–357). This basic conflict was crosscutting in nature and disrupted the party system in the 1932 and 1936 critical elections (Sundquist, 1973: 185–199). As Sundquist notes, there were certainly other highly controversial issues that raised partisan passions. The difference between these issues and critical or realigning issues is that issues such as immigration and Prohibition reinforce division between the major parties; critical issues divide and cut across the coalitions within each of the major parties (Sundquist, 1973: 199–204). Therefore, the salient cases represent the invalidation of policies that raise directly the crosscutting issues and not simply controversial questions.[43]

In sum, the salient state policies struck down by the Court between 1911 and 1932 raised the basic political question of business regulation and government management of economic interests. These cases constituted 54.6 percent of all state cases handed down in this period. The cases support the view that the Court contributed to the majority party's stance on the critical issues, which would eventually lead to realignment in the party system. Of course, one should not view these cases as somehow "anticipating" the New Deal realignment but only as conservative judicial policy relating to crosscutting issues of the depression years.

Figure 4.2 displays the total number of salient cases by year from 1911 to 1945. Simple inspection of the distribution of cases reveals that the largest number of cases over the entire series occurred in 1914 and 1915 when the Supreme Court voided thirteen and eleven statutes, respectively. The number dropped after 1915 to less than five for the remaining years of the decade. From 1920 to 1930, however, there is apparently an increase in the series. The number of salient cases rose to ten in both 1922 and 1927 and dropped below five cases a year in only three years. The salient cases did increase in the period before 1932, but this increase was neither straightforward nor linear. It is important to remember that the Progressive majority on the Court achieved in 1916 was soon reduced to a minority with President Harding's appointment of four conservative justices.

The examination of the number of salient cases and the higher incidence of cases in the 1920s suggests two points. First, these results are consistent with the conservative turn attributed to the Court in line with national politics in the 1920s. Second, and more important, the cases support the view that the Court helped to posture the Republican party on issues dealing with government management of the economy and economic interests. The state cases relating to labor-related issues and the regulation or taxation of businesses illustrate the general question of government management of the economy and economic interests. It may be that the vast majority of salient state policies were enacted primarily by Democratic legislatures.

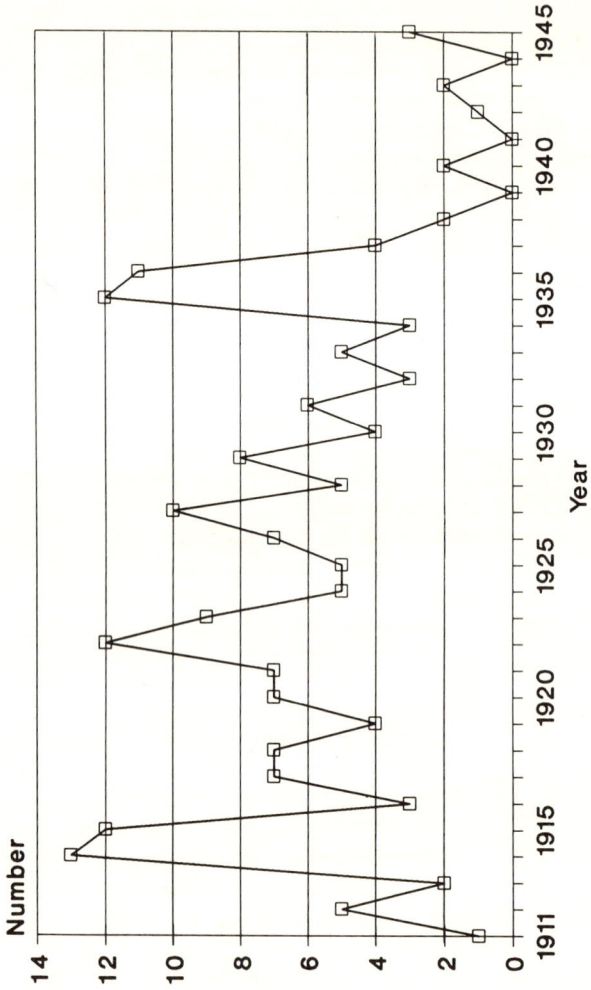

Figure 4.2
Number of Salient Policies
Declared Unconstitutional, 1911–1945

Source: Compiled by the author.

TABLE 4.2

Distribution of Salient and Nonsalient State Cases
by Partisan Control of State Governments
at Time of Policy Enactment and by Region,
1911-1932

Partisan Control by Region	Number of Salient[a]	Percent	Number of Nonsalient	Percent
Democratic				
New England & Middle Atlantic	0	0.0	0	0.0
Solid South & Border	48	42.1	23	43.4
East & West North Central	1	0.8	2	3.8
Pacific & Mountain	2	1.8	1	1.9
Mixed[b]				
New England & Middle Atlantic	4	3.5	4	7.5
Solid South & Border	5	4.4	1	1.9
East & West North Central	4	3.5	4	7.5
Pacific & Mountain	1	0.8	1	1.9
Republican				
New England & Middle Atlantic	12	10.5	5	9.4
Solid South & Border	2	1.8	0	0.0
East & West North Central	26	22.8	8	15.1
Pacific & Mountain	9	7.9	4	7.5
Total	114	100.0	53	100.0
Missing	30		49	

Percentage of all states ideologically opposed = 56.1

[a]The salient invalidation cases include cases of business regulation and taxation and labor, excluding the 13 cases where state policies were struck down on the basis of a federal statute.
[b]State governments classified as mixed in terms of partisan control had either a divided legislature or the partisanship of the governor and the legislature was different. Legislative control is signified by either a majority or a simple plurality.

Source: Clubb, Flanigan, and Zingale (1990); *United States Reports.*

An examination of the partisan status of the states enacting salient cases reveals that 44.7 percent of these statutes were enacted by Democratic state governments; 42.9 percent by Republican state governments; and 12.3 percent by state governments with mixed control. Table 4.2 displays the distribution of salient and nonsalient cases by region and by the partisan status of the state government enacting the policy. Democratic state governments in the solid South and the border states enacted over 42 percent of the salient policies. Similarly, these states accounted for over 43 percent of the nonsalient policies. Unlike in the period before 1896, the origin of the salient cases was not significantly different from the nonsalient cases. When the Court struck down state policies between 1911 and 1932, a large plurality of these policies were enacted by southern Democratic governments.

Table 4.2 also illustrates that the second largest grouping of salient as well as nonsalient policies were enacted by Republican governments in the midwestern or the eastern and northwest central regions. Over 22 percent of the salient policies and slightly over 15 percent of the nonsalient policies were enacted by Republican state governments in these regions. Again, there was not a substantial difference between the origin of salient and nonsalient policies. Nevertheless, the data show that the Court struck down 62.9 percent of the salient policies from southern Democratic and midwestern Republican governments. In terms of all states, 56.1 percent were ideologically opposed to the dominant majority on the Court.

These findings are quite consistent with the regional party system established in the late 1890s. With the election of President McKinley in 1896, the control of state governments returned to the regional party system of the post–Civil War period. The midwestern Republican states continued to contain Progressive elements after 1896. Ideologically, there are reasons to believe that these states as a region were the more progressive of the Republican states. This may account for these states' being the source of the second largest number of policies overturned by the conservative Supreme Court. In discussing the receptiveness of state governments to progressivism after 1896, Sundquist (1973: 161) notes:

> In the rural areas . . . a reform stream flowed into the Republican party. When the Populists returned to their original Republican allegiance, they carried their ideological baggage with them, and at once joined forces as an insurgent wing with the Republicans who, though Populist in sympathy, had remained behind in the old party when the more daring had bolted. The most renowned governors of the agrarian brand of Progressivism in the West—LaFollette of Wisconsin, Cummins of Iowa, and Hiram Johnson of California—were Republicans.

Indeed, throughout the 1920s, the Midwest was the center of such protest forces as the Farmer-Labor party in Minnesota and the Farmers' Non-Partisan League in North Dakota. Neither movement, however, was as intense or as large as the various Populist movements of the 1880s and 1890s.

In addition, the influence of progressivism did not spread to all areas of the Midwest. Yet, the salient midwestern Republican states, which have received mention as the more progressive, are the source of the salient policies denoted in Table 4.1.[44] The salient policies arose from Illinois, Kansas, Ohio, Minnesota, Nebraska, North Dakota, Wisconsin, Michigan, and South Dakota. Except for Michigan, which is the source of only one salient policy, these states are the heart of the agricultural belt, or the western Midwest, where progressivism had made the greatest inroads into the Republican party. In short, over 62 percent of the state policies struck down by the Court between 1911 and 1932 originated from southern Democratic states and midwestern Republican states.

At the national level, there are countless examples of groups entering the federal judicial system to obtain favorable rulings after defeat in the popularly elected branches (Wolfskill, 1962; Barker, 1967; Olson, 1981; Vose, 1981; Wasby, 1981). The cases of state policy invalidation suggest a similar pattern of interest mobilization. As noted, the salient policies declared unconstitutional were often enacted by state legislatures who were controlled by partisan majorities different from that of the Supreme Court. This suggests that societal interests and groups at the state level who are "losers" at the state level may turn to the federal court system for relief. The data support such a conjecture. In the vast majority of cases, state courts were the original trial court and nongovernmental interests were responsible for over 90 percent of the appeals brought to the federal courts.

The analysis of the 249 state policies declared unconstitutional by the Court between 1911 and 1932 has shown that over a majority were related to the general question of labor relations and business regulation and taxation. These types of policies are related to the crosscutting issue of government management that arose in the New Deal realignment. Although one should not view these decisions as the Supreme Court "anticipating" realignment, the policy stance of the Court is quite consistent with the policy stance the Republican party took in the 1930s. In addition, the partisan origin of these policies as well as the remaining policies overturned by the Court arose from Democratic states in the South and Republican states in the Midwest and perhaps illuminates the dynamics of legal mobilization.

The Federal Cases 1911–1932. The Supreme Court declared twenty-one federal policies unconstitutional between 1911 and 1932, or an average of only one policy per year. Table 4.1 shows that five of the cases dealt with labor policies.[45] Also, there were four cases of business regulation[46] and taxation policy.[47] The remaining cases included a variety of policies: a 1908 statute relating to the local tax status of Indian lands;[48] a 1912 statute that removed grand jury proceedings from the juvenile court for the District of Columbia;[49] an 1876 statute dealing with presidential removal of power;[50] and various political process reforms such as a 1911 limit to contributions for senatorial primary contests.[51]

The four federal cases dealing with business regulation and taxation illustrate the conservative nature of the Court as well as the "return to normalcy" in the 1920s. First, the Court voided an 1898 stamp tax on cargo carriers engaged solely in travel between U.S. ports and foreign ports as a tax on exports in *United States v. Hvoslef* (1915). More important, the impact of the Harding appointments in the early 1920s is perhaps evident in the three remaining business regulation and taxation cases. In *Eisner v. Macomber* (1920), the Supreme Court invalidated a 1916 income tax law that placed taxes on stock dividends. Conservatives committed to laissez-faire had hoped that despite adoption of the Sixteenth Amendment, which gave Congress authority to levy income taxes, they could persuade the judiciary to limit the reach of the amendment by narrowly defining income (Swindler, 1969: 209; Semonche, 1978: 384). The Court, speaking through Justice Pitney, invalidated the statute on the grounds that corporate stock dividends were not income for purposes of the Sixteenth Amendment.

In addition, the Supreme Court struck down wartime price controls established by the Lever Act in *United States v. Cohen Grocery Co.* (1922).

And in *Hill v. Wallace* (1922), the Court delivered another blow to congressional power in economic matters when it voided the Future Trading Act of 1921. Viewing the measure as an attempt to control the boards of trade through the levy of taxes, the Court held that the statute was a regulatory measure rather than a simple tax and therefore beyond the scope of congressional power.

The narrow view of congressional regulation is also seen in five labor cases handed down between 1911 and 1932. In *Hammer v. Dagenhart* (1918), the Court struck down the 1916 Keating-Owen Child Labor Law, which prohibited goods produced by child labor from passing in interstate commerce. The Court held that the statute extended federal power to matters of local concern beyond Congress's power to regulate interstate commerce (1918: 276). The Court voided similar state Progressive measures because of limits to state power over interstate commerce. When Congress attempted similar measures, the justices found these to be an infringement on the reserved powers of the states. This interesting doctrinal position produced sharp attacks on the Court. As Kelly, Harbinson, and Belz note (1983: 460): "The decision which ranks with *Lochner* as among the most politically notorious in Supreme Court history reflected the Court's belief that fundamental changes in the economic order must be stopped at almost any cost."

Two years later the Supreme Court invalidated a federal statute that sought to conform to an earlier decision by the Court involving workmen's compensation. The previous decision, *Southern Pacific Co. v. Jensen* (1917), held that maritime workmen's compensation claims could not be litigated on the basis of state laws. Congress responded by specifically delegating this authority to the states. The Court found this remedial statute to be an unconstitutional attempt to delegate legislative authority to the states in *Knickerbocker Ice Co. v. Stewart* (1920). This same issue led to another case of judicial nullification in 1924. Following *Knickerbocker*, Congress attempted to limit the impact of the decision, but the Court struck down this 1922 statute in *Washington v. Dawson & Co.* (1924).

The most notable labor cases of the era were *Bailey v. Drexel Furniture Co.* (1922) and *Adkins v. Children's Hospital* (1923). In *Bailey*, the Court nullified the second child labor law passed by Congress under President Woodrow Wilson. The 1919 statute based its regulation of child labor on the taxing power instead of the commerce power struck down in *Hammer v. Dagenhart* (1918). The Court, however, rejected Congress's attempt to find a new constitutional basis for regulating child labor; it overturned the policy as an invasion of the powers reserved to the states under the Tenth Amendment.

In *Adkins*, the Court struck down a congressional minimum-wage law for women in the District of Columbia. Although the Court upheld similar legislation in 1908 and 1917,[52] it declared these regulations unconstitutional as a violation of the freedom of contract under the due process clause of the Fifth Amendment. As some commentators have noted, "While the Supreme Court was willing to accept hours of labor legislation, it regarded prices and wages in a more direct sense as the foundation of the free enterprise system and hence in need of protection against government interference" (Kelly, Harbinson, and Belz, 1983: 460). Besides these cases of labor relations and business regulation and taxation,[53] the Court struck down a 1918 tax on judges' salaries;[54] the tax violated the constitutional guaranty that judges' salaries would not be reduced while in office.

The five cases dealing with labor and the four cases of business regulation and taxation relate directly to the important question of government management of economic interests. Therefore, the Supreme Court's invalidation of these Progressive policies was salient to the Republican policy stance of the 1930s. Of the twenty-one federal statutes, these nine, or 42.9 percent, contributed to the Republican party's posture in the midst of economic depression and realignment.

Figure 4.2 presents the yearly number of salient federal cases from 1911 to 1945. The fact that most were decided between 1914 and 1924 demonstrates that the Court's invalidations were primarily a response to the Progressive successes at the national level in the first twenty years of the twentieth century. Once these movements had lost momentum, there was a gradual decline in the salient invalidations from the mid-1920s to the mid-1930s (see Figure 4.2).

The invalidation of these federal statutes as well as the previously discussed state cases illustrate major as well as minor judicial policy consistent with the Court's conservative reputation. In sum, the 135 salient state cases and the 9 salient federal cases were 53.5 percent of all invalidations in the 1911–1932 period.

The Voting of the Justices, 1911–1932. The aggregate, or macrolevel, results certainly support the agenda-setting role ascribed to the Supreme Court before critical elections. The microlevel behavior of the individual justices may reveal important information that can help account for the results reported above. Hence, this section is an examination of the voting of the justices in the state and federal invalidation cases handed down between 1911 and 1932. The first question to address is the extent of division among the justices in deciding cases related to the realigning issues. The political issues precipitating critical elections and partisan realignment are volatile and cut across the existing ideological cleavages in the major parties. It would be surprising if the justices were not similarly divided, especially given the evidence of external pressures on judicial policymaking (e.g., Kuklinski and Stanga, 1979; Segal, 1990) and the evidence of heightened division in Congress (e.g., Brady, 1985). It is expected that the justices will divide more frequently in the salient cases noted above than in other types of cases. The percentage of salient invalidation cases decided nonunanimously is compared to the percentage of nonunanimous, nonsalient invalidation cases as well as to all cases decided with a full opinion.

The available data indicate that dissent ranged from 10 to 15 percent for cases decided with opinion by the White Court (1910–1921) and between 7 and 10 percent for the Taft Court (1921–1930) (Halpern and Vines, 1977;

Goldman, 1982). In all of the 270 invalidation cases, dissent was much higher than the average case decided by the Court under White or Taft. The dissent rate for all invalidation cases was 31.0 percent and 40.7 percent for the White and Taft Courts, respectively. As expected, the dissent rate of the justices in the salient cases was even higher. In these salient cases, the White Court decided 34.9 percent nonunanimously and the Taft Court decided 50.8 percent nonunanimously. Overall, the Court decided 42.7 percent of the salient cases with at least one formal dissent between 1911 and 1932 (p > t = 0.10).

The higher level of dissent in the salient and nonsalient cases reinforces the unique exercise of judicial authority involved in these cases. Unlike in other types of cases, the Court explicitly prohibits the exercise of governmental power. The high level of dissent found in the invalidation cases may indicate the concern of certain justices in overturning legislative choices. These declarations of unconstitutionality raise fundamental and perennial questions regarding the proper role of the judiciary in democratic governments.

A second microlevel question relates to party-line voting. Studies of congressional voting have shown that partisan voting is evident on votes related to the crosscutting issues (Brady and Stewart, 1982; Sinclair, 1982). Therefore, the role of the justices' partisan affiliations and their votes in deciding salient cases are explored. As one measure of the Court's response to the critical issues, the voting records may aid in understanding Supreme Court policymaking in times of critical elections.

Bloc analysis was possible in two periods of stable membership on the Supreme Court before 1932. In these "natural court" periods, there were a significant number of salient cases for analysis. The Court decided twenty-one nonunanimous salient cases between 1916 and 1921 and twenty-five cases between 1925 and 1930. Although far from ideal, the number of cases permits voting-bloc analysis and yields statistically significant pairwise agreement scores for the vast majority of voting pairs.[55] The results show a strong conservative bloc in each period. For the 1916–1921 period, the mean of the pairwise percentage of agreement between Chief Justice Edward White and Justices James McReynolds, Willis VanDevanter, William Day, and Joseph McKenna was 85.2 percent.[56] This is above the criterion index of 77.5 percent for inferring a voting bloc (Sprague, 1968). These justices' agreement as a bloc on the salient cases occurred more often than did overall agreement on the Court. These conservative justices confronted a Progressive bloc made up of Justices Brandeis and Clarke. Indeed, these two justices voted together in 81.0 percent of the salient cases. Although Justice Holmes is well known as a frequent dissenter, his agreement level with either Justice Brandeis or Clarke is not statistically significant.

The results are consistent with previous studies of the justices' voting on the White Court (Leavitt, 1974) and with a study by Handberg (1976) of all nonunanimous cases decided between 1916 and 1921. A comparison of the rankings of the justices favored the salient policies struck down with Handberg's (1976) data on the votes in all "economic liberalism" cases decided nonunanimously is revealing. The justices' rankings are almost identical to those in Handberg's analysis of all nonunanimous cases. Justices Brandeis and Clarke stand out as the most progressive justices followed by the moderate Progressives, Justices Holmes and Pitney. The most conservative justices composing the bloc identified in the salient invalidation cases give the least support for the claims of a broad class of "economic underdogs" (Handberg, 1976: 366).

The Court responded to the crosscutting issues along ideological rather than party lines. These results are surprising given the continuing focus on a united Court, which is part of the enduring partisan alliances during stable majority party rule. Although Presidents Taft and Wilson had made numerous appointments to the Court by 1916, the progressive justices failed to gain control of the Court. This may be due, in large part, to President Wilson's decision to appoint Justice McReynolds to the Court in an effort to remove him from his cabinet post (Binkley, 1958).

The justices' voting in the second period (1925–1930) allows for bloc analysis and demonstrates the continuing domination of the conservative, but not Republican, majority in the salient invalidation cases. Indeed, the analysis shows a clear six-justice bloc composed of the conservative justices McReynolds, VanDevanter, Taft, Butler, Sutherland, and Sanford. The mean interagreement level of this group was 91.1 percent, exceeding the criterion index of 80.8 percent. This group of justices joined in overturning salient policies. Again, Justice Brandeis had significant levels of disagreement with each member of the conservative bloc. Brandeis agreed with these justices in only 12.0 to 20.0 percent of the cases (significant at the .01 level). The oft-noted liberals, Justices Stone, Holmes, and Brandeis, did not form a bloc; their mean interagreement level was 67.4 percent. Moreover, the more moderate liberalism of Justice Holmes in the salient cases prevents a solid three-justice liberal bloc.

The justices' voting does not appear partisan based. For example, four Republicans and two Democrats composed the conservative bloc identified in the 1925–1930 period. Over the entire 1911–1932 period, the correlation between the dissent rate of the individual justices and their partisan affiliations produces a correlation of 0.302 (eta), but it is statistically insignificant. Using an index based on the partisan congruence between the justices and the appointing president also yields an insignificant correlation of 0.287 (gamma).[57]

The dissent rate for all justices in salient and nonsalient cases from 1911 to 1932 is presented in Table 4.3. The dissent rates illustrate the varied responses by both Democratic and Republican justices to the crosscutting issues. Although this method is imperfect (see Appendix B), more precise estimation strategies (i.e., regression and probit analysis) support the incongruence between justices' partisan affiliations and their voting in the salient cases. Before the critical election of 1932, partisan voting was rare on the realigning questions.

This extended discussion of the justices' voting has import for understanding the Court's role before the realignment of the 1930s. There is a

TABLE 4.3

Dissent Rates of the Justices in Salient Invalidation Cases
and All Invalidation Cases,
1911-1932

Justice (Party)	Dissent Rate in Salient Cases		Dissent Rate in All Cases	
	Percent	Number	Percent	Number
Brandeis, J. (D)	40.5	111	31.3	201
Clarke, J. (D)	35.7	42	32.2	59
Cardozo, J. (D)	33.3ᵃ	3	20.0ᵃ	5
Holmes, J. (R)	23.9	142	19.7	264
Stone, C.J. (R)	23.4	47	20.5	107
Pitney, J. (R)	16.7	78	13.1	123
Sanford, J. (R)	5.9	51	4.5	111
Hughes, J. (R)	5.7	35	4.3	70
Lurton, J. (D)	5.3ᵃ	19	4.9	41
McReynolds, J. (D)	4.8	145	7.5	22
McKenna, J. (R)	4.1	97	3.7	159
Day, J. (R)	3.8	78	2.3	130
White, J., C.J. (D)	3.2	63	1.8	113
Lamar, J. (D)	3.1	32	1.6	64
Taft, J. (R)	1.5	66	1.6	125
Van Devanter, J. (R)	0.0	144	0.7	268
Sutherland, J. (R)	0.0	68	3.5	141
Butler, J. (D)	0.0	64	2.2	137
Hughes, C.J. (R)	0.0ᵃ	13	0.0	27
Roberts, J. (R)	0.0ᵃ	9	5.0	20
Harlan, J. (R)	0.0ᵃ	1	0.0ᵃ	4

ᵃPercentages computed with less than 20 cases.

Source: Compiled by author from *United States Reports.*

solid conservative bloc on the Court from the progressive era to 1932, at least in the salient, nonunanimous cases. Although Progressive justices continuously dissented in cases raising the general question of government management of economic interests, five- and six-justice conservative blocs were found in two periods. The salient cases also divided the justices more often than nonsalient invalidation cases or the average case handed down by either the Taft or White Courts. Although the voting was not partisan based, the control of the Court by a majority of Republicans and conservative justices contributed to the perception of the Court as conservative. Indeed, the Court's conservative reputation became an issue in the Senate confirmation hearings on Chief Justice Hughes in 1930 when Democratic senators criticized the Court's conservative and Republican record (Murphy, 1972: 101–102).

Although further historical and interpretive analysis is needed to explore the Court's role in the period before 1932, the analysis of the invalidation cases and the justices' voting is somewhat consistent with Adamany's (1980: 251) argument. In the period before the New Deal realignment, the Court contributed to the Republican party's policy position regarding the critical issue of the government's role in the economy. These issues were not only apparent in the majority of invalidation cases but divided the justices into polar blocs with conservatives in firm control of the Court. It was this policy position that the Republican party maintained in the midst of economic crisis and political realignment in the 1930s. The precise impact of the cases awaits further analysis, but the data along with traditional studies (Swindler, 1969) provide further evidence that the Court contributed significantly to shaping the Republican party's position on the critical or crosscutting issues.

Finally, it is important to note that the results are quite similar to those for the period before 1896. The agenda-setting role is affirmed at the aggregate level, but the microlevel evidence suggests that the linkage of the Court to the majority coalition is not necessarily provided through presidential appointments during the stable years of the party system. Both Republican and Democratic justices voted to overturn state and federal policies aimed at economic regulation. Although the case outcomes were consistent with the policy views of the dominant party, the underlying causal structures appear much more complex than has previously been argued. Indeed, the voting of the justices is much more consistent with the view that the crosscutting moved several Democratic justices to a conservative position and a select number of Republican justices to a Progressive position, albeit there are many limitations imposed by the data. At a minimum, however, the data do not support the view that the agenda-setting role of the Court before critical elections is a product of presidential appointments by the majority coalition.

Conclusion: The Pre-1932 Period

In the years before the New Deal realignment, the Supreme Court invalidated very few federal statutes compared to the number of state policies struck down. Only 9 of the voided federal laws involved the question of the government's role in the economy compared to 135 state policies. The cases illustrate judicial animosity toward Progressive policies, and most important, the policy outcomes are consistent with the view that the Court contributed to the majority party's stance on those critical issues, a stance that was ultimately rejected in the critical elections of 1932 and 1936.

Some caution is necessary before specifying the exact impact of these judicial policies on the realignment of the 1930s. Unlike the period before 1896, the 1920s did not witness a slow and gradual polarization in response to protest movements. The salient cases did not gradually become a greater percentage of all instances of judicial review. The Court's invalidation agenda did not gradually become dominated by the salient cases. These results may reflect the different dynamics of the realignments of the 1890s and the 1930s. The realignment of the 1890s represented the culmination of long-term tensions in post–Civil War America. Midwestern farmers and eastern laborers periodically entered the political arena seeking reforms directed at corporate capitalism. These economic movements grew in intensity throughout the 1880s and the 1890s and were given further fuel by the panic of 1893. These developments represented increasing polarization in the party system and issue intensity among political groups.

The dominant tone of national politics before the crash of 1929, however, was one of "normalcy." Although Progressive groups such as the Farmer-Labor party in Minnesota were important in the Midwest, the 1920s was not a period of increasing issue intensity and strong political movements surrounding the critical issues. As Key (1959) and Sundquist (1973) have noted, the New Deal realignment was the result of a sudden and dramatic depression. This important difference in the nature of the rise of critical issues and party polarization in the 1890s and 1930s may contribute to understanding the lack of an increase in proportion of invalidations dealing with salient issues. Nevertheless, the salient policies were consistent with the long-term conservativism of the Republican party.

The analysis of the regional distribution and partisan origin of the salient policies lends added support to the ideological character of these cases. The salient policies struck down by the Supreme Court originated in southern Democratic and midwestern Republican states. In these states, populism and later progressivism were strong forces over the period. A majority of the remaining nonsalient state cases also arose from these regions. It appears that the Court's hostility to certain types of legislation extended beyond policies directly related to the control of economic interests.

The analysis of the justices' voting demonstrated that the issues related to the general question of government management divided the justices to a greater extent than either nonsalient invalidation cases or all cases handed down by either the White or Taft Courts. Contrary to expectations, there is little evidence of partisan voting. The Court did, however, divide into ideological blocs in the two periods permitting such an analysis. Conservative blocs are seen in the labor, business regulation, and tax cases in the 1916–1921 and 1925–1930 periods. These salient cases also provoked dissent among Progressive justices, including at various times Justices Louis Brandeis, John Clarke, Benjamin Cardozo, Oliver Holmes, and Harlan Stone. But only Justices Brandeis and Clarke constituted a consistent bloc of Progressive opponents to the Court's conservatism. Although ideological blocs are clear in these two periods, the crosscutting question precipitating the critical elections did not lead to party-line voting by the justices in the salient cases. Indeed, the absence of even a solid liberal bloc may suggest, but by no means prove, the disruptive nature of these issues.

The dissenting opinions of the justices in some of the salient cases decided between 1911 and 1932 are relevant in another vein. These opinions would later become rallying points for Democratic congresspeople and legal commentators when the Court blocked and overturned New Deal policies in the years following the critical election of 1932. This confrontation between a conservative Court and Democrats in the executive branch and Congress points to the second major role ascribed to the Supreme Court in periods of partisan realignment: The Court may delegitimate or overturn policies supported by the new majority party brought to power in a critical election. The following section is an examination of the Supreme Court's invalidation of state and federal policies between 1933 and 1945.

POLICY CONFLICT FOLLOWING
THE REPLACEMENT OF A MAJORITY PARTY

Most scholarly efforts at understanding the Supreme Court and partisan realignment concentrate on the possible policy conflict between the Court and the popularly elected branches following certain critical elections. Similar to the presidential election of 1860, the critical election of 1932—a victory for Franklin Roosevelt—resulted in a new majority party controlling the popularly elected branches. The Supreme Court, however, was still staffed by the conservative "Four Horsemen"—Sutherland, McReynolds, Butler, and VanDevanter—and the "swing" justice, Roberts, who often joined his conservative brethren. The role ascribed to the Court following the replacement of a majority party has been one of a delegitimizer of the new majority party's policies, because the Court represents the "old regime" position and the new majority party must await uncertain and slow turnover on the Court (Funston, 1975; Adamany, 1973). Indeed, the traditional policy "lag" period suggested by Funston (1975) and corrected by Beck (1976) extends from 1933 to 1940, at which time President Roosevelt had appointed a majority of new Democratic justices.

Most previous studies of policy conflict focus almost exclusively on the number of federal policies overturned by the Court (but see Adamany, 1973; 1980; Lasser, 1983). At least for the New Deal period, this approach to gauging policy conflict confirms the hypothesis that following critical elections replacing an old majority party with a new one will lead to a significant increase in the number of federal policies struck down by the Court. In no other period following a critical election, however, is there a statistically significant increase in the raw number of federal policies overturned (Canon and Ulmer, 1976). Policy conflict is, of course, seen in other ways including various attacks on the Court. In the post-1932 period, these included proposals by Democratic members of Congress and President Roosevelt's famous plan to enlarge the size of the Court and thus ensure a favorable new majority.

This analysis also explores the degree of policy conflict following the 1932 election through an examination of not only the federal statutes nullified by the Court but also the unconstitutional state policies. It could be that the number of salient state policies related to the critical issue of the government's role in managing the economy and economic interests increases significantly in the policy "lag" period. The conservative and primarily Republican Court may strike down a large number of policies dealing with the general government management question and thereby reflect judicial animosity to the liberal ideology of the new majority party at the state level. In addition, the partisan control of the state governments enacting the salient policies may also provide additional evidence of ideological conflict.

The voting of the justices in the salient state and federal cases is examined as well. The justices may divide more often in these salient cases than in the remaining invalidation cases or in all cases handed down by the Court. The volatile nature of realigning issues may also divide the justices along party lines, if the "old regime" position is a plausible explanation of policy conflict. Before turning to an examination of the cases invalidating state and federal policies, it is appropriate to describe the dynamics of change in the party system and the general characterizations of Court policymaking from 1932 to the end of World War II.

The New Deal Realignment and Democratic Dominance

The New Deal realignment brought many years of Democratic dominance in national policymaking. In Key's (1959) terms, the realignment was not a "secular" realignment in which the party system responded to long-term political tensions. Unlike the period before the critical election of 1896, the 1920s saw few strong protest movements and third parties. Instead, the New Deal realignment had a very abrupt phase because of the staggering economic depression that began in 1929 (Sundquist, 1973: 183). The sheer size of the economic problems produced demands for some form of government intervention. The Republicans were slow to respond, and President Herbert Hoover's program of limited intervention did not silence political leaders hoping to use government as a means of bringing stabilization and improvement to a wide variety of economic markets.

The presidential campaign of 1932 did not reflect a major polarization compared to the specific policies and programs in the campaign of 1896 such as the silver question. Instead, Franklin Roosevelt campaigned promising simply a more activist administration to cope with the economic problems. His election, as well as the election of a majority of Democratic members of Congress in both chambers of Congress, led to a flurry of legislation designed to provide aid to a wide-ranging set of interests including agricultural aid in the Agricultural Adjustment Act (AAA) and aid to business in the National Industrial Recovery Act (NIRA). The volume of legislation fostered an extremely activist image for the Democratic party despite the New Deal's often pragmatic and piecemeal approach (Hoftstadter, 1948: 315–352). Also, these policies reflected significant departures from the Republican commitment to limited government intervention in the economy and in economic matters generally. The interventionist, but hardly programmatic, stance of the Democratic party was ratified in the congressional election of 1934, and the polarization of the party system continued. In the presidential election of 1936, Roosevelt's reelection solidified Democratic gains and strengthened Democratic control in Congress. As some analysts note: "Policy action by the government that can be perceived as a meaningful and effective response to societal problems is a further and necessary component of the realignment" (Clubb, Flanigan, and Zingale, 1980: 39).

The New Deal realignment represents a long-term redirection in national policymaking away from the laissez-faire of the Gilded Age to a mixed system of welfare capitalism. The critical elections of 1932 and 1936 served to change the electoral base of the Democratic party as an influx of urban, working-class, and ethnic voters were mobilized to support the party or converted from Republican ranks (Anderson, 1979; Erikson and Tedin, 1981). The changing electoral coalitions and the strength of the Democratic party resulted in solid control of the presidency and Congress from 1932 to 1946. Also, at the state level, the party demonstrated strength in the traditional Republican North. For example, in 1930 and 1931, Democrats controlled the governments in 11 percent of nonsouthern states. In 1932 and 1933, the Democratic party controlled 42 percent of these states (Clubb, Flanigan, and Zingale, 1980: 199).

There has been considerable attention to the Supreme Court in the New Deal period ranging from portrayals of the Court's anti–New Deal rulings to major doctrinal changes in the period. Few observers would disagree that the Democratic party confronted an unsympathetic and conservative Court in the years after 1932. Initially, however, the Court was supportive of some Democratic or liberal policies at the state and national level. In *Nebbia v. New York* (1934), the Court upheld a New York price control on milk, and in *Home Building & Loan Association v. Blaisdell* (1934) it approved a Minnesota mortgage moratorium statute. Also, the Court upheld national legislation enabling the Tennessee Valley Authority and one aspect of the Democrats' monetary policy.[58] The Court was not unanimous or reserved in its rhetoric. Indeed, conservative Justice McReynolds strayed from his written dissent in the Court's monetary decision to announce that "The Constitution is gone," and "This is Nero at his worst" (Murphy, 1972: 138).

The Democratic party and Congress did face hostile treatment by the lower federal courts shortly after the 1932 election. By the end of 1933, the lower federal courts had issued over 1,600 injunctions forbidding the execution of New Deal–related policies by federal officers (Murphy, 1972: 141). It was in 1935 and 1936, however, that the Supreme Court struck at the core of New Deal legislation. The Court struck down ten federal provisions enacted by the Democrats (Library of Congress, 1978). The Agricultural Adjustment Act,[59] the National Industrial Recovery Act,[60] and other policies discussed further on were declared unconstitutional. Also, in 1936, the Court struck down New York's minimum-wage law in *Morehead v. New York ex rel. Tipaldo* (1936).

It was not until 1937 that the Court retreated from these positions and Justice Roberts joined the liberals on the Court and upheld New Deal policies.[61] In the midst of congressional attacks and President Roosevelt's attempt to "pack" the Court, the majority withdrew as an overseer of state and federal economic legislation. This "change of heart" in 1937 led E.S. Corwin to describe the transition as a "constitutional revolution" (Corwin, 1938).

The following sections are a further exploration of the period of policy conflict through an examination of the cases of state policy invalidation as well as the famous federal cases. It is expected that the analysis will

TABLE 4.4

Number and Percentages of State and Federal Cases
by Policy Area,
1933-1945

	Total Number of State Policies	Total Number of Federal Policies	Total Number of State & Federal Policies	Percent of Total
Business Regulation & Taxation	37	10	47	51.6
Labor	6	0	6	6.6
General Contracts & Debts	4	0	4	4.3
General Taxation	8	1	9	9.9
Civil Rights & Liberties	14	1	15	16.5
Banking	2	0	2	2.2
Alcohol Control	1	0	1	1.1
Political Process Reforms	0	0	0	0.0
Miscellaneous*	5	2	7	7.7
Total	77	14	91	100.0

*Includes the following types of policies: state protection of in-state businesses; education/nondiscrimination; federalism; public land disputes; and war risk insurance.

Source: Compiled by author from *United States Reports.*

demonstrate that the Court struck down policies that were not only inconsistent with Democratic policies at the national level but with similar types
of policies at the state level as well.

The Invalidation of State and Federal Policies
Following the Critical Election of 1932

Between 1933 and 1945, the Supreme Court struck down ninety-one
state and fourteen federal policies. Inspection of Table 4.4 reveals that the
two largest classes of invalidation cases dealt with business regulation and
taxation (49.5%) and civil rights and liberties (16.5%). The remaining cases
ranged from general taxation policies to banking. A closer examination of
the state and federal cases demonstrates that many of the state policies are
important indicators of policy conflict with the new majority party, but the
number of state policies does not mirror the number of federal invalidations
following the critical election of 1932, as discussed in the following section.
It is appropriate to examine the famous federal cases handed down in the
period of policy lag. Along with *Scott v. Sanford* (1857) and the income tax
cases of 1895, *Pollock v. Farmer's Loan and Trust Co.* (1895), these cases
represent some of the most controversial decisions in the history of the
Supreme Court.

The Federal Cases, 1933–1945. The Supreme Court's initial acceptance of a departure from a limited role for government in *Nebbia v. New York* (1934) vanished in January of 1935. In the next sixteen months, the Court upheld only two of the ten New Deal policies challenged (Kelly, Harbinson, and Belz, 1983: 487–490). Although the Court upheld the Tennessee Valley Authority Act[62] and emergency monetary policies,[63] these decisions were secondary to rejection of the Agricultural Adjustment Act, the National Industrial Recovery Act (NIRA), the Railroad Pension Act, and other statutes enacted by the victorious Democratic party.

In the first case, *Panama Refining Co. v. Ryan* (1935), the Court held provisions of the National Industrial Recovery Act (NIRA) unconstitutional. The provisions authorized the executive branch to establish fair codes of conduct for the oil industry including the power to prohibit the interstate transportation of oil produced or stored in excess of state imposed limits. Congress sought both to conserve oil and to control its price. The majority ruled that the statute was an unconstitutional delegation of legislative authority.

Four months after *Panama*, the Court voided the Railroad Retirement Pension Act in *Railroad Retirement Board v. Alton Railroad Co.* (1935). The statute provided a retirement program for the nation's older railway workers who were forced to retire because of age. Justice Roberts's majority opinion restricted Congress's important, if not vital, power over interstate commerce, a power that was the constitutional basis for a large part of the New Deal legislation. He ruled that the subject of pensions was outside of Congress's commerce power. This same restrictive reading of the commerce clause led a majority to declare the entire National Industrial Recovery Act unconstitutional in *Schechter Poultry Corp. v. United States* (1935). Chief Justice Charles Evans Hughes argued that the grave economic conditions did not enlarge or restrict Congress's power and that the statute exceeded congressional power over interstate commerce and was an unconstitutional delegation of legislative power.

The Supreme Court's hostility toward New Deal legislation continued throughout 1935 and 1936. The Court invalidated the Farm Mortgage Law, which provided for mortgage moratorium provisions similar to the Minnesota statute upheld in 1934.[64] In addition, the Court nullified crop-control provisions in the Agricultural Adjustment Act in two cases[65] and struck down price, wage, and hours provisions in the Bituminous Coal Act.[66]

The final two New Deal cases demonstrate how the Court could also find congressional policies unconstitutional on the grounds that federal authority had encroached on state authority contrary to the states' reserved powers under the Tenth Amendment. The Court ruled in *Ashton v. Cameron County District* (1936) that a provision of the Municipal Bankruptcy Act interfered with state sovereignty in providing for a readjustment of public corporation debts. A similar concern with state power and the Tenth Amendment is seen in *Hopkins Federal Savings & Loan Association v. Cleary* (1935). In *Hopkins*, the Court held a provision of the Home Owners' Loan

Act of 1933 unconstitutional. The statute established procedures for the conversion of state building and loan associations into federal associations.

In sum, of the fourteen cases involving the invalidation of federal policies, ten related to assorted provisions of New Deal legislation. The ten salient cases are found under business regulation and taxation in Table 4.4. The four remaining cases involved a 1926 federal tax on alcohol,[67] a 1933 repeal of war risk insurance,[68] a reduction in federal justices' retirement pay,[69] and a 1938 procedural statute for federal prosecutions for firearm possession.[70] After the "change of heart" in 1937, only one federal provision was struck down dealing with the general question of civil rights and liberties.

Figure 4.2 graphically presents the sudden and dramatic increase in the invalidation of salient federal policies and illustrates what is known quite well: There is a significant increase in the number of federal New Deal policies in the period following the critical election of 1932. The following section is an examination of the more frequent type of judicial review following the critical election of 1932: the overturn of state policies. To what extent did these cases contribute to the level of policy conflict following the critical election of 1932?

The State Cases, 1933–1945. Table 4.4 displays the number and distribution of the state cases by policy area. Of the seventy-seven state policies, the Supreme Court struck down thirty-seven, or 48.1 percent, dealing with business regulation or taxation; fourteen, or 18.2 percent, relating to various civil rights and civil liberties questions; six, or 7.8 percent, focusing on labor; four general debt and contract cases; and eight cases dealing with taxation. Federal statutes were the primary or secondary basis for invalidating only thirteen of these policies.

The Court also struck down six policies related to labor and labor rights. The labor cases do not illustrate policy conflict as suggested by the "old regime" thesis. Only the invalidation of a Washington workmen's compensation statute[71] was voided before 1940, and the remaining cases were prolabor. The Court struck down peonage laws[72] and restrictive state regulations on labor picketing and organizing.[73] Hence, the labor cases were consistent with the liberal position of the Roosevelt Court of the 1940s.

The remaining state policies invalidated between 1933 and 1945 related to general taxation, contractual and debt relationships, civil rights and liberties, and assorted or miscellaneous policy areas such as the repeal of tenure for state teachers.[74] In the area of contracts and debts, the Court voided policies dealing with the settlement of public contracts and land sales.[75] The fourteen cases dealing with civil rights and liberties are also nonsalient from the perspective of the partisan struggle of the 1930s. The Court struck down a wide range of state policies related to the rights of aliens, indigents,[76] and blacks[77] as well as policies dealing with criminal justice[78] and free speech.[79] The Court also voided state taxing policies involving property taxes,[80] sales taxes,[81] and income taxes.[82] Federal statutes were the basis for striking down only two of the eight taxation policies.[83]

As in the pre–New Deal period, the cases of business regulation and taxation dealt with policies aimed at oil, natural gas, and insurance companies.[84] Three cases involved state attempts to regulate railroads.[85] The Court also invalidated different types of taxes and fees levied on businesses.[86] A federal statutory ground was the basis for only three of these invalidations.[87] These cases represent conservative judicial policy related to the general question of government management of economic interests. Although 80 percent of these cases involved policies enacted after the beginning of the depression in 1929,[88] the substantive nature of the policies is similar to many state policies struck down in the 1920s. Undoubtedly, these cases reinforced the conservative image of the Supreme Court on the critical issue of government management.

The class of business regulation and taxation cases also includes notable state policies aimed at stabilizing industry and the economy in the depression years. Perhaps the most widely cited case is *Morehead v. New York ex rel. Tipaldo* (1936), which involved a New York minimum-wage law. The statute provided for wage levels that were not only fair and reasonable for the services rendered by labor but also that would provide for a standard of living necessary for minimum health. The "Four Horsemen" and Justice Roberts held that the New York law deprived employers and employees of the liberty of contract and so was contrary to due process. The decision provoked considerable outcry in the national and state press because the decision implicitly invalidated seventeen similar statutes in different states.

Equally renowned are decisions involving New York's Milk Control Board. In *Nebbia v. New York* (1934), the Court upheld the price-fixing provisions of the statute creating the board. The case is important because it marked an important doctrinal turn away from the idea that regulation of business was justified only when the business was "affected with a public interest." The decision marks the end of the restrictive use of that doctrine, which had been wielded to protect conservative interests. Nevertheless, the Supreme Court nullified several other policies of the Milk Control Board. One year after *Nebbia*, the Court in *Baldwin v. G.A.F. Seelig* (1935) struck down provisions controlling the price paid to producers from other states. The Court found such a regulation to be an invalid burden on interstate commerce. Also, the Court voided another milk-control provision in the following year in *Mayflower Farms v. Ten Eyck* (1936). With Justice Cardozo, Brandeis, and Stone in dissent, the majority ruled that New York could not allow retailers who did not have well-advertised trade names to sell their milk at one cent below the level charged to other competitors. The majority opinion reasoned that the provision denied the equal protection of the laws to milk dealers who did not have well-advertised trade names.

In *Morehead* and the New York price-control cases, the Court created further concern over the New Deal approach to the economic crisis. This concern is evident not only in the dissents of Progressive justices but also in the actions of the Democratic administration, which continued to fashion legislation to cope with the crisis (Murphy, 1972: 114). The less dramatic cases involving business regulation and taxation also contributed to the conservative reputation of the Court. When we combine the ten cases invalidating New Deal policies with the state cases, there is added support to the proposition regarding a period of policy conflict between the Court and the new majority party following the critical election of 1932.

Figure 4.2 presents graphically the yearly number of salient state and federal cases from 1911 to 1945. In the policy lag period of 1933 to 1940 there is, as expected, a major increase in the yearly number of salient cases. Recall that this so-called lag period was originally suggested by Funston (1975) and corrected by Beck (1976). The starting date for the period is 1933 because it is the first year of Democratic dominance in the popularly elected branches, and 1940 marks the year in which the new Democratic majority party had made five new appointments to the Court. Figure 4.2 suggests that there was a significant increase in the number of salient policies declared unconstitutional.

It is possible to test more precisely whether such an increase is statistically significant by estimating an equation through least-squares regression. As in the previous chapter, an interrupted time-series design is appropriate. The possible impact of the traditional policy lag period of 1933–1940 on the series of salient state cases can be formally tested by the following estimate:

$$I(s)_t = a + b_1 \text{ Time1}_t + b_2 \text{ Time2}_t + b_3 R_t + e_t,$$

where $I(s)_t$ is either the number of salient state policies or the estimated rate of invalidation in each year from 1911 to 1945; a is the constant term or intercept of the regression line; Time is the time trend from 1911 to 1945; R_t is a dummy variable representing the policy lag period on the series and takes the value of 1 from 1933 to 1940 and 0 in other years; and e_t is the error term. The coefficients to be estimated are b_1, b_2 and b_3. Given the context of the New Deal era, one would expect that b_3 is greater than 0, signifying increased policy conflict during the traditional policy lag period. In addition, it is expected that Time 2 will be less than 0, consistent with the Supreme Court's well-known retreat from the economic field in 1937.

Estimation of the equation by ordinary least-squares regression was not possible because serial- or auto-correlation marred the estimates as determined by the Durbin-Watson statistic. Therefore, adjustments in the estimates of the coefficients were necessary using the value of rho according to the Cochrane-Orcutt procedure (Pindyck and Rubinfeld, 1981: 456–457). The generalized least-squares results are shown in Table 4.5.

The table shows the estimated coefficients for the intercept, time trends, the dummy variable, and the accompanying t statistics. R^2 is the coefficient of multiple determination; D.W. is the Durbin-Watson statistic; and N is the number of cases. The first column displays the estimates for detecting a surge in the number of salient invalidations; the second column presents the results for the estimated rate of invalidation, which is based upon the number of salient cases and the number of opinions issued each year.

TABLE 4.5

Interrupted Time-Series Estimates for the
Total Number of Salient Policies and an Estimated Rate of Invalidation:
Traditional Policy Lag Period, 1933-1940

Variable		Total Number of Salient Policies	Estimated Rate of Invalidation
Constant	b	6.851[a]	1.195[a]
	SE	1.299	0.238
	t	5.272	5.005
Time 1	b	-0.032	0.002
	SE	0.094	0.017
	t	-0.347	0.124
Time 2	b	-0.573[a]	-0.158[b]
	SE	0.191	0.058
	t	-2.994	-2.714
R_t	b	0.125	-0.109
	SE	1.424	0.285
	t	0.088	-0.382
R^2 =		0.283	0.259
Adj. R^2 =		0.214	0.188
D.W. =		1.647	1.608
rho =		———	———
n = 35			

[a]$p > t = 0.01$
[b]$p > t = 0.05$

Source: Compiled by author.

By either measure, there is not an abrupt and statistically significant increase in policy conflict based on the state cases. Neither estimate for R_t is significant in a statistical sense.[89] Using the traditional period of policy lag suggested by Funston (1975) (see Beck, 1976), the state cases did not undergo a significant increase in the period between 1933 and 1940. The only significant estimates are for the postconflict period (Time 2), and the negative value is consistent with the expectations of a withdrawal from the economic field. One must conclude that the number of salient state cases does not increase significantly in the policy lag period suggested by Funston (1975) in a manner similar to the salient federal invalidations.

Yet, the policy lag period of 1933 to 1940 may not be appropriate for determining whether the number of salient state policies increased in periods of realignment. The basic difficulty is that the start date of the lag period may not coincide with changes at the state level. Indeed, electoral changes at the state level have often *preceded* changes at the national level (Burnham,

1970), and partisan change at the state level often occurred before 1932 (Sundquist, 1973: 171–182). Therefore, it is reasonable to examine whether the Supreme Court struck down a significant number of state laws before 1933. The period of greatest conflict with state policies begins in 1929 with the Great Depression. As previously discussed, the depression and the responses of party leaders to it represent the most important factors in the New Deal realignment. Additionally, over 80 percent of the salient policies identified were enacted in or shortly after 1929.

A second problem with the federal policy lag period (1933–1940) is the date when the policy conflict should recede. President Roosevelt made his fifth, or majority, appointment to the Court in 1940. The last year of the policy lag period is certainly consistent with Funston's (1975) logic: Namely, conflict will ensue following the installation of a new majority, and the conflict will continue until the new majority party appoints a majority of like-minded justices. Although 1940 seems reasonable as a date for expecting policy conflict to wane given Funston's straightforward logic, it does not square with historical evidence. The Supreme Court's "change of heart" in 1937 represents a dramatic turn in Court policymaking as Justice Roberts switched his earlier position to join the liberals in upholding New Deal policies rather than as a result of new appointments to the Court. Further, in a series of cases after 1937, the Court retreated from its long-time and active role in reviewing state and federal economic legislation (Kelly, Harbinson, and Belz, 1983: 501–510). Indeed, the dramatic change in 1937 occurred before President Roosevelt made a single appointment to the Supreme Court.

Therefore, an adjusted policy lag period for state policies is 1929 to 1936. During this period, there should be an abrupt and significant increase in the number of state policies related to government management. This hypothesis can be formally stated as

$$I(s)_t = a + b_1 \, Time1_t + b_2 \, Time2_t + b_3 \, R_t + e_t,$$

where the terms and values for all elements are the same as equation (4.1) except that the dummy variable (R_t) representing the expected period of potential conflict takes the value of 1 in the years 1929 through 1936 and 0 in all years of the 1911–1945 series, and the Time 2 trend begins earlier (1929). The results of estimating the equation through generalized least squares do confirm the hypothesis as shown in Table 4.6.

The estimated coefficients for R_t or the adjusted period of policy conflict, are greater than 0 and statistically significant at the 0.10 level. In addition, the negative estimates for the time period following the conflict (Time 2) are consistent with expectations.[90] One can conclude that there was a significant and abrupt increase in the number of salient state policies between 1929 and 1936.

Similar to the Supreme Court's famous clash with the Democratic party over national legislation, the exercise of judicial review of state policies

TABLE 4.6

Interrupted Time-Series Estimates for the
Total Number of Salient Policies and an Estimated Rate of Invalidation:
Adjusted Policy Lag Period, 1929-1937

Variable		Total Number of Salient Policies	Estimated Rate of Invalidation
Constant	b	4.685[a]	0.833[a]
	SE	1.546	0.290
	t	3.029	2.871
Time 1	b	-0.192	0.040
	SE	0.144	0.027
	t	-1.330	1.496
Time 2	b	-0.223[b]	-0.037
	SE	0.136	0.256
	t	-1.693	-1.453
R_t	b	2.679[c]	0.599[c]
	SE	1.568	0.294
	t	1.708	2.038
$R^2 =$		0.312	0.320
Adj. $R^2 =$		0.245	0.254
D.W. =		1.918	1.939
rho =		0.068	0.061
n = 35			

[a]$p>t = 0.01$
[b]$p>t = 0.05$
[c]$p>t = 0.10$

Source: Compiled by author.

reinforces and enhances the intensity of the conflict in the New Deal era. Although interpretative analysis of these cases highlighted the importance of state policies for understanding policy conflict, the time-series results show that this conflict is neither random nor sporadic. The increase in both the number of salient policies overturned and the estimated rate of invalidation show Supreme Court policymaking that is quite consistent with the policy conflict thesis.

The ideological character of the salient invalidations is further illuminated by an examination of the partisan status of the states that enacted the salient policies. As Table 4.7 illustrates, Democratic state governments in the West, South, and Midwest accounted for twenty-one of the thirty-three state policies where the date of enactment was available. The remaining policies arose from mixed and Republican state governments. Also, a majority of the nonsalient cases arose from Democratic state governments, primarily in

TABLE 4.7

Distribution of Salient and Nonsalient State Cases
by Partisan Control of State Governments
at Time of Policy Enactment and by Region,
1933-1945

Partisan Control by Region	Number of Salient	Percent	Number of Nonsalient	Percent
Democratic				
New England & Middle Atlantic	0	0.0	0	0.0
Solid South & Border	13	39.4	11	42.3
East & West North Central	2	6.1	0	0.0
Pacific & Mountain	6	18.2	3	11.5
Mixed[a]				
New England & Middle Atlantic	3	9.1	2	7.7
Solid South & Border	2	6.1	0	0.0
East & West North Central	0	0.0	3	11.5
Pacific & Mountain	1	3.0	1	3.8
Republican				
New England & Middle Atlantic	1	3.0	4	15.4
Solid South & Border	1	3.0	0	0.0
East & West North Central	2	6.1	2	7.7
Pacific & Mountain	2	6.1	0	0.0
Total	33	100.0	26	100.0[b]
Missing	6		12	

Percentage of all states ideologically opposed = 56.1

[a]State governments classified as mixed have either a divided legislature or the partisanship of the governor and the legislature differ. Legislative control is signified by either a majority or a simple plurality.

[b]This total does not precisley equal 100% because of rounding.

Source: Clubb, Flanigan, and Zingale (1990); *United States Reports.*

the South. These data demonstrate a weak but important relationship between the partisan character of the state governments and the invalidation of policies raising the general issue of government management. It is important to keep in mind, however, that the partisan control of state governments is not a perfect indicator of a policy's general ideological character. Indeed, the renowned minimum-wage and milk price-control laws were enacted in New York at a time of mixed control of that state's legislature and governorship. Nonetheless, it is true that only six, or 18.1 percent, of the policies struck down by the Court were enacted by state governments firmly controlled by the Republican party.

Finally, in contrast to the late nineteenth century, in the 1933–1945 period only two (6.1%) of the government management policies originated in midwestern Republican states. From the 1870s to the early 1930s, these states were the source of a substantial number of policies overturned by the Court. By the 1933–1945 period, however, the movements of populism and progressivism had ceased as powerful elements in midwestern politics. The fewer cases from these states in post-1932 years is quite consistent with changes in the national party system.

In sum, the analysis of the invalidation of state policies gives additional support to the hypothesis concerning a period of policy conflict between the Court and the new majority party. From the onset of the Great Depression to the turnaround in 1937, the Court struck down state minimum-wage legislation and various price controls aimed at stabilizing industry. The Court also continued to void several general business regulations and taxes. These cases reinforced the conservative reputation of the Court and in cases such as *Morehead* contributed to the growing concern over the Court's willingness to block attempts by the Democrats to deal with the economic crisis.

An examination of the Supreme Court's invalidation of federal and state policies supports the role ascribed to the Court in periods when a majority party is replaced (Adamany, 1973; 1980; Funston, 1975). The Court is likely to strike down many federal policies related to the critical issues of realignment as it confronts a new majority party. The number of state policy invalidations illustrates additional policy conflict, and the number of state policies increased abruptly during the traditional 1933–1940 policy lag period. Invalidations of state policies often pale in comparison to the dramatic New Deal invalidations including the Agricultural Adjustment Act and the National Industrial Recovery Act. Nonetheless, these salient state cases do illustrate judicial animosity toward departures from conservative Republican economic principles and serve as additional indicators of policy conflict. From 1929 to 1937, the Supreme Court stood as a barrier to reform at both the state and national level. Adamany (1980: 246) summarizes the implications of this period of conflict.

> The consequences of conflict for both legitimacy and policymaking become clear. The standing of the presidential wing of the party is diminished, and the legitimacy of the presidency itself may suffer. More important, the controversy over the Court diverts attention from substantive reform issues. And, finally, a division in both the electoral and the governmental wings of the majority party over the counterattack on the judiciary diminishes the coalition's ability to act in concert on other matters. . . . The Supreme Court stands as a reef on which the vessel of reform runs aground.

At the aggregate level, the cases involving the invalidation of state policies contribute to the level of conflict following a critical election. Although the patterns of federal and state cases are not parallel, there is a relationship between the number of policies struck down and the critical issues of government management of economic interests. It is necessary to examine the voting behavior of the justices in these salient state cases as well as the federal cases in order to explore the individual dynamics of the Court in resolving the dramatic cases related to the crosscutting issues of the New Deal realignment. The analysis gives further support to the ideological character of the justices' responses to both the federal and state salient policies.

The Voting of the Justices, 1933–1945. It is expected that the justices will decide salient cases nonunanimously more often than in the typical case or in the nonsalient invalidation cases following the critical election of 1932. These political questions presented the justices with not only volatile political questions dividing the party system but also more difficult legal questions (Kelly, Harbinson, and Belz, 1983: 487–494; Songer, 1986). In addition, bloc analysis affords an assessment of the partisan nature of the justices' voting. There is much documentation on the division of the Court in the New Deal cases. In most of these cases, Justice Roberts joined McReynolds, Butler, Sutherland, and VanDevanter in striking down the recently enacted New Deal policies. Extension of the voting analysis to the salient state cases may give further support to the volatile nature of these state-level policies.

First, the rate of dissent in all invalidation cases from 1933 to 1937 is higher than the dissent rate for all types of cases. The justices divided in 42.9 percent of these instances of judicial review. Perhaps the higher level for both salient and nonsalient relates to division over the proper judicial role. More important, in the salient or government management cases, the rate of dissent is 52.2 percent. Data were not available on the dissent of the justices in all cases decided in this period. A crude comparison is possible by assessing the level of disagreement using the percentage of all written opinions that were dissenting (Pritchett, 1948: 25, Table 1). In the 1933 to 1945 period, 20.6 percent of all written opinions were dissenting opinions. In the salient invalidation cases, 46.0 percent of written opinions were dissenting.

Given the many salient cases and the lack of membership changes from 1932–1937, it is possible to examine the voting blocs in these cases. As noted, the voting of the justices in the famous New Deal cases shows a closely divided Court with Justice Roberts usually joining the conservatives until 1937. A similar alignment is seen in the justices' voting in the salient state cases. Justices Butler, Sutherland, McReynolds, VanDevanter, and Roberts have a mean interagreement score of 96.1 percent in the salient federal cases handed down between 1932 and 1937. This is above the criterion index of 89.1 percent (see Appendix B). The liberal bloc, which dissented from the invalidation of state and federal policies, included Justices Stone, Cardozo, and Brandeis. Chief Justice Hughes is not included in the liberal bloc because he joined with the conservatives in 75 percent of the cases. Hughes's pairwise agreements with the three liberal justices constitute the only statistically insignificant scores in the 36 pairwise agreements in the interagreement matrix ($p > t = .05$ level).

The ideological alignment of the justices is very similar to Danelski's (1966: 734–735) study, which examined all nonunanimous cases handed down by the Court in the 1935 and 1936 terms. In cases related to government activity over economic matters, Justice Hughes was the least liberal of the justices who would later uphold New Deal policies, excluding Justice Roberts.

TABLE 4.8

Dissent Rates of the Justices in Salient Invalidation Cases
and All Invalidation Cases,
1933-1945

Justice (Party)	Dissent Rate in Salient Cases		Dissent Rate in All Cases	
	Percent	Number	Percent	Number
Cardozo, J. (D)	45.9	37	34.9	63
Douglas, J. (D)	42.9[a]	7	20.8	24
Black, J. (D)	38.5[a]	13	22.9	35
Frankfurter, J. (D)	37.5[a]	8	23.0	26
Brandeis, J. (D)	36.8	38	27.7	65
Stone, J. (R)	34.8	46	23.3	90
Murphy, J. (D)	28.6[a]	7	21.7	23
Hughes, J. (R)	9.8	41	6.8	74
Reed, J. (D)	9.1[a]	11	6.0	33
Roberts, J. (R)	6.7	45	5.6	89
McReynolds, J. (D)	4.9	41	10.9	73
Sutherland, J. (R)	0.0	35	3.4	58
Byrnes, J. (D)	0.0[a]	1	16.7[a]	6
Jackson, J. (D)	0.0[a]	5	0.0[a]	17
Rutledge, J. (D)	0.0[a]	4	0.0[a]	11
Van Devanter, J. (R)	0.0	33	3.6	56

[a]Percentages computed with less than 20 cases.

Source: Compiled by author from *United States Reports.*

Chief Justice Hughes voted a conservative position in 33.3 percent of all nonunanimous economic cases in these two terms compared to 4.2 percent for Justice Brandeis, 2.1 percent for Justice Cardozo, and 2.3 percent for Justice Stone (see Table 4.8).

Simple inspection of the composition of the conservative and liberal blocs does not, however, support the expectation of partisan voting by the justices. The conservative bloc consisted of three Republicans and two Democrats. The liberal bloc included one Republican and two Democrats. Table 4.8 also displays evidence on the lack of party-based voting based upon the dissent rates of individual justices in the salient and nonsalient cases handed down between 1932 and 1937. The correlation between the justices' dissent rates and their partisan affiliations yields an insignificant eta of 0.477. If we use an index of the congruence between the party affiliation of the justices and the appointing president, the correlation is 0.520 (significant at the .10 level). Both regression and probit analysis support this simple rank-ordering.

The analysis of the justices' voting raises a number of points with respect to the roles ascribed to the Court during periods of partisan realignment. First, the voting blocs identified provide empirical support at the individual level for the proposition that the invalidation of state policies related to the general question of government management divided the justices along lines similar to the famous federal cases. This finding gives further support to the saliency of state policies related to the critical issues. Although not all cases involving invalidation of state policies are deemed salient, invalidations increased during the famous period of conflict with Congress, when the justices divided in a similar fashion and at a higher rate than in other types of cases.

Second, the lack of support for party-line voting has implications for arguments advanced by Funston (1975) and Adamany (1980). Funston (1975), and to a lesser extent Adamany (1980), argue that one of the causes of policy conflict when a new majority party arises is that the Supreme Court remains a spokesperson for the vanquished regime. Adamany (1980: 251) notes that because of linkages provided by the appointment process and the chief executive's similar goals of policy enforcement, the Court's majority will side with the presidential wing of the vanquished party. However, the justices are often appointed before the rise of critical issues, and therefore, the appointing president lacks knowledge of the justices' policy position on these issues. The justices may behave in a somewhat erratic fashion reflecting the new cleavages created by the critical issues.

These microlevel results suggest that the internal dynamics of the Court during periods of partisan realignment reflect fluid and changing coalitions as opposed to cohesiveness and party-line voting. The analysis of the voting in the salient cases of federal and state policy invalidation shows that the justices divided along ideological lines as gauged by their rate of dissent and bloc analysis. The conservative bloc of justices, however, also contained Democratic justices. Justice Butler was nominally a Democrat, appointed by President Harding seven years before the depression. Also, Justice McReynolds was a Democrat appointed by President Wilson in 1914 when the president had sought to rid himself of a troublesome cabinet member. In the three-man liberal bloc, Justice Stone was a Republican appointed in 1925 by President Calvin Coolidge. Although there is little evidence of perfect party-line voting, the salient cases are nonetheless quite consistent with the conservative presidential wing of the Republican party in the depression years, as Adamany (1980: 251) argues. It is not clear, however, that this conservative majority was the direct result of the appointment process in the period before the critical election.

Although periods of partisan realignment provoked considerable party-line voting in Congress over bills related to the critical issues (Brady and Stewart, 1982; Sinclair, 1982), the division on the Court is not strongly partisan based in either the 1890s or the 1930s. The different results in congressional and Supreme Court voting reside in the different pathways for turnover in these institutions. In Congress, the combination of issue intensity and rapid turnover led to increased party-line voting (Sinclair, 1982). Most especially, this increased turnover often brought newly recruited candidates from polarized and ideological party organizations at the state and local levels (Brady, 1978: 84–86).

However, the Supreme Court's membership does not change with the travails and turnout of critical elections. Instead, presidents must await uncertain turnover on the high bench, and many appointments occur during the stable phases of the party system when the parties are not as ideologically polarized as in times of critical elections (compare Ulmer, 1982 and King, 1987). This turnover and the uneven appointment pattern serve to weaken the role of partisanship on the Court. In addition, Carp and Rowland (1983: 93–117) have shown that partisan voting on federal district courts varies with certain historical periods, which is suggestive that the extent of party polarization at the time of appointment is an important consideration in understanding voting behavior.

The turnover pattern and the role of party voting in the salient cases does not present overwhelming support for the notion that the justices of the old regime will join the presidential wing of the majority party *because* of linkages provided between the Court and the executive branch. The fact does remain, however, that the Democratic party inherited a conservative majority on the Supreme Court that was willing to strike down many state and federal policies that departed from the Court's conservative economic philosophy.

CONCLUSION:
THE NEW DEAL REALIGNMENT

The analysis of these cases in which the Supreme Court invalidated state and federal policies supports the two roles ascribed to the Court in periods of realignment. One argument is that the Court will contribute to the policy stance of the majority party in the period before a critical election (Adamany, 1980). The analysis of the cases of state policy invalidation supports this proposition. The other argument is that there will be policy conflict between the Supreme Court and the new majority party following a critical election. The findings on this score are somewhat mixed outside of the renowned federal cases but generally consistent with the view that policy conflict between the "old regime" and the new majority coalition extended beyond national legislation to the province of state policies. A brief discussion of some important qualifications as well as the implications of these findings appear in order.

From 1911 to 1932, conservatives and mostly Republicans dominated the Court. At the same time, the Court invalidated a staggering number of state and federal policies. More than half of the state invalidation cases related in some way to the important issue of government management of economic interests. The Court struck down state attempts to regulate or tax businesses and to enact prolabor policies. Also, over 40 percent of the overturned federal policies were Progressive measures. In policy terms, these cases represented conservative judicial decisions regarding government management, and the decisions contributed to the Republican party's posture in the period of crisis and eventual realignment. The state policies overturned were enacted primarily by Democratic state governments in the South and Republican states in the Midwest. This not only reinforces the political implications of the decisions but suggests that political groups who are "losers" at the state level may seek relief through litigation in the federal court system.

It is impossible to view the cases decided in the years before the critical election of 1932 as somehow anticipating the realignment. Unlike the Court's invalidations in the 1880s and 1890s when the Court blunted demands for reform, these cases are more appropriately viewed as conservative judicial policy regarding the critical issues, which served to posture the Republican party as a party dedicated to laissez-faire.

The justices' voting in the period before 1932 demonstrated the volatility of government management questions. The cases of business regulation and taxation as well as labor clearly divided the justices more often than the nonsalient invalidation cases or the average case handed down by the Court. Bloc analysis confirmed that in two periods (1916–1921, 1925–1930) the Court contained a conservative five- or six-justice bloc. The justices did not, however, divide along partisan lines in the decade of "normalcy" in the 1920s. Ideological division is evident, but a congruence between ideology and party is not found in these cases. From the 1920s to 1932, the Court contained a solid majority of conservative justices who struck down several policies raising basic government management questions. This control contributed to the anti-Progressive rhetoric of the Supreme Court (Murphy, 1972: 98–102).

Following the critical election of 1932, the conflict between the Court and the popularly elected branches is clear in the famous New Deal cases. This policy conflict, however, can also be seen in the cases of state policy invalidations related to business regulation and taxation. The pattern of the state cases does not perfectly parallel the significant increase in unconstitutional federal policies. Instead, state-level realignment occurred earlier, and an abrupt increase in the salient state cases was seen between 1929 and 1936. In short, the analysis of the cases of state policy invalidation shows how these cases contributed to partisan conflict between the Supreme Court and a new majority party. Moreover, the pattern of the state cases is very similar to the well-known clash over Roosevelt's New Deal legislation.

In any attempt to establish a relationship between the Supreme Court and partisan realignment, we must be wary of the central underlying issue dynamics of the realignment. Identifying the salient and nonsalient cases in the New Deal period gives some support to the roles ascribed to the Court. Nevertheless, the tremendous increase in the yearly number of cases, salient as well as nonsalient, in the 1920s points to the difficulties in understanding the Court's invalidation agenda. The staggering number of state policies overturned by the White and Taft Courts illustrates that any attempt must account for internal factors such as leadership, personnel, and institutional procedures as well as various external factors such as the willingness of interests and groups to mobilize and use judicial forums. The role of interest groups is especially apparent in the period following World War II (e.g., O'Connor and Epstein, 1983). This is evident in the Supreme Court's invalidation of state and federal policies from 1946 to 1964. The following chapter is an examination of these cases to determine whether the policies contributed to the agenda of the critical elections of 1960 and 1964—elections that induced a major decomposition of the New Deal party system.

NOTES

1. The electoral changes solidified by the Democratic party in this period began much earlier. Indeed, the changes in the Democratic party's electoral coalition appeared as early as 1924 (Pomper, 1975; Adamany, 1973).

2. E.g., *Bunting v. Oregon*, 243 U.S. 426 (1917).

3. *Hipolite E Co. v. United States*, 220 U.S. 45 (1911).

4. *Pittsburgh Melting Co. v. Totten*, 248 U.S. 1 (1918).

5. *I.C.C. v. Chicago, Rock Island, and Pacific Railway Co.*, 218 U.S. 88 (1910).

6. *McCabe v. Atchison, T & S. F. Railway Co.*, 235 U.S. 151 (1914).

7. *Guinn v. United States*, 238 U.S. 347 (1915); *Mayers v. Anderson*, 238 U.S. 268 (1915); *Nixon v. Herndon*, 273 U.S. 536 (1927); *Nixon v. Condon*, 286 U.S. 73 (1932).

8. *Traux v. Raich*, 239 U.S. 33 (1915); *Meyer v. Nebraska*, 262 U.S. 390 (1923); *Bartels v. Iowa*, 262 U.S. 404 (1923); *Bohning v. Ohio*, 262 U.S. 404 (1923).

9. *Near v. Minnesota ex rel. Olson*, 283 U.S. 697 (1931); *Santovincenzo v. Egan*, 284 U.S. 30 (1931).

10. *Stromberg v. California*, 283 U.S. 359 (1931).

11. E.g., *Globe Bank v. Martin*, 236 U.S. 288 (1915). See e.g., *Coe v. Armour Fertilizer Works*, 237 U.S. 413 (1915); *Bank of Minden v. Clement*, 256 U.S. 126 (1921); *Missouri ex rel. Robertson v. Miller*, 276 U.S. 174 (1928).

12. *Frick v. Pennsylvania*, 268 U.S. 473 (1925); *Rhode Island Trust Co. v. Doughton*, 270 U.S. 69 (1926); *Childers v. Beaver*, 270 U.S. 55 (1926); *Farmers Loan Co. v. Minnesota*, 280 U.S. 204 (1930); *First National Bank v. Maine*, 284 U.S. 312 (1932).

13. E.g., *Safe Deposit & T. Co. v. Virginia*, 280 U.S. 83 (1929); *Turner v. Wade*, 254 U.S. 64 (1920); *Brooke v. Norfolk*, 277 U.S. 27 (1928); *Hoeper v. Tax Commission*, 284 U.S. 206 (1931).

14. *Chicago, Rhode Island and Pacific Railway Co. v. Hardwick Elevator Co.*, 226 U.S. 426 (1913).

15. One could possibly question the exclusion of the five alcohol-control cases from the class of salient cases. Together with religious questions, Prohibition was an issue in the presidential election of 1928 when Democrat Al Smith made what many see as the first inroads into the urban vote, which was important in the elections of 1932 and 1936. As Sundquist (1973: 81-82) argues, however, the issue dynamics of the 1930s were different from the dominant issues of the 1928 campaign. Therefore, it appears prudent to exclude these cases.

16. E.g., *Atchison, Topeka, and Santa Fe Railway Company v. O'Conner*, 223 U.S. 280 (1912); *Oklahoma v. Wells Fargo and Co.*, 223 U.S. 298 (1912); *Crenshaw v. Arkansas*, 227 U.S. 389 (1913); *Stewart v. Michigan*, 232 U.S. 665 (1914); *Singer Sewing Machine Co., v. Brickell*, 233 U.S. 304 (1914); *Heyman v. Hays*, 236 U.S. 178 (1915); *Davis v. Virginia*, 236 U.S. 697 (1915); *Looney v. Crane Co.*, 245 U.S. 178 (1917); *Cheney Brothers Co. v. Massachusetts*, 246 U.S. 147 (1918); *Askren v. Continental Oil Co.*, 252 U.S. 444 (1920); *Bethlehem Motors Co. v. Flynt*, 256 U.S. 421 (1921); *Champlain Co. v. Brattleboro,*

260 U.S. 366 (1922); *Tampa Interocean Steamship Co. v. Louisiana*, 266 U.S. 594 (1925); *Ozark Pipe Line v. Monier*, 266 U.S. 555 (1925); *Alpha Cement Co. v. Massachusetts*, 268 U.S. 203 (1925); *Hughes Brothers Co. v. Minnesota*, 272 U.S. 469 (1926); *Miller v. Milwaukee*, 272 U.S. 713 (1927); *Cudahy Co. v. Hinkle*, 278 U.S. 460 (1929); *Interstate Transit Inc. v. Lindsey*, 283 U.S. 183 (1931).

17. E.g., *Provident Savings Association v. Kentucky*, 239 U.S. 103 (1915); *New York Life Insurance Co. v. Dodge*, 246 U.S. 357 (1918); *Newton v. Consolidated Gas Co.*, 258 U.S. 165 (1922); *Texas Co. v. Brown*, 258 U.S. 466 (1922); *St. Louis Compress Co. v. Arkansas*, 260 U.S. 346 (1922); *Ottinger v. Consolidated Gas Co.*, 272 U.S. 576 (1926); *Standard Pipe Line v. Highway District*, 277 U.S. 160 (1928); *Panhandle Oil Co. v. Missouri ex rel. Knox*, 277 U.S. 218 (1928); *Graysburg Oil Co. v. Texas*, 278 U.S. 582 (1929); *Carson Petroleum Co. v. Vial*, 279 U.S. 95 (1929); *Home Insurance Co. v. Dick*, 281 U.S. 397 (1930); *State Tax Commission v. Interstate Natural Gas Co.*, 284 U.S. 41 (1931); *Western Union Telegraph Co. v. Brown*, 234 U.S. 542 (1914); *Southwestern Telephone Co. v. Danaher*, 238 U.S. 482 (1915); *New Jersey Telegraph Co. v. Tax Board*, 280 U.S. 338 (1930).

18. E.g., *Wisconsin v. Philadelphia and Reading Coal Co.*, 241 U.S. 329 (1916); *Terral v. Burke Construction Co.*, 257 U.S. 529 (1922); *Furst v. Brewster*, 282 U.S. 493 (1931).

19. E.g., *Sioux Remedy Co. v. Cope*, 235 U.S. 197 (1914).

20. *Dahnke-Walker Co. v. Bondurant*, 257 U.S. 282 (1921).

21. *Oklahoma Operating Co. v. Love*, 252 U.S. 331 (1920); *Ohio Valley Co. v. Ben Avon Borough*, 253 U.S. 287 (1920).

22. E.g., *Adams v. Tanner*, 244 U.S. 590 (1917); *Ribnik v. McBride*, 277 U.S. 350 (1928).

23. E.g., *Weaver v. Palmer Brothers Co.*, 270 U.S. 402 (1926); *Burns Baking Co. v. Bryan*, 264 U.S. 504 (1924).

24. E.g., *Russell v. Sebastian*, 233 U.S. 195 (1914); *Carondelet Canal Co. v. Louisiana*, 233 U.S. 362 (1914); *Forbes Pioneer Boat Line v. Everglades Drainage District*, 258 U.S. 338 (1922); *Georgia Railway Co. v. Decatur*, 262 U.S. 432 (1923); *New State Ice Co. v. Liebmann*, 285 U.S. 262 (1932); *Coombes v. Getz*, 285 U.S. 434 (1932).

25. E.g., *Tyson and Brother v. Banton*, 273 U.S. 418 (1927); *Fairmont Co. v. Minnesota*, 274 U.S. 1 (1927). There were also four cases involving state policies that regulated businesses, but the policies were clearly enacted to protect certain in-state businesses. These four cases are included in the miscellaneous category in Table 4.1. An Oklahoma statute of 1907 was struck down in 1911 which prevented foreign corporations from building natural gas pipelines in favor of local businesses (*Oklahoma v. Kansas Natural Gas Co.*, 221 U.S. 229 [1911]). Also, the Court voided a Louisiana law of 1926 that regulated the shipment of seafood in a manner designed to favor the state's canning industry (*Foster-Fountain Packing Co. v. Haydel*, 278 U.S. 1 [1928]). These cases cannot be included in the general class of conservative business regulation and taxation causes because it is clear that these policies sought to protect selected industries or companies. See also *Buck v. Kuykendall*, 267 U.S. 307 (1925); *Bush Co. v. Maloy*, 267 U.S. 317 (1925). Undoubtedly, there may have been state policies aimed at business regulation and taxation that were viewed by certain legislators as having some incidental benefit on a local or in-state business. The favoritism of the Oklahoma and Louisiana statutes, however, was explicitly discussed by the Court.

26. Of the twenty state policies aimed at labor relations and labor rights struck down by the Court, ten were struck down on the basis of a federal statute. The Court struck down four state policies dealing with employer liability for injury. The justices found these policies superseded by the Federal Employer Liability Act (E.g., *St. Louis, S. F. & T. Railway Co. v. Seale*, 228 U.S. 156 [1913]; *New York Central Railway*

Co. v. Winfield, 244 U.S. 147 [1917]; *Erie Railroad Company v. Winfield,* 244 U.S. 170 [1917]). Also, state attempts to regulate either the hours of labor or the remedies available to labor were held void on the basis of the Federal Hours of Service Act (*Northern Pacific Railway Co. v. Washington,* 222 U.S. 370 [1912]; *Erie Railroad Co. v. New York,* 233 U.S. 671 [1914]; and various maritime and bankruptcy statutes such as *Chicago, B. & Q. R. v. Hall,* 229 U.S. 511 [1913]; *Lindgren v. United States,* 281 U.S. 38 [1930]; *Baizley Iron Works v. Span,* 281 U.S. 222 [1930]).

27. *McDermott v. Wisconsin,* 228 U.S. 115 (1913).

28. *Sperry Oil Co. v. Chisholm,* 264 U.S. 488 (1924).

29. *Buck v. Kuykendall,* 267 U.S. 307 (1925); *Bush Co. v. Maloy,* 267 U.S. 317 (1925).

30. E.g., *American Express Company v. Caldwell,* 244 U.S. 617 (1917); *Postal Telegraph-Cable Co. v. Warren Grodwin Co.,* 251 U.S. 27 (1919); *Western Union Telegraph Co. v. Boegli,* 251 U.S. 315 (1920); *Lancaster v. McCarty,* 267 U.S. 427 (1925); *Oregon-Washington Co. v. Washington,* 270 U.S. 87 (1926). See also *Macallen Co. v. Massachusetts,* 279 U.S. 620 (1929).

31. E.g., *First National Bank v. Hartford,* 273 U.S. 548 (1927); *Minnesota v. First National Bank,* 273 U.S. 561 (1927); *Keating v. Public National Bank,* 284 U.S. 587 (1932).

32. E.g., *Southern Railway Co. v. Reid,* 222 U.S. 424 (1912); *Chicago, Rhode Island & Pacific Railway Co. v. Hardwick Elevator Co.,* 226 U.S. 426 (1913); *St. Louis, Iron Mt. & S. Railway v. Edwards,* 227 U.S. 265 (1913).

33. *Adams Express Co. v. Croninger,* 226 U.S. 491 (1913); *Chicago, B. & Q. Railway v. Miller,* 226 U.S. 513 (1913); *Chicago, St. Paul, M. & O. Railway Co. v. Latta,* 226 U.S. 519 (1913); *Missouri K & T Railway v. Harriman Brothers,* 227 U.S. 657 (1913); *Charleston & W. C. Railway Co. v. Varnville Co.,* 237 U.S. 597 (1915).

34. *Pennsylvania Railway Co. v. Public Service Commission,* 250 U.S. 566 (1919); *Missouri Pacific Railway Co. v. Stroud,* 267 U.S. 404 (1925); *Missouri Pacific v. Porter,* 273 U.S. 341 (1927).

35. *International Harvester Co. v. Kentucky,* 234 U.S. 216 (1914). See also *Davis v. Cohen,* 268 U.S. 638 (1925); *Napier v. Atlantic Coast Line,* 272 U.S. 605 (1926).

36. *Missouri Pacific Railway Co. v. Tucker,* 230 U.S. 340 (1913); *Chicago, M. & St. P. Railway Co. v. Polt,* 232 U.S. 165 (1914); *Northern Pacific Railway v. North Dakota ex rel. McCue,* 236 U.S. 585 (1915); *Norfolk & Western Railway v. Conley,* 236 U.S. 605 (1915); *Rowland v. Boyle,* 244 U.S. 106 (1917).

37. E.g., *St. Louis, Iron Mt. and S. Railway Co. v. Wynne,* 224 U.S. 354 (1912); *Charleston & W. C. Railway Co. v. Varnville Co.,* 237 U.S. 597 (1915); *Davis v. Farmers Cooperative Co.,* 262 U.S. 313 (1923); *Atchison, T. & S. F. Railway Co. v. Wells,* 265 U.S. 101 (1924); *Western & Atlantic Railway Co. v. Henderson,* 279 U.S. 639 (1929).

38. *Wright v. Central of Georgia Railway,* 236 U.S. 674 (1915); *Union Pacific Railway v. Public Service commission,* 248 U.S. 67 (1918); *Central of Georgia Railway Co. v. Wright,* 248 U.S. 525 (1919); *Wallace v. Hines,* 253 U.S. 66 (1920); *Kansas City Southern Railway v. Road Improvement District No. 6,* 256 U.S. 658 (1921); *Southern Railway Co. v. Kentucky,* 274 U.S. 76 (1927); *Road Improvement v. Missouri Pacific Railway Co.,* 274 U.S. 188 (1927).

39. E.g., *Harrison v. St. L., S. F. & T. R. Co.,* 232 U.S. 318 (1914); *Smith v. Texas,* 233 U.S. 630 (1914); *Chicago B. & Q. Railway v. Wisconsin Railroad Commission,* 237 U.S. 220 (1915); *Atchison, T. & S. F. Railway Co. v. Vosburg,* 238 U.S. 56 (1915); *Detroit United Railway v. Michigan,* 242 U.S. 238 (1916); *Seaboard Air Line Railway v. Blackwell,* 244 U.S. 310 (1917); *Georgia v. Cincinnati Southern Railway,* 248 U.S. 26 (1918).

40. *Connally v. General Construction Co.,* 269 U.S. 385 (1926).

41. *Frost Trucking Co. v. Railroad Commission,* 271 U.S. 583 (1926); *Hughes Brothers Co. v. Minnesota,* 272 U.S. 469 (1926).

42. E.g., *United States v. Reynolds,* 235 U.S. 133 (1914).

43. It is inappropriate to consider all types of economic policies as salient because the basic question of management of business interests is not explicit and the litigants are nonbusiness interests in many of the cases involving general types of policies (see Appendix B). State policies aimed at the conditions for real estate transfers by individuals or inheritance taxes are not central to the critical question of this particular critical election period. The general class of economic cases often referred to as the "E-scale" is overinclusive (Schubert, 1974). In addition, there is little evidence provided by major historical accounts that these more general types of economic legislation related indirectly to the basic crosscutting question precipitating the critical elections of 1932 and 1936 (Swindler, 1969; Murphy, 1972)

44. As Mowry (1958: 71) notes: "It was not until Robert LaFollette defeated the Wisconsin regular Machine in 1900 that the reform movement really got started. LaFollette's election as governor seemed to start a chain reaction of revolt in the agricultural Middle West. A year afterward reform spread to Iowa, then to Minnesota and Missouri, and eventually down the entire tier of states immediately West, from North Dakota to Kansas."

45. *Hammer v. Dagenhart,* 247 U.S. 251 (1918); *Knickerbocker Ice Co. v. Stewart,* 253 U.S. 149 (1920); *Bailey v. Drexel Furniture Co.,* 259 U.S. 20 (1922); *Adkins v. Children's Hospital,* 261 U.S. 525 (1923); *Washington v. Dawson & Co.,* 264 U.S. 219 (1924).

46. *United States v. Hvoslef,* 237 U.S. 1 (1915); *Eisner v. Macomber,* 256 U.S. 189 (1920); *United States v. Cohen Grocery Co.,* 255 U.S. 81 (1921); *Hill v. Wallace,* 259 U.S. 44 (1922).

47. *Nicholds v. Coolidge,* 274 U.S. 531 (1927); *Untermeyer v. Anderson,* 276 U.S. 440 (1928); *Heiner v. Donnan,* 258 U.S. 312 (1932); *National Life Insurance v. United States,* 277 U.S. 508 (1928).

48. *Choate v. Trapp,* 224 U.S. 665 (1912).

49. *United States v. Moreland,* 258 U.S. 433 (1922).

50. *Myers v. United States,* 272 U.S. 52 (1926). See also *Muskrat v. United States,* 219 U.S. 346 (1911); *Keller v. Potomoc Electric Co.,* 261 U.S. 428 (1923).

51. *Newberry v. United States,* 256 U.S. 232 (1921).

52. *Muller v. Oregon,* 208 U.S. 412 (1908); *Bunting v. Oregon,* 243 U.S. 426 (1917).

53. E.g., *Nicholds v. Coolidge,* 274 U.S. 531 (1927); *Untermeyer v. Anderson,* 276 U.S. 440 (1928).

54. *Evans v. Gore,* 253 U.S. 245 (1920).

55. In the 1916–1921 bloc, 50 percent of the pairwise proportions of agreements were statistically significant at either the .05 or the .01 level. In the 1925–1930 period, 69.4 percent of the 36 pairwise proportions were statistically significant (Willetts, 1972).

56. Justice McKenna should be considered a marginal member of this bloc because his percentage of agreement with Chief Justice White is statistically insignificant at the .05 level.

57. The justice-president index is as follows: 4 = justice and appointing president are Democratic; 3 = justice is Democratic but the appointing president is Republican; 2 = justice is Republican but the appointing president is Democratic; and 1 = justice and appointing president are Republican (Tate, 1981).

58. The Supreme Court's validation of monetary policy involves the administration's repeal of clauses in private and public bonds that promised redemption in gold. The

Court, with Justice Roberts joining the liberals, held that these suspensions were valid as applied to private contracts and gold certificates. The Court did technically rule that the provision modifying the government's obligation to its own gold bonds was unconstitutional. The majority noted, however, that bondholders were not entitled to damages. The decision was hailed as a victory for the Democratic administration. The Gold Clause cases (*Norman v. Baltimore & O. Railroad Co.*, 294 U.S. 240 [1935], and *Perry v. United States*, 294 U.S. 330 [1935]) represent an upholding of New Deal policy, although technically a minor provision was declared unconstitutional. Although the Library of Congress (1978) includes *Perry* in its listing of federal statutes declared unconstitutional, the following analysis does not treat this case as a salient invalidation representing conflict with the new majority party. Indeed, the evidence is overwhelming in support of this approach (Jackson, 1941: 98–104). For the sake of clarity, the case is presented in tabular summaries but is omitted from all statistical analyses using the salient or crosscutting federal cases.

59. *Rickert Rice Mills v. Fontenot*, 297 U.S. 110 (1936); *United States v. Butler*, 297 U.S. 1 (1936).

60. *Panama Refining Co. v. Ryan*, 293 U.S. 388 (1935); *Schechter Poultry Corp. v. United States*, 295 U.S. 495 (1935).

61. E.g., *NLRB v. Jones and Laughlin Steel Corp.*, 301 U.S. 1 (1937); *West Coast Hotel Co. v. Parrish*, 300 U.S. 379 (1937).

62. *Answander v. T.V.A.*, 297 U.S. 288 (1936).

63. E.g., *Nortz v. United States*, 294 U.S. 317 (1935).

64. *Louisville Bank v. Radford*, 295 U.S. 555 (1935).

65. *Rickert Rice Mills v. Fontenot*, 297 U.S. 110 (1936); *United States v. Butler*, 297 U.S. 1 (1936).

66. *Carter v. Carter Coal Co.*, 298 U.S. 238 (1936).

67. *United States v. Constantine*, 296 U.S. 287 (1935).

68. *Lynch v. United States*, 292 U.S. 571 (1934).

69. *Booth v. United States*, 291 U.S. 339 (1934).

70. *Tot v. United States*, 319 U.S. 463 (1943).

71. *Murray v. Gerrick & Co.*, 291 U.S. 315 (1934).

72. *Taylor v. Georgia*, 315 U.S. 25 (1942); *Pollack v. Williams*, 322 U.S. 4 (1944).

73. *Thornhill v. Alabama*, 310 U.S. 88 (1940); *Thomas v. Collins*, 323 U.S. 516 (1945); *Hill v. Florida ex rel. Watson*, 325 U.S. 538 (1945).

74. *Missouri ex rel. Gaines v. Canada*, 305 U.S. 337 (1938). Other cases include: *Best v. Maxwell*, 311 U.S. 454 (1940) and *United States v. Allegheny County*, 322 U.S. 174 (1944).

75. *International Steel & Iron Company v. National Surety Co.*, 297 U.S. 657 (1936); *Wood v. Lovett*, 313 U.S. 362 (1941). See also *W. B. Worthen Co. v. Thomas*, 292 U.S. 426 (1934); *Broderick v. Rosner*, 294 U.S. 629 (1935).

76. *Morrison v. California*, 291 U.S. 82 (1934); *Hines v. Davidowitz*, 312 U.S. 52 (1941); *Edwards v. California*, 314 U.S. 160 (1941).

77. *Missouri ex rel. Gaines v. Canada*, 305 U.S. 337 (1938); *Lane v. Wilson*, 307 U.S. 268 (1939).

78. *Lindsey v. Washington*, 301 U.S. 397 (1937); *Lanzetta v. New Jersey*, 306 U.S. 451 (1939); *Skinner v. Oklahoma ex rel. Wilwinson*, 316 U.S. 535 (1942).

79. *Grosjean v. American Press Co.*, 297 U.S. 233 (1936); *Arizona Publishing Co. v. O'Neil*, 304 U.S. 543 (1938); *Herndon v. Lowry*, 301 U.S. 242 (1937); *Cantwell v. Connecticut*, 310 U.S. 296 (1940); *Taylor v. Mississippi*, 319 U.S. 583 (1943).

80. *Manley v. Georgia*, 279 U.S. 1 (1929).

81. *Graves v. Texas Company*, 298 U.S. 393 (1936).

82. *Colgate v. Harvey,* 296 U.S. 404 (1935); *New York ex rel. Rogers v. Graves,* 299 U.S. 401 (1937).

83. E.g., *Lawrence v. Shaw,* 300 U.S. 345 (1937); *Federal Land Bank v. Bismarck Co.,* 314 U.S. 95 (1941).

84. *Johnson Oil Co. v. Oklahoma ex rel. Mitchell,* 290 U.S. 158 (1933); *Standard Oil Co. v. California,* 291 U.S. 242 (1934); *Hartford Accident & Insurance Co. v. Delta Pine Land Co.,* 292 U.S. 143 (1934); *Concordia Insurance Co. v. Illinois,* 292 U.S. 535 (1934); *Panhandle Co. v. Highway Commission,* 294 U.S. 613 (1935); *Oklahoma v. Barnsdall Corp.,* 296 U.S. 521 (1936); *Bingaman v. Golden Eagle Lines,* 297 U.S. 626 (1936); *Hartford Insurance Co. v. Harrison,* 301 U.S. 459 (1937); *McCarroll v. Dixie Lines,* 309 U.S. 176 (1940).

85. *Southern Railway v. Virginia,* 290 U.S. 190 (1933); *Georgia Railway & Electric Co. v. Decatur,* 295 U.S. 165 (1935); *Southern Pacific Co. v. Arizona,* 325 U.S. 761 (1945).

86. *Anglo-Chilean Corp. v. Alabama,* 288 U.S. 218 (1933); *Cooney v. Mountain States Telephone Co.,* 294 U.S. 384 (1935); *Fisher's Blend Station v. State Tax Commission,* 297 U.S. 650 (1936); *Ingels v. Morf,* 300 U.S. 290 (1937); *Puget Sound Co. v. Tax Commission,* 302 U.S. 90 (1937); *Connecticut General Life Insurance Co. v. Johnson,* 303 U.S. 77 (1938).

87. *McKnett v. St. Louis & San Francisco Railroad Co.,* 292 U.S. 230 (1934); *Cloverleaf Butter Co. v. Patterson,* 315 U.S. 148 (1942); *Tulee v. Washington,* 315 U.S. 681 (1942).

88. Three cases are missing because the date of enactment or the citation date could not be located from the federal court records.

89. The estimates for the number of salient policies using Poisson regressions are substantively very similar to least-squares regression. The estimates are constant (b = 1.528; S.E. = 0.187); Time 1 (b = 0.010; S.E. = 0.0150); Time 2 (b = 0.098; S.E. = 0.0941); and R_t (b = 0.0142; S.E. = 0.0079).

90. The Poisson regression estimates for number of salient policies are constant (b = 1.592; S.E. = 0.172); Time 1 (b = 0.030; S.E. = 0.0144); Time 2 (b = −0.0835; S.E. = 0.025); and R_t (b = 0.791; S.E. = 0.222).

5

The Critical Elections
of 1960 and 1964

Wherever the civil rights issue became heated, . . . resistance took on the character of a polar force, more concerned with resisting black demands—for housing integration, for equal employment opportunities, for police review boards, for the end of de facto school segregation, or whatever—than with the unity of the Democratic party. The realignment crisis once confined to the South became a crisis everywhere.

—James Sundquist
Dynamics of the Party System (1973)

[E]vidence of dealignment is readily apparent almost everywhere one looks in public attitudes and behavior. The belief that one should vote the man rather than the party has now become part of the American consensus, and split-ticket voting has risen markedly. Fewer people now identify themselves with the parties, and the percentage of those who have neither likes nor dislikes regarding the two parties has more than tripled since the 1950s.

—Martin P. Wattenberg
"From a Partisan to a Candidate-centered Electorate" (1990)

This chapter is an examination of the Supreme Court's invalidation of state and federal policies between 1946 and 1964 and an assessment of the relationship between the political issues in these cases and the crosscutting issues of the critical presidential elections of 1960 and 1964. These elections changed the coalitional base of the Democratic majority party (Pomper, 1975) and eventually prompted major changes in electoral behavior. The presidential elections of 1960 and 1964 were critical elections because they marked a "durable and significant redistribution of party support" (Trilling and Campbell, 1980: 6). In previous critical election periods, this redistribution of party support produced either a new majority party (1860s and the 1930s) or a restrengthening of support for a declining majority party (1890s). The aftermath of the critical elections of 1960 and 1964 was much more complex.

The critical elections of 1960 and 1964 focused on partisan differences on the crosscutting issues of civil rights for blacks as well as the "social issue," which encompassed a diffuse set of concerns including rising crime and perceived lawlessness, liberal domestic programs, and matters of lifestyle (Scammon and Wattenberg, 1970; Sundquist, 1973: 308–331). At the national level, these issues unsettled traditional partisan loyalties and the electorate became increasingly ambivalent toward the major parties. This ambivalence is striking both in terms of citizens' attitudes and in terms of voting behavior. Several developments illustrate this major and long-term change: The number of individuals professing independence from both parties rose; the incidence of split-ticket voting swelled; and the electorate increasingly focused on candidates and issues instead of the party label as voting cues (e.g., Crotty, 1984). Hence, the critical elections at 1960 and 1964 mark the beginning of dealignment in the national party system. These major changes in electoral support began in one particular region, the South (Beck, 1977; Gatlin, 1975). Indeed, there is evidence that a full-scale reorientation had been completed in the South as certain population groups within the region rejected the traditional majority party status of the Democratic party (Hadley and Howell, 1980; Swansbrough and Brodsky, 1988; Campbell, 1977). Gradually, the changes following the critical elections of 1960 and 1964 took on national significance and produced a significant and durable change in the parties' support by the electorate. These major changes ensued without establishing a majority party in the popularly elected branches.

The agenda-setting role ascribed to the Supreme Court in periods before critical elections suggests that Supreme Court policymaking will contribute to the policy position of the majority party before these elections. The partisan character of the Court over the 1946–1964 period reinforces the likelihood of such a role; the Court was composed of a majority of justices appointed primarily by Democratic presidents given the dominance of the Democratic party from the New Deal to 1960. Several Supreme Court decisions also justify this role. In dealing with issues of racial equality, the rights of criminal defendants, and school prayer, the Supreme Court aligned itself with the liberal wing of the Democratic party and contributed to the policy stance of the party in the electoral battles of 1960 and 1964. Adamany (1980: 254–256) argues that several Supreme Court decisions played an important role in shaping these issues and, in the process, the critical elections of 1960 and 1964.

As noted below, reliance on the Court's major decisions does yield considerable support to the Supreme Court's role in shaping the critical issues. The primary goal, however, is to examine all cases in which the Supreme Court struck down state or federal policies from 1946 to 1964 in order to address a number of related questions. First, to what extent are the cases of invalidation related to the critical issues and is there a significant increase in the number of salient cases immediately preceding 1964 or during polarization? Second, are the salient state policies enacted primarily by state governments whose partisan character and ideology are different from the Warren Court's in the 1950s and 1960s? Third, is the volatility and intensity of these issues reflected in the rate of division among the justices in the salient cases identified compared to other types of cases? Finally, do the justices divide along party lines in deciding these cases and what are the implications for understanding the internal dynamics of the Court on the eve of a critical election? An examination of all cases invalidating state and federal policies follows the next section, which is a discussion of the rise of the critical issues, the response of other party leaders, and general characterizations of Supreme Court policymaking under Chief Justices Fred Vinson and Earl Warren.

CROSSCUTTING ISSUES

The Great Depression and the New Deal wrought a fundamental reorientation in party ideology on economic policy. More specifically, there was a realignment of partisan debate on the proper relationship between government and the marketplace. The strict laissez-faire Republicanism of the 1890s and 1920s was not expressed by any large segment of Republican leadership in the years after the New Deal. Partisan conflict did occur in the 1940s and 1950s over macroeconomic matters and policy instruments. Republican attacks on government spending were rarely premised, however, on a wholesale rejection of government intervention in economic matters. Most differences focused on the principles of fiscal austerity and the scale of interventionist policies (Sundquist, 1973: 214–227; Ladd, 1972: 210–224). These older economic issues were not central to the 1960s period of dealignment. Instead, the party system confronted the rise of new, crosscutting issues from 1945 to 1964 including civil rights, the threat of communism, and the "social issue" (Sundquist, 1973: 315–317; Scammon and Wattenberg, 1970).

Shortly after World War II, President Harry Truman introduced the controversial issue of racial equality. In the State of the Union message in 1948 and in proposals to establish a committee on civil rights, Truman raised an issue that could alienate southern Democrats. Truman's call for racial justice and a "fair deal" was not highlighted but downplayed four years later by moderates in firm control of the Democratic party. These included the party's 1952 presidential nominee, Adlai Stevenson. The election of Republican Eisenhower also contributed to silencing the race issue as moderates in both parties straddled the volatile and crosscutting issues.

Another potentially crosscutting issue grew in intensity during the cold war era as national attention focused on the possible threat of communism. McCarthyism and the concern about Communist regimes were potentially crosscutting for the New Deal party system. Because of the nature of these issues, however, party leaders on both sides did not take polar positions. There simply was not a major difference on the basic policy objective of stopping the "march of communism."

In 1954, the Supreme Court reintroduced the race issue into national politics by declaring state-enforced racial segregation in public schools unconstitutional. In *Brown v. Board of Education* (1954), the Court rejuvenated the programmatic liberal wing of the Democratic party, a move that later served to alienate southern Democrats. As Sundquist (1973: 316) observes:

> If centrist politicians had succeeded in healing (or perhaps more accurately papering over the party rupture), the Supreme Court in 1954 reopened it. With the decree that year outlawing dual school systems, the polar forces in the Democratic party regrouped. The Northern zealots demanded that the Supreme Court decision be carried out forthwith, with full support of the executive and legislative branches. The southern polar forces solidified under the banner of "massive resistance." . . . [The] continuing turmoil over school integration in the South increased polarization throughout the country. The lunch counter "sit-ins" heightened it. When the 1960 Democratic convention met, the polar forces demanding unqualified commitment to civil rights regardless of the consequences to the party were in clear control.

The movement by southern Democrats away from the national party was also precipitated by the economic conservatism of southern Democrats regarding domestic spending and, in the 1960s, regarding domestic social programs. Moreover, by 1960 and 1964 this issue had become intertwined with a concern for crime and lawlessness and the growing countercultural movements. These diffuse, nonracial concerns were termed the "social issue" by Scammon and Wattenberg (1970). Along with the issue of racial equality, the social issue served to divide the New Deal coalition established in the depression years.

With the election of John Kennedy in 1960 and Lyndon Johnson in 1964, the liberal programmatic wing of the Democratic party was in control of the party. The party was committed to broad scale "Great Society" domestic programs and measures aimed at remedying the perceived inequalities between labor and management. Legislative successes such as the Civil Rights Act of 1964 and the Voting Rights Act of 1965 initially signaled a full-scale partisan realignment where the declining Democratic party would be strengthened and dominant for many years in national policymaking, similar to the fortune of the Republican party in the 1890s. The election of Richard Nixon in 1968 and 1972 demonstrates, however, the lack of long-term Democratic dominance following the critical election of 1964 (Brady and Stewart, 1986).

The critical elections represented a major long-term change in the parties' electoral support, but these changes represented dealignment and a weakening of party loyalties in contrast to the 1890s. The Democratic party continued its considerable post–New Deal strength in the North, but the "solid South" witnessed tremendous disaffection (Beck, 1977; Campbell, 1977). Indeed, Republican Barry Goldwater received 87 percent of the vote in Mississippi and over 54 percent of the total vote in Alabama, South Carolina, Louisiana, and Georgia. In 1952, the Republican party was able to muster only an average of 40.1 percent in these five states, and no state supported the Republican presidential candidate with over 50 percent of its votes. Nevertheless, such changes did not signal permanent reorientation to a new majority party but constituted the early signs of dealignment. For example, after 1965 the number of political independents and the incidence of split-ticket voting increased dramatically as party ties weakened (Nie, Verba, and Petrocik, 1979: 47–73; Crotty, 1984: 34–36).

Critical elections arise because of crosscutting issues, polarization in the party system, and long-term change in the electorate's support for the major parties. A complete realignment to a new majority party did not follow the critical elections of 1960 and 1964 for two interrelated reasons. According to Sundquist (1973: 324–328), the social issue was intense enough to disrupt or sever many voters from their existing partisan attachments, but it lacked the intensity of the economic issues of the depression years. Second, the issues were diffuse or lacked the character that produces single-peaked preferences; that is, the issues did not present a single policy dimension underlying the preferences of voters or party leaders, and hence, policy alternatives could not be ordered along a single dimension (e.g., Black, 1958; Arrow, 1963; Sen, 1970; Riker and Ordeshook, 1973). The social issue, for example, was so diffuse that a clear line of cleavage along a single axis was not possible for either the electorate or party leaders. Voters and politicians could support both a "law and order" position as well as increased spending for liberal domestic programs. Liberal members of Congress also often found it difficult to vote against law and order measures such as the Safe Streets Act of 1968. The diffuse nature of these issues allowed Democratic leaders after President Lyndon Johnson to straddle and avoid polar positions. In sum, the critical elections of 1960 and 1964 did not lead to full-scale realignment of the party system because the diffuse and less volatile character of the critical issues could not ignite polar groups in each party as seen so vividly in the 1850s, 1890s, and 1930s.

In its very broad outlines, the Supreme Court's agenda from 1946 to 1964 reflected the issues of postwar politics, the social issue, and the question of civil rights for blacks. With the possible exception of foreign policy, the Court entertained many controversial issues. The rise of racial equality questions in the Vinson Court (1946–1953) and Warren Court (1953–1969) is apparent in several cases in the 1946–1964 period. Symbolically, in the same year President Truman raised the civil rights issue, the Court upheld state antidiscrimination statutes and struck down court enforcement of racially restrictive covenants that prohibited white homeowners from selling their homes to nonwhites.[1] The Vinson Court (1946–1953) also struck down segregation in professional education in *Sweatt v. Painter* (1950) when there was evidence that the state had separate, but not necessarily equal, facilities.

It was the Warren Court, however, that raised the question of racial equality to the forefront of national concern. In the historic decision of *Brown v. Board of Education* (1954), the Court ruled that state-enforced dual school systems violated the equal protection clause of the Fourteenth Amendment. Chief Justice Warren's opinion noted, in part, that segregation in public schools was inherently unequal because of the psychological problems imposed on public school students. Warren's opinion mustered a unanimous vote as he brought three potential dissenters to support the ruling (Douglas, 1980: 113–115; Ulmer, 1971), but the decision met with silence from President Dwight Eisenhower. In contrast to the president, southern members of Congress and state legislatures erupted in a program of "massive resistance." Conservatives in Congress launched a series of attacks on the Court in response to the *Brown* decision as well as to the Court's liberal decisions involving cold war issues (Pritchett, 1961; Murphy, 1962; Schmidhauser and Berg, 1972). Southern states, most notably Louisiana, resurrected dual sovereignty notions of federalism and argued that states should reject the constitutional interpretations of the federal judiciary.

Issues of racial equality and the Warren Court before 1964 have been a subject of much study and debate. From the perspective of critical elections and partisan realignment, many of the major cases illustrate Court policymaking consistent with the programmatic liberal wing of the Democratic party under both John Kennedy and Lyndon Johnson. The notable decisions reflect a consistency with the policies and issue positions that led to Democratic victories in 1960 and to President Johnson's landslide victory in 1964. For example, in *Heart of Atlanta Motel v. United States* (1964) and *Katzenbach v. McClung* (1964), the Court upheld the expansive powers of Congress exercised in the Civil Rights Act of 1964 and also upheld the act's debatable constitutional basis.

In addition to issues of racial equality, the conservative concern with crime and perceived lawlessness met with some notable liberal rulings by the Court in the field of criminal justice. In *Mapp v. Ohio* (1961), the Court ruled that illegally seized evidence could not be admitted in a criminal trial at the state level. The decision marks only one federal criminal procedure rule that the Warren Court applied as a limit on state criminal proceedings (Fellman, 1976). In addition, the Court ruled that criminal defendants have a right to state-provided counsel in *Gideon v. Wainwright* (1963). *Gideon* was the subject of national media attention; law enforcement leaders protested that the decision would be the basis for "opening the jailhouse doors to hundreds of prisoners" (Murphy, 1972: 280). The Court's liberal decisions in the field of criminal justice became a campaign issue for the strong "law and order" position of Republican Barry Goldwater in 1964. In the early fall, he announced "that a criminal defendant must be given a sporting chance to go free, even though nobody doubts in the slightest he is guilty." Further, he argued, "No wonder that our law enforcement officers have been demoralized and rendered ineffective in their jobs" (Murphy, 1972: 381).

Equally controversial were the Supreme Court's decisions outlawing school prayer. In *Engle v. Vitale* (1962) and *Abington School District v. Schempp* (1963), the Court fueled partisan passions. A southern congressman announced, "They put the Negroes in the schools and now they've driven God out" (Pritchett, 1977: 406). Members of Congress introduced several constitutional amendments designed to overturn the school prayer rulings.

Public opinion polls showed that the Supreme Court received unfavorable ratings from a majority of respondents to national surveys from 1963 to

1966 (Wasby, 1978: 44). The few supporters of the Court were blacks, northerners, and the college-educated segment of the general public. Not surprisingly, the Court's sharpest critics in the early 1960s were conservative Republicans and southerners. In Congress, attempts to curb the Court's power had the strongest support among Republicans and southerners; liberal Democrats such as Senate majority leader Lyndon Johnson defended the Court (Pritchett, 1961).

The oft-noted liberalism of the Warren Court contributed to the partisan clash in the critical elections of 1960 and 1964. The Court's major rulings focusing on racial equality and the social issue represented a policy stance consistent with the northern, programmatic liberal wing of the Democratic party—a position that was central to the major electoral change in 1960 and 1964.

A systematic examination of the Supreme Court's invalidation of federal and state policies contributes further empirical support to the role ascribed to the Court by Adamany (1980) in the years before critical elections. The analysis illustrates the increasing number of salient policies struck down by the Court in the years surrounding critical elections. As in the 1890–1900 period, the exercise of judicial review related to highly volatile issues on which critical elections depend. Further, there is a significant, abrupt, and sustained increase in the number of salient policies struck down in the years between the *Brown* decision and the critical elections of 1960–1964.

THE INVALIDATION OF STATE AND
FEDERAL POLICIES, 1946–1964

Between 1946 and 1964, the Supreme Court struck down 155 state policies but only 8 federal policies. The small number of federal policies struck down is perhaps not surprising given the Democratic character of the Roosevelt Court and the fact that the Democrats controlled both chambers of Congress in all but two terms during this time (Dahl, 1957). In addition, the number of state and federal invalidations did not reach the Court's highest level seen in the 1920s. The Court struck down an average of 11.8 policies per year between the 1911–1932 period compared with an average of only 8.6 policies per year from 1946–1964. Figure 5.1 displays the total number of state and federal invalidations between 1946 and 1964.

The important issues for the critical elections of 1960 and 1964, civil rights for blacks and the social issue, were found in a significant minority of cases. In contrast to the periods before the critical elections of 1896 and 1932, in 1960 and 1964 the salient policies did not constitute a majority of the cases overturning state and federal policies. Table 5.1 shows that fifty-two of the cases raised issues of civil rights for blacks or the rights of criminal defendants. The Court struck down forty-six state policies aimed at restricting the civil rights of black citizens and six state policies related to criminal justice. Also of importance to the "social issue" were the two school prayer rulings included in the nonracial civil rights and liberties

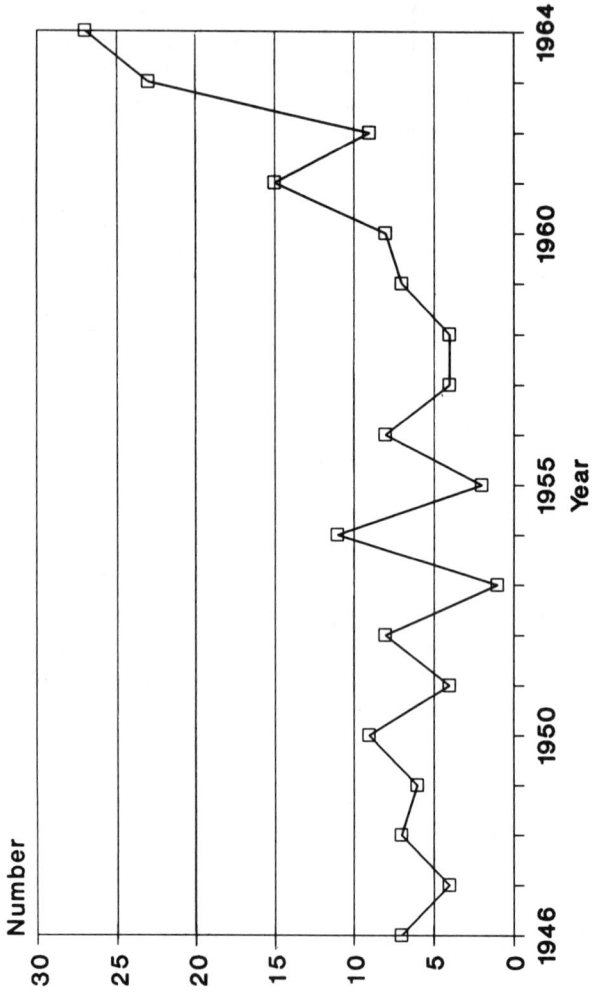

Figure 5.1
Number of Federal and State Policies
Declared Unconstitutional, 1946-1964

Source: Library of Congress (1978).

TABLE 5.1

Number and Percentage of State and Federal Cases
by Policy Area,
1946-1964

	Number of State Cases	Number of Federal Cases	Total Number of Cases	Percent of Total Cases
Civil Rights-Blacks	46	0	46	28.2
Civil Rights & Liberties, nonracial	26	7	33	20.2
Civil Rights & Liberties, rights of criminal defendants	6	0	6	3.7
Labor Rights	20	0	20	12.3
Business Regulation & Taxation	28	1	29	17.8
General, Nonbusiness Taxation	5	0	5	3.1
Federalism/Public Land Disputes	8	0	8	4.9
Miscellaneous[a]	16	0	16	9.8
Total	155	8	163	100.0

[a]Includes state policies dealing with alcohol control, general contracts and debts, banking, state protectionism regulation of the legal profession.

Source: Compiled by author from *United States Reports.*

category. These cases are discussed in detail below. The remaining policies struck down raised a wide variety of political issues. Some of these cases dealt with some politically volatile but nonrealigning issues such as free speech and religious freedom.

The State Cases, 1946-1964. As displayed in Table 5.1, the state cases raised many different policy questions between 1946 and 1964. The cases directly related to the critical issues of the 1960 and 1964 elections are included under the civil rights–blacks and criminal justice policy areas. The second largest class of policies related to business regulation and taxation. The Court struck down twenty-eight state policies related to business regulation or taxation. Of these, over 43 percent were struck down because of a conflict with federal legislation. The Court invalidated gross receipts taxes,[2] privilege taxes,[3] and other forms of business taxation.[4] Also, state policies dealing with regulations and licensing requirements for business were struck down, usually on the basis of an overriding federal statute.[5] In addition, the Court voided state policies relating to labor negotiations and unions. The basis of the invalidations was, however, a federal statute in each of the twenty labor cases shown in Table 5.1. The cases dealt with state infringement on the jurisdiction of the National Labor Relations Board.[6] The statutory basis of the overturn of business regulation stands in stark contrast to the constitutional basis for such violations in the earlier realigning eras. Both the character of the Supreme Court and the extent of involvement in economic regulation by the national government were fundamentally different in the period following World War II. By the 1940s, there were literally thousands of federal rules that could serve as a basis for striking down state policies.

In addition, the Supreme Court struck down statutes related to nonracial civil rights and liberties such as policies affecting religious freedom,[7] free speech,[8] and anti-Communist loyalty oaths.[9] The remaining cases related to general, nonbusiness taxation,[10] public land disputes,[11] general contractual and debt policies,[12] and state attempts to protect in-state business.[13]

The salient cases involved the overturn of state policies dealing with issues of racial equality, criminal justice, and school prayer. The outcomes represented liberal rulings consistent with the northern wing of the Democratic party in the 1950s and the stance of Presidents Kennedy and Johnson in the early 1960s. Undoubtedly, *Brown v. Board of Education* (1954) represents the classic case that supports the view that the Supreme Court helps to shape the policy stance of the majority party on the eve of a critical election.

In *Brown* and subsequent school desegregation cases, the Court announced highly controversial doctrines that raised political issues disruptive of the New Deal coalition. Southerners viewed school desegregation as hostile and as an intrusive national intervention upon states' rights as well as an attack on the entire dual social system of the South. *Brown* led to many attempts to block or to impede desegregation. Although the national Republican party continued to straddle the race issue, it could announce sympathy with the southern cause on states' rights grounds. The congruence between the ideology of southern Democratic members of Congress and Republican members of Congress on this issue found expression in the "conservative coalition" (Manley, 1973; Ladd, 1972: 212–218).

The invalidations of state policies related to issues of racial equality actually predate the historic decision in *Brown*. As many note, the Supreme Court began an incremental attack on segregation and voided five state policies before 1954. In three of these cases, the Vinson Court gradually moved to a stronger commitment to racial equality by firmly enforcing the guarantee of the "separate but equal" doctrine. In *Sipuel v. Board of Regents* (1948), the Court overturned an Oklahoma law that barred blacks from the only law school in the state. The Court ruled that states could not exclude blacks from white institutions if separate but equal facilities were not available. Similarly, in *Sweatt v. Painter* (1950) the Court invalidated a Texas segregation statute because the separate law school facilities afforded to blacks were inferior to those provided to whites. And in *McLaurin v. Oklahoma State Regents* (1950), the Court ruled that segregation of a black graduate student within a white institution unconstitutionally inhibited his right to an equal education.[14]

The race relations cases after *Brown* illustrate a wide ranging set of state policies. First, the Court extended its desegregation ruling in a number of cases to areas outside of education. For instance, in 1956 the Court invalidated an Alabama statute requiring segregation on motor buses[15] and in 1959 voided a Louisiana statute prohibiting interracial athletic contests.[16] The Court also struck down state segregation statutes relating to bus terminals[17] and restaurants.[18]

Second, the invalidations of race-related policies after *Brown* illustrate the Supreme Court's battle with southern forces and the "massive resistance" movement against its school desegregation rulings. In many cases the Court overturned southern policies designed to avoid or block compliance with judicial policy.[19] For example, in *Bush v. Orleans School Board* (1961), the Court invalidated a Louisiana statute that declared the *Brown* decision unconstitutional and interposed state sovereignty in race matters.

From 1960 to 1964, the Court also protected the rights of black demonstrators and organizations such as the National Association for the Advancement of Colored People (NAACP). The Court invalidated state trespass laws applied to punish "sit-in" demonstrators,[20] statutes designed to uncover membership lists of black groups,[21] and policies limiting participation of third parties in litigation.[22]

The remaining cases dealing with racial equality concerned the rights of blacks in the electoral process.[23] The Court struck down statutes requiring notice of race on election ballots[24] and voter registration.[25] Beginning in 1960, the Court attacked the subtle forms of discrimination such as racial gerrymandering[26] and apportionment (Claude, 1970). In *Wesberry v. Sanders* (1964), the Court struck down statutes establishing congressional districts of unequal proportions and announced the important "one man-one vote" rule. The reapportionment decisions led to the voiding of numerous state apportionment schemes in 1964.[27] The drawing of congressional districts in the South was often a deliberate attempt to dilute black voting strength. Hence, black groups were supportive of the reapportionment movement against rural power and saw it as a means to ensure racial equality in the political arena (Claude, 1970).[28] Pro–civil rights groups such as the NAACP praised the Court's historic decisions in *Reynolds* and *Baker v. Carr* (1962). Indeed, the NAACP had previously sought such a ruling in third party amici, or "friend of the Court," briefs (Claude, 1970: 149–169).

The Supreme Court's invalidation of state policies relating to race provoked considerable outcry from southerners who would move away from the liberal wing of the party in the critical election of 1960 and 1964. Although the liberal record of the Warren Court has received much comment, the cases relating to racial equality precipitated the disaffection of the South within the Democratic party and reinforced the policy position of the liberal wing of the Democratic party.

Many have noted that the diffuse "social issue" contributed to the dealignment in the party system begun in the 1960 and 1964 presidential elections (Sundquist, 1973; Pomper, 1975; Scammon and Wattenberg, 1970). The Supreme Court's decisions relating to the rights of criminal defendants and school prayer contributed to the policy stance of the northern wing of the Democratic party on the critical "social issue." Indeed, the Supreme

Court's criminal justice decisions (e.g., Fellman, 1976) stand in contrast to the demands of conservatives for increased law and order in response to perceptions of rising crime and lawlessness. There were six state criminal justice policies struck down by the Court from 1956 to 1963. The most notable cases are *Griffin v. Illinois* (1956) and *Gideon v. Wainwright* (1963). In *Griffin*, the Court nullified an Illinois statute that restricted the rights of indigent defendants to obtain a free transcript of trial court proceedings for effecting an appeal. A similar Washington statute was invalidated two years later,[29] and the appellant rights to appeal were expanded by another invalidation in 1963.[30]

In *Gideon*, a Florida statute denying indigent defendants the right to free legal services in noncapital felonies was held to deprive the defendant of due process. In this and other such prodefendant rulings on issues of trial court proceedings[31] and harsh narcotics prosecution procedures,[32] the Court came under fire from conservatives. This included attacks by Republican Goldwater in the 1964 campaign.

The Court also raised school prayer in public schools as an issue of national concern in the case of *Abington School Dist. v. Schempp* (1963). In so doing, the Court fueled southern hostility toward the federal judiciary as it overturned a state law that required Bible reading at the beginning of each school day. It may be that the increasing southern hostility to the Court's stance on school prayer was a factor in Chief Justice Warren's decision to assign the writing of the majority opinion to Justice Tom Clark, a deeply religious man and one of only two southern justices on the Court.

The regional distribution of the salient policies and the partisan character of the state governments enacting the policies show that most arose from southern Democratic states. Over 75 percent of the salient cases arose from southern Democratic states, as shown in Table 5.2. This figure is especially revealing when one considers that only 54.5 percent of all states were either Republican or southern in this period. The few salient Republican policies (18.0%) included two state segregation statutes struck down in *Brown v. Board of Education* (1954) as well as state policies dealing with criminal justice, school prayer, and reapportionment. Few observers of the Warren Court will be surprised by the concentration of the salient policies in the Democratic South. In combination with the analysis of crosscutting issues before 1896 and 1932, however, these results show that the Court was prone to invalidate salient state policies enacted by state governments whose partisan and ideological orientation was different from the dominant majority's on the Court.

Also, the South was the source for the largest number of nonsalient policies, but the percentage of total policies is much lower (32.8%) and close to the level of nonsalient policies enacted by midwestern Republican states (29.7%). Republican state governments were the source for 48.5 percent of the nonsalient policies compared to 37.5 percent from mixed states. This higher level of nonsalient Republican policies may reflect a general ideological conflict between the Democratic Court along the New Deal–issue dimensions

TABLE 5.2

Distribution of Salient and Nonsalient State Cases
by Partisan Control of State Governments
at Time of Policy Enactment and by Region,
1946-1964

Partisan Control by Region	Number of Salient	Percent	Number of Nonsalient	Percent
Democratic				
New England & Middle Atlantic	2	5.1	0	0.0
Solid South & Border	29	74.4	21	32.8
East & West North Central	0	0.0	1	1.6
Pacific & Mountain	1	2.6	2	3.1
Mixed[a]				
New England & Middle Atlantic	0	0.0	5	7.8
Solid South & Border	0	0.0	1	1.6
East & West North Central	0	0.0	2	3.1
Pacific & Mountain	0	0.0	1	1.6
Republican				
New England & Middle Atlantic	3	7.7	6	9.4
Solid South & Border	0	0.0	0	0.0
East & West North Central	3	7.7	19	29.7
Pacific & Mountain	1	2.6	6	9.4
Total	39	100.0	64	100.0[b]
Missing	19		41	

Percentage of all states ideologically opposed = 54.5

[a]State governments classified as mixed had either a divided legislature or the partisanship of the governor and legislature were different. A majority or a simple plurality constitutes legislative control.
[b]This total does not precisley equal 100% because of rounding.

Source: Clubb, Flanigan, and Zingale (1990); *United States Reports.*

established in the 1930s rather than the crosscutting and diffuse character of the social issue and the regional character of the racial equality issue.

The cases related to school prayer, the rights of criminal defendants, and racial equality give support to the agenda-setting role attributed to the Court in periods before critical elections. In this period, the Supreme Court appears firmly part of the majority coalition as suggested by Dahl (1957). At least through its exercise of judicial review of state policies, a majority of the Court joined the northern liberal wing of the Democratic party. These decisions reinforced the liberal cast of the Democratic party.

Moreover, one could argue that the Court's agenda-setting role in the critical elections of 1960 and 1964 was even greater than in the previous realigning eras before the elections of 1896 and 1932–36. The Supreme Court in *Brown* and its subsequent decisions brought the issue of racial equality to the forefront of national concern and debate. Before the critical elections of 1896 and 1932, the Court served to reinforce the most conservative wing of the then dominant Republican party (Westin, 1953). In the 1950s and into the 1960s, the Court was almost solely responsible for the resurgence of a critical issue similar in importance to *Dred Scott* before the Civil War realignment.

The Federal Cases, 1946–1964. From the end of World War II to 1964, the Supreme Court invalidated only eight federal statutes, a record consistent with the Democratic character of the Court and Congress in the postwar era. The Democrats controlled both houses of Congress except during the 1947–48 and 1950–56 terms. The federal cases did not reflect the salient issues of the critical elections of 1960 and 1964. For example, the Court voided a 1938 provision of the Federal Food, Drug, and Cosmetic Act, which prohibited businesses from refusing to allow federal inspectors to enter their premises. This case, *United States v. Cardiff* (1952), was unrelated to any of the critical issues.

The remaining cases dealt with military court martials and various internal security matters. In two cases, the Court overturned separate provisions of the strict 1950 Uniform Code of Military Justice. In *Toth v. Quarles* (1955), the court martial of discharged servicemen for crimes committed abroad was declared unconstitutional on the basis of the Fifth and Sixth Amendments. And in *Reid v. Covert* (1957) the Court voided a provision of the code allowing court martials of the civilian dependents of servicemen who were alleged to have committed crimes abroad while accompanying servicemen. Finally, the Court struck down war-related measures aimed at the prosecution of "subversives" during the cold war. In *Trop v. Dulles* (1958), a 1944 statute prescribing loss of citizenship for desertion from the armed services in times of war was nullified. Further, the justices voided similar penalties imposed on individuals who either left the country or remained on foreign soil to avoid military service.[33]

In three cases, the Court struck down anti-Communist measures such as a 1943 statute directed at withholding the pay of three federal employees. In 1946, the Court held this provision of an appropriation measure to be an unconstitutional bill of attainder.[34] Similarly, a 1952 statute withdrew citizenship from naturalized citizens who lived three years in their country of origin, and the Court invalidated this provision in 1964.[35] Finally, in *Aptheker v. Secretary of State* (1964), the Court overturned section 6 of the 1950 McCarran Act, which established criminal sanctions for any member of a Communist organization who attempted to use a passport for foreign travel.

The three anti-Communist rulings and other noninvalidation cases produced a short-lived but volatile period of conflict between the Court and members of Congress such as Joseph McCarthy. The cold war issues and Supreme Court policymaking quickly subsided with the decline of McCarthyism. The decisions are clearly consistent with the liberal reputation of the Vinson and Warren Courts on civil rights and liberties issues (Murphy, 1972). The cases were not, however, salient to the law and order issue on which Goldwater and others attacked the Court or to other crosscutting issues (Murphy, 1972: 370; Sundquist, 1973: 322–325).

The examination of the cases of federal policy invalidation does not contribute support to the Court's probable role in shaping the issues surrounding the critical elections of 1960 and 1964. Indeed, the analysis of the Court's activism regarding federal policies is consistent with Dahl's analysis of the relationship between the Court and Congress. As Dahl (1957: 293) argued, the Court is "inevitably a part of the dominant national alliance." In contrast, analysis of the cases of state policy invalidation is the source for the thesis that judicial policy contributes to the majority party's stance on the critical issues. In striking down state policies dealing with racial equality, school prayer, and the rights of criminal defendants, the Supreme Court strengthened the programmatic liberal wing of the Democratic party and provoked harsh comment from conservatives, especially from the South.

The number of salient state cases from 1946 to 1964 is illustrated in Figure 5.2. The graph depicts a rather drastic increase in cases dealing with civil rights for blacks and the social issue in the late 1950s and especially between 1960 and 1964. This is compelling testimony not only to the Warren Court's invalidation of state laws but to a rather dramatic turn from the moderate course of the Vinson Court to a strong Progressive position.

A precise estimate of the increase in the number of salient invalidations in the period surrounding the critical elections of 1960 and 1964 is possible through least-squares regression analysis. Formally stated, the expectation of a significant increase is

$$I_t = a + b_1 \text{ Time1}_t + b_2 \text{ Time2}_t + b_3 R_t + e_t,$$

where I_t is the simple number of cases striking down salient policies from 1946 to 1980; a is a constant term; Time1_t is the time trend before *Brown* (1954), which raised the issue of racial equality to national prominence; and Time2_t is the time trend from 1946 to 1980; R_t is a bivariate qualitative variable signifying polarization and takes the value of 1 from 1955 to 1968 and 0 in other years' polarization (Sundquist, 1973; Ginsberg, 1972); and e_t is an error term. The coefficients to be estimated are b_1, b_2, and b_3.

This interrupted time-series design is identical to the one employed in previous critical election periods. Two points should be noted. First, it was necessary to extend the time series through to 1980 in order to provide both a "before" and "after" trend in the salient invalidations.[36] Second, this extension allows for the inclusion of the 1968 presidential election in the series of elections precipitating dealignment in the American party system (e.g., Sundquist, 1973:314–328; Campbell, 1977). Hence, the intervention term (R_t) denoting the period of most intense polarization over the crosscutting issues extends from 1955 to 1968.[37] It is expected that the value of the coefficient for this bivariate qualitative variable (b_3) will be greater than 0.

Least-squares regression provides the estimates for the impact of the realignment period except in the presence of serial-, or auto-, correlation.

156

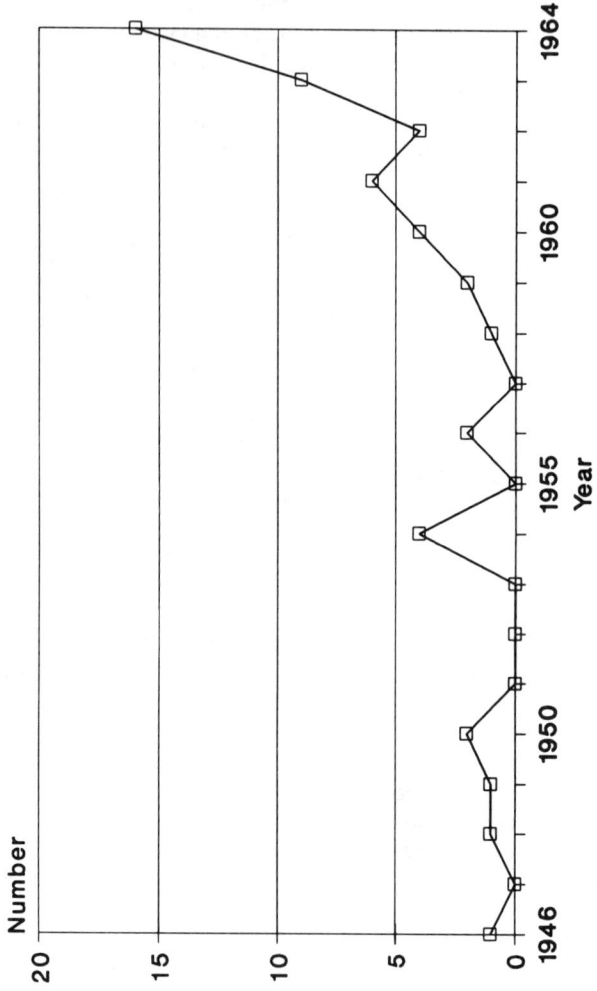

Figure 5.2
Number of Salient Policies
Declared Unconstitutional, 1946-1964

Source: Compiled by the author.

TABLE 5.3

Interrupted Time-Series Estimates for the
Total Number of Salient Policies and an Estimated Rate of Invalidation:
1946-1980

Variable		Total Number of Salient Policies	Estimated Rate of Invalidation
Constant	b	0.801	0.162
	SE	2.152	0.476
	t	0.372	0.340
Time 1	b	-0.054	-0.0001
	SE	0.359	0.0795
	t	-0.043	-0.0016
Time 2	b	0.220	0.0445
	SE	0.424	0.0937
	t	0.521	0.4753
R_1	b	3.225[a]	0.702[a]
	SE	1.389	0.307
	t	2.321	2.285
R^2 =		0.342	0.338
Adj. R^2 =		0.277	0.274
D.W. =		2.097	1.821
rho =			
n = 34			

[a]p>t = 0.05

Source: Compiled by author.

Table 5.3 displays the estimates for the dealigning era of the 1960s and Supreme Court policymaking. Note as well that Table 5.3 displays estimates for both the total number of salient policies and an estimated rate of invalidation. Once again, the estimated rate of invalidation is based on a measure of the changing workload of the Supreme Court, the log of the number of written opinions handed down by the Court (Blaustein and Mersky, 1978:137).

The results indicate that there was a statistically significant increase in the number of salient cases from 1955 to 1968. Indeed, the coefficient for the intervention term for party polarization shows that between 1955 and 1968 the Court struck down a much larger number of salient policies than in other years. This is true for both the number of policies and the estimated rate of invalidation.[38] Regardless of the measure, judicial review of state policies underwent a dramatic surge that coincided with the most intense period of partisan rivalry since the 1930s. These results are significant statistically and substantively.

Judicial review is not only related to the critial issues but the pattern of these cases over time points to an intimate connection between developments in the American party system and judicial policymaking. Similar to Supreme Court policymaking in the 1890s, the Court's exercise of judicial review, most especially over state policies, reflected and contributed to public and partisan concern. The well-known liberalism of the Warren Court cannot be ignored if we are to understand the dynamics of dealignment in the 1960s. The findings dramatically reinforce the Court's potential role in shaping the issues on which critical elections depend.

In sum, the analysis of the cases of state policy invalidations at the aggregate or macrolevel provide support for the agenda-setting role through an analysis of select cases. Through its exercise of judicial review over state legislation, the Supreme Court appears to have contributed to the policy stance of the northern liberal wing of the Democratic party. These aggregate or macrolevel results should be supplemented with data regarding the individual dynamics of the Court. This can be provided in part by an analysis of the voting records of the justices.

The Voting of the Justices, 1946–1964. There has been only one study of the internal dynamics of the Supreme Court in response to crosscutting issues (Schmidhauser, 1961). This is unfortunate because many of the previous studies of the Court and critical elections make important assumptions premised upon the relationship between the justices and the majority party. Given the paucity of studies on the Supreme Court and realignment, these assumptions are quite understandable.

Most argue that during the long stable phase of majority party dominance, the Court is composed of a majority of justices appointed by presidents of the majority party. The asserted roles for the Supreme Court before and after certain critical elections place the Court as part of the "relatively cohesive alliances that endure for long periods of time" (Dahl, 1957: 280). In broad terms, this seems clearly to be the case following the New Deal realignment of the 1930s. President Roosevelt appointed eight new justices before 1943, and President Truman followed with four additional appointments. Only two of these twelve justices were Republican. Although President Eisenhower had an opportunity to appoint five justices, Republican Chief Justice Warren, and the only Democrat appointed, Justice Brennan, eventually became two of the most liberal justices on the postwar Court.

The Democratic and liberal cast of the Court deserves more detailed analysis from the perspective of critical elections and partisan realignment. The voting records of the justices can serve as one indicator of the Court's response to new, crosscutting issues. First, these highly volatile issues may serve to divide the justices more often than in other types of cases. Second, and more important, the justices' voting may reflect partisan division on the Court consistent with the view that presidential appointments provide an important linkage between the policy views of the justices and the dominant majority party before realigning elections. Alternatively, one could argue that the justices will divide along new lines of cleavage as these new and explosive issues disrupt the traditional ideological division on the Court and more fluid or erratic coalitions develop (Gates, 1989).

The expectation of increased division among the justices in salient cases is not validated by the percentage of nonunanimous cases. In the salient cases from 1946–1964, the justices decided 50.0 percent nonunanimously. Surprisingly, over 63 percent of the nonsalient invalidation cases were also nonunanimous and over 53 percent of all cases decided with opinion had registered dissent. This finding contrasts with earlier realigning eras. In the 1896 and New Deal realignment, the salient cases were more likely to produce dissent than were other types of cases.[39]

The higher level of dissent in the nonsalient cases and all cases with opinion is perhaps due to a number of factors. One reason is the presence of a number of controversial cases that were not directly related to the critical issues of dealignment such as the demonstration and solicitation rights of religious groups.[40] Also, the dramatic role of the Court in reigniting the question of racial equality perhaps led to a desire to stand united in these matters as the public and conservatives attacked the Court. In addition, Chief Justice Warren was clearly concerned with obtaining a unanimous decision in *Brown* (Ulmer, 1971). The prominent role of the Court in race matters and Chief Justice Warren's leadership (Goldman, 1982: 418–419) may account for the lower level of dissent in the salient cases—a class of cases dominated by questions of racial equality. Nonetheless, the data do not support the proposition that the justices will divide more often in deciding to strike down a policy related to a crosscutting issue.

A second reason for examining the voting of the justices is to determine whether the justice's divide along partisan lines consistent with the view of the Court as a member of the "old regime." Given the evidence of increasing polarization and party-line voting among members of Congress (Sinclair, 1982; Brady and Stewart, 1982; Brady, 1985), it may be that the justices will polarize in a similar fashion. An examination of the dissent rates and bloc analysis may provide insight into the cleavages created by salient issues.

Table 5.4 presents the dissent rates for all justices serving on the Court between 1946 and 1964 in salient and nonsalient cases. A higher level of dissent in the salient cases represents disagreement with the liberal outcome of the salient cases. Consistent with general characterizations of the Warren Court, the justices with the higher dissent rates have generally been considered conservatives or moderates.[41] Conservative Justice Harlan has the highest dissent rate (43.2%). This is compared to low levels of dissent by the traditional liberals. Justices Earl Warren, William Douglas, and William Brennan did not cast a single dissent in any of the salient cases and Justices Hugo Black and Arthur Goldberg also dissented in very few cases. Further, the conservative justices appear to have dissented more frequently in the salient than in the nonsalient cases.

The dissent rates of the justices are consistent with ideological charac-terizations of the Court, and there is a stronger relationship between the

TABLE 5.4

Dissent Rates of the Justices in Salient
Cases of Invalidation Compared to All Cases of Invalidation,
1946-1964

Justice (Party)	Dissent Rate in Salient Invalidation Cases		Dissent Rate in All Cases of Invalidation	
	Percent	Number	Percent	Number
Harlan II, J. (R)	43.2	34	23.3	63
Stewart, J. (R)	22.0	41	10.4	48
Reed, J. (D)	18.2[a]	11	22.2	54
Burton, J. (R)	16.7[a]	12	22.6	62
Minton, J. (D)	14.3[a]	7	21.2	33
Clark, J. (D)	14.0	50	20.0	90
Whittaker, J. (R)	13.3[a]	15	12.5	24
White, J. (D)	11.1	27	10.0	30
Goldberg, J. (D)	3.8	26	15.4	26
Frankfurter, J. (D)	3.7	27	17.9	84
Black, J. (D)	1.9	53	24.5	109
Douglas, J. (D)	0.0	53	17.3	110
Brennan, J. (D)	0.0	43	0.0	57
Warren, C.J. (R)	0.0	48	7.2	69
Murphy, J. (D)	0.0[a]	3	20.0	20
Jackson, J. (R)	0.0[a]	9	12.8	47
Rutledge, J. (D)	0.0[a]	3	25.0	20
Vinson, C.J. (D)	0.0[a]	4	0.0	36

[a]Percentages computed with less than 20 cases.

Source: Compiled by author from *United States Reports.*

nominal partisan affiliations of the justices and the dissent rates than found in previous realigning eras. The correlation between the dissent rate of the justices' party is 0.589 (eta). This is the strongest evidence of partisan voting found in the four periods of realignment covered in this study.[42]

The dissent rates do not pertain to the level of agreement between justices but only to the dissenting behavior of the justices. Ideally, one should examine the changing voting blocs over time within "natural court" periods or periods of stable membership on the Court. Unfortunately, the small number of salient nonunanimous cases allows for such analysis for only the 1962–1964 period. Given available data, it is impossible to examine the possible changes in the coalitions on the Court because the critical issues increase in intensity and polarization occurs in the political parties in the years before 1964.

If we use the standard interagreement matrix based upon the proportion of pairwise agreements for each possible pair of justices (Dubois, 1980: 173–175) and a criterion for inferring a voting bloc (Sprague, 1968: 33–39), voting blocs are found in the salient cases decided between 1962–1964. These blocs remain stable using other nonlinear alignment methods (Bolner,

Feldman, and Gates, 1982). The results show there is a solid seven-justice bloc composed of Chief Justice Warren and Justices Black, Goldberg, Douglas, Brennan, Clark, and White. The remaining two justices, Republicans Potter Stewart and John Harlan, do not form a bloc. All members of the bloc are Democrats, with the exception of the Republican Earl Warren.

Hence, there is evidence of partisan voting in the salient cases. Indeed, the pre-1964 period shows a fairly cohesive Supreme Court supporting the policy stance of the liberal wing of the dominant party. This is not to suggest that the evidence is conclusive. There is some evidence that supports the view that the critical issues of realignment create new alignments on the Supreme Court. For example, Goldman (1982: 419, Table 7.3) reports that there were three voting blocs for all nonunanimous civil liberties and civil rights cases in 1962 in contrast to only two voting blocs in the salient cases handed down between 1962 and 1964. In the salient cases, Justice White's voting placed him within the strong liberal bloc. His voting in all cases of civil liberties and civil rights cases, however, placed White as a member of a moderate bloc composed of Justices Stewart and White.

Nevertheless, the strongest evidence is consistent with the agenda-setting role ascribed to the Supreme Court in times of partisan realignment. In contrast to Supreme Courts in previous realigning eras, the Warren Court demonstrated cohesiveness and ideological consistency with the majority party. In confronting the critical issues of electoral realignment, the Supreme Court was united behind a policy position that produced significant and enduring shifts in electoral support for both the Democratic and Republican parties.

CONCLUSION:
THE CRITICAL ELECTIONS OF THE 1960s

The Supreme Court's invalidation of state policies between 1946 and 1964 gives strong support to the agenda-setting role ascribed to the Court in the years before a critical election. As a member of the majority coalition during the long and stable phase of majority party dominance, the Supreme Court issued decisions dealing with the new crosscutting issues and contributed to the posture of the majority party (Adamany, 1980). On the critical issues of racial equality, the rights of criminal defendants, and school prayer, the Court invalidated state policies, which provoked partisan outcry and rejuvenated the programmatic liberal wing of the Democratic party. In a fashion similar to the period before the critical election of 1896, the invalidation of state policies in this period supports the proposition that the Court contributes to the policy stance of the majority party. Indeed, the national Democratic party and the Court stood together in a Progressive position on the critical issues in both 1960 and 1964. Moreover, in the pre-1960 period, the Supreme Court was responsible for reigniting the issue of racial equality when party leaders were attempting to silence the issue.

Analysis of the few cases nullifying federal statutes does not yield a single case related directly to the critical issues of the 1960 and 1964 elections.

Although the policy outcome of the federal cases is consistent with the liberal character of the Warren Court, the cases do not touch upon either civil rights for blacks or the social issue. The few federal cases are consistent with Dahl's (1957) analysis, which concluded that the Court was "inevitably" part of the majority coalition. The federal cases illustrate a congruence at the national level between the Court and the popularly elected branches.

Nevertheless, the Court participated in the agenda of the critical elections of 1960 and 1964 by striking down state-level policies in such cases as *Brown v. Board of Education* (1954) and *Gideon v. Wainwright* (1963). These major cases are similar to the dramatic invalidation cases before 1896 such as *Chicago, Milwaukee, and St. Paul Railway Co. v. Minnesota* (the Minnesota Rate Case) (1890). The analysis also shows that the class of salient cases underwent an abrupt and sustained increase from the mid-1950s to 1964. The Court was also more "willing" or prone to strike down all types of state and federal policies as shown by the estimated rate of invalidation. The number of state policies related directly to civil rights for blacks and the social issue increased significantly in the period surrounding the critical election and left a dramatic impact on the entire series. This sudden surge is very similar to the aggregate level findings in the pre-1896 period. In the years before the critical elections of 1896 and 1960–64, the Court's invalidation of policies related to the central issues polarizing the party system and contributed to partisan debate and controversy.

At the individual level, or microlevel, the analysis of the justices' voting responses yields somewhat mixed results. Unlike in any of the previous periods before critical elections, the justices were less likely to dissent in invalidating salient policies than in other types of cases. The percentage of nonunanimous cases related to civil rights for blacks and the social issue provoked even less dissent than the nonsalient invalidations. Chief Justice Warren's strong leadership and the collective concern for a united Court could have contributed to the lower level of dissent in the salient cases. Regardless of the reason, it is clear that the Court was more prone to unanimity in deciding the crosscutting political questions in this realigning era than in other critical election periods.

In sum, the examination of the invalidation of state and federal laws gives support to the agenda-setting role ascribed to the Court before critical elections. The Court, as a member of the national majority coalition, made important policy directly related to the issues leading to polarization and did so with increasing frequency from the mid-1950s through 1964. The Supreme Court's invalidation of state policies in the period before the critical election of 1960 illustrates vividly how judicial policy focused attention on the position of the Democratic majority party in the critical election of 1964. This period parallels the period before the critical election of 1896 when the Court struck down policies related to the demands of Populists and reformers. In each period, the Court took an extreme position by declaring salient policies unconstitutional. In the 1890s, the Court took a conservative position compared to the Progressive extremist decisions of the 1950s and early 1960s.

This agenda-setting role is evident in these two eras, but one must be cautious in generalizing this role to all realigning eras. The Court clearly contributed to the policy stance of the majority party, but it is not certain which group the Court will support within the majority party. As Sundquist (1973: 275–298) shows, crosscutting issues divide each party into three groups—moderates attempting to straddle the issue, conservative extremists arguing for no change in government policy, and Progressive extremists arguing for reform and policy changes. The Supreme Court's liberal position on the racial and social issues certainly contributed to the Progressive "extremist" position of the Democratic party. This position, however, does not appear inevitable.

The study of the justices' voting across the four critical election periods points to a more unpredictable Court, at least in its response to the crosscutting issues. Only one period (1962–1964) saw strict, party-line voting, and there is some evidence of changing coalitions. Moreover, although the Court was composed primarily of Democratic justices appointed by Democratic presidents, the liberal bloc contained two Republican appointments, Chief Justice Warren and Associate Justice Brennan. Most important, the appointments by Democratic and Republican presidents in the precritical election period were unlikely to be made on the basis of the justices' probable response to issues most party leaders were attempting to avoid, straddle, or silence. Indeed, it was the Supreme Court that reintroduced the important and explosive issue of racial equality after moderates in the Democratic party had sought to downplay the issue.

As Dahl (1957) noted, the Supreme Court can make important policy when the majority coalition is unstable. It is not clear, however, that Court policymaking will inevitably support one particular wing of the party or whether it will follow a new course. It is evident that the Supreme Court has often made important policy related to the critical issues and helped to posture the majority party in the critical elections.

In contributing to the agenda on which critical elections depend, the Court's impact on national policymaking may be much greater at certain junctures in American history than originally suggested by Dahl (1957). At least through its power to declare state statutes and constitutional provisions unconstitutional, the Supreme Court contributed to a reshuffling of voter allegiance and long-term support for the major political parties. From its historic desegregation decision to decisions relating to criminal justice and school prayer, the Supreme Court reinforced the perception of a liberal national Democratic party and national government—a position that led to a major and durable redistribution of electoral support for the major parties.

NOTES

1. *Bob-Lo Excursion Co. v. Michigan,* 333 U.S. 28 (1948); *Shelley v. Kraemer,* 334 U.S. 1 (1948).

2. *Greyhound Lines v. Mealey,* 334 U.S. 653 (1948); *Norton Co. v. Dept. of Revenue,* 340 U.S. 534 (1951); *Richfield Oil Corp. v. State Board,* 329 U.S. 69 (1946).

3. E.g., *Spector Motor Service v. O'Connor*, 340 U.S. 602 (1951); *Memphis Steam Laundry v. Stone*, 342 U.S. 389 (1952); *Railway Express Agency v. Virginia*, 347 U.S. 359 (1954).

4. E.g., *Michigan-Wisconsin Pipe Line Co. v. Calvert*, 347 U.S. 157 (1954); *Miller Bros. Co. v. Maryland*, 347 U.S. 340 (1954); *Society for Savings v. Bowers*, 349 U.S. 143 (1955); *Federal Land Bank v. Kiowa County*, 368 U.S. 146 (1961); *United States v. Union Central Life Ins. Co.*, 368 U.S. 291 (1961); *State Board of Ins. v. Todd Shipyards*, 370 U.S. 451 (1962); *Halliburton Oil Well Co. v. Reily*, 373 U.S. 64 (1963).

5. E. g., *First Iowa Hydro-Electric Corp. v. FPC*, 328 U.S. 152 (1946); *Rice v. Sante Fe Elevator Corp.*, 331 U.S. 218 (1947); *Hood and Sons v. DuMond*, 336 U.S. 525 (1949); *Paul v. United States*, 371 U.S. 245 (1963); *Sears, Roebuck & Co. v. Stiffel Co.*, 376 U.S. 225 (1964).

6. E.g., *Bethlehem Steel Co. v. New York Employment Relations Board*, 330 U.S. 767 (1947); *La Crosse Tel. Corp. v. WERB*, 336 U.S. 18 (1949); *United Automobile Workers v. O'Brien*, 339 U.S. 454 (1950); *Guss v. Utah Labor Board*, 353 U.S. 1 (1957); *Teamsters Union v. Oliver*, 358 U.S. 283 (1959); *DeVries v. Baumgartner's Electric Co.*, 359 U.S. 498 (1959); *Marine Engineers v. Interlake Co.*, 370 U.S. 173 (1962); *Waxman v. Virginia*, 371 U.S. 4 (1962); *Construction Laborers v. Curry*, 371 U.S. 542 (1963); *Journeymen and Plumbers' Union v. Borden*, 373 U.S. 690 (1962); *Iron Workers v. Perko*, 373 U.S. 701 (1963).

7. E.g., *Marsh v. Alabama*, 326 U.S. 501 (1967); *Tucker v. Texas*, 326 U.S. 517 (1946); *Torasco v. Watkins*, 367 U.S. 488 (1961); *Bus Employees v. Missouri*, 374 U.S. 74 (1963); *Sherbet v. Verner*, 374 U.S. 398 (1963); *Chamberlin v. Dade County Board of Public Instruction*, 377 U.S. 402 (1964).

8. E.g., *Winters v. New York*, 333 U.S. 507 (1948); *Joseph Burstyn, Inc. v. Wilson*, 343 U.S. 495 (1952); *Butler v. Michigan*, 352 U.S. 380 (1957); *Speiser v. Randall*, 357 U.S. 513 (1958); *Kingsley Pictures Corp. v. Regents*, 360 U.S. 684 (1959); *Marcus v. Search Warrant*, 367 U.S. 717 (1961); *Cramp v. Board of Public Institution*, 368 U.S. 278 (1961); *A Quantity of Copies of Books v. Kansas*, 378 U.S. 205 (1964).

9. E. g., *Wieman v. Updegraff*, 344 U.S. 183 (1952); *Pennsylvania v. Nelson*, 350 U.S. 497 (1956); *Baggett v. Bullitt*, 377 U.S. 360 (1964).

10. E.g., *Dameron v. Brodhead*, 345 U.S. 322 (1953).

11. E.g., *United States v. Louisiana*, 339 U.S. 699 (1950); *United States v. Texas*, 339 U.S. 707 (1950); *United States v. California*, 332 U.S. 19 (1947).

12. E.g., *Wissner v. Wissner*, 338 U.S. 655 (1950).

13. E.g., *Seaboard R. Co. v. Daniel*, 333 U.S. 118 (1948); *Toomer v. Witsell*, 334 U.S. 385 (1948).

14. The two remaining pre-1954 race cases are *Morgan v. Virginia*, 328 U.S. 373 (1946), voiding a Virginia statute requiring segregation on motor buses, and *Schnell v. Davis*, 336 U.S. 933 (1949), voiding an Alabama constitutional provision giving unlimited authority to election officials in determining the successful completion of the state's literacy test for voting.

15. *Gayle v. Browder*, 352 U.S. 903 (1956).

16. *State Athletic Commission v. Dorsey*, 359 U.S. 533 (1959).

17. *Bailey v. Patterson*, 369 U.S. 31 (1962).

18. *Turner v. City of Memphis*, 369 U.S. 350 (1962).

19. *Faubus v. Aaron*, 361 U.S. 197 (1959); *Bush v. Orleans School Board*, 364 U.S. 500 (1961); *Tugwell v. Bush*, 367 U.S. 907 (1961); *Legislature of Louisiana v. United States*, 367 U.S. 908 (1961); *St. Helena Parish School Board v. Hall*, 368 U.S. 515 (1962).

20. E.g., *Boynton v. Virginia*, 364 U.S. 454 (1960); *Peterson v. City of Greenville*, 373 U.S. 244 (1963); *Wright v. Georgia*, 373 U.S. 284 (1963); *Gober v. City of Birmingham*, 373 U.S. 374 (1963).

21. E.g., *Shelton v. Tucker*, 364 U.S. 479 (1960); *Louisiana v. NAACP ex rel. Gremillion*, 366 U.S. 293 (1961).

22. *NAACP v. Button*, 371 U.S. 415 (1963).

23. There is also one case involving a Virginia miscegenation statute voided in *McLaughlin v. Florida*, 379 U.S. 184 (1964).

24. *Anderson v. Martin*, 375 U.S. 399 (1964).

25. *Tancil v. Woolls* and *Virginia Board of Elections v. Hamm*, 379 U.S. 19 (1964).

26. *Gomillion v. Lightfoot*, 364 U.S. 339 (1960).

27. E.g., *Martin v. Bush*, 376 U.S. 222 (1964); *Maryland Committee for Fair Representation v. Tawes*, 377 U.S. 656 (1964); *Wesberry v. Sanders*, 376 U.S. 1 (1964); *Reynolds v. Sims*, 377 U.S. 533 (1964).

28. The policies involved in the reapportionment decisions were indirectly related to the salient issues; that is, apportionment schemes overturned by the Court were enacted primarily to preserve rural as opposed to urban power in state politics. In combination with explicit state attempts at racial gerrymandering, black groups such as the NAACP lobbied for the overturn of these policies. Participating through amici in many cases relating to reapportionment, these groups viewed the demands for reapportionment favorably given the high concentration of black voters in under-represented urban centers (Claude, 1970: 149–169).

29. *Eskridge v. Washington Prison Bd.*, 357 U.S. 214 (1958).

30. *Lane v. Brown*, 372 U.S. 477 (1963).

31. *Ferguson v. Georgia*, 365 U.S. 570 (1961).

32. *Robinson v. California*, 370 U.S. 660 (1962).

33. *Kennedy v. Mendoza-Martinez*, 372 U.S. 144 (1963).

34. *United States v. Lovett*, 328 U.S. 303 (1946).

35. *Schneider v. Rusk*, 377 U.S. 163 (1964).

36. The author appreciates the funding of the Committee on Research of the Davis Division of the Academic Senate of the University of California, which allowed for extension of the content analysis of issue saliency.

37. This is quite consistent with Sundquist (1973) and with Ginsberg's "index of critical conflict," which is based on a content analysis of party platforms (1972: 619–620).

38. The number of salient policies overturned by the Supreme Court is an event count. Some argue that the most precise estimation strategy is Poisson regression (King, 1989) as opposed to some variant of least-squares regression. Poisson estimates of the equation for the total number of salient policies yield estimates that are very similar to those provided by least-squares regression: constant (b = −0.685; S.E. = 0.808); Time 1 (b = 0.1117; S.E. = 0.1115); Time 2 (b = −0.052; S.E. = 0.123); and R_t (b = 0.900; S.E. = 0.269).

If one is willing to make certain debatable assumptions, poisson regression may also be applied to the estimated rate of invalidation. Poisson estimates of the equation for the estimated rate of invalidation also yields very similar estimates compared to the least-squares estimates: constant (b = −2.262; S.E. = 1.748); Time 1 (b = 0.122; S.E. = 0.240); Time 2 (b = −0.065; S.E. = 0.265); and R_t (b = 0.879; S.E. = 0.572).

39. This figure is computed from data in the *Harvard Law Review*, volumes 68–79, issue no. 1 of each volume.

40. E.g., *Aptheker v. Secretary of State*, 378 U.S. 500 (1964); *Torasco v. Watkins*, 367 U.S. 488 (1961).

41. The few number of salient cases decided by the Vinson Court does yield a few unstable percentages for some justices.

42. Ulmer (1986) presents evidence that social background models of judicial decisionmaking may be time-bound. The political party of judges is often a key variable in such models. He found in an examination of the justices' percentage of support for the government that social background indicators could account for 72.3 percent of the variation in the justices' support for the government's position in the 1936–1968 period. The same indicators, however, could account for only 18.4 percent of the variation in the 1903–1935 period.

6

Toward an Understanding of the Supreme Court and Partisan Realignment

The ultimate function of the Supreme Court is nothing less than the arbitration between fundamental and ever-present rival forces or trends in our organized society.

—Robert H. Jackson
The Struggle for Judicial Supremacy

Critical realignment . . . drastically reshuffles the coalitional bases of the two parties, but it does far more than this. It constitutes a political decision of the first magnitude and a turning point in the mainstream of national policy formation. Characteristically, the relationships among policymaking institutions, their relative power and decisionmaking capacity, and the policy outputs they produce are profoundly affected by critical realignments. . . . [C]ritical realignment may well be regarded as America's surrogate for revolution.

—Walter Dean Burnham
Critical Elections and the Mainsprings of American Politics

Realignment of the American party system is provocative for students of democratic societies. Partisan realignment signals clear linkages between elections, institutions, and public policy. Scholars continue to uncover the precise dynamics of these linkages (Brady, 1985: 28–29; e.g., McDonald and Rabinowtz, 1987); there are clear and significant connections between electoral change, congressional policymaking, and the broad contours of national policymaking.

The linkages between Supreme Court policymaking and partisan realignment are less straightforward. The evidence drawn from the cases of judicial review of state and federal policies at the aggregate level as well as the evidence of individual or microlevel behavior does not consistently support either the policy conflict role following critical elections or the agenda-setting role before critical elections. Before summarizing the macro- and microlevel findings and the roles most commonly ascribed to the Supreme

Court, it is important to examine briefly how the wider range of cases covered in this study enhances the importance of the Supreme Court as a national policy maker. Dahl (1957), in his analysis of the role of the Supreme Court in national policymaking, concluded that the role of the Supreme Court is to legitimize the policies of the popularly elected branches based upon his analysis of judicial review of federal statutes. According to Dahl, the main "task of the Court is to confer legitimacy on the fundamental policies" of the "enduring alliances" at the national level (1957: 291, 294). It appears, however, that a wider range of evidence supports a much broader and more complex impact on national policymaking. If realignments are the fundamental means of "tension management" as Burnham (1970:10) argues, then Supreme Court policymaking is much more important to the course of national politics than portrayed by Dahl's classic analysis.

THE SUPREME COURT AS A NATIONAL POLICYMAKER AND JUDICIAL REVIEW OF STATE POLICIES

Previous studies of the Supreme Court and realignment have focused on either an interpretative analysis of select, yet major, decisions or a more precise accounting through an analysis of the cases overturning federal statutes. Funston (1975), for example, limited his test of the policy conflict thesis to only decisions overturning recently enacted federal statutes. He reasoned, for example, that these policies were the acts of current or contemporary majorities. Unfortunately, recently enacted federal statutes are only a partial indicator of Supreme Court policymaking (e.g., Casper, 1976). Party leaders may consider older statutes salient or important to the scope of partisan conflict, such as the Missouri Compromise of 1820, which was overturned in *Dred Scott* (1857) (Casper, 1976; Schattschneider, 1975).

Further, important and politically salient policymaking is evident in several other types of cases, most especially the cases overturning state policies. Indeed, the preceding chapters show how excluding the hundreds of cases striking down state policies is troublesome for several reasons. First, state legislatures were the primary forums for most economic legislation until the early part of the twentieth century (Friedman, 1973; Keller, 1977). These issues were central to realignment in the 1890s and 1930s.

Second, policies enacted by partisan majorities at the state level often provoke a national response when the policies deal with realigning issues or simply with volatile political issues (Gates, 1987; 1989; Lasser, 1983). The Court's invalidation of state policies repeatedly alarms party leaders in Congress (e.g., Murphy, 1972; Goldman, 1982: 527–574).[1] The issues provoking congressional attacks on the Supreme Court in the last twenty-five years, for example, include school prayer, school desegregation, and abortion. Indeed, the most recent decisions provoking national attention by the Supreme Court related to cases involving state, and not federal, legislation (i.e., abortion). In the period studied, judicial review of state policies either began or prolonged partisan controversy, and this occurred either through a dramatic decision or a series of decisions whose cumulative impact was to posture the Supreme Court in the partisan struggle.

In sum, analysis of the state cases reinforces Casper's critique of Dahl's thesis that the Court merely reinforces the position of the majority. These cases show that it is important to consider a wider range of evidence than the much debated and oft-cited cases overturning federal statutes. The following sections summarize and highlight how the aggregate and individual analyses of the cases of state policy invalidation illuminate the Supreme Court as an important national policymaker when approached from the perspective of partisan realignment.

Unconstitutional State Policies
and the Crosscutting Issues of Realignment

The importance of the cases invalidating state policies is perhaps most clear in the content analysis of the political issues raised in these cases. A substantial portion of the cases invalidating state policies raised the salient political and legal issues that disrupted party systems and set the tone of political debate in the ensuing decades. In some periods, the salient cases were a substantial majority of the policies struck down by the Supreme Court. Table 6.1 is a summary of the results of the content analysis of the state and federal cases across the four periods of realignment. The first column displays the number of salient cases by different realigning eras. This tabular summary shows vividly how the Supreme Court often overturned state laws connected to the political issues that realigned the American party system.

In the Civil War era, the issues included slavery, the Civil War, and Reconstruction. In the Second Republican era, the salient issues were the government's proper role in regulating economic interests and the economy. Similar types of issues provoked partisan division during the onslaught of the Great Depression and the New Deal realignment. The issues of racial equality, counter-cultural "lifestyles," and the rights of criminal defendants produced the final period of electoral "dealignment."

Of the seventy-two state policies declared unconstitutional in the Civil War era (1837–1878), only eight, or 11.1 percent, raised critical issues. As Caldeira and McCrone (1982: 115–121) showed, however, judicial review was nonsystematic before the Civil War. Therefore, judicial review of state policies may not be a suitable indicator of Court policymaking and critical elections in this era. Following the war, judicial review of state policies became much more commonplace or "institutionalized" (Polsby, 1968).

In the three remaining periods of electoral realignment, judicial review often centered on the critical issues. During the Second Republican party era (1879–1910), the divisive issues of government control of economic interests, the money supply, and labor rights were at the center of this major electoral change (Sundquist, 1973). Throughout the period, a solid majority of Republican and conservative justices sat on the Court. The Supreme Court's invalidation of state policies during this period reflected

TABLE 6.1

The Number of Salient and Nonsalient Cases of
Federal and State Policy Invalidation
1837-1964

Period	Salient		Nonsalient		Total	
Civil War Era						
(1837-1878)						
State Policies	8	(11.1%)	64	(88.9%)	72	(100.0%)
Federal Policies	4	(36.3%)	7	(63.7%)	11	(100.0%)[a]
Second Republican Era						
(1879-1910)						
State Policies	81	(72.3%)	31	(27.7%)	112	(100.0%)
Federal Policies	2	(10.5%)	17	(89.5%)	19	(100.0%)[a]
New Deal Era						
(1911-1945)						
State Policies	183	(56.7%)	140	(43.3%)	323	(100.0%)
Federal Policies	17	(48.6%)	18	(51.4%)	35	(100.0)%
Dealignment						
(1946-1964)						
State Policies	58	(35.6%)	105	(64.4%)	163	(100.0%)
Federal Policies	5	(62.5%)	3	(37.5%	8	(100.0%)[a]
TOTAL						
State Policies	330		340		670	
Federal Policies	28		45		73	

Source: Library of Congress (1978) and *United States Reports.*

the realigning political questions. Between 1879 and 1910, the Court struck down 112 state policies; 72.3 percent related to business regulation and taxation as well as to the repudiation of municipal bond indebtedness.[2] In short, when the Court struck down state policies in this era, the policies were usually state attempts to control economic interests.

The Supreme Court's invalidation of state policies from 1911 to 1932 also dealt with the salient question of government management of the economy. The Supreme Court struck down 248 state statutes or constitutional provisions. The majority of these statutes (59.3%) dealt with the regulation and taxation of businesses.[3] In addition, the Court struck down twenty state policies favorable to labor interests or labor unions.[4] In sum, 135 cases, or 54.2 percent, were salient to the basic question of government management. These cases illustrate an unwillingness by the conservative Court to depart from the Republican party's traditional laissez-faire position.

Following 1932, the Supreme Court initially upheld New Deal legislation and similar state policies. In 1935 and 1936, however, the Court struck down several New Deal statutes. In several cases, the Court also moved against liberal domestic policies aimed at regulating the economy. The Supreme Court struck down ninety-one state policies between 1933 and 1945. Of these, thirty-seven involved business regulation and taxation.[5] These cases contributed to the growing concern over the Court's attempt to block Democratic policies controlling economic interests and the economic crisis.

The 1960s witnessed electoral realignment because there was a durable and significant redistribution of partisan support (McMichael and Trilling, 1980: 23). The issues included civil rights for blacks and the "social issue." The social issue encompassed a diffuse set of concerns including rising crime, perceived lawlessness, liberal domestic programs, and matters of lifestyle (Scammon and Wattenberg, 1970). In sum, Supreme Court policymaking, as gauged by judicial review of state policies, is clearly connected to the forces of realignment.

Unconstitutional State Policies and the Partisan Character of State Legislatures

Not only is the overturn of state policies often related to the underlying political questions of realignment but the partisan composition of the states enacting the unconstitutional policies illustrates how the Supreme Court was viewed as an important actor that would perhaps be responsive to certain types of claims. The state policies were usually enacted by state legislatures whose partisan composition or regional location conflicted ideologically with the partisan majority on the Court. The findings from the period surrounding the critical election of 1896 serve as an excellent reminder of this fact.

Of the salient policies overturned by the Supreme Court between 1879 and 1910, 50.0 percent were enacted by Democratic states in the West and solid South. Further, the Republican states in the Midwest were the source of an additional eighteen, or 28.1 percent, of the salient policies. The states in this region—Indiana, Illinois, Minnesota, Michigan, and Nebraska—had moderate to strong Populist movements (Swindler, 1969: 61–68; Mowry, 1958). In short, 78.1 percent of the policies that raised the central political question in this period of electoral realignment were enacted by states controlled by a party opposed to the dominant majority on the Court or from regions that evidenced ideological incongruence with the national party. The large percentage of salient invalidations stands out in contrast to the percentage of all states classified as ideologically opposed to the Court. Over the entire period, 58.4 percent of all states were either Democratic or midwestern Republican states. In sum, a disproportionate number of the ideological dissimilar states enacted the salient state policies.

The pattern of invalidations across the states and by region illuminates the importance of the mobilization of the law by societal interests affected by the most pressing issues of the day. Given the Supreme Court's passive agenda, individuals, groups, and governmental interests must approach the

Supreme Court before it can decide a policy question. Political "losers" in the state political system may expand the scope of conflict over realigning issues through appeal to the more favorable federal court system. This is a real possibility given the pattern of appeals and the type of litigants in the salient cases. During the period when judicial review became "institutionalized" or a regular part of the Court's agenda (1860–1900), only 11.3 percent of business litigants who were eventually successful in their pleas before the U.S. Supreme Court had received favorable rulings by their respective state supreme courts. These figures are in sharp contrast to the 80 percent victory rate of government litigants before the states' highest courts. In addition, 73.3 percent of all litigants invoking federal jurisdiction for the original trial were nongovernmental interests. Indeed, of the salient cases appealed from the state court of last resort, government interests appealed only 3.6 percent of the cases, and in cases where the original trial court was federal, the government appealed only 12.2 percent (p > 0.001).

Interests who confront hostile state governments mobilized into the federal court system and in the process expanded the scope of conflict over the most pressing partisan issues of the period. The increasing frequency of judicial review of state policies appears dependent upon legal mobilization by private and organized interests. Although after 1925 the Court could deny such appeals, it is evident that taking into account the political "losers" at the state level may be crucial for understanding Supreme Court policymaking in periods of partisan realignment. Understanding legal mobilization during party polarization and realignment could be an important avenue for future research.

This portrayal of the importance of legal mobilization awaits more rigorous confirmation, but the available data are consistent with the thesis that those who received unfavorable outcomes from their state court system were willing to bring their claims to the Supreme Court—an institution they perceived as a more favorable judicial forum. In much the same vein, the factors underlying legal mobilization could provide insight into the increasing incidence of judicial review of state policies in the late nineteenth century. Given available evidence, it may be most appropriate to view the institutionalization of judicial review as a dynamic process wherein each invalidation sent important messages to societal interests who were in a situation similar to that of former (and now successful) plaintiffs. There are several reasons to suggest that these speculations on the growth in judicial review may have merit.

First, each invalidation on salient issues sent important cues to potential litigants on the probability that certain types of state policies would receive a veto by the Supreme Court. Individuals, organized interests, and the legal community are attentive to recent decisions and trends. Research on contemporary interest-group litigation, for example, shows how Supreme Court decisions are important signals in group litigation. Groups often seek judge-made policy as an end in itself (O'Connor, 1980; Epstein, 1985) as well as for advancing their agenda before other institutions (McIntosh, 1985) or their constituency (Vose, 1981; Gates and McIntosh, 1990). In so doing, the litigation strategy is often dependent on cues taken from the Court's earlier decisions.

Second, this interpretation of the institutionalization of judicial review is bolstered by historical studies that argue that Supreme Court decisions are important signals to those seeking judicial remedies. This is especially evident in the economic field in the late nineteenth century (e.g., Warren, 1932; Twiss, 1942). The rise of substantive due process, for example, was a major doctrinal development that advertised the Supreme Court's laissez-faire posture. As Twiss (1942) persuasively shows, the Court's decisions were crucial in the development of group strategy and subsequent Supreme Court litigation during the late nineteenth century.

How and why societal interests decide to expand the scope of conflict during realignment into the courts is an exciting area for future research. Indeed, much work remains on these dynamics including the response of the attentive public to Supreme Court decisions relating to the critical issues. It is important to examine how cases come before the Court, the factors associated with the decision to litigate, and how the Court's decisions affect the public, opinion leaders, and party leaders. The dynamics of mobilizing the legal system to expand the scope of political conflict is important.[6] Although scattered historical accounts exist (e.g., Westin, 1953; Lasser, 1983), there is a need to understand more precisely the dynamics between legal mobilization, Supreme Court policymaking, and partisan realignment.

Despite these speculations and gaps in our knowledge, the presence of the realigning issues on the Supreme Court's agenda and the partisan origin of these salient cases demonstrate rather conclusively the merits of Casper's (1976) argument that an analysis of the Supreme Court as a national policymaker cannot be limited to judicial review of federal statutes. The analysis results of the state policies struck down by the Court are in direct opposition to Dahl's characterization of the Court as a weak institution limited to upholding the policies of the dominant coalition and providing regime legitimacy (1957: 291, 294).[7]

The state cases establish a Court intimately engaged with the political process. Moreover, the salient cases are not limited to regional or local issues but deal with the fundamental political questions disrupting and realigning the American party system. Once judicial review of state policies became a common feature of the Court's agenda following the Civil War, the cases frequently touched upon issues with national consequences (e.g., Westin, 1953). Casper's (1976: 60) observations on Dahl's limited portrayal of Court policymaking is particularly apt: "[I]f we are to identify the crucial participants in the policy-development process, to minimize the role of the Court, as Dahl is inclined to do, provides a view of policymaking that does not do justice to the potential or actual contributions of the Court."

Once we have shown that the evidence of state policy invalidation enhances the scope and importance of Supreme Court policymaking, it is necessary to examine the implications for the two most common roles ascribed to the Court during partisan realignment. The following section is a summary and assessment of the evidence on whether the pattern of these important cases consistently supports either an agenda-setting role before critical elections or a policy conflict role following certain critical elections.

The Policy Conflict and Agenda-Setting Roles

The focus of almost every analysis of the Supreme Court and realignment has been on determining a clear, consistent, and empirically verifiable role for the Supreme Court either before or immediately following critical elections. Funston (1975) asserted, for example, that policy conflict is most probable during the "lag" between the election of a new party and the point in time when this party appoints a majority of like-minded justices.[8] Earlier studies found only partial support for the policy conflict role following critical elections (i.e., the New Deal period; see Adamany, 1973).

Expanding the scope of Supreme Court policymaking to the universe of cases invalidating state policies provides little additional evidence of such a role except during the New Deal period. The evidence is quite simply mixed that the Supreme Court will make policy in conflict with a new majority party following a critical election. The evidence of conflict following the critical election of 1932 is unequivocal: The Supreme Court struck down thirteen provisions of New Deal legislation and provoked a Supreme Court crisis comparable to the reaction to *Dred Scott*. Some have also found evidence of conflict following the critical election of 1860 (e.g., Adamany, 1973: 831–836). But the evidence of conflict with a new majority party is not conclusive and the old Scottish verdict of "not proved" remains true even after expanding the range of Supreme Court policymaking to include the cases of state policy invalidation.

Another line of research focuses on Supreme Court policymaking before critical elections (Westin, 1953; Adamany, 1980). These studies examine whether Court policymaking shapes the majority party position on the crosscutting issues upon which polarization and realignment depend. Before critical elections, the Supreme Court is presumed to be a firm and reliable ally of the majority party because of numerous appointments by the majority party. The premiere example is *Dred Scott v. Sanford* (1857), a decision that is generally viewed as pivotal to the onslaught of war and realignment in the 1860s.[9]

In sum, some argue that the Supreme Court is an ally of the majority party before critical elections. During this period, the Supreme Court will often help shape the majority party's position on the critical issues (Adamany, 1980). It is, however, very difficult to ascribe a consistent role to Supreme Court policymaking across all realignments. The Supreme Court played different roles in the four periods of electoral realignment from 1837 to 1964. In several periods, the Court proved to be an important actor during transformations in the party system. Before 1860, 1896, and 1964, for example, the Supreme Court handed down several decisions that fueled partisan debate and controversy on the realigning questions. In *Dred Scott* (1857), the Court declared the Missouri Compromise of 1820 unconstitutional and limited congressional power to regulate slavery in the territories. This major pronouncement drastically reduced the constitutional options for reconciliation or compromise between Democrats and Republicans.

Before the critical election of 1896, the Supreme Court also enlarged the scope of conflict in several decisions. In 1895, for example, the Court handed down three major cases dealing with the realigning question of government control of economic interests. The Court restricted the scope of the Sherman Antitrust Act in *U.S. v. E.C. Knight Co.* (1895) (Westin, 1953). In addition, the conservative and Republican Supreme Court further polarized the party system as it struck down a Democratic-Populist income tax. The Court also effectively used the Sherman Antitrust Act as a legal tool for obstructing labor picketing.[10] Moreover, in a series of decisions invalidating state policies, the Supreme Court restricted state power over economic interests. These included cases central to the development of substantive due process[11] as well as restrictions on state business regulation and taxation.[12] In sum, the Supreme Court struck down several state and selected federal laws that contributed to the Republican party's conservative position. In these decisions, the Court reinforced the laissez-faire stance of the Republican party before the critical election of 1896.

This important role of shaping the majority party's response to the critical issues before realignment is less clear in the years preceding 1932. Although the Court continued a "return to normalcy" following the challenges of progressivism, the New Deal realignment was the result of the dramatic and sudden Great Depression. Supreme Court policymaking did reinforce the conservative, laissez-faire position of the Republicans, but there were no cases similar to either *Dred Scott, Pollock,* or *Brown* that served to rally partisan forces on the basic question. It was not until the clash between the Court and the Democratic party in 1934 and 1935 that partisan passions were aroused. Indeed, in 1934, the Court gave a signal that it might uphold the innovative New Deal measures in *Nebbia v. New York* (1934).

In contrast to the pre-1932 period, the Supreme Court was fundamental in contributing to the majority party's posture before the dealignment of the 1960s. The Court's decisions on racial equality and the rights of criminal defendants disaffected southern Democrats, and these issues became part of the debate in the presidential campaign of 1964 (Campbell, 1977; Adamany, 1980). From the desegregation ruling of *Brown v. Board of Education* (1954) to its mandate of state enforcement of the exclusionary rule in *Mapp v. Ohio* (1961), the Supreme Court publicized the position of the most liberal wing of the Democratic party, a position that would soon change the coalitions of the Democratic party, most especially in the South. Supreme Court policymaking contributed to the posture of majority parties before *some* critical elections. This is not an inevitable role, however, as the period before the New Deal shows. In sum, the Supreme Court's policy decisions do not consistently demonstrate either an agenda-setting or a conflict role surrounding critical elections and realignment, albeit the data point more often to an agenda-setting role than to the widely heralded policy conflict thesis.

Aggregate data on the Court's policy outputs are important but do not provide insights into the individual-level behavior that may account for the aggregate-level findings. The microlevel evidence presented in earlier chapters provides considerable insight into the reasons for the mixed results in support of either an agenda-setting or policy conflict role.

The Voting of the Justices on Realigning Issues

In addition to an analysis of the timing and issues raised by the Supreme Court's exercise of judicial review, this study has also been an examination of the individual, or microlevel, behavior of the justices in these cases. Two questions guided the analysis. First, would the justices divide more often in cases raising the crosscutting realigning issues than in other types of cases? Second, to what extent do the partisan affiliations of the justices structure their votes in cases raising the critical issues? These questions are important because of the underlying assumptions of both the agenda-setting and policy conflict roles. Dahl (1957: 293) wrote: "The Supreme Court is inevitably a part of the dominant national alliance." He argues that the Supreme Court shares the policy perspectives of the popularly elected branches because presidents of the majority party have many opportunities to appoint like-minded justices. The Court will be a supportive ally of the prevailing majority coalition during the "enduring alliances" or party eras. Underlying this perspective are important assumptions about how the individual justices will behave. Adamany (1973: 824–825) notes: "Command of the Court by men of the old majority, slow turnover on the bench, and the added reluctance of justices to resign after a new lawmaking majority is inaugurated all set the stage for conflict between the Supreme Court and the new, dominant electoral coalitions."[13]

Other analysts share Dahl's perspective. These analysts, however, have sought a more precise understanding of the role of Supreme Court policymaking *before* critical elections. Adamany (1980) and Westin (1953) argue that the Supreme Court helps shape the position of the majority party as the critical election approaches. In so doing, some of the Court's decisions contribute to the realignment agenda and party polarization. In sum, the theories regarding agenda-setting and policy conflict roles assume a fairly cohesive Court that either marches in step with the prevailing majority party before a critical election or stands as a barrier to reform following the defeat of the old majority party.

This portrayal of the Supreme Court as a solid member of the majority party before critical elections or as a proponent of the "old regime" after critical elections may be inappropriate because of the issue dynamics of partisan realignment. Realigning issues are intense and volatile and disrupt traditional lines of partisan division. The issue of slavery before 1860, for example, split the Democratic party of Jackson into northern and southern factions. The Court may not support the majority party on the realigning issues before a critical election nor will it inevitably oppose the new majority party following critical elections. This is because realigning issues divide the justices in new and uncertain ways. Unlike Congress, the Court's membership changes slowly and almost randomly (Ulmer, 1982; cf. King, 1987).[14] Moreover, the appointment of most justices is before the critical issues arise or when party leaders are attempting to silence or straddle these issues. The justices may not divide along partisan lines but may divide in new and fairly unpredictable ways as the new crosscutting issues arrive at the Court's doorstep (see especially Sundquist, 1973: 11–25; McDonald and Rabinowitz, 1987). Hence, a definitive role to Supreme Court policy-making across all periods of electoral realignment may be problematical.[15] A summary of the evidence supporting this interpretation is appropriate.

Realigning Issues and Dissent on the Supreme Court. To what extent do the salient issues divide the justices more often than in other types of cases? Table 6.2 is a summary of the number and percentage of salient cases with dissent discussed in previous chapters. The table also displays the percentage of dissent in the nonsalient invalidation cases and in all cases decided with opinion. Finally, the last column shows the percentage of total opinions with dissent in all cases. The salient policies produce greater dissent among the justices than other types of cases. In six of the seven pre- and postcritical election periods, the salient cases show the highest level of nonunanimous cases of judicial review. Between 1897 and 1945, for example, nonunanimous cases raising realigning issues range from 23.4 percent to 83.3 percent. The Court's level of dissent in all cases decided with opinion (including the salient cases) ranges from only 16.7 to 40.5 (p < 0.001).

The level of nonunanimous salient cases is not a product of solo dissents or of a persistent lone dissenter. The realigning issues divide the Supreme Court more often than other types of issues, at least based on the Court's invalidation of state policies from 1837 to 1964. In sum, the rise of critical issues promotes conflict on the Supreme Court similar to that in Congress. The data give convincing testimony to the divisiveness of issues surrounding realignment. The Court confronts volatile political issues and novel legal questions arising from the underlying socioeconomic and political change.

Partisan Voting and Realigning Issues. The justices clearly divide more often in cases dealing with the critical, realigning issues. It is also important to determine whether this division reflects partisan voting. As noted, studies of the Supreme Court's policy outputs often assume a connection between the partisan affiliation of the justices and their voting before critical elections. The question remains: To what extent do the justices' partisan affiliations structure their response to critical issues?

In this research a simple, imperfect, but intuitively appealing approach was used.[16] The justices were rank ordered based on their level of dissent in the cases dealing with the realigning issues in the period before a critical election.[17] Table 6.3 presents this rank-ordering in three periods before the critical elections of 1896, 1932, and before the 1960–1964 period. More

TABLE 6.2

Percent Nonunanimous Cases:
Salient Invalidation, Nonsalient, and All Cases with Opinion,
1837-1964

	Invalidation Cases				
Pre- & Post- *Critical Election* *Periods*	*Percent* *Nonunanimous,* *Salient Cases*		*Percent* *Nonunanimous,* *Nonsalient Cases*	*Percent* *Nonunanimous, All* *Cases With Opinion* [a]	*Percent of* *Total* *Opinions With* *Dissent* [b]
Civil War Era					
1837-1860	83.3	(6)	50.0 (8)	16.0 1840- 1860	25.4
1861-1878	80.0	(10)	26.3 (57)	10.1 (1870) 11.0 (1872- 1873)	26.6
Second					
Republican Era					
1879-1896	23.4	(47)	47.8 (23)	10.0 (1874- 1888)	16.7
1897-1910	59.5	(43)	54.5 (20)	20.0 (1888- 1910)	31.53
New Deal Era					

1911-1932	42.7	(178)	20.0 (93)	12.5 (1910-
				       1921)
				 8.5 (1921-
				       1930)
					18.8

1933-1945	53.1	(49)	33.3 (42)	20.6 (1933- 1945)	40.5
Dealignment					
1946-1964	50.0	(62)	63.4 (101)	53.2 (1946- 1964	37.28

[a]The percentage of nonunanimous decisions in all cases decided with opinion is not available by year from 1837 to 1964. Instead, the available evidence is used. The following list represents the data sources for the selected periods that appear in parantheses in the fourth column: Goldman (1982, and references cited); Halpern and Vines (1977); and the Harvard Law Review (1946-1964). In addition, Stephen Halpern provided unpublished data.
[b]See Blaustein and Mersky (1978). The cases of judicial review are not included in these figures.

Source: Cited in notes and *United States Reports.*

precise methods support this approach. Regression results of the justices' percentage of support for the case outcome with their political party is consistent with these simple dissent rates. Moreover, correlation and probit analysis of individual votes for and against the case outcome are also consistent with the dissent rates. In terms of correlation statistics, the relationship between the justices' party and their vote seldom reached 0.20 in any period before or after a critical election. The probit results using a pooled cross-sectional time series also do not support the notion of a cohesive

TABLE 6.3

Dissent Rates of the Justices in Salient
Cases of Invalidation Compared to All Cases of Invalidation,
1879-1896

Justice (Party)	Dissent Rate in Salient Invalidation Cases		Dissent Rate in All Cases of Invalidation	
	Percent	Number	Percent	Number
White, J. (D)	22.2[a]	9	18.2[a]	11
Fuller, C.J. (D)	21.0[a]	19	15.4	26
Gray, J. (R)	16.7	36	15.7	66
Brewer, J. (R)	12.5[a]	16	21.7	23
Waite, C.J. (R)	10.0	20	12.2	41
Shiras, J. (R)	10.0[a]	10	8.3[a]	12
Lamar, J. (D)	8.3[a]	12	5.3[a]	19
Bradley, J. (R)	6.5	31	8.6	57
Miller, J. (R)	3.6	28	7.4	54
Harlan, J. (R)	2.4	41	8.6	70
Field, J. (D)	00.0	41	4.3	70
Blatchford, J. (R)	00.0	27	00.0	50
Brown, J. (R)	00.0[a]	13	00.0[a]	16
Matthews, J. (R)	00.0[a]	17	00.0	35
Jackson, J. (D)	00.0[a]	6	00.0[a]	6
Peckham, J. (D)	00.0[a]	4	00.0[a]	6
Strong, J. (R)	00.0[a]	3	00.0[a]	6
Clifford, J. (D)	00.0[a]	5	11.1[a]	9
Hunt, J. (R)	00.0[a]	5	00.0[a]	9
Swayne, J. (R)	00.0[a]	3	00.0[a]	7
Woods, J. (R)	00.0[a]	14	00.0	31

and highly partisan Supreme Court in dealing with the critical issues. The probit estimates are not shown because it was not possible to obtain statistically significant relationships across all three periods of realignment. Significant results were found in two of the three periods, and these were consistent with the simple dissent rates. In every instance of statistically significant findings, the results support the simple rank-ordering in Table 6.3.

The partisan affiliations of the justices are only marginally related to the justices' voting. Democratic and Republican justices do not rank order across any precritical election period. The political party of each justice appears as a very poor predictor of the dissenting votes in cases involving the crosscutting issues surrounding electoral realignment. This casts some doubt on the plausibility of an "old regime" position for the Court's majority. The findings are most consistent with the view that partisan voting is rare on questions that cut across the party system and divide the parties along new regional and ideological lines. In each era, justices from both political parties are strong and weak supporters of the conservative and progressive positions. The results presented in Table 6.3 are not a perfect test of the "old regime"

TABLE 6.3 (Continued)

Dissent Rates of the Justices in Salient
Cases of Invalidation Compared to All Cases of Invalidation,
1911-1932

Justice (Party)	Dissent Rate in Salient Invalidation Cases		Dissent Rate in All Cases of Invalidation	
	Percent	Number	Percent	Number
Brandeis, J. (D)	40.5	111	31.3	201
Clarke, J. (E)	35.7	42	32.2	59
Cardozo, J. (D)	33.3[a]	3	20.0[a]	5
Holmes, J. (R)	23.9	142	19.7	264
Stone, C.J. (R)	23.4	47	20.5	107
Pitney, J. (R)	16.7	78	13.1	123
Sanford, J. (R)	5.9	51	4.5	111
Hughes, J. (R)	5.7	35	4.3	70
Lurton, J. (D)	5.3[a]	19	4.9	41
McReynolds, J. (D)	4.8	145	7.5	22
McKenna, J. (R)	4.1	97	3.7	159
Day, J. (R)	3.8	78	2.3	130
White, J. C.J. (D)	3.2	63	1.8	113
Lamar, J. (D)	3.1	32	1.6	64
Taft, C.J. (R)	1.5	66	1.6	125
VanDevanter, J. (R)	0.0	144	0.7	268
Sutherland, J. (R)	0.0	68	3.5	141
Butler, J. (D)	0.0	64	2.2	137
Hughes, C.J. (R)	0.0[a]	13	0.0	28
Roberts, J. (R)	0.0[a]	9	5.0	20
Harlan, J. (R)	0.0[a]	1	0.0[a]	4

hypothesis and suffer from some intractable methodological problems. Nevertheless, the findings cast considerable doubt on the thesis of a united and partisan Supreme Court before or following critical elections. Understanding Supreme Court policymaking in times of partisan realignment entails more than simply asserting that the justices are inevitably a member of the majority coalition because of presidential appointments (Dahl, 1957). This position has some support from a review of the Court's policy outputs, but individual-level data illustrate that the realigning questions are extremely volatile and crosscutting. Most important, the justices' partisan affiliations do not appear to structure the justices' responses to the realigning issue as most assume.[18]

CONCLUSION

Some argue that the Supreme Court is an ally of the majority party before critical elections. During this period, the Supreme Court will often help shape the majority party's position on the critical issues (Adamany, 1980). The second role suggests that following critical elections the Supreme

TABLE 6.3 (Continued)

Dissent Rates of the Justices in Salient
Cases of Invalidation Compared to All Cases of Invalidation,
1946-1964

Justice (Party)	Dissent Rate in Salient Invalidation Cases		Dissent Rate in All Cases of Invalidation	
	Percent	Number	Percent	Number
Harlan II, J. (R)	43.2	34	23.3	63
Stewart, J. (R)	22.0	41	10.4	48
Reed, J. (D)	18.2[a]	11	22.2	54
Burton, J. (R)	16.7[a]	12	22.6	62
Minton, J. (D)	14.3[a]	7	21.2	33
Clark, J. (D)	14.0	50	20.0	90
Whittaker, J. (R)	13.3[a]	15	12.5	24
White, J. (D)	11.1	27	10.0	30
Goldberg, J. (D)	3.8	26	15.4	26
Frankfurter, J. (D)	3.7	27	17.9	84
Black, J. (D)	1.9	53	24.5	109
Douglas, J. (D)	0.0	53	17.3	110
Brennan, J. (D)	0.0	43	0.0	57
Warren, C.J. (R)	0.0	48	7.2	69
Murphy, J. (D)	0.0[a]	3	20.0	20
Jackson, J. (R)	0.0[a]	9	12.8	47
Rutledge, J. (D)	0.0[a]	3	25.0	20
Vinson, C.J. (D)	0.0[a]	4	0.0	36

[a]Percentages computed with less than 20 cases.

Source: Compiled by author from *United States Reports.*

Court will forcefully pursue the "old regime" position, and policy conflict with the new majority party will ensue. Several studies attempted to gauge quantitatively Supreme Court policymaking and policy conflict following each critical election (Funston, 1975; cf. Canon and Ulmer, 1976). This study expanded the range of Supreme Court policymaking to include all cases invalidating state policies, and neither role appears inevitable, albeit the agenda-setting role appears most frequently. It may be very difficult to ascribe a consistent role to Supreme Court policymaking across all realignments. The Supreme Court may move in step with the voices of the majority; it may even anticipate the echo chamber of elections; or it may stand as a barrier to, or protector against, majoritarian reform.

The post–Civil War period illustrates vividly why a definitive role is difficult to ascribe to the Court during party polarization and realignment. President Lincoln appointed a new majority of Republican justices in only four years after 1860. Unlike in any other postcritical election periods, turnover was very rapid and resembled congressional turnover. Nevertheless, the Supreme Court was not a consistent supporter of either Lincoln's position or the new Republican majority party during the following years. On some issues such as the question of the constitutionality of legal tender, the Supreme Court disappointed the Lincoln administration. On other issues such as the suspension of habeas corpus, the Republican party found support among the justices.

The conduct of the Civil War was a central concern during Lincoln's fortuitous appointments to the Supreme Court between 1860 and 1864. The Civil War realignment was solidified, however, on other issues as well. These included the issues surrounding Reconstruction and the constitutional rights of the former slaves (Sundquist, 1973). These questions were not salient until after there was the new Republican majority on the Court. In making his appointments during the war, Lincoln could not anticipate how these appointed justices would respond to the complicated political and legal issues surrounding Reconstruction. Hence, the argument that the Court will stand as a barrier to realigning reforms following a critical election is problematical even when there is very rapid turnover and several new appointments by the victorious party.

Although the Court, like Congress, reflects external pressures in its policymaking, the clear and consistent linkages between policymaking and realignment found in congressional behavior are often lacking in the study of the Supreme Court. The answer may be found in the dynamics of the individual justice's responses to these issues. The data suggest a much different process at the individual justice level than at the individual Congress-member level (Gates, 1989). Indeed, the fact that the evidence does not support each role traditionally ascribed to the Court is important for understanding the differences between congressional and Supreme Court policymaking.

The reasons for congressional policy change are clear. Realigning elections produce massive turnover in Congress (Brady, 1978; Sinclair, 1982). Combined with new paths of candidate recruitment (Brady, 1978), there are many new and ideological congress members who were elected based primarily on their party's position on the critical issues. However, the membership of the Supreme Court does not change automatically with polarization and realignment. Turnover on the Court is often slow and almost random. Party polarization and realignment does not produce a new majority of justices appointed during the height of polarization over the realigning issues.[19] Moreover, presidents usually appoint justices during the stable party eras or during polarization. These justices are not recruited on the basis of their probable stance on the realigning political questions. Before the rise of critical issues, presidents most often appoint justices to represent their policy position on issues that were usually defined in the previous critical election.[20] It is impossible to predict which issues will arise and cut across the existing lines of ideological cleavage. Even when these new issues become salient, party leaders attempt to silence or downplay the issues to maintain their party's coalitions. Finally, there is little evidence that the salient issues divide the justices along partisan lines (Gates, 1989). The justices' voting in the salient cases before a critical election does not appear to represent a solid and cohesive "old regime" position. From the perspective of partisan realignment, Chief Justice Rehnquist's observation is particularly appropriate (Taylor, 1988: 9).

> History teaches us . . . that even a "strong" president determined to leave his mark on the Court, like Lincoln or Franklin Roosevelt, is apt to be only partly successful. . . . Neither the President nor his appointees can foresee what issues will come before the Court during the tenure of their appointees, and it may be that none had thought very much about these issues. Even though they agree as to the proper resolution of current issues, they may well disagree as to future cases involving other questions.

The findings reported herein support this argument. Before several critical elections, the Supreme Court moved against state majorities ideologically opposed to the Court and reinforced the position of the majority party at the national level. Following the New Deal, the Court also struck down policies of the new majorities consistent with its oft-cited role as a defender of minorities. In sum, the Supreme Court has not been a consistent defender of minorities or a dependable ally of new majorities during periods that are arguably the most majoritarian in American political history. The reasons rest on the different long- and short-term factors precipitating realignments, the constitutional detachment of the Court from electoral processes, the changing nature of issues over a justice's tenure on the Court, and the reactive nature of the Court's agenda. Several constitutional theorists point to the unique "historical" role of the Court in national policymaking (e.g., Dahl, 1957; Perry, 1982). If we approach the role question from the perspective of the democratic principles inherent in realignment processes, there is no consistent role. This adds additional difficulties to the quest for an adequate theory of the proper mode or judicial role in constitutional interpretation.[21]

Nevertheless, the pattern of cases suggests that future research may profit from exploring the similarities and differences between the Supreme Court and the popularly elected branches before and after realignment in the American party system. If Burnham is correct that realignments have "profound" effects on institutional elites, then it appears that Supreme Court policymaking is an area ripe for further investigation. The precise dynamics of socioeconomic change, legal mobilization, as well as the justices' responses must be examined with a broader class of cases than presented here. Nevertheless, Robert Jackson's (1941) observation that the ultimate role of the Supreme Court is the arbitration of "rival forces or trends" in society is especially important and intriguing from the perspective of partisan realignment. Through historical and more precise quantitative estimates, we may come to understand the role or, more likely, the roles served by the Supreme Court before and after partisan realignment.

NOTES

1. It is important to recall that these decisions may also fuel partisan controversy because the overturn of a state policy often implicitly invalidates similar policies

enacted by other states. Each case may raise partisan concerns in many states whose policies become either invalid or, at the very least, constitutionally suspect.

2. The latter was of particular concern to western farmers (Westin, 1953:17). E.g., *Pickard v. Pullman Southern Car Co.*, 117 U.S. 34 (1886); *Norfolk and Western Railway Co. v. Pennsylvania*, 136 U.S. 628 (1890); *Illinois Central Railway v. Illinois*, 163 U.S. 142 (1896); *Mobile v. Watson*, 116 U.S. 289 (1886); *Chicago, Milwaukee, and St. Paul Railway Co. v. Minnesota*, 134 U.S. 418 (1890); *Wabash St. Louis and Pacific Railway Co. v. Illinois*, 118 U.S. 557, (1886); *Smyth v. Ames*, 169 U.S. 466 (1898); *Ohio v. Thomas*, 173 U.S. 176 (1899); *Louisville and Nashville Railway Co. v. Eubank* (1902); *Schollenberger v. Pennsylvania*, 171 U.S. 1 (1898); *Lochner v. New York*, 198 U.S. 45 (1905); *St. Louis S.W. Railway v. Arkansas*, 217 U.S. 136 (1910).

3. E.g., *New York Life Insurance Co. v. Dodge*, 246 U.S. 357 (1918); *Wolff Packing Co. v. Industrial court*, 262 U.S. 522 (1923); *Ottinger v. Consolidated Gas Co,*, 272 U.S. 576 (1926); *Ribnick v. McBride*, 277 U.S. 350 (1928).

4. E.g., *Connally v. General Construction Co.*, 296 U.S. 587 (1926); *Frost Trucking Co. v. Railroad Commission*, 271 U.S. 583 (1926); *United States v. Reynolds*, 235 U.S. 933 (1914).

5. E.g., *Morehead v. New York ex rel. Tipaldo*, 298 U.S. 587 (1936); *Baldwin v. G.A.F. Seelig*, 294 U.S. 511 (1935); *Mayflower Farms v. Ten Eyck*, 297 U.S. 266 (1936).

6. As Zemans (1983) argues, research in judicial politics has been concerned primarily with the decisions and their impact on societal interests rather than focused on how the activities of both private individuals and organized interests relate to court decisions (but see Peltason, 1955; Epstein, 1985; Gates and McIntosh, 1990).

7. Dahl (1957:294) noted, however, that the Supreme Court can engage in controversial and important policymaking when the national coalition is divided. This is, according to Dahl, extremely risky for the institution's power to legitimate.

8. This is a restatement of Funston's thesis as corrected by Beck (1976).

9. Although the aggregate analysis extends previous analyses, it is important to note some of the limitations of the time-series analysis. Most important, it was not possible to obtain a rate of invalidation for salient or nonsalient issue areas. Ideally, the rate measure would gauge the propensity to overturn policies using yearly data on the number of challenges to policies in each issue area. Instead, only a measure of the Court's workload was used as a control variable. This has several disadvantages as discussed in detail in Appendix B.

10. *Pollock v. Farmer's Loan and Trust Co.*, 157 U.S. 429 (1895). *In re Debs*, 58 U.S. 564 (1895).

11. E.g., *Chicago, Milwaukee, and St. Paul Railway Co. v. Minnesota*, 134 U.S. 418 (1890).

12. E.g., *Pickard v. Pullman Southern Car Co.*, 117 U.S. 34 (1886); *Norfolk and Western Railway Co. v. Pennsylvania*, 136 U.S. 114 (1890); *Mobile and Ohio Railroad v. Tennessee*, 153 U.S. 486 (1894); *New York, L.E. and W. Railroad Co. V. Pennsylvania*, 153 U.S. 628 (1894); *Illinois Central Railway v. Illinois*, 163 U.S. 142 (1896).

13. Adamany is careful to note that only the probability of conflict is greater following a critical election. This is in contrast to the position of Funston (1975).

14. King (1987) finds that realigning periods are marginally associated with turnover on the Supreme Court, but that does not guarantee a new majority of justices appointed by the "new regime." An exception to this argument is the Civil War realignment. Lincoln was able to obtain a new majority on the Court in four short years because of vacancies and Justice Campbell's resignation. Lincoln's appointments in these years include Salmon Chase, Samuel Miller, Noah Swayne, David Davis, and Stephen Field.

15. This would, of course, be of little surprise and perhaps of some comfort to the framers of the Constitution, who sought to divorce the federal judiciary from electoral politics.

16. The role of party voting in congressional research is often measured by V coefficients. This procedure requires many votes or observations in a given year. The few Supreme Court cases in one year or across "natural courts" obviates this type of analysis as well as other forms of analysis such as bloc (e.g., Bolner, Feldman, and Gates, 1982) or cluster voting methods (e.g., Brady and Stewart, 1982).

17. This method is imperfect because it does not measure the extent to which each justice on the Court voted together *in a particular case*. It is not a measure of partisan voting blocs in each period. This approach does, however, align justices on a continuum of support and nonsupport for different positions on the realigning issues. There is no resolution to this common problem in judicial research except to expand the number of cases in each year. Resources are currently not available for such an enterprise. Appendix B presents a more thorough discussion of this dilemma.

18. On some of the methodological issues surrounding this conclusion, see Appendix B.

19. King (1987) shows how realignments are associated with increased turnover on the Court. His analysis examines the Court's entire history and shows that turnover is marginally structured by realignment. The pace of turnover across realignments, however, is very uneven. The time it takes for the victorious party to appoint a new majority to the Court varies tremendously.

20. On these "older" partisan issues, presidents are successful in obtaining justices supportive of their position (Rohde and Spaeth, 1976). Presidents are even more successful on the issues they feel are most important during their administration (Gates and Cohen, 1988; 1989).

21. Tushnet (1988) paves an interesting, provocative, and arduous path toward resolving the apparent normative impasse.

7

Epilogue

This study of Supreme Court policymaking and partisan realignment concludes in 1964, a year that marks the beginning of dealignment as voters became increasingly ambivalent toward the two major parties. Dealignment is continuing. The proportion of the electorate expressing a neutral view toward both parties, for example, increased from 74 percent of the electorate polled in 1952 to 92 percent in 1984 (Wattenberg, 1990: 146). The issues, including the social issue, that disrupted party loyalties in the 1960s have also ebbed in the public mind. Today, there are few major, highly salient issues threatening to cut across the existing lines of ideological division between the parties.[1]

Since 1964, the Supreme Court has undergone dramatic personnel changes that transformed the liberal, Democratic Warren Court into a Republican body. In the 1970s, the "Nixon Court" moved gradually away from important Warren Court doctrine. Yet, the dramatic doctrinal shifts occurred in only a few selected areas. The 1980s, however, saw the emergence of a more decisively conservative Supreme Court in a variety of policy areas. This is especially true of the early Rehnquist Court, which aligns itself with increasing frequency to the most conservative wing of the Republican party. Indeed, the recent appointments of Justices Antonio Scalia and Anthony Kennedy may be two of the five most conservative, Republican appointments in this century.

One could envision a shift away from dealignment to realignment in the 1990s and the establishment of a new majority party.[2] This future realignment scenario would have to be based on some new issue or set of issues around which party leaders would polarize. The Supreme Court would presumably confront these new and divisive issues. The literature on the Supreme Court's agenda-setting role would suggest that Court policymaking, given the Republican party's good fortune in having had the opportunity to make so many appointments to the Court in the past two decades, would help to posture the Republican party on these new issues before such a hypothetical critical election. Should the Democratic party be victorious in a critical election, others would suggest this conservative Court would be ideally situated for a clash resembling the crisis of the New Deal period.

Either scenario is possible. But it is not at all clear that the appointments by Richard Nixon, Gerald Ford, Ronald Reagan, or George Bush were based on the justices' positions on the unknown crosscutting, realigning issues of the future. Although research must continue to expand the range of Supreme Court policymaking, it appears that neither role is inevitable, nor is one role more likely as the Supreme Court moves into the 1990s. Prognostication on the future of the Supreme Court is always risky. The Supreme Court's role is perhaps nowhere more uncertain than on the issue of partisan realignment because of the almost random turnover on the Court and, most important, because of the crosscutting quality of the political issues that historically have transformed the American party system and national policymaking.

NOTES

1. The issue of state regulation of abortion services is a possible exception. Whether the single abortion issue could lead to realignment is debatable. Certainly, the distribution of opinion suggests the potential for abortion to cut across and divide both Republicans and Democrats (Ladd, 1990: 11–13).

2. There is considerable debate on the Reagan era and whether realignment did occur. The scholarly community is divided but the survey evidence continues to point to the fact that voters are much more concerned with candidates than with parties (e.g., Wattenberg, 1990: 145–151).

Bibliography

Abraham, Henry. 1974. *Justices and Presidents*. New York: Oxford University Press.

Abramson, Paul R., John H. Aldrich, and David W. Rohde. 1982. *Continuity and Change in the 1980 Elections*. Washington, D.C.: Congressional Quarterly Press.

Adamany, David. 1969. The Party Variable in Judge's Voting: Conceptual Notes and a Case Study. *American Political Science Review* 63:57–73.

_____. 1973. Legitimacy, Realigning Elections, and the Supreme Court. *Wisconsin Law Review* 3:790–846.

_____. 1977. Public and Activist Attitudes Toward the U.S. Supreme Court. Paper delivered at the Annual Meeting of the American Political Science Association, Washington, D.C.

_____. 1980. The Supreme Court's Role in Critical Elections. In *Realignment in American Politics*, ed. B. Campbell and R. Trilling. Austin: University of Texas Press.

Adamany, David, and Joel B. Grossman. 1983. Support for the Supreme Court as a National Policymaker. *Law & Policy Quarterly*, 5:405–437.

Agresto, John. 1984. *The Supreme Court and Constitutional Democracy*. Ithaca, N.Y.: Cornell University Press.

Anckar, Dag, and Viveca Ramstedt-Silen. 1981. Relating Preferences to Policy: Three Problem Areas. In *Advances in Content Analysis*, ed. K.E. Rosengren. Beverly Hills: Sage.

Anderson, Kristi. 1979. *The Creation of a Democratic Majority*. Chicago: University of Chicago Press.

Arnold, Thurman. 1935. *The Symbols of Government*. New Haven: Yale University Press.

Arrow, Kenneth J. 1963. 2nd ed. *Social Choice and Individual Values*. New Haven: Yale University Press.

Atkins, Burton, and Henry Glick. 1976. Environmental and Structural Variables as Determinants of Issues in State Courts of Last Resort. *American Journal of Political Science* 20:97–115.

Baas, Larry R., and Dan Thomas. 1984. The Supreme Court and Policy Legitimation: Experimental Tests. *American Politics Quarterly* 12:335–360.

Barker, Lucius. 1967. Third Parties in Litigation. *Journal of Politics* 29:41–69.

Barnum, David G. 1985. The Supreme Court and Public Opinion: Judicial Decision Making in the Post–New Deal Period. *Journal of Politics* 47:652–665.

Baum, Lawrence. 1977. Policy Goals in Judicial Gatekeeping: A Proximity Model of Discretionary Jurisdiction. *American Journal of Political Science* 21:13–35.

_____. 1988. Measuring Policy Change in the U.S. Supreme Court. *American Political Science Review* 82:905–912.

————. 1989. *The Supreme Court*. 3rd. ed. Washington, D.C.: Congressional Quarterly Press.

Baum, Lawrence, Sheldon Goldman, and Austin Sarat. 1982. The Evolution of Litigation in the Federal Courts of Appeals, 1895–1975. *Law and Society Review* 16:291–309.

Beach, Charles, and James McKinnon. 1978. A Maximum Likelihood Procedure for Regression with Autocorrelated Errors. *Economics* 46:51–58.

Beck, Nathaniel. 1983. Time-Varying Parameter Regression Models. *American Journal of Political Science* 27:557–600.

Beck, Paul Allen. 1976. Communication—Critical Elections and the Supreme Court: Putting the Cart After the Horse. *American Political Science Review* 70:930–932.

————. 1977. Partisan Dealignment in the Postwar South. *American Political Science Review* 71:477–496.

————. 1979. The Electoral Cycle and Patterns of Policy Changes. *British Journal of Political Science* 9:129–156.

————. 1986. Micropolitics in Macro Perspective: The Political History of Walter Dean Burnham. *Social Science History* 10:221–244.

Beiser, Edward N., and Jonathan J. Silberman. 1971. The Political Party Variable: Workmen's Compensation Cases in the New York Court of Appeals. *Polity* 3:521–531.

Berger, Raoul. 1977. *Government by Judiciary*. Cambridge: Harvard University Press.

Beth, Loren P. 1971. *The Development of the American Constitution, 1877–1917*. New York: Harper and Row.

Binkley, Wilfred. 1958. *American Political Parties: Their Natural History*. New York: Knopf.

Black, Charles. 1960. *The People and the Court*. Englewood Cliffs, New Jersey: Prentice-Hall.

Black, Duncan. 1958. *Theory of Committees and Elections*. Cambridge: Cambridge University Press.

Blaustein, Albert P., and Roy M. Mersky. 1978. *The First Hundred Justices: Statistical Studies on the Supreme Court of the U.S.* Hamden, New Jersey: Shoestring Press.

Bolner, James; Arnold Feldman; and John Gates. 1982. A New Method of Bloc Analysis of Judicial Voting. *Political Methodology* 7:109–130.

Bonadio, Felice A. (ed.). 1974. *Political Parties in American History: 1828–1890*. New York: Putnam.

Bork, Robert H. 1990. *The Tempting of America: The Political Seduction of the Law*. New York: Free Press.

Boudin, Louis B. 1911. Government by Judiciary. *Political Science Quarterly* 26:238–270.

Boyum, Jenneth O., and Samuel Krislov (eds.). 1980. *Forecasting the Impact of Legislation on Courts*. Washington, D.C.: National Academy Press.

Brady, David W. 1978. Critical Elections, Congressional Parties, and Clusters of Policy Changes. *British Journal of Political Science* 8:79–99.

————. 1985. A Reevaluation of Realignments in American Politics: Evidence from the House of Representatives. *American Political Science Review* 79:28–49.

————. 1988. *Critical Elections and Congressional Policy Making*. Stanford, CA: Stanford University Press.

Brady, David W., and Joseph Stewart, Jr. 1982. Congressional Party Realignment and Transformations of Public Policy in Three Realigning Eras. *American Journal of Political Science* 26:333–360.

_____ . 1986. When Elections Matter: Realignments and Changes in Public Policy. In *Do Elections Matter*, ed. B. Ginsberg and A. Stone. Armonk, New York: M. E. Sharpe, Inc.

Brenner, Saul. Fluidity on the United States Supreme Court: A Reexamination. *American Journal of Political Science* 24:526–535.

Burnham, Walter Dean. 1965. The Changing Shape of the American Political Universe. *American Political Science Review* 59:7–28.

_____ . 1970. *Critical Elections and the Mainsprings of American Politics*. New York: Norton.

_____ . 1981. The System of 1896: An Analysis. In *The Evolution of American Electoral Systems*, ed. P. Gleppner, et al. Westport, Connecticut: Greenwood Press.

_____ . 1982. *The Current Crisis in American Politics*. New York: Oxford University Press.

_____ . 1986. Periodization Schemes and 'Party Systems': The 'System of 1896' as a Case in Point. *Social Science History* 10:263–314.

Caldeira, Gregory A. 1981. The U.S. Supreme Court in Criminal Cases, 1935–1976: Alternative Models of Agenda Building. *British Journal of Political Science* 11:449–470.

_____ . 1982. A Tale of Two Reforms: On the Workload of the U.S. Supreme Court. In *The Analysis of Judicial Reform*, ed. P. L. Dubois. Lexington: D. C. Heath.

_____ . 1986. Neither the Purse nor the Sword: The Dynamics of Public Confidence in the United States Supreme Court. *American Political Science Review* 80:1209–1226.

Caldiera, Gregory A., and Donald J. McCrone. 1982. Of Time and Judicial Activism: A Study of the U.S. Supreme Court, 1800–1973. In *Supreme Court Activism and Restraint*, ed. S. Halpern and C. Lamb. Lexington: D. C. Heath.

Cameron, A. Colin, and Pravin K. Trivedi. 1986. Econometric Models Based on Count Data: Comparisons and Applications of Some Estimators and Tests. *Journal of Applied Econometrics* 1:29-53.

Campbell, Angus. 1966. A Classification of Presidential Elections. In *Elections and the Political Order*, ed. A. Campbell, P. Converse, W. Miller, and D. Stokes. New York: John Wiley.

Campbell, Angus; Philip P. Converse; Warren E. Miller; and Donald E. Stokes. 1960. *The American Voter*. New York: John Wiley.

Campbell, Bruce A. 1977. Change in the Southern Electorate. *American Journal of Political Science* 21:37–64.

Canon, Bradley, and Dean Jaros. 1970. External Variables, Institutional Structure, and Dissent on State Supreme Courts. *Polity* 3:175–200.

Canon, Bradley, and S. Sidney Ulmer. 1976. The Supreme Court and Critical Elections: A Dissent. *American Political Science Review* 70:1215–1218.

Cardozo, Benjamin N. 1921. *The Nature of the Judicial Process*. New Haven: Yale University Press.

Carmines, Edward, and James Stimson. 1981. Issue Evolution, Population Replacement, and Normal Partisan Change. *American Political Science Review* 75:107–118.

_____ . 1986. On the Structure and Sequence of Issue Evolution. *American Political Science Review* 80:901–920.

Carp, Robert A., and C.K. Rowland. 1983. *Policymaking and Politics in the Federal District Courts*. Knoxville: University of Tennessee Press.

Carr, Robert K. 1942. *The Supreme Court and Judicial Review*. New York: Farrar and Rinehart.

Cartwright, Bliss. 1975. Conclusion: Disputes and Reported Cases. *Law and Society Review* 9:369–384.

Casper, Gerhard, and Richard Posner. 1974. A Study of the Supreme Court's Caseload. *Journal of Legal Studies*. 3:339–375.

———. 1976. *The Workload of the U.S. Supreme Court*. Chicago: American Bar Foundation.

Casper, Jonathan. 1976. The Supreme Court and National Policy Making. *American Political Science Review* 70:50–63.

Castle, David, and Harold W. Stanley. 1982. Partisan Realignment in the South: Making Sense of Scholarly Dissonance. Paper delivered at the 1982 meeting of the Southern Political Science Association.

Chambers, William Nisbet, and Walter Dean Burnham (eds.). 1975. *The American Party Systems: Stages of Political Development*, 2nd edition. New York: Oxford.

Chatterjee, Sungit, and Frederick Wiseman. 1983. Use of Regression Diagnostics in Political Science Research. *American Journal of Political Science* 25:601–613.

Choper, Jesse H. 1980. *Judicial Review and the National Political Process*. Chicago: University of Chicago Press.

Chubb, John E., and Paul E. Peterson (eds.). 1985. *New Directions in American Politics*. Washington, D.C.: Brookings.

Claude, Richard P. 1970. *The Supreme Court and the Electoral Process*. Baltimore: The Johns Hopkins Press.

Clausen, Aage. 1973. *How Congressmen Decide: A Policy Focus*. New York: St. Martins.

Clubb, Jerome; William H. Flanigan; and Nancy Zingale. 1980. *Partisan Realignment*. Beverly Hills: Sage.

———. 1990. *Partisan Realignment: Voters, Parties, and Government in American History*. Encore edition. Boulder: Westview Press.

Corwin, Edward S. 1932. Social Planning Under the Constitution: A Study in Perspectives. *American Political Science Review* 26:1–27.

———. 1936. The Constitution as Instrument and as Symbol. *American Political Science Review* 30:1071–1085.

———. 1938. *Court Over Constitution*. Princeton, New Jersey: Princeton University Press.

———. 1941. *Constitutional Revolution Ltd.* Claremont, California: Claremont College.

Cox, Archibald. 1987. *The Court and the Constitution*. Boston: Houghton Mifflin.

Coxe, Brinton. 1970. *An Essay on Judicial Power and Unconstitutional Legislation*. New York: DaCapo Press.

Crewe, Ivor, and David Denver (eds.). 1985. *Electoral Change in Western Democracies: Patterns and Sources of Electoral Volatility*. London: Croom Helm.

Crotty, William. 1984. *American Parties in Decline*. 2nd edition. Boston: Little Brown.

Curry, Richard (ed.). 1969. *Radicalism, Racism, and Party Realignment*. Baltimore: Johns Hopkins University Press.

Dahl, Robert. 1957. Decision-making in a Democracy: The Supreme Court as a National Policymaker. *Journal of Public Law* 6:279–295.

Dalton, Russell J., Scott Flanagan, and Paul Allen Beck (eds.). 1984. *Electoral Change in Advanced Industrial Democracies: Realignment or Dealignment*. Princeton, N.J.: Princeton University Press.

Danelski, David J. 1966. Values as Variables in Judicial Decision-Making: Notes Toward a Theory. *Vanderbilt Law Review* 19:721–740.

Davis, Horace. 1914. *The Judicial Veto*. New York: Houghton-Mifflin.

Dean, H. 1966. *Judicial Review and Democracy*. New York: Random House.

DeTocqueville, Alexis. 1973. *Democracy in America*. New York: Mentor.

Dolan, Paul. 1964. Dissent in the Taney Court. *Dickinson Law Review* 68:281–306.

Dolbeare, Kenneth, and Philip Hammond. 1968. The Political Party Basis of Attitudes Toward the Supreme Court. *Public Opinion Quarterly* 32:16–30.

Dougherty, J.H. 1912. *The Power of the Federal Judiciary Over Legislation*. New York: Putnams.

Douglas, William O. 1980. *The Court Years, 1939–1975: The Autobiography of William O. Douglas*. New York: Random House.

Dubois, Philip. 1980. *From Ballot to Bench*. Austin: University of Texas Press.

Dubois, Philip, and Paul Dubois. 1980. Measuring Dissent Behavior on State Courts, *Polity* 13:147–158.

Durkheim, Emile. 1966. *The Division of Labor in Society*. New York: Free Press.

Edgerton, Henry W. 1937. The Incidence of Judicial Control Over Congress. *Cornell Law Review* 22:299–348.

Ely, John Hart. 1980. *Democracy and Distrust: A Theory of Judicial Review*. Cambridge: Harvard University Press.

Epstein, Lee. 1985. *Conservatives in Court*. Knoxville: University of Tennessee Press.

Erikson, Robert, and Kent Tedin. 1981. The 1928–1936 Partisan Realignment: The Case for the Conversion Hypothesis. *American Political Science Review* 75:951–962.

Ernst, Morris L. 1937. *The Ultimate Power*. Garden City, N.Y.: Doubleday, Doran, and Company.

Fairman, Charles. 1966. *Mr. Justice Miller and The Supreme Court: 1862–1890*. New York: Russell and Russell.

Feeley, Malcolm. 1979. *The Process is the Punishment: Handling Cases in a Lower Criminal Court*. New York: Russell Sage Foundation.

Fellman, David. 1976. *The Defendant's Rights Today*. Madison: University of Wisconsin Press.

Fisher, Louis. 1988. *Constitutional Dialogues: Interpretation as Political Process*. Princeton, N.J.: Princeton University Press.

Flango, Victor, and Nora Blair. 1980. Creating an Intermediate Appellate Court. *Judicature* 64:74–84.

Frank, John D. 1964. *Justice Daniel Dissenting*. Cambridge: Harvard University Press.

Frankfurter, Felix. 1938. *Mr. Justice Holmes and the Supreme Court*. Cambridge: Harvard University Press.

Frankfurter, Felix, and James Landis. 1928. *The Business of the Supreme Court*. New York: McMillan.

Franklin, Charles H., and Liane C. Kosaki. 1989. The Republican Schoolmaster: The Supreme Court, Public Opinion, and Abortion. *American Political Science Review* 83:751–772.

Friedman, Lawrence M. 1973. *A History of American Law*. New York: Touchstone.

Funston, Richard. 1975. The Supreme Court and Critical Elections. *American Political Science Review* 69:795–811.

Galanter, Marc. 1975. Afterword: Explaining Litigation. *Law and Society Review* 9:347–368.

Gates, John B. 1984. The American Supreme Court and Electoral Realignment: A Critical Review. *Social Science History* 8:267–290.

———. 1987. Partisan Realignment, Unconstitutional State Policies, and the U.S. Supreme Court:1837–1964. *American Journal of Political Science* 31:259–280.

———. 1989. Supreme Court Voting and Realigning Issues: A Microlevel Analysis of Supreme Court Policy Making and Electoral Realignment. *Social Science History* 13:255–283.

———. 1991. Theory, Methods, and the New Institutionalism in Judicial Research. In *The American Courts: A Critical Assessment*, ed. J.B. Gates, and C.A. Johnson. Washington, D.C.: Congressional Quarterly Press.

Gates, John B., and Jeffrey E. Cohen. 1988. Presidents, Justices, and Racial Equality Cases. *Political Behavior* 10:22–36.

———. 1989. Presidential Policy Preferences and Supreme Court Appointment Success. *Policy Studies Review* 8:800–811.

———. 1991. The Motivations for Interest Group Litigation in a Changing Interest Group Environment. University of California, Davis, University of Maryland, mimeo.

Gatlin, Douglas S. 1975. Party Identification, Status, and Race in the South: 1952–1974. *Public Opinion Quarterly* 39:39–51.

Gibson, James L. 1977. Discriminant Functions, Role Orientations and Judicial Behavior: Theoretical and Methodological Linkages. *Journal of Politics* 39:984–1007.

———. 1978. Judge's Role Orientations, Attitudes, and Decisions: An Interactive Model. *American Political Science Review* 72:911–924.

———. 1980. Environmental Constraints on the Behavior of Judges: A Representational Model of Judicial Decision-Making. *Law and Society Review* 14:343–370.

———. 1983. From Simplicity to Complexity: The Development of Theory in the Study of Judicial Behavior. *Political Behavior* 5:7–49.

———. 1986. The Social Science of Judicial Politics. *Political Science: The Science of Politics*, ed. H.F. Weisberg. New York: Agathon Press.

Ginsberg, Benjamin. 1972. Critical Elections and the Substance of Party Conflict. *Midwest Journal of Political Science* 16:603–625.

———. 1976. Elections and Public Policy. *American Political Science Review* 70:41–49.

Glass, Gene V. 1968. Analysis of Data on the Connecticut Speeding Crackdown as a Time Series Quasi-Experiment. *Law and Society Review* 3:55–76.

Goldman, Sheldon. 1975. Voting Behavior on the U.S. Court of Appeals, Revisited. *American Political Science Review* 69:491–506.

———. 1982. *Constitutional Law and Supreme Court Policymaking*. New York: Harper and Row.

———. 1985. *The Federal Courts as a Political System*. Second Edition. New York: Harper and Row.

Goldman, Sheldon, and Charles M. Lamb (eds.). 1986. *Judicial Conflict and Consensus: Behavioral Studies of American Appeallate Courts*. Lexington: University of Kentucky Press.

Goodwyn, Lawrence. 1976. *Democratic Promise: The Populist Movement in America*. New York: Oxford University Press.

Grossman, Joel. 1967. Social Backgrounds and Judicial Decisions: Notes for a Theory. *Journal of Politics* 29:334–351.

Grossman, Joel B., and Austin D. Sarat. 1975. Litigation in the Federal Courts: A Comparative Perspective. *Law and Society Review* 9:321–346.

Gunther, Gerald. 1980. *Constitutional Law: Cases and Materials*, 10th Edition. Mineola, N.Y.: Foundation Press.

Hadley, Charles D., and Susan E. Howell. 1980. The Southern Split Ticket Voter, 1952–1976: Republican Conversion or Democratic Decline? In *Party Politics in the South*, ed. R. Steed, L. Moreland, and T. Baker. New York: Praeger.

Haines, Charles G. 1932. *The American Doctrine of Judicial Supremacy*. Revised Edition. Berkeley: University of California Press.

Hall, Kermit (ed.). 1985. *The Supreme Court and Judicial Review in American History.* Washington, D.C.: American Historical Association.

Halpern, Stephen C. n.d. Selected Percentages of Nonunanimous Supreme Court Cases, 1837–1964. Raw Data.

Halpern, Stephen C., and Charles M. Lamb (eds.). 1982. *Supreme Court Activism and Restraint.* Lexington: D. C. Heath.

Halpern, Stephen C., and Kenneth V. Vines. 1977. Institutional Disunity, the Judges' Bill and the Role of the U.S. Supreme Court. *Western Political Quarterly* 30:471–483.

Handberg, Roger. 1976. Decision-Making in a Natural Court, 1916–1921. *American Politics Quarterly* 4:357–378.

Handberg, Roger and Harold Hill. 1980. Court-Curbing, Court Reversal, and Judicial Review: The Supreme Court versus Congress. *Law and Society Review* 14:309–322.

Harris, Robert J. 1940. *The Judicial Power of the United States.* Baton Rouge, LA: Louisiana State University Press.

———. 1948. The Decline of Judicial Review. *Journal of Politics* 10:1–19.

Hartz, Louis. 1955. *The Liberal Tradition in America.* New York: Harcourt, Brace, and World.

Harvard Law Review. 1946–1964. Cambridge, MA: Harvard University.

Hay, Richard, and Richard McCleary. 1979. Box-Tiao Time Series Models for Impact Assessments. *Evaluation Quarterly* 3:277–314.

Hayes, Samuel P. 1980. *American Political History as Social Analysis.* Knoxville: University of Tennessee Press.

Hibbs, Douglas, Jr. 1974. Problems of Statistical Estimation. In *Sociological Methodology,* ed. H. Costner. San Francisco: Jossey-Bass.

———. 1977a. Political Parties and Macroeconomic Policy. *American Political Science Review* 71:1467–1487.

———. 1977b. On Analyzing the Effects of Policy Interventions: Box-Tiao vs. Structural Equation Models. In *Sociological Methodology 1977,* ed. H. Costner. San Francisco: Jossey-Bass.

Hildreth, C. and J. Lu. 1960. Demand Relations with Autocorrelated Disturbances. *Research Bulletin 276.* Lansing, MI: Michigan State University Agricultural Station.

Hofstadter, Richard. 1948. *The American Political Tradition.* New York: Vintage.

Holcombe, Arthur N. 1916. *State Government in the U.S.* New York: Houghton-Mifflin.

Holmes, Oliver Wendell. 1920. *Collected Legal Papers.* New York: Harcourt.

Horowitz, Donald L. 1977. *The Courts and Social Policy.* Washington, D.C.: Brookings.

Howard, J. Woodford. 1968. On the Fluidity of Judicial Choice. *American Political Science Review* 62:43–56.

———. 1981. *Courts of Appeal in the Federal Judicial System.* Princeton: Princeton University Press.

Huntington, Samuel P. 1965. Political Development and Political Decay. *World Politics* 17:386–430.

———. 1968. *Political Order in Changing Societies.* New Haven: Yale University Press.

Hurst, James Willard. 1950. *The Growth of American Law: The Lawmakers.* Boston: Little Brown.

———. 1977. *Law and Social Order in the United States.* Ithaca, New York: Cornell University Press.

———. 1982. *Law and Markets in United States History.* Madison: The University of Wisconsin Press.

Hyman, Harold M., and William M. Wiecek. 1982. *Equal Justice Under the Law*. New York: Harper and Row.

Jackman, Robert W. 1985. Cross-National Statistical Research and the Study of Comparative Politics. *American Journal of Political Science* 29:161–182.

Jackson, Robert H. 1941. *The Struggle for Judicial Supremacy*. New York: Vintage.

Jahnigne, Thomas. 1971. Critical Elections and Social Change. *Polity* 9:465–500.

Jensen, Richard. 1986. The Changing Shape of Burnham's Political Universe. *Social Science History* 10:209–219.

Johnson, Bruce, and Kirk H. Porter (comps.). 1970. *National Party Platforms: 1840–1968*. Urbana, Illinois, University of Illinois Press.

Johnson, Charles A. 1981. Stare Decisis and Precedents: Using Citations to Explore Judicial Behavior and Policy Making. Paper delivered at the Annual Meeting of the Southern Political Science Association, Atlanta, Georgia.

———. 1982. Content Analytic Techniques in Judicial Research. Paper delivered at the 1982 Annual Meeting of the American Political Science Association.

———. 1987. Content-Analytic Techniques and Judicial Research. *American Politics Quarterly* 15:169–197.

Johnston, Richard E. 1972. Some Comparative Statistics on U.S. Chief Justice Courts. *Rocky Mountain Social Science Journal* 9:89–100.

Kagan, Robert A.; Bliss Cartwright; Lawrence M. Friedman; and Stanton Wheeler. 1977. The Business of State Supreme Courts, 1870–1970. *Stanford Law Review* 30:121–156.

———. 1978. The Evolution of State Supreme Courts. *Michigan Law Review* 76:961–1005.

Keller, Morton. 1977. *Affairs of State*. Cambridge: Harvard University Press.

Kelly, Alfred; Winfred A. Harbinson; and Herman Belz. 1983. 6th edition. *The American Constitution*. New York: Norton.

Kessel, John. 1966. Public Perception of the Supreme Court. *Midwest Journal of Political Science* 10:167–191.

Key, V.O. 1955. A Theory of Critical Elections. *Journal of Politics* 17:3–18.

———. 1959. Secular Realignment and the Party System. *Journal of Politics* 21:198–210.

King, Gary. 1987. Presidential Appointments to the Supreme Court: Adding Systematic Explanation to Probabilistic Description. *American Politics Quarterly* 15:373–386.

———. 1988. Statistical Models for Political Science Event Counts: Bias in Conventional Procedures and Evidence for The Exponential Poisson Regression Model. *American Journal of Political Science* 32:838–863.

———. 1989. *Unifying Political Methodology: The Likelihood Theory of Statistical Inference*. New York: Cambridge University Press.

King, Willard L. 1967. *Melville Weston Fuller: Chief Justice of U.S., 1888–1910*. Chicago: University of Chicago Press.

Kleppner, Paul; W.D. Burnham; R.P. Formisano; S.P. Hayes; R. Jensen; and W.G. Shade (eds.). 1979. *The Third Electoral System, 1853–1892: Parties, Voters, and Political Culture*. Chapel Hill: University of North Carolina Press.

———. 1981. *The Evolution of American Electoral Systems*. Westport, Conn.: Greenwood Press.

Krippendorff, Klaus. 1980. *Content Analysis: An Introduction to its Methodology*. Beverly Hills: Sage.

Kuklinski, James, and John Stanga. 1979. Political Participation and Government Responsiveness: The Behavior of California Superior Courts. *American Political Science Review* 73:1090–1099.

Kutler, Stanley. 1958. *Judicial Power and Reconstruction Politics*. Chicago: University of Chicago Press.

Ladd, Everett C. 1972. *American Political Parties*. New York: W. W. Norton.

_____ . 1990. *The Ladd Report #8: Abortion*. New York: W. W. Norton.

Ladd, Everett C., and Charles D. Hadley. 1975. *Transformations of the American Party System*. New York: W. W. Norton.

Landis, J.R., and G.G. Koch. 1977. The Measurement of Observer Agreement for Category Data. *Biometrics* 33:159–174.

Lasser, William. 1983. *Crisis and the Supreme Court: Judicial Politics in Periods of Critical Realignment*. Ph.D. Diss., Harvard University.

_____ . 1985. The Supreme Court in Periods of Critical Realignment. *Journal of Politics* 47:1174–1187.

Leavitt, D. 1974. Changing Issues, Ideological and Political Influences on the U.S. Supreme Court, 1893–1945. Paper delivered at the Annual Meeting of the American Political Science Association.

Lewis-Beck, Michael S. 1979. Some Economic Effects of Revolution: Models, Measurements, and the Cuban Revolution. *American Journal of Sociology* 84:1127–1149.

_____ . 1986. Interrupted Time Series. In *New Tools for Social Scientists*, ed. W. Berry and M. Lewis-Beck. Beverly Hills: Sage Publications.

Library of Congress. 1978. *The Constitution of the United States: Analysis and Interpretation*. Washington, D.C.: Government Printing Office.

Likens, Thomas W. 1979. "The Supreme Court's Agenda: A Dynamic Model." Unpublished manuscript.

Lindkvist, Kent. 1981. Approaches to Textual Analysis. In *Advances in Content Analysis*, ed. K.E. Rosengren. Beverly Hills: Sage.

Lipsey, Richard G., and Peter O. Steiner. 1987. *Economics*, 8th ed. New York: Harper and Row.

Llewellyn, Karl. 1962. *Jurisprudence: Realism in Theory and Practice*. Chicago: University of Chicago Press.

Longaker, Richard P. 1956. Andrew Jackson and the Judiciary. *Political Science Quarterly* 71:341–364.

Lowery, David, and William D. Barry. 1983. The Growth of Government in the U.S. *American Journal of Political Science* 27:665–694.

Magrath, L. Peter. 1963. *Morrison R. Waite: The Triumph of Character*. New York: McMillan.

Manley, John F. 1973. The Conservative Coalition in Congress. *American Behavioral Scientist* 17:223–247.

Marshall, Thomas. 1989. *Public Opinion and the Supreme Court*. New York: Longman.

Mason, Alpheus T. 1964. *The Supreme Court from Taft to Warren*. Baton Rouge: Louisiana State University Press.

McCleary, Richard, and Richard Hay. 1980. *Applied Time Series Analysis for the Social Sciences*. Beverly Hills: Sage.

McCleskey, Clifton. 1966. Judicial Review in a Democracy: A Dissenting Opinion. *Houston Law Review* 3:354–366.

McCloskey, Robert G. 1951. *American Conservatism in the Age of Enterprise*. Cambridge: Harvard University Press.

_____ . 1960. *The American Supreme Court*. Chicago: University of Chicago Press.

_____ . 1962. Economic Due Process and the Supreme Court: An Exhumation and Reburial. In *The Supreme Court Review*, ed. P. Kurland. Chicago: University of Chicago Press.

McCormick, Richard L. 1986. Walter Dean Burnham and the 'System of 1896'. *Social Science History* 10:245–262.

McDonald, Stuart Elaine, and George Rabinowitz. 1987. The Dynamics of Structural Realignment. *American Political Science Review* 81:775–796.

McIntosh, Wayne. 1980–81. 150 Years of Litigation and Dispute Settlement: A Court Tale. *Law and Society Review* 15:823–848.

———. 1983. Private Use of a Public Forum: A Long Range View of the Dispute Processing Role of Courts. *American Political Science Review* 77:991–1010.

———. 1985. Litigating Scientific Creationism, or 'Scopes' II, III, ... *Law and Policy Quarterly* 7:375–394.

McLauchlan, William P. 1984. *Federal Court Caseloads.* New York: Praeger.

McMichael, Lawrence G., and Richard Trilling. 1980. The Structure and Meaning of Critical Realignment. In *Realignment in American Politics,* ed. B. Campbell and R. Trilling. Austin: University of Texas Press.

Melone, Albert P., and George Mace. 1988. *Judicial Review and American Democracy.* Ames, Iowa: Iowa State University Press.

Mendelson, Wallace. 1947. Sectional Politics and the Rise of Judicial Supremacy. *Journal of Politics* 9:255–272.

———. 1961. The Politics of Judicial Supremacy. *Journal of Law and Economics* 4:175–185.

Miller, Arthur S. 1968. *The Supreme Court and American Capitalism.* New York: Free Press.

Moore, Blaine R. 1913. *The Supreme Court and Unconstitutional Legislation.* New York: Columbia University Press.

Mowry, George E. 1958. *The Era of Theodore Roosevelt.* New York: Harper and Brothers.

Murphy, Paul L. 1972. *The Constitution in Crisis Times, 1918–1969.* New York: Harper and Row.

Murphy, Walter. 1962. *Congress and the Supreme Court.* Chicago: University of Chicago Press.

———. 1964. *Elements of Judicial Strategy.* Chicago: University of Chicago Press.

Murphy, Walter, and Joseph Tannenhaus. 1968. Public Opinion and the United States Supreme Court: A Preliminary Mapping of Some Prerequisities for Court Legitimation of Regime Changes. *Law and Society Review* 2:357–382.

———. 1972. *The Study of Public Law.* New York: Random House.

———. 1981. Patterns of Public Support for the Supreme Court: A Panel Study. *Journal of Politics* 43:24–39.

Murphy, Walter; Joseph Tannenhaus; and Daniel Kastner. 1973. *Public Evaluations of Constitutional Courts.* Beverly Hills: Sage.

Nagel, Robert F. 1989. *Constitutional Cultures: The Mentality and Consequences of Judicial Review.* Berkeley: University of California Press.

Nagel, Stuart. 1961. Political Party Affiliation and Judges' Decisions. *American Political Science Review* 55:843–850.

———. 1965. Political Parties and Judicial Review in American History. *Journal of Public Law* 4:328.

———. 1969. Curbing the Court: The Politics of Congressional Reaction. In *The Legal Process from a Behavioral Perspective,* ed. S. Nagel. Homewood, Illinois: Dorsey Press.

Nanenwirth, J.Z. 1973. Wheels of Time and Interdependence of Value Change in America. *Journal of Interdisciplinary History* 3:649–683.

Newmyer, R. Kent. 1968. *The Supreme Court Under Marshall and Taney.* Arlington Heights, Illinois: Harlan Davidson, Inc.

Nexon, David. 1980. Methodological Issues in the Study of Realignment. In *Realignment in American Politics*, ed. B. Campbell and R. Trilling. Austin: University of Texas Press.

Nie, Norma; Sidney Verba; and John R. Petrocik. 1976. *The Changing American Voter*. Cambridge: Harvard University Press.

————. 1979. *The Changing American Voter*. Enlarged edition. Cambridge: Harvard University Press.

Norpoth, Helmut, and Thom Yantek. 1983. Macroeconomic Conditions and Fluctuations of Presidential Popularity. *American Journal of Political Science* 25:785–807.

O'Connor, Karen. 1980. *Women's Organizations' Use of the Courts*. Lexington, Mass.: Lexington Books.

————. 1981. A View of Three U.S. Solicitor General Participation as Amicus Curiae in Supreme Court Litigation. Paper delivered at the 1981 Annual Meeting of the American Political Science Association, New York, New York.

O'Connor, Karen, and Lee Epstein. 1983. Court Rules and Workload: A Case Study of Rules Governing Amicus Curiae Participation. *Justice System Journal* 8:35–45.

Olson, Susan. 1981. The Political Evolution of Interest Group Litigation. Paper delivered at the 1980 meeting of the American Political Science Association.

O'Neil, William L. 1975. *The Progressive Years*. New York: Dodd and Mead.

Ostrom, Charles W., and Renee M. Smith. 1990. Presidential Popularity and the Economy: Contrasting VAR and SEQ Approaches. Paper delivered at the 1990 meeting of the Midwest Political Science Association.

Pacelle, Richard, Jr. 1986. The Supreme Court Agenda Across Time: Toward a Theory of Agenda Building. Paper delivered at the 1986 annual meeting of the Midwest Political Science Association, Chicago, Illinois.

Paul, Arnold M. 1969. *Conservative Crisis and the Rule of Law*. New York: Cornell University Press.

Peltason, Jack W. 1955. *Federal Courts in the Political Process*. New York: Random House.

Pennock, J. Roland. 1979. *Democratic Political Theory*. Princeton, N.J.: Princeton University Press.

Perry, Michael J. 1982. *The Constitution, the Courts, and Human Rights: An Inquiry into the Legitimacy of Constitutional Policymaking*. New Haven: Yale University Press.

Petrocik, John R. 1981. *Party Coalitions: Realignment and the Decline of the New Deal Party System*. Chicago: University of Chicago Press.

Phillips, Kevin P. 1969. *The Emerging Republican Majority*. New Rochelle, New York: Arlington House.

Pindyck, Robert S., and Daniel L. Rubinfeld. 1981. *Economic Models and Economic Forecasts*. 2nd edition. New York: McGraw Hill.

Pitkin, Hanna Fenichel. 1967. *The Concept of Representation*. Berkeley: University of California Press.

Polsby, Nelson. 1968. The Institutionalization of the U.S. House of Representatives. *American Political Science Review* 62:144–168.

Pomper, Gerald. 1967. A Classification of Presidential Elections. *Journal of Politics* 29:535–566.

————. 1968. *Elections in America*. New York: Dodd and Mead.

————. 1975. *Voter's Choice*. New York: Dodd and Mead.

Pomper, Gerald M., and Susan M. Lederman. 1980. *Elections in America: Control and Influence in Democratic Politics*, 2nd ed. New York: Longman.

Porter, Mary Cornelia. 1975. Politics, Ideology, and the Workload of the Supreme Court: Some Historical Perspectives. Paper delivered at the 1975 annual meeting of the Midwest Political Science Association, Chicago, Illinois.

Powell, Thomas Reed. 1956. *Vagaries and Varieties in Constitutional Interpretation.* New York: Columbia University Press.

Pritchett, C. Herman. 1948. *The Roosevelt Court: A Study in Judicial Politics, 1937–1947.* New York: MacMillan.

———. 1961. *Congress Versus the Supreme Court, 1957–1960.* Minneapolis: University of Minnesota Press.

———. 1977. *The American Constitution,* 3rd edition. New York: McGraw-Hill.

Provine, Doris Marie. 1980. *Case Selection in the United States Supreme Court.* Chicago: University of Chicago Press.

Puro, Steven. 1981. The United States as Amicus Curiae. In *Courts, Law and Judicial Processes,* ed. S. Ulmer. New York: Free Press.

Rao, Potluri, and Roger L. Miller. 1971. *Applied Econometrics.* Belmont, California: Wadsworth Publishing Company.

Ratner, S. 1935. Was the Supreme Court Packed by President Grant? *Political Science Quarterly* 50:343–358.

Riker, William H., and Peter S. Ordeshook. 1973. *An Introduction to Positive Political Theory.* Englewood Cliffs, N.J.: Prentice-Hall.

Rodell, Fred. 1955. *Nine Men.* New York: Random House.

Rohde, David, and Harold Spaeth. 1976. *Supreme Court Decisionmaking.* San Francisco: Freeman.

Rosenstone, Steven J., Roy L. Behr, and Edward H. Lazarus. 1984. *Third Parties in America.* Princeton: Princeton University Press.

Sandel, Michael J. 1982. *Liberalism and the Limits of Justice.* New York: Cambridge University Press.

Scammon, Richard M., and Benjamin J. Wattenberg. 1970. *The Real Majority.* New York: Coward-McCann.

Schattschneider, E.E. 1975. *The Semi-Sovereign People.* Hinsdale, Illinois: Dryden Press.

Schlesinger, Arthur M., Jr. 1941. *The Age of Jackson.* Boston: Boston University Press.

Schmidhauser, John R. 1958. *The Supreme Court as Final Arbiter in Federal-State Relations.* Chapel Hill: University of North Carolina Press.

———. 1961. Judicial Behavior and the Sectional Crisis of 1837–1860. *Journal of Politics* 23:615–640.

Schmidhauser, John R., and Larry L. Berg. 1972. *The Supreme Court and Congress: Conflict and Interaction, 1945–1968.* New York: Free Press.

Schubert, Glendon. 1963. *Constitutional Politics.* New York: Holt, Rinehart, and Winston.

———. 1974. *The Judicial Mind Revisited.* New York: Oxford University Press.

Scigliano, Robert. 1971. *The Supreme Court and the Presidency.* San Francisco: Free Press.

Scott, William A. 1955. Reliability of Content Analysis. The Case of Normal Scale Coding. *Public Opinion Quarterly* 19:321–325.

Segal, Jeffrey A. 1984. Predicting Supreme Court Cases Probabilistically: The Search and Seizure Cases, 1962–1981. *American Political Science Review* 78: 891–900.

———. 1986. Supreme Court Justices as Human Decision Makers: An Individual-Level Analysis of the Search and Seizure Cases. *Journal of Politics* 48:938–955.

———. 1988. Amicus Curiae Briefs by the Solicitor General During the Warren and Burger Courts. *Western Political Quarterly* 41:135–144.

_____. 1991. Courts, Executives, and Legislatures. In *The American Courts: A Critical Assessment*, ed. J. B. Gates and C. A. Johnson. Washington, D.C.: Congressional Quarterly Press.

Semonche, John E. 1978. *Charting the Future: The Supreme Court Responds to a Changing Society, 1890–1920*. Westport, Conn.: Greenwood Press.

Sen, Amartya K. 1970. *Collective Choice and Social Welfare*. San Francisco: Holden-Day.

Shamir, Michael. 1983. Investigating Causal Relationships: A New Time Series Methodology and a Political Application. *Political Methodology* 9:171–199.

Shapiro, Martin M. 1978. The Supreme Court from Warren to Burger. In *The New American Political System*, ed. A. King. Washington, D.C.: American Enterprise Institute.

_____. 1988. *Who Guards the Guardians? Judicial Control of Administration*. Athens: University of Georgia Press.

Sheldon, Charles. 1974. *The American Judicial Process*. New York: Dodd and Mead.

Siegan, Bernard H. 1987. *The Supreme Court's Constitution: An Inquiry into Judicial Review and Its Impact on Society*. New Brunswick, N.J.: Transaction Books.

Sinclair, Barbara. 1982. *Congressional Realignment, 1925–1978*. Austin: University of Texas Press.

Songer, Donald R. 1978/79. The Relevance of Policy Values for the Confirmation of Supreme Court Nominees. *Law and Society Review* 13:927–948.

_____. 1979. Concern for Policy Outputs as a Cue for Supreme Court Decisions on Certiorari. *Journal of Politics* 41:1185–1194.

_____. 1986. Factors Affecting Variation in Rates of Dissent in the U.S. Courts of Appeals. In *Judicial Conflict and Consensus: Behavioral Studies of American Appellate Courts*, ed. S. Golman and C.M. Lamb. Lexington: University of Kentucky Press.

Spaeth, Harold. 1976. *Supreme Court Policymaking*. San Francisco: Freeman.

Sprague, John. 1968. *Voting Patterns of the United States Supreme Court: Cases in Federalism, 1889–1959*. Indianapolis: Bobbs-Merrill.

Stookey, John A. 1982. Creating an Intermediate Court of Appeals: Workload and Policymaking Consequences. In *The Analysis of Judicial Reform*, ed. P. Dubois. Lexington: D. C. Heath.

Sulfridge, Wayne. 1980. Ideology as a Factor in Senate Consideration of Supreme Court Nominations. *Journal of Politics* 42:560–567.

Sundquist, James. 1973. *Dynamics of the Party System*. Washington, D.C.: Brookings.

Swansbrough, Robert H., and David M. Brodsky (eds.). 1988. *The South's New Politics: Realignment and Dealignment*. Columbia, S.C.: University of South Carolina Press.

Swindler, William F. 1969. *Court and Constitution in the Twentieth Century: The Old Legality, 1889–1932*. New York: Bobbs-Merrill.

Swisher, Carl Brent. 1954. *American Constitutional Development*. 2nd edition. New York: Houghton-Mifflin.

Tate, C. Neal. 1981. Personal Attribute Models of the Voting Behavior of U.S. Supreme Court Justices: Liberalism in Civil Liberties and Economic Decisions, 1946–1978. *American Political Science Review* 75:355–367.

Taylor, Stuart. 1988. Re: Shaping the Court. *New York Times*, July 2, 1988.

Trilling, Richard, and Bruce Campbell. 1980. Toward a Theory of Realignment: An Introduction. In *Realignment in American Politics*, ed. B. Campbell and R. Trilling. Austin: University of Texas Press.

Truman, David B. 1959. *The Congressional Party: A Case Study*. New York: John Wiley and Sons.

Tushnet, Mark V. 1980a. Darkness on the Edge of Town: The Contributions of John Hart Ely to Constitutional Theory. *Yale Law Journal* 89:1037–1062.

———. 1980b. Post-Realist Legal Scholarship. *Wisconsin Law Review* 1980:1383–1401.

———. 1988. *Red, White, and Blue: A Critical Analysis of Constitutional Law.* Cambridge: Harvard University Press.

Twiss, Benjamin R. 1942. *Lawyers and the Supreme Court: How Laissez-faire Came to the Supreme Court.* Princeton: Princeton University Press.

Ulmer, S. Sidney. 1971. Earl Warren and the Brown Decision. *Journal of Politics* 33:689–702.

———. 1972. The Decision to Grant Certiorari as an Indicator to Decision 'On the Merits'. *Polity* 4:429–447.

———. 1973. Revising the Jurisdiction of the Supreme Court: Mere Administrative Reform or Substantive Policy Change. *Minnesota Law Review* 58:121–155.

———. 1982. Supreme Court Appointments as a Poisson Distribution. *American Journal of Political Science* 26:113–116.

———. 1984. The Supreme Court's Certiorari Decisions: Conflict as a Predictive Variable. *American Political Science Review* 78:901–911.

———. 1986. Are Social Background Models Time-Bound? *American Political Science Review* 80: 957–968.

Unger, Roberto M. 1976. *Law and Modern Society.* San Francisco: Free Press.

United States Reports. Washington, D.C.: Government Printing Office.

Vose, Clement. 1981. Interest Groups and Litigation. Paper delivered at the 1981 meeting of the American Political Science Association, New York, New York.

Walker, Thomas G., Lee Epstein, and William J. Dixon. 1988. On the Mysterious Demise of Consensual Norms in the United States Supreme Court. *Journal of Politics* 50:361–389.

Warren, Charles. 1913. The Progressiveness of the United States Supreme Court. *Senate Document* 30, 63d Congress.

———. 1932. *The Supreme Court in United States History,* Volume 2. Boston: Little Brown.

Wasby, Stephen L. 1981. Interest Group Litigation in an Age of Complexity. Paper delivered at the 1981 meeting of the American Political Science Association, New York.

———. 1979. *Volume and Delay in State Appellate Courts.* Williamsburg, Virginia: National Center for State Courts.

Wasby, Stephen; Thomas Marvell; and Alexander Aikman. 1978. *The Supreme Court in the Federal Judicial System.* New York: Holt, Rinehart, and Winston.

Wattenberg, Martin P. 1990. From a Partisan to a Candidate-Centered Electorate. In *The New American Political System,* ed. A. King. Washington, D.C.: The American Enterprise Institute Press.

Westin, Alan. 1953. The Supreme Court, the Populist Movement, and the Campaign of 1896. *Journal of Politics* 15:3–41.

Wiecek, William M. 1969. The Reconstruction of Federal Judicial Power, 1863–1875. *American Journal of Legal History* 13:333–359.

———. 1978. Slavery and Abolition Before the U.S. Supreme Court, 1820–1860. *Journal of American History* 65:34–59.

———. 1988. *Liberty under Law: The Supreme Court in American Life.* Baltimore: Johns Hopkins University Press.

Willetts, Peter, 1972. Cluster-Bloc Analysis and Statistical Inference. *American Political Science Review* 66:569–582.

Wilson, James Q. 1975. *Thinking About Crime.* New York: Basic Books.

Wolfe, Christopher. 1986. *The Rise of Modern Judicial Review: From Constitutional Interpretation to Judge-Made Law*. New York: Basic Books.

Wolfskill, George. 1962. *The Revolt of the Conservatives: A History of the American Liberty League, 1934–1940*. Boston: Houghton Mifflin Company.

Zemans, Frances Kahn. 1983. Legal Mobilization: The Neglected Role of the Law in the Political System. *American Political Science Review* 77:609–703.

Zimring, F.E. 1975. Firearms and Federal Law: The Gun Control Act of 1968. *Journal of Legal Studies* 4:133–194.

Appendix A:
Cases Cited in Text

Abington School District v. Schempp, 374 U.S. 361 (1963).
Adkins v. Children's Hospital, 261 U.S. 523 (1923).
Allgeyer v. Louisiana, 165 U.S. 578 (1897).
Aptheker v. Secretary of State, 378 U.S. 500 (1964).
Ashton v. Cameron County District, 298 U.S. 513 (1936).
Bailey v. Drexel Furniture Co., 259 U.S. 20 (1922).
Baker v. Carr, 369 U.S. 186 (1962).
Baldwin v. G.A.F. Seelig, 294 U.S. 511 (1935).
Barron v. Burnside, 121 U.S. 186 (1887).
Brown v. Board of Education, 347 U.S. 483 (1954).
Bush v. Orleans School Board, 364 U.S. 569 (1961).
Chicago, Milwaukee, and St. Paul Railway Co. v. Minnesota, 134 U.S. 418 (1890).
Connolly v. Union Sewer Pipe Co., 184 U.S. 540 (1902).
Coppage v. Kansas, 236 U.S. 1 (1915).
Cummings v. Missouri, 4 Wall. (71 U.S.) 277 (1867).
Delmas v. Insurance Company, 14 Wall. (81 U.S.) 661 (1872).
Dennis v. United States, 339 U.S. 162 (1950).
Eisner v. Macomber, 252 U.S. 189 (1920).
Engel v. Vitale, 370 U.S. 421 (1962).
Ex parte Garland, 4 Wall. (71 U.S.) 277 (1867).
Ex parte McCardle, 7 Wall. (74 U.S.) 506 (1869).
Ex parte Merryman, 17 F. Cas. 144 (No. 9487) (C.C. MD. 1861).
Ex parte Milligan, 4 Wall. (71 U.S.) 2 (1866).
Ex parte Yerger, 8 Wall. (75 U.S.) 85 (1869).
Ex parte Young, 209 U.S. 123 (1908).
Fairbank v. United States, 181 U.S. 283 (1901).
Fiske v. Kansas, 274 U.S. 380 (1927).
Gideon v. Wainwright, 372 U.S. 335 (1963).
Griffin v. Illinois, 351 U.S. 12 (1956).
Groves v. Slaughter, 15 Pet. (40 U.S.) 449 (1841).
Hall v. DeCuir, 95 U.S. 485 (1878).

Hammer v. Dagenhart, 247 U.S. 251 (1918).
Heart of Atlanta Motel v. United States, 379 U.S. 241 (1964).
Hepburn v. Griswold, 8 Wall. (75 U.S.) 603 (1870).
Hill v. Wallace, 259 U.S. 44 (1922).
Home Building & Loan Assn. v. Baisdell, 290 U.S. 398 (1934).
Hopkins Federal Savings & Loan Assn. v. Cleary, 296 U.S. 315 (1935).
In re Debs, 58 U.S. 564 (1895).
Katzenbach v. McClung, 379 U.S. 294 (1964).
Keith v. Clark, 97 U.S. 454 (1878).
Knickerbocker Ice Co. v. Stewart, 253 U.S. 149 (1920).
Knox v. Lee, 12 Wall. (79 U.S.) 457 (1871).
Lochner v. New York, 198 U.S. 45 (1905).
Louisville and Nashville Railway Co. v. Eubank, 184 U.S. 27 (1902).
Manly v. Georgia, 279 U.S. 1 (1929).
Mapp v. Ohio, 367 U.S. 643 (1961).
Marbury v. Madison, 1 Cranch 60 (1803).
Marshall v. Baltimore & Ohio Railroad Co., 16 How. (57 U.S.) 314 (1853).
Mayflower Farms v. Ten Eyck, 297 U.S. 266 (1936).
McCray v. United States, 195 U.S. 27 (1904).
McLaurin v. Oklahoma State Regents, 339 U.S. 637 (1950).
Monongahela Navigation Co. v. United States, 148 U.S. 312 (1893).
Morehead v. New York ex. rel. Tipaldo, 298 U.S. 587 (1936).
Munn v. Illinois, 94 U.S. 113 (1877).
Nebbia v. New York, 291 U.S. 502 (1934).
Osborne v. Nicholson, 13 Wall. (80 U.S.) 654 (1872).
Panama Refining Co. v. Ryan, 293 U.S. 388 (1935).
Passenger Cases, 7 How. (48 U.S.) 283 (1849).
Pierce v. Carskador, 16 Wall. (83 U.S.) 234 (1873).
Plessy v. Ferguson, 163 U.S. 537 (1896).
Pollock v. Farmer's Loan and Trust Co., 157 U.S. 429 (1895).
Prigg v. Pennsylvania, 16 Pet. (41 U.S.) 539 (1842).
Prize Cases, 2 Bl. (67 U.S.) 635 (1862).
Railroad Retirement Board v. Alton Railroad Co., 295 U.S. 330 (1935).
Reid v. Covert, 354 U.S. 1 (1957).
Ribnick v. McBride, 277 U.S. 350 (1928).
Schechter Poultry Corp. v. United States, 295 U.S. 495 (1935).
School District v. Schempp, 374 U.S. 203 (1963).
Second Employers' Liability Case, 233 U.S. 1 (1912).
Scott v. Sandford, 19 How. (60 U.S.) 393 (1857).
Sipwel v. Board of Regents, 332 U.S. 631 (1948).
Smyth v. Ames, 169 U.S. 466 (1898).
Southern Pacific Co. v. Jensen, 244 U.S. 205 (1917).
Sweatt v. Painter, 339 U.S. 629 (1950).
Swift v. United States, 196 U.S. 375 (1905).
Toth v. Quarles, 350 U.S. 11 (1955).
Trade Mark Cases, 100 U.S. 82 (1879).

Trop v. Dulles, 356 U.S. 86 (1958).
Truax v. Corrigan, 257 U.S. 312 (1921).
Tyson Brothers v. Bantom, 273 U.S. 418 (1927).
U.S. v. Klein, 13 Wall. (80 U.S.) 128 (1872).
U.S. v. Reese, 92 U.S. 214 (1876).
United States v. Cardiff, 344 U.S. 174 (1952)
United States v. Cohen Grocery Co., 255 U.S. 81 (1922).
United States v. E.C. Knight Co., 156 U.S. 1 (1895).
United States v. Hvoslef, 237 U.S. 1 (1915).
Wabash, St. Louis & Pacific Railway Co. v. Illinois, 118 U.S. 557 (1886).
Washington v. Dawson & Co., 264 U.S. 219 (1924).
Wesberry v. Saunders, 377 U.S. 533 (1964).
White v. Hart, 13 Wall. (80 U.S.) 646 (1872).
Wolff Packing Co. v. Industrial Court, 262 U.S. 522 (1923).

Appendix B:
Data Sources and
Research Methods

The theorist must straddle the fence between two desirable characteristics of a theory: reality and testability. The theory can be made increasingly realistic by adding to its complexity. But at some point it becomes too complex to be tested. The only resolution to this very real practical problem that we can visualize is through a theory-construction process that allows for many more complexities than possibly can be handled in any single piece of research. In effect this implies that our theories must "lead" our data-collection capabilities by a reasonable amount and must be sufficiently flexible to allow for additional complications introduced whenever measurement is crude or highly indirect. . . . Given the more complete and more general theory, a critic of any particular piece may then see more easily just where the shortcomings lie. . . . This, of course, makes the job of the critic much easier, but it also facilitates the process of linking the results of diverse pieces of research.

—Hubert M. Blalock and Paul Wilken
Intergroup Processes: A Micro-Macro Perspective

This appendix is an examination of the types of information and methods used in this study of Supreme Court policymaking, the invalidation of state and federal policies, and partisan realignment. The focus is primarily on research strategies employing quantification and statistical procedures. Interpretative and historical sources have also been utilized. The citations for these original and secondary historical sources appear throughout the book.

One of the central premises of this research is that the study of judicial policymaking and realignment should focus on the issue dynamics that underlie change in the party system. This raises a number of methodological concerns examined here. In addition, this appendix is a discussion of the methods used to investigate macrolevel relationships and the justices' voting. The final section is a brief review of the data and procedures for analyzing the partisan character of the states whose policies were subsequently overturned by the Supreme Court.

THE CASES OF STATE AND
FEDERAL POLICY INVALIDATIONS

The *Constitution of the United States: Analysis and Interpretation* (Library of Congress, 1978) provides a list of Supreme Court decisions declaring federal and state policies unconstitutional. It has become the standard sourcebook in the study of judicial review (e.g., Funston, 1975; Caldeira and McCrone, 1982). One clarification, however, is necessary with respect to the number of cases and the number of policies declared unconstitutional.

There are slight differences between the Library of Congress study and other studies in the number of policies struck down and the number of decisions listed. This is because the Supreme Court may dispose of several cases under a single opinion. Most studies (e.g., Caldeira and McCrone, 1982) treat such decisions as a single instance of judicial review. This study also employs this procedure but only when all of the policies overturned by a single opinion involve the same state and the policies relate to only one substantive legal or political issue. In those multiple disposition cases invalidating policies from different states, each policy is treated as a separate invalidation. The differences between the number of cases and the number of overturned policies are minor. There were six cases that invalidated policies enacted by different states. These cases are distributed rather evenly over the time frame of the study (i.e., 1849, 1876, 1913, 1923, 1954, 1964). This treatment of multiple dispositions is reasonable given the focus on the substantive issues over time and the partisan composition of the state governments. Throughout the book, however, the terms "case" and "policy" are used interchangeably. Appendix C lists the decisions striking down federal and state policies.

CONTENT ANALYSIS OF THE CASES

A central premise of this research is that judicial policymaking and partisan realignment must be issue focused. This requires identifying cases that raise issues relating to the basic question or cluster of issues surrounding realignment. The cases of judicial nullification were classified into issue categories. The cases were read in their entirety by a panel of researchers. Each policy was categorized into two different sets of issue areas that are related to the issues surrounding each party system. The first set of issue categories was previously used in Ginsberg's study of party platforms (1972) and federal statutes (1976). A more refined set of issue categories was also developed. As noted below, Ginsberg's issue categories proved to have serious problems of overinclusiveness and underinclusiveness when applied to Supreme Court decisions.

The classification of judicial decisions into issue areas appears intuitively straightforward and is widely used in some form (e.g., Goldman, 1975; Rohde and Spaeth, 1976; Tate, 1981). Nonetheless, it raises the question of whether the classification process is reliable or replicable by other analysts.

Quantitative content analysis assures reliable classification (Krippendorff, 1980; Johnson, 1987). As a field of social science inquiry, content analysis allows for reliable inferences regarding symbolic, verbal, or communicative data. This reliability is sought through the use of a panel of coders, explicit decision rules, limits on group discussions for purposes of classification, and other requirements necessary for replicating the analysis (Krippendorff, 1980: 20).

As noted, the content analysis involved classifying each policy as raising one of the seven issue or value categories developed by Ginsberg in his analysis of party platforms and federal statutes. These categories were initially appealing because a direct comparison could be made with the Supreme Court's invalidations and changes in party platforms and federal statutes. The seven issue categories are defined by Ginsberg (1972: 607) as follows:

(1) Capitalism, the aggregation of wealth and control over the distribution of wealth by business, financial and mercantile elites;

(2) Internal Sovereignty, the exercise of the power and increase of sphere of action of the central government *vis a vis* states, localities and individuals;

(3) Redistribution, the reallocation of wealth in favor of the economically disadvantaged;

(4) International Cooperation, open ended cooperation with and friendship toward foreign objects,

(5) Universalism, equality of rights and privileges for domestic minorities,

(6) Labor, labor and labor organizations; and,

(7) Ruralism, farms, and farmers and the rural way of life.

In addition, Ginsberg classifies each platform or statute as promoting or detracting from the value, such as Capitalism-Positive or Universalism-Negative. This second dimension is also used, which results in a twenty-one-fold classification scheme. This is seen in Table B.1. The "neither" category refers to instances when the issue or value was raised but the Supreme Court's decision could not be interpreted as either promoting or detracting from the value.[1]

Table B.1 also presents the distribution of cases in the various issue dimensions. The first column displays the percentage of the total cases classified by the author as raising one of the seven Ginsberg values and the twenty-one refined categories denoting the direction of value advocacy. Of the 743 policies, 660, or 88.8 percent, could be classified as raising six of the seven general value categories. No redistribution cases were found by more than one coder on the three-coder panel. Of the cases classified, the majority of cases raise the value of capitalism (65.5%). The second largest class of cases are universalism cases (11%). The remaining values are seen in even fewer instances: labor (5.6%), internal sovereignty (5.4%), ruralism (0.1%) and internal cooperation (0.3%).

Capitalism cases include a diverse group of cases ranging from issues of price and wage controls to general contractual relations. A capitalism-positive

TABLE B.1

Distribution of Ginsberg Issue Classification
and Percentage of Coder Agreement

	Percent of Total Cases		Coder Agreement
Capitalism	65.8	n=489	87.1
positive	59.9		86.8
negative	2.4		00.0
neither	3.2		00.0
Universalism	10.9	n=81	81.6
positive	9.8		78.1
negative	1.1		100.0
neither	-------		------
Labor	6.3	n=47	53.9
positive	2.7		65.0
negative	2.9		00.0
neither	.7		00.0
Internal Sovereignty	5.4	n=40	40.0
positive	-------		------
negative	5.4		40.0
neither	-------		------
Redistribution	00.0	n=0	00.0
positive	-------		------
negative	-------		------
neither	-------		------
Ruralism	00.1	n=1	00.0
positive	00.1		00.0
negative	-------		------
neither	-------		------
International Cooperation	00.3	n=2	50.0
positive	00.3		50.0
negative	-------		------
neither	-------		------
Not Classifiable by Ginsberg Issue Areas	11.2	n=83	64.0
Total	100.00	743	100.0

pi (coefficient of reliability) = 0.597
Overall Percentage of Agreement on Value Raised = 78.4
Overall Percentage of Agreement on Value and Direction of Value Advocacy = 74.8

Source: Compiled by author from *United States Reports.*

case supports the claims of a business subject to government taxation or regulation. For consistency with Ginsberg's classification scheme, cases of contractual relations favoring the contractual claim of a business, individual, or government are also treated as capitalism-positive. These cases raise questions of stable market relations. As will become evident, the inclusion of nonbusiness contractual cases in the broad category of capitalism raises problems of overinclusiveness in studying the relationship between the Supreme Court's invalidation of state and federal policies and realigning issues.

The capitalism-negative cases are rare. In one case, a state statute provided for a business monopoly and the claimant in the case was not another business interest. Negative advocacy was also found in cases denying a business an injunction in labor-management conflicts. These cases obviously raise issues of labor rights and capitalism. One procedure for dealing with this problem is to examine the nature of the litigants at the trial level. Although this is not an ideal resolution, this approach has been used in the study of state courts of last resort (Cartwright, 1975; Kagan, Cartwright, Friedman, and Wheeler, 1977; 1978). Hence, in cases raising both labor and capitalism issues, the names of the plaintiff and defendant at the trial level were recorded and the appropriate decision criteria were used.

In contrast to the value of capitalism, Ginsberg's universalism value is seen in only a narrow class of Supreme Court decisions usually subsumed under the broader class of "civil rights and civil liberties" (e.g., Goldman, 1975). Ginsberg uses this category for party platforms and federal statutes that are directed explicitly at "domestic minorities." Issues of the rights of criminal defendants and prisoners were not considered by Ginsberg as questions related to domestic minorities. Moreover, the value of universalism does not include cases dealing with free expression of religion or the media. The omission of these issues limits the connection of this class of cases to the "social issue," which was important in the critical elections of 1960 and 1964. The absence of this class of interests in Ginsberg's categories may reside in his focus on federal statutes and national party platforms. Many of these volatile issues have been the province only of state law.

Cases advocating the value of universalism in a positive direction include the invalidation of policies requiring racial segregation in various areas of national life such as transportation, education, and public accommodations. The overturning of policies restricting the employment rights of aliens are also classified universalism-positive. Universalism-negative cases include the invalidation of policies enforcing various political rights for blacks.

The labor cases center on laborers' rights including workmen's compensation and general labor-management relations. Labor interests in these cases represent the plaintiffs at the trial level. The value of labor is promoted in a positive fashion in cases that restrict the liability of employers from the claims of injured workers. The invalidation of policies limiting a labor union's ability to strike or reducing the possibilities for compulsory arbitration are also labor-positive. Alternatively, labor-negative cases involve the invalidation of policies enhancing the position of labor interests, such as a state statute outlawing the use of "yellow-dog" contracts by employers.

In some cases, the result of a decision could not be classified as either positive or negative advocacy of the labor value. These "labor-neither" cases involve the invalidation of state laws, but the Court did not rule in favor of either party. Instead, the Court remanded the case for reconsideration by lower courts. Hence, it is difficult to assign a direction to these labor cases because either party could have eventually been successful in the lower courts. The vast majority of "labor-neither" cases strike down state laws on the grounds that the laws infringed on the federal jurisdiction of the National Labor Relations Board.

The category of internal sovereignty is similar to the general constitutional area of federalism or the distribution of federal and state power. Although all of the cases of state law invalidation raise *doctrinal* issues of federalism, this category includes only those cases in which the *result* of the case and the state policy in question did not involve societal interests such as individuals, businesses, or interest groups. Hence, cases of internal sovereignty are limited to disputes in which the only parties in the case are governmental and the policy does not relate explicitly to other interests. The cases of internal sovereignty, for example, include the invalidation of state laws relating to state claims over the control of coastal waterways and state taxes levied on national financial instruments or national land. The direction of advocacy in these cases is inevitably negative because the legislative power of the state is limited.

The second column of Table B.1 presents the percentage of agreement between my classification and those of one other coder on each policy. The panel agreed that the value of capitalism was found in over 87 percent of the 743 cases. One would expect slightly less agreement in assigning the advocacy direction because this requires a more subtle judgment. Surprisingly, the panel agrees in nearly 87 percent of the capitalism-positive cases. The lowest level of agreement for a class of cases constituting more than one percent of the total cases is 40 percent agreement for internal sovereignty. This is an important difference in agreement as noted below. It is necessary to test the reliability of the classification process.

The test of reliable data in content analysis usually focuses on the extent of agreement between coders. The percentage of agreement is often reported in research using a panel of coders for content analysis. This measure, however, does not account for the level of agreement one would expect on the basis of chance (Krippendorff, 1980: 135). A variety of more rigorous reliability statistics are available including sophisticated weighting procedures for ordinal categories (Landis and Koch, 1977). Given the nominal nature of the Ginsberg categories, the pi statistic is used.[2] The value of pi ranges from 0 to 1. The value of 1 signifies the highest level of agreement. The content analysis of the cases yields an initial pi of 0.597. This coefficient represents a moderate level of agreement above what one would expect on the basis of random agreement given the number of cases, categories, and coders. Krippendorff (1980: 147) reports that an arbitrary convention has developed in communication research that requires a value greater than 0.670.[3]

Krippendorff argues that unreliable data are not unusable, especially when the source of unreliability can be located. Various factors can affect the level of agreement. These include structural and case-specific factors. A structural factor inherent in the classification process is the months of analysis and panel meetings designed to discuss generic problems of classification.[4] It may be that the level of agreement increased over time due to increased familiarity with the classification process.

To investigate this possibility, a three-point summary scale of agreement was developed and correlated with the sequence number of the cases. The sequence number represents the order in which the cases were analyzed. If the level of agreement increases over time, one would expect a high positive correlation with the sequence number and the scale of agreement. The Pearsonian correlation coefficient is -0.160. This is not only low but its value is not in the expected direction. This result shows that time or familiarity with the coding procedure is not a factor in coder agreement.

Agreement among the coders may be affected by certain case characteristics. Four case characteristics perhaps contribute to case complexity and coder disagreement: the number of written dissents, the number of concurrences, the total number of opinions, and the page length of the entire case. Again the results of correlational analysis show that these case-specific factors are not collinear with the level of agreement among coders. None of the coefficients were above 0.05, and only one was statistically significant.

Aside from structural and case-specific factors, the source of unreliability in the data may reside in differences between coders on one or more issue areas. Some coders may be more careful, thorough, or simply more understanding of the coding scheme (Krippendorff, 1980: 149–152). Individual reliability becomes suspect when one examines the number of errors by each value category. The errors or disagreements with the author and Coder A are rather evenly distributed over the twenty-one categories as a proportion of all cases. This even error distribution across issue categories is not found in the errors of Coder B; 22 percent of the total errors occur among the sixteen cases under the value of redistribution. Neither the author nor Coder A classified a single case under the rubric of redistribution. Further, an additional 20 percent of the errors occur in cases the author identified as either not-classifiable or as internal sovereignty cases. The classification of internal sovereignty was reserved for cases that presented the constitutional issue of federalism without the presence of other issues and when the only parties were government interests. This distinction had proven difficult during the pretest and apparently confused Coder B.

Krippendorff recommends that when there is a problem of category unreliability, the problem categories can be eliminated from the data and a new coefficient of reliability computed. After removing the internal sovereignty and redistribution categories from the data, the value of pi increased from 0.597 to 0.655. This is encouraging because these categories are not salient to partisan realignment, which strongly suggests that the remaining issue classifications are replicable by other analysts. This is not to argue for the objective character of the data but only to say that other analysts can achieve very similar or identical results.

The content analysis of the cases of judicial review is successful. There is, however, a major problem in relating Ginsberg's categories to critical or realigning issues. The categories of capitalism and universalism are especially troubling when the focus is on judicial policies and realignment. First, the cases classified as capitalism include an extremely diverse class of economic disputes and policies. The category includes policies related to the regulation of business, contracts, and debt. The salient economic issues of the 1890s, however, relate to the control of economic interests. Ginsberg's capitalism value is simply too broad for the diverse set of state and federal policies and the critical issues of the 1890s and 1930s. Fortunately, the panel of coders also recorded the types of litigants at the original trial and before the Supreme Court. This provides a reliable filter for excluding personal contract and debt cases and preserves the integrity of the content analysis using Ginsberg's categories.

The value of universalism is also restrictive for discussing the social issue of the 1950s and 1960s. Ginsberg limits the definition of *universalism* to federal statutes or party platforms relating to "domestic minorities." Unfortunately, the "social issue" of relevance to the critical elections of 1960 and 1964 includes many other issues. This problem led to the development of many refined issue categories that could be grouped into a few broad issue areas. Table B.2 displays the broader areas.

The largest class of cases are those raising policy issues of business taxation and regulation. This category contains 33.1 percent, or 246, of the 743 cases. The cases range from disputes dealing with state repeal of charter tax provisions to regulation of railroad practices. This category also includes conflicts regarding price controls on selected products, business license fees, and issues of general business taxation. Further, questions concerning the exercise and extent of governmental power over individual businesspersons or companies in the conduct of business are found in this category. The major difference between this category and the previously discussed capitalism category is that it does not include cases of contractual relations between individuals and nonbusiness taxation.

The second largest issue category is civil rights and civil liberties. The 134 cases constitute 18.0 percent of all cases. This category includes the famous school desegregation cases as well as other civil rights and civil liberties cases such as nineteenth-century controversies over the sterilization of habitual criminals.

The third largest category of cases raises issues of general nonbusiness taxation and contractual relations and constitutes 13.5 percent of the total cases. The types of policies range from personal and property tax statutes to those establishing rights in real estate transfer proceedings.

TABLE B.2

Distribution of the Invalidation of Federal and State Policies
by Policy Area, 1836-1964

	Number	Percent of Total
Business Regulation and Taxation	327	44.0
Civil Rights and Liberties	131	17.6
General Nonbusiness Taxation, Contracts & Debts	101	13.6
Labor Rights	57	7.7
Slavery, Civil War, and Reconstruction	20	2.7
National Banking	18	2.4
Public Land Disptues	14	1.9
Alcohol Control	13	1.7
Municipal Bonds	13	1.7
State Banking	10	1.3
Immigration Policy	4	0.5
Miscellaneous[a]	35	4.7
Total	743	100.0

[a]Some of the issues included in this category focus on federal court removal and receivership, the distribution of power between the branches of the national government, and questions of state versus national control of coastal waterways. There was no miscellaneous category in the content analysis. Miscellaneous is used only for tabular presentation.

Source: Compiled by author from *United States Reports.*

The fourth largest category of cases, regulation and taxation of railroads, is analyzed in Chapters 2, 3, and 4 under the more general category of business regulation and taxation. The significance of railroad regulation in the realignment of the 1890s merits separate tabular presentation. The cases classified in this category range from policies dealing with state attempts to regulate the rates charged by railroads to general damage remedies and safety practices.

The only other category of cases constituting more than 3 percent of the total cases is labor rights (7.6%). The policies include several regulatory schemes such as peonage laws, compulsory arbitration statutes, the rights of labor unions in contract negotiations, and picketing.[5]

This classification allows one to examine only those cases raising realigning or salient issues for each period of realignment. As Sundquist (1973) elaborates, the realigning issues are different in each period. One example illustrates this important point. A select number of civil rights and liberties policies are found in cases of invalidation before 1900. These issues are of little importance to the realigning or critical issues of the 1890s. These types of cases are, however, especially important to the critical issues of race and the "social issue" in the late 1950s and early 1960s. Each chapter includes a discussion of the relevance of the various policy areas.

This lengthy explanation of the issue classification of the cases of judicial review is important. A fundamental assumption of this work is that only certain judicial policies are relevant or salient to partisan realignment. It is important to establish that the cases were not classified in an ad hoc or nonreplicable manner.

The following sections examine the methodological issues in the study of Supreme Court outcomes over time and the justices' voting.

ASSESSING CHANGE
IN THE LEVEL OF INVALIDATIONS

The study of Supreme Court policymaking and partisan realignment focuses a great deal of attention on the relationship between decisions by the Court and critical elections. Most studies examine whether invalidations increase significantly following these elections. Interpretative analyses also focus on decisions before a critical election. Neither approach examines precisely the pattern of salient decisions over time. It is possible to arrive at precise estimates for inferring relationships through statistical time-series methods.

In fact, one can conceptualize the various periods of realignment as events, or "shocks," to the normal policymaking of the Supreme Court. In this light, the most appropriate measurement strategy is an interrupted time-series design (e.g., Lewis-Beck, 1986). This type of time-series analysis is used extensively in various contexts including the assessment of the impact of psychological treatment on patient behavior and the impact of legal changes on certain types of criminal behavior (Zimring, 1975; cf. Glass, 1968; Hibbs, 1977b: Caldeira and McCrone, 1982). The goal is to arrive at precise estimates of the change in the time series in a quasi-experimental or a "before and after" fashion. In this study, specific periods during realignment are conceptualized as impacts on the Supreme Court's invalidation of salient federal and state laws.

Estimating change in an interrupted time-series design has received considerable attention (Beck, 1983; McCleary and Hay, 1980; Hibbs, 1974; 1977a; 1977b; Lewis-Beck, 1986; Shamir, 1983). Least-squares regression is a common tool but it is often inappropriate in its standard form in a time-series design. The major problem resides in the error component of the general linear model. The error term represents the unspecified elements of the theoretical model. Least-squares regression assumes that the error component is a series of truly random shocks to the observations. Least-squares estimates of a series of observations will be accurate only when these shocks or errors are distributed randomly and independently over time. This is often a problem in time-series analysis of political and economic data because the error component in year 1 is likely to be correlated with the error in year 2; social processes often change cumulatively and gradually over time. This is the problem of autocorrelation.

The presence of autocorrelation means that the same distribution of events or shocks at one point in time also arises at another point. If autocorrelation is present, least-squares regression may lead to erroneous estimates and substantive conclusions. When autocorrelation is detected in the ordinary least-squares estimates, efficient and unbiased estimates can be achieved by using generalized least-squares regression (Hibbs, 1977a; 1977b). This method is a two-step process of estimation. First, ordinary least-squares regression provides estimates of the disturbances. Second, these values are transformed by a value of rho and reestimated through ordinary least squares.

The generalized least-squares method is based on a linear statistical model. There is evidence that a different estimation strategy may provide more efficent and unbiased estimates when the dependent variable is basically an event count and other conditions are found. This is relevant to this research because the yearly number of policies declared unconstitutional is a typical event count. Such event-count models appear to be more precisely estimated using some version of the exponential Poisson regression model (e.g., Cameron and Trivedi, 1986; King, 1988). Although Poisson regression is more precise and should always be used to examine the robustness of estimates derived from a linear estimation technique, I chose not to present Poisson regression results in tabular form because the overall substantive results are the same as those provided with a linear statistical model. The linear or least-squares results are more readily interpretable for social scientists who are only now becoming aware of Poisson regression. Undoubtedly, it is a superior statistical estimator for event counts (King, 1988; 1989: 14–37). In the present context and time, however, it serves more appropriately as a check on the substantive thrust of the findings. Hence, linear models are presented in the text to estimate the macrolevel models. Nevertheless, results based upon Poisson regression are presented in footnotes.[6]

Regardless of the statistical estimation strategy, an interrupted time-series design provides a model for assessing change in the series of invalidations and can be formally stated as

$$I_t = a + b_1 \text{ Time1}_t + b_2 \text{ Time2}_t + b_3 R_t + e_t$$

where, I_t is the number of salient cases decided by the Court in each year of the time series considered; a is the constant term; Time1_t is the overall time trend; Time2_t is the time trend after the period of theoretical interest; R_t is a bivariate qualitative variable and takes the value of 1 during the years when the number of salient policies should increase and 0 in the remaining years; and e_t is the error term. The parameters to be estimated are represented by the coefficients b_1, b_2, and b_3. The values of the coefficients determine the degree of change in the series of invalidations. The change in the number of invalidations may range from no change over the series to major transformational change; that is, the event has a long-term impact on the series of observations following the event.

The precise logic of this design is that the coefficients estimate trends before, during, and after a particular event. If, for example, all of the parameter estimates are positive and significant in a statistical sense, then an analyst could conclude that the event had a positive and major impact on the entire trend of increasing events or phenomena. However, a negative value for the time trend after the event suggests a major negative impact following the event even though the coefficient detecting its impact is positive (showing a significant but brief increase in the dependent variable during the event).

THE VOTING PATTERNS OF THE JUSTICES

The voting records of the seventy-five justices serving on the Supreme Court from 1837 to 1964 provides important information on the Supreme Court and partisan realignment. Microlevel, or individual-level, information aids in testing the various assumptions underlying many theories that posit a connection between policy outputs and realignment. Funston (1975) and, to a lesser extent, Adamany (1973, 1980) argue that there will be policy conflict between the Supreme Court and the popularly elected branches following a critical election. At this time, the Court will be a holdover from the "old regime" confronting a new and victorious opposition. Adamany (1973: 824–825) writes: "Command of the Court by men of the old majority, slow turnover on the bench, and the added reluctance of the justices to resign after a new lawmaking majority is inaugurated all set the stage for conflict between the Supreme Court and the new dominant electoral co-alition."[7] The argument that there will be policy conflict between the Supreme Court and a new majority party emphasizes the connection between the justices' party affiliations and their decisionmaking.

There have been no attempts to provide empirical support for these arguments other than historical and interpretive analysis of selected major decisions.[8] By examining the justices' voting in cases of invalidation, various assumptions underlying this argument can be tested.

An alternative hypothesis has been suggested by William Lasser in his analysis of the New Deal cases,[9] the *Income Tax Case* of 1895,[10] and *Dred Scott* (1983a; 1983b).[11] Lasser argues that the political party affiliation of the justices becomes less important as a guide to decisionmaking in the years surrounding critical elections. He found in these select cases that the justices came to divide along new lines of cleavage that did not necessarily reflect their previous partisan affiliations. The crosscutting nature of critical issues divided the justices in new ways similar to the impact of these issues on the party system (Sundquist, 1973). If this argument is correct, one would not expect the justices to divide along party lines.

In order to address these alternative hypotheses, data were collected on the voting records of each justice in all cases of judicial review. Moreover, comparative data on the Supreme Court's rate of dissent in all cases decided with opinion were culled from various sources (Blaustein and Mersky, 1978; Johnston, 1972; Goldman, 1982; Fairman, 1966; Magrath, 1963; Frank, 1964; Frankfurter, 1938; Halpern, n.d.). These dissent rates allow a comparison of the dissent in the realigning or salient and nonsalient cases as well as in all cases decided with opinion.

Clearly, the partisan affiliation of the justices is an incomplete guide to decisionmaking on judicial bodies.[12] Within the context of the Court and partisan realignment, however, the *degree* of partisan division assumes importance for understanding the internal dynamics on the Court. Certainly, there are a host of factors that affect a justice's voting including informal norms, leadership, environmental factors, and institutional procedures and structure (e.g., Gibson, 1980; Adamany, 1969; Canon and Jaros, 1970; Walker, Epstein, and Dixon, 1988). Nevertheless, these factors may be of secondary importance in cases decided at times of intense political party polarization and national concern with the critical or realigning issues. Hence, the role of the justices' partisan affiliation is examined and compared in the salient and nonsalient cases.

The small number of salient cases in a given year also raises other issues. Some of these issues are discussed throughout the book. Because one aim of the research is to examine the relationship between the justices' partisan affiliations and voting in salient cases, the method used deserves elaboration. First, it would be ideal if there were a large number of cases during "natural courts" when membership did not change, because sophisticated voting-bloc techniques could be applied (e.g., Bolner, Feldman, and Gates, 1982). Unfortunately, this is not the case. It is nonetheless possible to examine the justices' rates of dissent and their partisan affiliations across both salient and nonsalient cases. Although admittedly imperfect, it is a reasonable approach given the limited alternatives.

More precise methods also support this approach. Regression results based on the justices' percentage of party-line support for the case outcome is consistent with these simple dissent rates. Moreover, correlation and probit analysis of individual votes for and against the case outcome are also consistent with the dissent rates. These results are not shown because it was not possible to obtain statistically significant relationships across all three periods of realignment. Significant and consistent results were found in two of the three periods. Unfortunately, the insignificant results varied across different periods depending upon the different estimation strategy. In every instance of statistically significant findings, however, the results support the simple rank-ordering of the justice's simple rate of dissent in each period.[13]

Another methodological issue is sparse measurement. It is expected that dissent writing and party-line voting will be evident in the cases related to the critical, realigning issues. Although such comparisons across realigning eras appear straightforward, there is a complicating factor. If the level of nonunanimous cases is computed on a yearly basis, the number of such cases is small throughout most of the nineteenth century. This sparseness of measurement could introduce instability in the data because the rate could fluctuate greatly with only an increase of one or two cases. One means of determining whether the changes in the rate over time are due to the small number of cases is to examine the correlation between the magnitude of change in the rate for every other year in the series and the number of cases in that year or the total number of cases in the two-year period (Sprague, 1968: 63–68). The results show virtually no correlation using Spearman's rank-order coefficient (rho = −0.178 and −0.218; sig. = 0.05). The rate changes are not due to the small number of cases but to some other factor or combination of factors. It was necessary to exclude the period 1836 to 1864 because of the presence of only one or two cases in several years.

THE PARTISAN CONTROL OF STATE GOVERNMENTS AND INVALIDATED STATE POLICIES

This research shows how state policies often relate to partisan realignment. Although previous studies focus almost exclusively on the invalidation of federal statutes, state policies often reflect the party ideology. As expected, the salient state policies struck down by the Supreme Court are often enacted by state partisan majorities contrary to the partisan character of the Court (Gates, 1987). The data on the partisan character of states were collected based on the partisan composition of state governments in the year in which the law was enacted. Given the date of enactment, each state was classified as either Democratic, Republican, or mixed on the basis of plurality control of both houses of the state legislature and the governorship (Clubb, Flanigan, and Zingale, 1980). These data serve as a measure of majority preferences at the state level.[14]

NOTES

1. Following the general guidelines provided by Krippendorff (1980), the process began with a two-week period of training the research associates and pretesting the coding rules. Each coder read several works dealing with realignment (Sundquist, 1973; Brady and Stewart, 1982) and the Supreme Court's role in relignment (Adamany, 1980). One hundred cases were read by the author and two research associates during the pretest, and meetings were held every other day to discuss problems with the coding rules. The second period involved dividing all of the cases equally between the two research associates. Each coder read roughly one-half of the cases. Their classification of the cases was then compared with my classification of all cases. At no time did any of the coders discuss classification problems even in a generic sense. The coders were recent graduates of prominent law schools with an interest in political history. One coder majored in political science as an undergraduate and the other coder majored in history.

2. In formal terms, pi can be stated as

$$pi = P\ (O)\ \text{-}P\ (E)\ /\ (1\ \text{-}P\ (E)),$$

where

P (O) = the proportion of observed agreement; and

P (E) = the proportion of expected agreement based on the marginals of an interagreement matrix formed by the cases and categories.

3. The reliability statistic can be significantly affected by two conditions that inflate its value: (1) the presence of a large number of categories for each case; and

(2) an even distribution of case assignments to the various categories (Scott, 1955; Johnson, 1987). These two conditions change the expected agreement part of the pi coefficient. The pi reported is robust because the data meet only one of these conditions, the large number of categories. Further, there is not an even distribution of assignments. There is a maldistribution of assignments to one category (59.9 percent).

4. In these meetings, the researchers did not reach agreement on specific cases. This preserved the integrity of the written coding instructions, which are available from the author (46 pp.).

5. The different number of labor cases in Tables B.1 and B.2 is because the cases involving a remand to lower courts are not classified as either supporting or detracting from the claims of labor.

6. The computations were provided through two different statistical software progams. The least-squares and generalized least-squares results were computed using the Time Series Processor (TSP) (v. 4.1a). The software program COUNT (v. 2.1 by Gary King) computed the Poisson results. (All other statistical analyses reported in the book were obtained using one of the following computing programs: SHAZAM (version 6.1); SPSSX (version 3.1); SYSTAT (version 2).

7. See King (1987) for evidence that turnover on the Court is related to the extent of change in the membership of Congress. But the relationship is not extremely strong.

8. But see Schmidhauser (1961), who did examine partisan voting before the critical election of 1860.

9. E.g., *Schechter Poultry Corporation v. U.S.*, 295 U.S. 4–95 (1935); *Carter v. Carter Coal Co.*, 298 U.S. 238 (1936).

10. *Pollock v. Farmers' Loan & Trust Co.*, 158 U.S. 601 (1895).

11. *Dred Scott v. Sanford*, 19 Howard 393 (1857).

12. The studies of judicial voting are voluminous and encompass a variety of theoretical perspectives (e.g., Segal, 1984; Schmidhauser, 1961; Sprague, 1968; Goldman, 1975; Gibson, 1977; 1978; 1980; Tate, 1981; Goldman and Lamb, 1986). The role of the judge's political party affiliation has been a major concern for American judicial scholars because of what Pitkin (1967) has termed "standing for" representation. Further, the political party affiliation of judges has been examined as one of the various social background factors in the attempt to build explanatory models. The incomplete and uneven explanation afforded by a simple attitude-behavior model has led to greater complexity such as incorporating the normative orientations of the judge to the role of judging and to external or environmental factors (Gibson, 1983; 1978; 1977; Howard, 1981; Atkins and Glick, 1976) and consideration of the changing mix of case factors (Segal, 1984; Baum, 1988).

13. After nearly two years of attempting to overcome these methodological problems and provide multivariate voting analysis, it may not be surprising that I quote the following: "Rather than introduce 'new' techniques in an either/or manner, future political methodologists should pay some attention to the possible complementaries that exist. After all, the goal of political science is explanation and understanding not seeing who has the most impressive method" (Ostrom and Smith, 1990:24).

14. There are some missing-data problems. In 211, or 31.5 percent, of the cases, the date of enactment could not be located because the Court did not give the citation of the statute. In another 165 instances, the state code citation of the statute did not yield the actual date of enactment. When the date of enactment is missing, the Court's decision date was used for classifying the partisan character of a state.

Undoubtedly, this introduces some unreliability into the partisan-control data. Nevertheless, partisan control in the states is rather stable (Clubb, Flanigan, and Zingale, 1980). There is strong evidence of partisan stability within states. The correlation between the partisan composition of a state at the time of actual enactment and the partisan status at the time of the Court's decision is 0.857. Moreover, over 80 percent of the policies were under ten years of age.

Appendix C: U.S. Supreme Court Cases Invalidating Federal Statutes, State Statutes, and State Constitutional Provisions, 1837–1964

A Quantity of Copies of Books v. Kansas, 378 U.S. 205 (1964).
Abington School Dist. v. Schempp, 374 U.S. 203 (1963).
Achison v. Huddleson, 12 How. (53 U.S.) 293 (1852).
Adair v. United States, 208 U.S. 161 (1908).*
Adams Express Co. v. Croninger, 226 U.S. 491 (1913).
Adams Express Co. v. Kentucky, 206 U.S. 129 (1907).
Adams Express Co. v. Kentucky, 214 U.S. 218 (1909).
Adams Mfg. Co. v. Storen, 304 U.S. 307 (1938).
Adams v. Tanner, 244 U.S. 590 (1917).
Adkins v. Children's Hospital, 261 U.S. 525 (1923).*
Aetna Life Ins. Co. v. Dunken, 266 U.S. 389 (1924).
Air-Way Corp. v. Day, 266 U.S. 71 (1924).
Allen v. Galveston Truck Line Corp., 289 U.S. 708 (1933).
Allen v. Pullman Company, 191 U.S. 171 (1903).
Allgeyer v. Louisiana, 165 U.S. 578 (1897).
Almy v. California, 24 How. (65 U.S.) 169 (1861).
Alpha Cement Co. v. Massachusetts, 268 U.S. 203 (1925).
American Express Company v. Caldwell, 244 U.S. 617 (1917).
American Smelting Co. v. Colorado, 204 U.S. 103 (1907).
Anderson v. Martin, 375 U.S. 399 (1964).
Anglo-Chilean Corp. v. Alabama, 288 U.S. 218 (1933).
Appleby v. City of New York, 271 U.S. 365 (1926).
Aptheker v. Secretary of State, 378 U.S. 500 (1964).*
Arizona Publishing Co. v. O'Neil, 304 U.S. 543 (1938).
Asher v. Texas, 128 U.S. 129 (1888).

---

*Asterisks following cites throughout this list indicate that a federal statute was declared unconstitutional.

Ashton v. Cameron County Dist., 298 U.S. 513 (1936).*
Askren v. Continental Oil Co., 252 U.S. 444 (1920).
Asylum v. New Orleans, 105 U.S. 362 (1881).
Atchison, T. & S.F. Railway Co. v. O'Connor, 223 U.S. 280 (1912).
Atchison, T. & S.F. Railway Co. v. Vosburg, 238 U.S. 56 (1915).
Atchison, T. & S.F. Railway Co. v. Wells, 265 U.S. 101 (1924).
Baggett v. Bullitt, 377 U.S. 360 (1964).
Bailey v. Alabama, 219 U.S. 219 (1911).
Bailey v. Drexel Furniture Co., 259 U.S. 20 (1922).*
Bailey v. Patterson, 369 U.S. 31 (1962).
Baizley Iron Works v. Span, 281 U.S. 222 (1930).
Baldwin v. G.A.F. Seelig, 294 U.S. 511 (1935).
Baldwin v. Missouri, 281 U.S. 586 (1930).
Bank Tax Case, 2 Wall. (69 U.S.) 200 (1865).
Bank of Commerce v. New York City, 2 Bl. (67 U.S.) 620 (1863).
Bank of Commerce v. Tennessee, 161 U.S. 134 (1896).
Bank of Minden v. Clement, 256 U.S. 126 (1921).
Bank v. Supervisors, 7 Wall. (74 U.S.) 26 (1868).
Barings v. Dabney, 19 Wall. (86 U.S.) 1 (1873).
Barnitz v. Beverly, 163 U.S. 118 (1896).
Barron v. Burnside, 121 U.S. 186 (1887).
Bartels v. Iowa, 262 U.S. 404 (1923).
Beidler v. South Carolina Tax Comm., 282 U.S. 1 (1930).
Bell v. Burson, 402 U.S. 535 (1971).
Berryman v. Whitman College, 222 U.S. 334 (1912).
Best v. Maxwell, 311 U.S. 454 (1940).
Bethlehem Motors Co. v. Flynt, 256 U.S. 421 (1921).
Bethlehem Steel Co. v. New York Employment Relations Board, 330 U.S. 767
    (1947).
Bibb v. Navajo Freight Lines, 359 U.S. 520 (1959).
Bingaman v. Golden Eagle Lines, 297 U.S. 626 (1936).
Binney v. Long, 299 U.S. 280 (1936).
Blake v. McClung, 172 U.S. 239 (1898).
Bogle v. Jakes Foundry Co., 362 U.S. 401 (1960).
Bohning v. Ohio, 262 U.S. 404 (1923).
Booth v. United States, 291 U.S. 339 (1934).*
Bowman v. Chicago & Nw. Railway Co., 125 U.S. 465 (1888).
Bowman v. Continental Oil Co., 256 U.S. 642 (1921).
Boyd v. United States, 116 U.S. 616 (1886).*
Boynton v. Virginia, 364 U.S. 454 (1960).
Bradley v. Illinois, 4 Wall. (71 U.S.) 459 (1867).
Bradley v. Lightcap, 195 U.S. 1 (1904).
Brimmer v. Rebman, 138 U.S. 78 (1891).
Broderick v. Rosner, 294 U.S. 629 (1935).
Bronson v. Kinzie, 1 How. (42 U.S.) 311 (1843).
Brooke v. Norfolk, 277 U.S. 27 (1928).

Brown v. Board of Education, 347 U.S. 483 (1954).
Browning v. Hooper, 269 U.S. 396 (1926).
Buck v. Kuykendall, 267 U.S. 307 (1925).
Bucks Stove Co. v. Vickers, 226 U.S. 205 (1912).
Bunch v. Cole, 263 U.S. 250 (1923).
Burns Baking Co. v. Bryan, 264 U.S. 504 (1924).
Bus Employees v. Missouri, 374 U.S. 74 (1963).
Bus Employees v. WERB, 340 U.S. 383 (1951).
Bush Co. v. Maloy, 267 U.S. 317 (1925).
Bush v. Orleans School Board, 364 U.S. 500 (1961).
Butler v. Michigan, 352 U.S. 380 (1957).
California v. Pacific Railroad Co., 127 U.S. 1 (1888).
Callan v. Wilson, 127 U.S. 540 (1888).*
Campbell v. Hussey, 368 U.S. 297 (1961).
Cantwell v. Connecticut, 310 U.S. 296 (1940).
Carondelet Canal Co. v. Louisiana, 233 U.S. 362 (1914).
Carpenter v. Shaw, 280 U.S. 363 (1930).
Carr v. City of Attus, 385 U.S. 35 (1966).
Carrington v. Rash, 380 U.S. 89 (1965).
Carson Petroleum Co. v. Vial, 279 U.S. 95 (1929).
Carson v. Roane-Anderson Co., 342 U.S. 232 (1952).
Carter v. Carter Coal Co., 298 U.S. 238 (1936).*
Case of the State Freight Tax, 15 Wall. (82 U.S.) 232 (1873).
Castle v. Hayes Freight Lines, 348 U.S. 61 (1954).
Central Railroad Co. v. Pennsylvania, 370 U.S. 607 (1962).
Central of Georgia Railway Co. v. Murphey, 196 U.S. 194 (1905).
Central of Georgia Railway Co. v. Wright, 248 U.S. 525 (1919).
Central of Georgia Railway v. Wright, 207 U.S. 127 (1907).
Chalker v. Birmingham & N.W. Railway Co., 249 U.S. 522 (1919).
Chamberlin v. Dade County Board of Public Instruction, 377 U.S. 402 (1964).
Champlain Co. v. Brattleboro, 260 U.S. 366 (1922).
Champlin Rfg. Co. v. Corporation Comm., 286 U.S. 210 (1932).
Charleston & W. C. Railway Co. v. Varnville Co., 237 U.S. 597 (1915).
Cheney Brothers Co. v. Massachusetts, 246 U.S. 147 (1918).
Chicago & N.W. Railway v. Nye Schneider Fowler Co., 260 U.S. 35 (1922).
Chicago, B. & Q. Railway v. Wisconsin R. R. Com., 237 U.S. 220 (1915).
Chicago, B. & Q. Railway v. Hall, 229 U.S. 511 (1913).
Chicago, B. & Q. Railway v. Miller, 226 U.S. 513 (1913).
Chicago, M. & St. P. Railway Co. v. Minnesota, 134 U.S. 418 (1890).
Chicago, M. & St. P. Railway Co. v. Polt, 232 U.S. 165 (1914).
Chicago, M. & St. P. Railway v. Wisconsin, 238 U.S. 491 (1915).
Chicago, R.I. & P. Railway Co. v. Hardwick Elevator Co., 226 U.S. 426 (1913).
Chicago, St. P., M. & O. Railway Co. v. Latta, 226 U.S. 519 (1913).
Chicago, St. P., M. & P. Railway v. Holmberg, 282 U.S. 162 (1930).
Childers v. Beaver, 270 U.S. 555 (1926).
Choate v. Trapp, 224 U.S. 665 (1912).*

Choctaw & Gulf Railroad v. Harrison, 235 U.S. 292 (1914).
Christmas v. Russell, 5 Wall. (72 U.S.) 290 (1867).
Chy Lung v. Freeman, 92 U.S. 275 (1876).
Cipriano v. City of Houma, 395 U.S. 701 (1969).
City of New Orleans v. Barthe, 376 U.S. 189 (1964).
Civil Rights Cases, 109 U.S. 3 (1883).*
Clallam County v. United States, 263 U.S. 341 (1923).
Cleveland, C. C. & St. L. Railway Co. v. Illinois, 177 U.S. 514 (1900).
Cline v. Frink Dairy Co., 274 U.S. 445 (1927).
Cloverleaf Butter Co. v. Patterson, 315 U.S. 148 (1942).
Coe v. Armour Fertilizer Works, 237 U.S. 413 (1915).
Cole v. La Grange, 113 U.S. 1 (1885).
Colgate v. Harvey, 296 U.S. 404 (1935).
Collins v. New Hampshire, 171 U.S. 30 (1898).
Collins v. Yosemite Park Co., 304 U.S. 518 (1938).
Columbia R., Gas & Electric Co. v. South Carolina, 261 U.S. 236 (1923).
Commercial National Bank v. Custer County, 275 U.S. 502 (1927).
Concordia Ins. Co. v. Illinois, 292 U.S. 535 (1934).
Connolly v. Union Sewer Pipe Co., 184 U.S. 540 (1902).
Consolidated Flour Mills Co. v. Muegge, 278 U.S. 559 (1928).
Consolidated Textile Co. v. Gregory, 289 U.S. 85 (1933).
Construction Laborers v. Curry, 371 U.S. 542 (1963).
Cook v. Pennsylvania, 97 U.S. 566 (1878).
Coolidge v. Long, 282 U.S. 582 (1931).
Coombes v. Getz, 285 U.S. 434 (1932).
Cooney v. Mountain States Tel. Co., 294 U.S. 384 (1935).
Coppage v. Kansas, 236 U.S. 1 (1915).
Corson v. Maryland, 120 U.S. 502 (1887).
Coyle v. Smith, 221 U.S. 559 (1911).*
Cotting v. Kansas City Stock Yards Co., 183 U.S. 79 (1901).
Covey v. Town of Somers, 351 U.S. 141 (1956).
Covington & Cincinnati Bridge Co. v. Kentucky, 154 U.S. 204 (1894).
Cramp v. Board of Public Institutions, 368 U.S. 278 (1961).
Crandall v. Nevada, 6 Wall. (73 U.S.) 35 (1868).
Crenshaw v. Arkansas, 227 U.S. 389 (1913).
Crew Levick v. Pennsylvania, 245 U.S. 292 (1917).
Crutcher v. Kentucky, 141 U.S. 47 (1891).
Cudahy Co. v. Hinkle, 278 U.S. 460 (1929).
Cummings v. Missouri, 4 Wall. (71 U.S.) 277 (1867).
Curran v. Arkansas, 15 How. (56 U.S.) 304 (1854).
Dahnke-Walker Co. v. Bondurant, 257 U.S. 282 (1921).
Dameron v. Brodhead, 345 U.S. 322 (1953).
Darnell & Son v. Memphis, 208 U.S. 113 (1908).
Davis v. Cohen, 268 U.S. 638 (1925).*
Davis v. Farmers Co-operative Co., 262 U.S. 313 (1923).
Davis v. Mann, 377 U.S. 678 (1964).

Davis v. Virginia, 236 U.S. 697 (1915).

DeJonge v. Oregon, 299 U.S. 353 (1937).

DeVries v. Baumgartner's Electric Co., 359 U.S. 498 (1959).

Delmas v. Insurance Company, 14 Wall. (81 U.S.) 661 (1872).

Dept. of Alcoholic Beverage Control of California v. Ammex Warehouse Co., 378 U.S. 124 (1964).

Dept. of Revenue v. James B. Beam Distilling Co., 377 U.S. 341 (1964).

Detroit United Railway v. Michigan, 242 U.S. 238 (1916).

Dewey v. Des Moines, 173 U.S. 193 (1899).

DiSanto v. Pennsylvania, 273 U.S. 34 (1927).

Dobbins v. The Commissioners of Erie County, 16 Pet. (41 U.S.) 435 (1842).

Dodge v. Woolsey, 18 How. (59 U.S.) 331 (1856).

Dozier v. Alabama, 218 U.S. 124 (1910).

Duluth & I. Railroad Co. v. St. Louis County, 179 U.S. 302 (1900).

Edwards v. California, 314 U.S. 160 (1941).

Edwards v. Kearzey, 96 U.S. 595 (1878).

Effinger v. Kenney, 115 U.S. 566 (1885).

Eisner v. Macomber, 256 U.S. 189 (1920).*

Employers' Liability Assurance Co. v. Cook, 281 U.S. 233 (1930).

Erie Railroad Co. v. Winfield, 244 U.S. 170 (1917).

Erie Railroad Co. v. New York, 233 U.S. 671 (1914).

Eskridge v. Washington Prison Bd., 357 U.S. 214 (1958).

Ettor v. Tacoma, 228 U.S. 148 (1913).

Eureka Pipe Line Co. v. Hallanan, 256 U.S. 265 (1921).

Evans v. Gore, 253 U.S. 245 (1920).*

Ex parte Garland, 4 Wall. (71 U.S.) 333 (1867).*

Ex parte Young, 209 U.S. 123 (1908).

Fairbank v. United States, 181 U.S. 283 (1901).*

Fairmont Co. v. Minnesota, 274 U.S. 1 (1927).

Fargo v. Michigan, 121 U.S. 230 (1887).

Farmers Bank v. Minnesota, 232 U.S. 516 (1914).

Farmers Loan Co. v. Minnesota, 280 U.S. 204 (1930).

Farrington v. Tennessee, 95 U.S. 679 (1878).

Faubus v. Aaron, 361 U.S. 197 (1959).

Federal Land Bank v. Bismarck Co., 314 U.S. 95 (1941).

Federal Land Bank v. Crosland, 261 U.S. 374 (1923).

Federal Land Bank v. Kiowa County, 368 U.S. 146 (1961).

Ferguson v. Georgia, 365 U.S. 570 (1961).

Fidelity & Deposit Co. v. Tafoya, 270 U.S. 426 (1926).

First Iowa Hydro-Electric Coop. v. FPC, 328 U.S. 152 (1946).

First National Bank v. Anderson, 269 U.S. 341 (1926).

First National Bank v. California, 262 U.S. 366 (1923).

First National Bank v. Hartford, 273 U.S. 548 (1927).

First National Bank v. Maine, 284 U.S. 312 (1932).

First National Bank v. United Air Lines, 342 U.S. 396 (1952).

Fisher's Blend Station v. State Tax Comm., 297 U.S. 650 (1936).

Fiske v. Jefferson Police Jury, 116 U.S. 131 (1885).
Fiske v. Kansas, 274 U.S. 380 (1927).
Flanagan v. Federal Coal Co., 267 U.S. 222 (1925).
Flexner v. Farson, 248 U.S. 289 (1919).
Foote v. Maryland, 232 U.S. 495 (1914).
Forbes Pioneer Boat Line v. Everglades Drainage Dist., 258 U.S. 338 (1922).
Foster v. Masters of New Orleans, 94 U.S. 246 (1877).
Foster-Foundation Packing Co. v. Haydel, 278 U.S. 1 (1928).
Franklin National Bank v. New York, 347 U.S. 373 (1954).
Free v. Bland, 369 U.S. 663 (1962).
Freedman v. Maryland, 380 U.S. 51 (1965).
Frick v. Pennyslvania, 268 U.S. 473 (1925).
Frost v. Corporation Commission, 278 U.S. 515 (1929).
Frost Trucking Co. v. Railroad Comm., 271 U.S. 583 (1926).
Furman v. Nichol, 8 Wall. (75 U.S.) 44 (1869).
Furst v. Brewster, 282 U.S. 493 (1931).
Galveston, H. & S.A. Railway Co. v. Texas, 210 U.S. 217 (1908).
Garrison v. Louisiana, 379 U.S. 64 (1964).
Gayle v. Browder, 352 U.S. 903 (1956).
General Electric Co. v. Washington, 347 U.S. 909 (1954).
Georgia Railway & Electric Co. v. Decatur, 295 U.S. 165 (1935).
Georgia Railway Co. v. Decatur, 262 U.S. 432 (1923).
Georgia v. Cincinnati So. Railway, 248 U.S. 26 (1918).
Gibson v. Chouteau, 13 Wall. (80 U.S.) 92 (1872).
Gideon v. Wainwright, 372 U.S. 335 (1963).
Gillespie v. Oklahoma, 257 U.S. 501 (1922).
Globe Bank v. Martin, 236 U.S. 288 (1915).
Gloucester Ferry Co. v. Pennsylvania, 114 U.S. 196 (1885).
Gober v. City of Birmingham, 373 U.S. 374 (1963).
Gomillion v. Lightfoot, 364 U.S. 339 (1960).
Gordon v. Appeal Tax Court, 3 How. (44 U.S.) 133 (1845).
Gordon v. United States, 2 Wall (69 U.S.) 561 (1865).*
Graves v. Texas Company, 298 U.S. 393 (1936).
Gray v. Sanders, 372 U.S. 368 (1963).
Graysburg Oil Co. v. Texas, 278 U.S. 582 (1929).
Greyhound Lines v. Mealey, 334 U.S. 653 (1948).
Griffin v. Illinois, 351 U.S. 12 (1956).
Grosjean v. American Press Co., 297 U.S. 233 (1936).
Guinn v. United States, 238 U.S. 347 (1915).
Gulf, C. & S.F. Railway Co. v. Ellis, 165 U.S. 150 (1897).
Gulf, C. & S.F. Railway Co. v. Hefley, 158 U.S. 98 (1895).
Gunn v. Barry, 15 Wall. (82 U.S.) 610 (1873).
Guss v. Utah Labor Board, 353 U.S. 1 (1957).
Guy v. Baltimore, 100 U.S. 434 (1880).
Gwin, White & Prince, Inc. v. Henneford, 305 U.S. 434 (1939).
Hale v. Bimco Trading Co., 306 U.S. 375 (1939).

Hall v. DeCuir, 95 U.S. 485 (1878).

Hall v. Wisconsin, 103 U.S. 5 (1880).

Halliburton Oil Well Co. v. Reily, 373 U.S. 64 (1963).

Hammer v. Dagenhart, 247 U.S. 251 (1918).*

Hannibal & St. Joseph Railroad Co. v. Husen, 95 U.S. 465 (1878).

Hanover Ins. Co. v. Harding, 272 U.S. 494 (1926).

Hans Rees' Sons v. North Carolina ex rel. Maxwell, 283 U.S. 123 (1931).

Harrison v. St. Louis, S.F. & T. Railroad Co., 232 U.S. 318 (1914).

Hartford Accident & Insurance Co. v. Delta Pine Land Co., 292 U.S. 143 (1934).

Hartford Ins. Co. v. Harrison, 301 U.S. 459 (1937).

Hartman v. Greenhow, 102 U.S. 672 (1880).

Haskell v. Kansas Natural Gas Co., 224 U.S. 217 (1912).

Hawke v. Smith (No. 1), 253 U.S. 221 (1920).

Hawthorne v. Calef, 2 Wall., (69 U.S.) 10 (1865).

Hays v. The Pacific Mail Steamship Co., 17 How. (58 U.S.) 596 (1855).

Heiner v. Donnan, 285 U.S. 312 (1932).*

Helson v. Kentucky, 279 U.S. 245 (1929).

Henderson et al. v. Mayor of New York, 92 U.S. 259 (1876).

Hedrickson v. Apperson, 245 U.S. 105 (1917).

Henkel v. Chicago, St. P., M. & O. Railway Co., 284 U.S. 444 (1932).

Hepburn v. Griswold, 8 Wall. (75 U.S.) 603 (1870).*

Herndon v. Chicago, R.I. & P. Railway Co., 218 U.S. 135 (1910).

Herndon v. Lowry, 301 U.S. 242 (1937).

Heyman v. Hays, 236 U.S. 178 (1915).

Hill v. Davis, 378 U.S. 565 (1964).

Hill v. Florida ex rel. Watson, 325 U.S. 538 (1945).

Hill v. Wallace, 259 U.S. 44 (1922).*

Hines v. Davidowitz, 312 U.S. 52 (1941).

Hodges v. United States, 203 U.S. 1 (1906).*

Hoeper v. Tax Commission, 284 U.S. 206 (1931).

Home Ins. Co. v. Dick, 281 U.S. 397 (1930).

Home of the Friendless v. Rouse, 8 Wall. (75 U.S.) 430 (1869).

Home Savings Bank v. Des Moines, 205 U.S. 503 (1907).

Hood and Sons v. Du Mond, 336 U.S. 525 (1949).

Hoover and Allison Co. v. Evatt, 324 U.S. 652 (1945).

Hopkins Savings Assn. v. Cleary, 296 U.S. 315 (1935).*

Hostetter v. Idlewild Bon Voyage Liquor Corp., 377 U.S. 324 (1964).

Houston & Texas Central Railway v. Mayes, 201 U.S. 321 (1906).

Houston and Texas Central Railroad Co. v. Texas, 170 U.S. 243 (1898).

Houston and Texas Central Railroad Co. v. Texas, 177 U.S. 66 (1900).

Howard v. Bugbee, 24 How. (65 U.S.) 461 (1861).

Hughes Bros. Co. v. Minnesota, 272 U.S. 469 (1926).

Hughes v. Fetter, 341 U.S. 609 (1951).

Humphrey v. Pegues, 16 Wall. (83 U.S.) 244 (1873).

Hunt v. United States, 278 U.S. 96 (1928).

Illinois Central Railway v. Illinois, 163 U.S. 142 (1896).

Indian Oil Co. v. Oklahoma, 240 U.S. 522 (1916).
Indiana ex rel. Anderson v. Brand, 303 U.S. 95 (1938).
Ingels v. Morf, 300 U.S. 290 (1937).
Inman Steamship Co. v. Tinker, 94 U.S. 238 (1877).
Insurance Company v. Morse, 20 Wall. (87 U.S.) 445 (1874).
International Harvester Co. v. Kentucky, 234 U.S. 216 (1914).
International Paper Co. v. Massachusetts, 246 U.S. 135 (1918).
International Shoe Co. v. Pinkus, 278 U.S. 261 (1929).
International Steel & I. Co. v. National Surety Co., 297 U.S. 657 (1936).
International Textbook Co. v. Pigg, 217 U.S. 91 (1910).
Interstate Transit, Inc. v. Lindsey, 283 U.S. 183 (1931).
Iron Workers v. Perko, 373 U.S. 701 (1963).
James v. Bowman, 190 U.S. 127 (1903).*
James v. Dravo Contracting Co., 302 U.S. 134 (1937).
Jaybird Mining Co. v. Wier, 271 U.S. 609 (1926).
Jennings v. United States Fidelity & Guaranty Co., 294 U.S. 216 (1935).
Johnson Oil Co. v. Oklahoma ex rel. Mitchell, 290 U.S. 158 (1933).
Johnson v. Maryland, 254 U.S. 51 (1920).
Jones v. Meehan, 175 U.S. 1 (1899).*
Joseph Burstyn, Inc. v. Wilson, 343 U.S. 495 (1952).
Journeymen & Plumbers' Union v. Borden, 373 U.S. 690 (1962).
Kansas City So. Railway v. Road Imp. Dist. No. 6, 256 U.S. 658 (1921).
Keating v. Public National Bank, 284 U.S. 587 (1932).
Kedroff v. St. Nicholas Cathedral, 344 U.S. 94 (1952).
Keith v. Clark, 97 U.S. 454 (1878).
Keller v. Potomac Elec. Co., 261 U.S. 428 (1923).*
Keller v. United States, 213 U.S. 138 (1909).*
Kennedy v. Mendoza-Martinez, 372 U.S. 144 (1963).*
Kentucky Co. v. Paramount Exch., 262 U.S. 544 (1923).
Kern-Limerick, Inc. v. Scurlock, 347 U.S. 110 (1954).
Kingsley Pictures Corp. v. Regents, 360 U.S. 684 (1959).
Kirby v. United States, 174 U.S. 47 (1899).*
Kirmeyer v. Kansas, 236 U.S. 568 (1915).
Knickerbocker Ice Co. v. Stewart, 253 U.S. 149 (1920).*
Kring v. Missouri, 107 U.S. 221 (1883).
La Crosse Tel. Corp. v. WERB, 336 U.S. 18 (1949).
Lake Shore & Mich. S. Railway Co. v. Smith, 173 U.S. 684 (1899).
Lancaster v. McCarty, 267 U.S. 427 (1925).
Lane v. Brown, 372 U.S. 477 (1963).
Lane v. Wilson, 307 U.S. 268 (1939).
Lanzetta v. New Jersey, 306 U.S. 451 (1939).
Lassiter v. United States, 371 U.S. 10 (1962).
Lawrence v. Shaw, 300 U.S. 245 (1937).
Lee v. Osceola Imp. Dist., 268 U.S. 643 (1925).
Legislature of Louisiana v. United States, 367 U.S. 908 (1961).
Leisy v. Hardin, 135 U.S. 100 (1890).

Lemke v. Farmers Grain Co., 258 U.S. 50 (1922).
Leslie Miller, Inc. v. Arkansas, 352 U.S. 187 (1956).
Lindgren v. United States, 281 U.S. 38 (1930).
Lindsey v. Washington, 301 U.S. 397 (1937).
Loan Association v. Topeka, 20 Wall. (87 U.S.) 655 (1875).
Lochner v. New York, 198 U.S. 45 (1905).
Lombard v. Louisiana, 373 U.S. 267 (1963).
London Guarantee & Accident Co. v. Industrial Comm., 279 U.S. 109 (1929).
Long v. Rockwood, 277 U.S. 142 (1928).
Looney v. Crane Co., 245 U.S. 178 (1917).
Louis K. Liggett Co. v. Baldridge, 278 U.S. 105 (1928).
Louis K. Liggett Co. v. Lee, 288 U.S. 517 (1933).
Louisiana ex rel. Hubert v. New Orleans, 215 U.S. 170 (1909).
Louisiana v. J. Ferry Co. v. Kentucky, 188 U.S. 385 (1903).
Louisiana v. NAACP ex rel. Gremillion, 366 U.S. 293 (1961).
Louisville & Nashville Railroad Co. v. Cook Brewing Co., 223 U.S. 70 (1912).
Louisville & Nashville Railroad Co. v. Eubank, 184 U.S. 27 (1902).
Louisville & Nashville Railroad Co. v. Stock Yards Co., 212 U.S. 132 (1909).
Louisville Bank v. Radford, 295 U.S. 555 (1935).*
Louisville Gas Co. v. Citizens' Gas Co., 115 U.S. 683 (1885).
Louisville Gas Co. v. Coleman, 277 U.S. 32 (1928).
Lucas v. Forty-Fourth General Assembly of Colorado, 377 U.S. 713 (1964).
Ludwig v. Western Union Tel. Co., 216 U.S. 146 (1910).
Lynch v. United States, 292 U.S. 571 (1934).*
Lyng v. Michigan, 135 U.S. 161 (1890).
Macallen Co. v. Massachusetts, 279 U.S. 620 (1929).
Manley v. Georgia, 279 U.S. 1 (1929).
Marchetti v. United States, 390 U.S. 39 (1968).*
Marcus v. Search Warrant, 367 U.S. 717 (1961).
Marine Engineers v. Interlake Co., 370 U.S. 173 (1962).
Marsh v. Alabama, 326 U.S. 501 (1946).
Martin v. Bush, 376 U.S. 222 (1964).
Maryland Committee for Fair Representation v. Tawes, 377 U.S. 656 (1964).
Matter of Heff, 197 U.S. 488 (1905).*
Mayers v. Anderson, 238 U.S. 268 (1915).
Mayflower Farms v. Ten Eyck, 297 U.S. 266 (1936).
Mayo v. United States, 319 U.S. 441 (1943).
McCabe v. Atchison, T. & S.F. Railway Co., 235 U.S. 151 (1914).
McCarroll v. Dixie Lines, 309 U.S. 176 (1940).
McCracken v. Hayward, 2 How. (43 U.S.) 608 (1844).
McDermott v. Wisconsin, 228 U.S. 115 (1913).
McFarland v. American Sugar Co., 241 U.S. 79 (1916).
McGahey v. Virginia, 135 U.S. 662 (1890).
McKnett v. St. Louis & S. F. Railway Co., 292 U.S. 230 (1934).
McLaughlin v. Florida, 379 U.S. 184 (1964).
McLaurin v. Oklahoma State Regents, 339 U.S. 637 (1950).

McLeod v. Dilworth Co., 322 U.S. 327 (1944).

McMahon v. Milam Manufacturing Company, 368 U.S. 7 (1961).

Medley, Petitioner, 134 U.S. 160 (1890).

Memphis Steam Laundry v. Stone, 342 U.S. 389 (1952).

Mercantile National Bank v. Langdeau, 371 U.S. 555 (1963).

Merchant's National Bank v. Richmond, 256 U.S. 635 (1921).

Meyer v. Nebraska, 262 U.S. 390 (1923).

Meyers v. Thigpen, 378 U.S. 554 (1964).

Michigan Commission v. Duke, 266 U.S. 570 (1925).

Michigan National Bank v. Robertston, 372 U.S. 591 (1963).

Michigan-Wisconsin Pipe Line Co. v. Calvert, 347 U.S. 157 (1954).

Miller Bros. Co. v. Maryland, 347 U.S. 340 (1954).

Miller v. Milwaukee, 272 U.S. 713 (1927).

Minnesota v. Barber, 136 U.S. 313 (1890).

Minnesota v. First National Bank, 273 U.S. 561 (1927).

Missouri Pacific Railroad Co. v. Stroud, 267 U.S. 404 (1925).

Missouri Pacific Railway v. Nebraska, 164 U.S. 403 (1896).

Missouri Pacific Railway Co. v. Larabee, 234 U.S. 459 (1914).

Missouri Pacific Railway Co. v. Tucker, 230 U.S. 340 (1913).

Missouri Pacific Railway v. Nebraska, 217 U.S. 196 (1910).

Missouri Pacific v. Porter, 273 U.S. 341 (1927).

Missouri ex rel. Burnes National Bank v. Duncan, 265 U.S. 17 (1924).

Missouri ex rel. Gaines v. Canada, 305 U.S. 337 (1938).

Missouri ex rel. Missouri Ins. Co. v. Gehner, 281 U.S. 313 (1930).

Missouri ex. rel. Robertson v. Miller, 276 U.S. 174 (1928).

Missouri, K. & T. Railway v. Harriman Bros., 227 U.S. 657 (1913).

Mobile & Ohio Railroad v. Tennessee, 153 U.S. 486 (1894).

Mobile v. Watson, 116 U.S. 289 (1886).

Monongahela Navigation Co. v. United States, 148 U.S. 312 (1893).*

Montana National Bank v. Yellowstone County, 276 U.S. 479 (1928).

Moore v. Mitchell, 281 U.S. 18 (1930).

Morehead v. New York ex rel. Tipaldo, 298 U.S. 587 (1936).

Morey v. Doud, 354 U.S. 457 (1957).

Morgan v. Virginia, 328 U.S. 373 (1946).

Morrill v. Wisconsin, 154 U.S. 626 (1877).

Morrison v. California, 291 U.S. 82 (1934).

Mullane v. Central Hanover Bank & Trust Co., 339 U.S. 306 (1950).

Murray v. Gerrick & Co., 291 U.S. 315 (1934).

Muskrat v. United States, 219 U.S. 346 (1911).*

Myers v. United States, 272 U.S. 52 (1926).*

NAACP v. Button, 371 U.S. 415 (1963).

Napier v. Atlantic Coast Line, 272 U.S. 605 (1926).

National Life Ins. Co. v. Ohio, 277 U.S. 508 (1928).

Near v. Minnesota ex rel. Olsen, 283 U.S. 697 (1931).

Neil, Moore & Co. v. Ohio, 3 How. (44 U.S.) 720 (1845).

Nelson v. St. Martin's Parish, 111 U.S. 716 (1884).

New Brunswick v. United States, 276 U.S. 547 (1928).

New Jersey Insurance Co. v. Div. of Tax Appeals, 338 U.S. 665 (1950).

New Jersey Te. Co. v. Tax Board, 280 U.S. 338 (1930).

New Jersey v. Yard, 95 U.S. 104 (1877).

New Orleans & N.E.R.R. Co. v. Scarlet, 249 U.S. 528 (1919).

New State Ice Co. v. Liebmann, 285 U.S. 262 (1932).

New York Central Railroad Co. v. Winfield, 244 U.S. 147 (1917).

New York ex rel. Rogers v. Graves, 299 U.S. 401 (1937).

New York v. Compagnie Gen. Transatlantique, 107 U.S. 59 (1882).

New York, L. E. & W. Railroad Co. v. Pennsylvania, 153 U.S. 628 (1894).

New York Life Ins. Co. v. Dodge, 246 U.S. 357 (1918).

Newberry v. United States, 256 U.S. 232 (1921).*

Newton v. Consolidated Gas Co., 258 U.S. 165 (1922).

Nicholds v. Coolidge, 274 U.S. 531 (1927).*

Nielsen v. Johnson, 279 U.S. 47 (1929).

Nielson v. Oregon, 212 U.S. 315 (1909).

Nixon v. Condon, 286 U.S. 73 (1932).

Nixon v. Herndon, 273 U.S. 563 (1927).

Norfolk & West Railway v. Conley, 236 U.S. 605 (1915).

Norfolk & Western Railroad Co. v. Pennsylvania, 136 U.S. 114 (1890).

North Dakota ex rel. Flaherty v. Hanson, 215 U.S. 515 (1910).

Northern Central Railway Co. v. Jackson, 7 Wall. (74 U.S.) 262 (1869).

Northern Pac. Railway Co. v. North Dakota ex rel McCue, 236 U.S. 585 (1915).

Northern Pacific Railway Co. v. Washington, 222 U.S. 370 (1912).

Northwestern Ins. Co. v. Wisconsin, 275 U.S. 136 (1927).

Northwestern University v. Illinois ex rel. Miller, 99 U.S. 309 (1878).

Norton Co. v. Dept. of Revenue, 340 U.S. 534 (1951).

Norwood v. Baker, 172 U.S. 269 (1898).

Ohio Pub. Service Co. v. Ohio ex rel. Fritz, 274 U.S. 12 (1927).

Ohio Valley Co. v. Ben Avon Borough, 253 U.S. 287 (1920).

Ohio v. Thomas, 173 U.S 276 (1899).

Oklahoma Operating Co. v. Love, 252 U.S. 331 (1920).

Oklahoma v. Barnsdall Corp., 296 U.S. 521 (1936).

Oklahoma v. Kansas Natural Gas Co., 221 U.S. 229 (1911).

Oklahoma v. Wells, Fargo & Co., 223 U.S. 298 (1912).

Old Company's Lehigh v. Meeker, 294 U.S. 227 (1935).

Order of Travelers v. Wolfe, 331 U.S. 586 (1947).

Oregon-Washington Co. v. Washington, 270 U.S. 87 (1926).

Orleans Parish School Board v. Bush, 365 U.S. 569 (1961).

Osborne v. Nicholson, 13 Wall. (80 U.S.) 654 (1872).

Ottinger v. Consolidated Gas Co., 272 U.S. 576 (1926).

Oyama v. California, 332 U.S. 633 (1948).

Ozark Pipe Line v. Monier, 266 U.S. 555 (1925).

Pacific Coast Dairy v. Dept. of Agriculture, 318 U.S. 285 (1943).

Pacific Railroad Company v. Maguire, 20 Wall. (87 U.S.) 36 (1874).

Panama Refining Co. v. Ryan, 293 U.S. 388 (1935).*

Panhandle Co. v. Highway Comm., 294 U.S. 613 (1935).
Panhandle Oil Co. v. Missouri ex rel. Knox, 277 U.S. 218 (1928).
Parkersburg v. Brown, 106 U.S. 487 (1882).
Passenger Cases, 7 How. (48 U.S.) 283 (1849).
Paul v. United States, 371 U.S. 245 (1963).
Peete v. Morgan, 19 Wall. (86 U.S.) 581 (1874).
Pennoyer v. McConnaughy, 140 U.S. 1 (1891).
Pennsylvania Coal Co. v. Mahon, 260 U.S. 393 (1922).
Pennsylvania Railroad Co. v. Public Service Comm., 250 U.S. 566 (1919).
Pennsylvania v. Nelson, 350 U.S. 497 (1955).
Pennyslvania v. West Virginia, 262 U.S. 553 (1923).
Pensacola Tel. Co. v. Western Union Tel. Co., 96 U.S. 1 (1878).
Perry v. United States, 294 U.S. 330 (1935).*
Peterson v. City of Greenville, 373 U.S. 244 (1963).
Philadelphia Steamship Co. v. Pennsylvania, 122 U.S. 326 (1887).
Phillips Co. v. Dumas School District, 361 U.S. 376 (1960).
Phipps v. Cleveland Refg. Co., 261 U.S. 449 (1923).
Pickard v. Pullman Southern Car Co., 117 U.S. 34 (1886).
Pierce v. Carskadon, 16 Wall. (83 U.S.) 234 (1873).
Pierce v. Society of Sisters, 268 U.S. 510 (1925).
Pinney v. Butterworth, 378 U.S. 564 (1964).
Plankington Packing Co. v. WERB, 338 U.S. 953 (1950).
Planters' Bank v. Sharp, 6 How. (47 U.S.) 301 (1848).
Polar Ice Cream & Creamery Co. v. Andrews, 375 U.S. 361 (1964).
Pollack v. Williams, 322 U.S. 4 (1944).
Pollock v. Farmers' Loan & Trust Co., 157 U.S. 429 (1895).*
Postal Tel.-Cable Co. v. Warren-Godwin Co., 251 U.S. 27 (1919).
Power Mfg. Co. v. Saunders, 274 U.S. 490 (1927).
Powers v. Detroit & Grand Haven Railway, 201 U.S. 543 (1906).
Prigg v. Pennsylvania, 16 Pet. (41 U.S.) 539 (1842).
Provident Savings Assn. v. Kentucky, 239 U.S. 103 (1915).
Public Utility Comm. v. United States, 355 U.S. 534 (1958).
Puget Sound Co. v. Tax Commission, 302 U.S. 90 (1937).
Quaker City Cab Co. v. Pennsylvania, 277 U.S. 389 (1928).
Railroad Retirement Board v. Alton R. Co., 295 U.S. 330 (1935).*
Railway Employees' Dept. v. Hanson, 351 U.S. 225 (1956).
Railway Express Agency v. Virginia, 347 U.S. 359 (1954).
Ralls County Court v. United States, 105 U.S. 733 (1881).
Rassmussen v. United States, 197 U.S. 516 (1905).*
Ratterman v. Western Union Tel. Co., 127 U.S. 4111 (1888).
Reichart v. Felps, 6 Wall. (73 U.S.) 160 (1868).*
Reid v. Covert, 354 U.S. 1 (1957).*
Reitman v. Mulkey, 387 U.S. 369 (1967).
Republic Pictures Corp. v. Kappler, 327 U.S. 757 (1946).
Reynolds v. Sims, 377 U.S. 533 (1964).
Rhode Island Trust Co. v. Doughton, 270 U.S. 69 (1926).

Ribnik v. McBride, 277 U.S. 350 (1928).

Rice v. Sante Fe Elevator Corp., 331 U.S. 218 (1947).

Richfield Oil Corp. v. State Board, 329 U.S. 69 (1946).

Rickert Rice Mills v. Fontenot, 297 U.S. 110 (1936).*

Road Improvement Dist. v. Missouri Pacific R. Co., 274 U.S. 188 (1927).

Robbins v. Shelby Taxing District, 120 U.S. 489 (1887).

Robinson v. California, 370 U.S. 660 (1962).

Rohr Corp. v. San Diego County, 362 U.S. 628 (1960).

Roman v. Sincock, 377 U.S. 695 (1964).

Rosenberger v. Pacific Express Co., 241 U.S. 48 (1916).

Rossi v. Pennsylvania, 238 U.S. 62 (1915).

Rowland v. Boyle, 244 U.S. 106 (1917).

Royall v. Virginia, 116 U.S. 572 (1886).

Royster Guano Co. v. Virginia, 253 U.S. 412 (1920).

Russell v. Sebastian, 233 U.S. 195 (1914).

Safe Deposit & T. Co. v. Virginia, 280 U.S. 83 (1929).

San Diego Unions v. Garmon, 359 U.S. 236 (1959).

Santovincenzo v. Egan, 284 U.S. 30 (1931).

Schechter Poultry Corp. v. United States, 295 U.S. 495 (1935).*

Schlesinger v. Wisconsin, 270 U.S. 230 (1926).

Schneider v. Rusk, 377 U.S. 163 (1964).*

Schnell v. Davis, 336 U.S. 933 (1949).

Schollenberger v. Pennsylvania, 171 U.S. 1 (1898).

Schuylkill Trust Co. v. Pennsylvania, 296 U.S. 113 (1935).

Scott v. Donald, 165 U.S. 58 (1897).

Scott v. Sandford, 19 How. (60 U.S.) 393 (1857).*

Seaboard Air Line Railway v. Blackwell, 244 U.S. 310 (1917).

Seaboard R. Co. v. Daniel, 333 U.S. 118 (1948).

Searight v. Stokes, 3 How. (44 U.S.) 151 (1845).

Sears, Roebuck & Co. v. Stiffel Co., 376 U.S. 225 (1964).

Seibert v. Lewis, 122 U.S. 284 (1887).

Senior v. Braden, 295 U.S. 422 (1935).

Shafer v. Farmers Grain Co., 268 U.S. 189 (1925).

Shelton v. Tucker, 364 U.S. 479 (1960).

Sherbet v. Verner, 374 U.S. 398 (1963).

Singer Sewing Machine Co. v. Brickell, 233 U.S. 304 (1914).

Sinnot v. Davenport, 22 How. (63 U.S.) 227 (1860).

Sioux Remedy Co. v. Cope, 235 U.S. 197 (1914).

Sipuel v. Board of Regents, 332 U.S. 631 (1948).

Skinner v. Oklahoma ex rel. Wilwinson, 316 U.S. 535 (1942).

Smith v. Cahoon, 283 U.S. 553 (1931).

Smith v. Texas, 233 U.S. 630 (1914).

Smyth v. Ames, 169 U.S. 466 (1898).

Society for Savings v. Bowers, 349 U.S. 143 (1955).

Southern Pacific Co. v. Arizona, 325 U.S. 761 (1945).

Southern Pacific Co. v. Jensen, 244 U.S. 205 (1917).

Tennessee Coal Co. v. George, 233 U.S. 254 (1914).
Terral v. Burke Constr. Co., 257 U.S. 529 (1922).
Texas Co. v. Brown, 258 U.S. 466 (1922).
The Alicia, 7 Wall. (74 U.S.) 571 (1869).*
The Belfast, 7 Wall. (74 U.S.) 624 (1869).
The Binghamton Bridge, 3 Wall. (70 U.S.) 51 (1866).
The Employers' Liability Cases, 207 U.S. 463 (1908).*
The Hine v. Trevor, 4 Wall. (71 U.S.) 555 (1867).
The Justices v. Murray, 9 Wall. (76 U.S.) 274 (1870).*
The Kansas Indians, 5 Wall. (72 U.S.) 737 (1867).
The Moses Taylor, 4 Wall. (71 U.S.) 411 (1867).
The New York Indians, 5 Wall. (72 U.S.) 761 (1867).
The Robert W. Parsons, 191 U.S. 17 (1903).
The Roanoke, 189 U.S. 185 (1903).
Thomas v. Collins, 323 U.S. 516 (1945).
Thomas v. Kansas City So. Railway, 261 U.S. 481 (1923).
Thompson v. Utah, 170 U.S. 343 (1898).
Thornhill v. Alabama, 310 U.S. 88 (1940).
Tiernan v. Rinkler, 102 U.S. 123 (1880).
Toomer v. Witsell, 334 U.S. 385 (1948).
Torasco v. Watkins, 367 U.S. 488 (1961).
Tot v. United States, 319 U.S. 463 (1943).*
Toth v. Quarles, 350 U.S. 11 (1955).*
Trade-Mark Cases, 100 U.S. 82 (1879).*
Truax v. Raich, 239 U.S. 33 (1915).
Travis v. Yale & Towne Mfg. Co., 252 U.S. 60 (1920).
Treichler v. Wisconsin, 338 U.S. 251 (1949).
Treigle v. Acme Homestead Assn., 297 U.S. 189 (1936).
Trop v. Dulles, 356 U.S. 86 (1958).*
Traux v. Corrigan, 257 U.S. 312 (1921).
Trustees for Vincennes University v. Indiana, 14 How. (55 U.S.) 268 (1853).
Tucker v. Texas, 326 U.S. 517 (1946).
Tugwell v. Bush, 367 U.S. 907 (1961).
Tulee v. Washington, 315 U.S. 681 (1942).
Tumey v. Ohio, 273 U.S. 510 (1927).
Turner v. City of Memphis, 369 U.S. 350 (1962).
Turner v. Fouche, 396 U.S. 346 (1970).
Turner v. Wade, 254 U.S. 64 (1920).
Tyson & Brother v. Banton, 273 U.S. 418 (1927).
Union National Bank v. Lamb, 337 U.S. 38 (1949).
Union Pacific Railroad Co. v. Public Service Comm., 248 U.S. 67 (1918).
Union Tank Line Co. v. Wright, 249 U.S. 275 (1919).
Union Transit Co. v. Kentucky, 199 U.S. 194 (1905).
United Automobile Workers v. O'Brien, 339 U.S. 454 (1950).
United States ex rel. Wolff v. New Orleans, 103 U.S. 358 (1881).
United States v. Allegheny County, 322 U.S. 174 (1944).

United States v. Buffalo Savings Bank, 371 U.S. 228 (1963).
United States v. Butler, 297 U.S. 1 (1936).*
United States v. California, 332 U.S. 19 (1947).
United States v. Cardiff, 344 U.S. 174 (1952).*
United States v. Cohen Grocery Co., 255 U.S. 81 (1921).*
United States v. Constantine, 296 U.S. 287 (1935).*
United States v. Dewitt, 9 Wall. (78 U.S.) 41 (1870).*
United States v. Evans, 213 U.S. 297 (1909).*
United States v. Fox, 95 U.S. 670 (1878).*
United States v. Harris, 106 U.S. 629 (1883).*
United States v. Hvoslef, 237 U.S. 1 (1915).*
United States v. Klein, 13 Wall. (80 U.S.) 128 (1872).*
United States v. Louisiana, 339 U.S. 699 (1950).
United States v. Lovett, 328 U.S. 303 (1946).*
United States v. Moreland, 258 U.S. 433 (1922).*
Unites States v. Oregon, 366 U.S. 643 (1961).
United States v. Reese, 92 U.S. 214 (1876).*
United States v. Reynolds, 235 U.S. 133 (1914).
United States v. Shimer, 367 U.S. 374 (1961).
United States v. Texas, 339 U.S. 707 (1950).
United States v. Union Central Life Ins. Co., 368 U.S. 291 (1961).
Untermeyer v. Anderson, 276 U.S. 440 (1928).*
Valentine v. A. & P. Tea Co., 299 U.S. 32 (1936).
Van Allen v. The Assessors, 3 Wall. (70 U.S.) 573 (1866).
Van Brocklin v. Tennessee, 117 U.S. 151 (1886).
Van Huffel v. Harkelrode, 284 U.S. 225 (1931).
Vicksburg v. Waterworks Co., 202 U.S. 453 (1906).
Virginia Coupon Cases, 114 U.S. 269 (1885).
Voight v. Wright, 141 U.S. 62 (1891).
Von Hoffman v. Quincy, 4 Wall. (71 U.S.) 535 (1867).
W. B. Worthen Co. v. Thomas, 292 U.S. 426 (1934).
WMCA, Inc. v. Lomenzo, 377 U.S. 633 (1964).
Wabash, St. L. & P. Railway Co. v. Illinois, 118 U.S. 557 (1886).
Wachovia Trust Co. v. Doughton, 272 U.S. 567 (1926).
Walker v. Hutchison City, 352 U.S. 112 (1956).
Walker v. Whitehead, 16 Wall. (83 U.S.) 314 (1873).
Wallace v. Hines, 253 U.S. 66 (1920).
Walling v. Michigan, 116 U.S. 446 (1886).
Ward v. Maryland, 12 Wall. (79 U.S.) 418 (1871).
Washington v. Dawson & Co., 264 U.S. 219 (1924).*
Waxman v. Virginia, 371 U.S. 4 (1962).
Weaver v. Palmer Bros. Co., 270 U.S. 402 (1926).
Webber v. Virginia, 103 U.S. 344 (1881).
Welton v. Missouri, 91 U.S. 275 (1876).
Wesberry v. Saunders, 376 U.S. 1 (1964).
Western & Atlantic Railroad Co. v. Henderson, 279 U.S. 639 (1929).

Western Oil Refg. Co. v. Lipscomb, 244 U.S. 346 (1917).
Western Union Telegraph Co. v. Alabama, 132 U.S. 472 (1889).
Western Union Telegraph Co. v. Boegli, 251 U.S. 315 (1920).
Western Union Telegraph Co. v. Brown, 234 U.S. 542 (1914).
Western Union Telegraph Co. v. Kansas, 216 U.S. 1 (1910).
Western Union Telegraph Co. v. Massachusetts, 125 U.S. 530 (1888).
Western Union Telegraph Co. v. Pendleton, 122 U.S. 347 (1887).
Western Union Telegraph Co. v. Texas, 105 U.S. 460 (1881).
Wheeling Steel Corp. v. Glander, 337 U.S. 562 (1949).
White v. Hart, 13 Wall. (80 U.S.) 646 (1872).
Wieman v. Updegraff, 344 U.S. 183 (1952).
Willcox v. Consolidated Gas Co., 212 U.S. 19 (1909).
Williams v. Moss, 378 U.S. 558 (1964).
Williams v. Standard Oil Co., 278 U.S. 235 (1929).
Willner v. Committee on Character, 373 U.S. 96 (1963).
Wilmington & Weldon R. Co. v. King, 91 U.S. 3 (1875).
Wilmington Railroad v. Reid, 13 Wall. (80 U.S.) 264 (1872).
Winters v. New York, 333 U.S. 507 (1948).
Wisconsin v. Philadelphia & Reading Coal Co., 241 U.S. 329 (1916).
Wissner v. Wissner, 338 U.S. 665 (1950).
Wolff Packing Co. v. Industrial Court, 262 U.S. 522 (1923).
Wong Wing v. United States, 163 U.S. 228 (1896).*
Wood v. Lovett, 313 U.S. 362 (1941).
Woodruff v. Trapnall, 10 How. (51 U.S.) 190 (1851).
Worthen Co. v. Kavanaugh, 295 U.S. 56 (1935).
Wright v. Central of Georgia Railway, 236 U.S. 674 (1915).
Wright v. Georgia, 373 U.S. 284 (1963).
Wuchter v. Pizzuti, 276 U.S. 13 (1928).

About the Book and Author

New issues rise and fall every day on the American political landscape. Some issues, however, do not fade. Rather, they seem fixed on that landscape, polarizing the public and affecting electoral support. Eventually such issues may precipitate a realignment, cause a shift in institutional control, and, in effect, transform the party system.

Much has been written about the effects of realignment on the electorate and on congressional policymaking. Less is known about its effects on judicial policymaking. Does Supreme Court policymaking reflect the volatile issues that can polarize parties? Does it stand as a barrier to realignment of the party system following a critical election? In short, does the Supreme Court use its power of judicial review to legitimate or to oppose the political agenda of a new majority party?

In addressing these questions, John B. Gates is the first to offer a complete array of relevant data. Ranging across four party eras (1837–1964), he examines 743 cases in which federal statutes, state statutes, and state constitutional provisions were declared unconstitutional. In combination with interpretive and historical analysis, his study of these dramatic cases yields important information about the connections between Supreme Court policymaking and the process of realignment. Moreover, it makes an important contribution to our understanding of the dynamic processes that effect change in American politics.

John B. Gates is associate professor of political science at the University of California–Davis.

Index